America's

Black Musical

Heritage

America's Black Musical Heritage

TILFORD BROOKS

Washington University
St. Louis, Missouri

PRENTICE HALL, Englewood Cliffs, New Jersey 07632

Library of Congress Cataloging in Publication Data

BROOKS, TILFORD.
   America's Black musical heritage.

   "List of compositions by composers included in this
study": p.
   "List of recordings of compositions by composers in-
cluded in this study": p.
   Bibligraphy: p.
   Includes index.
   1. Afro-Americans—Music—History and criticism.
I. Title.
ML3556.B76 1984   781.7'296073   83-11184
ISBN   0-13-024315-9
ISBN   0-13-024307-8 (pbk.)

Editorial/production supervision and
   interior design: Chrystena Chrzanowski
Cover design: Diane Saxe
Manufacturing buyer: Harry P. Baisley

Printed in the United States of America

10 9 8 7 6 5 4

ISBN   0-13-024315-9 {c}

ISBN   0-13-024307-8 {p}

Prentice-Hall International (UK) Limited, *London*
Prentice-Hall of Australia Pty. Limited, *Sydney*
Prentice-Hall Canada Inc., *Toronto*
Prentice-Hall Hispanoamericana, S. A., *Mexico*
Prentice-Hall of India Private Limited, *New Delhi*
Prentice-Hall of Japan, Inc., *Tokyo*
Simon & Schuster Asia Pte. Ltd., *Singapore*
Editora Prentice-Hall do Brasil, Ltda., *Rio de Janeiro*

To the women in my life:
 my wife,
  my mother,
   and my daughters

Contents

chapter four:

The Black Musician in American Society 164

Foreword

It is probable that mature readers of these remarks can remember when the word "Black" was perjorative and when "Negro music" was thought to be quaint and certainly not worth serious study by anyone other than a few highly specialized ethnomusicologists. Such readers may also remember a time when children's songbooks (and other children's materials) were illustrated exclusively with White, rosy-cheeked little girls and boys living in comfortable houses with lovely green lawns. White people did sing "Negro music" (mainly spirituals, often with an ersatz Negro dialect), but it was not taken seriously as "art music." We also enjoyed singing "Mammy's little baby loves sho'tnin' bread" and other songs of this ilk.

One could continue endlessly with this sort of reminiscence and perhaps be brought up short by the realization that quite possibly a large portion of our citizenry, if they think about it at all, continues to carry the old stereotypes in their heads. Racial bigotry among Whites (and sadly, among Blacks) is probably as strong as it ever was.

Of all the stereotyped views of Blacks as musicians, none is more absurd and harmful than the belief that Niggers just "naturally got rhythm." Carlton Putnam, in his *Race and Reason* (Public Affairs Press, Washington, D.C., 1961) allowed that Negroes often could sing well, but so could his canary.

White Americans were by no means the first to accept the Black musician, not as a performing seal or as a "primitive" (a word I detest), but simply as a musician, like other musicians, no better, no worse than his White counterpart, not more or less gifted as a whole, but a person able to express himself through music as might a Hungarian, a German, a Chinese, or a White American. As Brooks reminds us, it was Europeans such as Dvořák and Debussy who pioneered in the recognition of artistic significance in music composed and performed by people with skins darker than their own.

None of the above is intended to suggest that most music composed by Blacks is the *same* as that composed by Whites. This is particularly true of jazz, which, of course, would not exist were it not for the Black musician having lived the Black experience in America. (In this connection it is worth noting that a large part, if not the majority, of serious writing about jazz has been done by European scholars.) On the other hand, it is impossible, at least for me, to detect any "Blackness" in the music of a Swanson or the electronic sounds of an Olly Wilson, his protestations to the contrary not withstanding. It is *music* and could have been written just as easily by a gifted and well-educated White American or Frenchman.

In the United States, the serious study of music written and/or performed by musicians who call themselves Black became generally respectable only very recently, at first at the graduate level by "ethno" majors and their professors (in that order). Then it became trendy to include some Black music (usually not of the best quality) in elementary and secondary school music books along with pictures of children with White features colored Black.

Black music and the Black studies movement date, for the most part, only back to the sixties, and at first were the province of specialists, accounting for the relative paucity of erudite yet readable texts on the subject. Brooks has succeeded in his goal: to add a work of scholarly significance to the growing corpus of such studies. While there is other extant literature written for the purpose of educating both Black and White students in the role the American Black musician has played historically and at present in world musics, Brooks is singularly skillful in offering a wealth of information written in a style that is not condescending nor so technical as to make it valuable only to the expert.

I hope that the book has a wide readership and that it will be followed by other writings by Blacks and Whites, expanding in some instances, and probing more deeply in others, into what, *fautede mieux*, we call the study of *Black* music.

Washington University
St. Louis, Missouri

Lewis B. Hilton
Professor Emeritus of Music

Preface

In the last decade, Black music has begun to receive the attention it deserves through intensive scholarly research and study. From this research and study has grown an awareness of this art form and why it is peculiar to America. As one examines the cultural milieu in which Black music took place, it becomes apparent that it is impossible to separate the music from the societal and religious influences that were in evidence during all periods of its development. It is also evident that Black music is a continually developing and viable art form, as exemplified by the *gospel song* eventually developing from the *spiritual,* and *jazz/rock fusion* evolving decades later from *New Orleans jazz.* Performance practices associated with Black music have had continuing influence on American music and are heard each time one listens to the music indigenous to the United States. Thus, this study examines an art form that is not only continually changing but that is continually influencing the American music we hear each day.

This discussion is a comprehensive, indexed study of Black music that makes readily available to the reader all aspects of Black music in the United States. There is a skillful offering of a wealth of information written in a style that is not patronizing to the reader, yet not so technical as to make it valuable only to the professional.

One of the more salient features of this study is the manner in which it is organized. Each Black music genre is discussed in depth in a separate section. Therefore, should the reader desire to identify information regarding a particular genre, it is not necessary to read several chapters to gain an overview of that genre, but simply to read that section in which the genre is discussed.

Within each section on the various Black music genres, selected Black composers and representative compositions of each are discussed and analyzed. There is extensive discussion of the role of the Black musician in American society, tracing that role from the early days of slavery to the present. There is also an examination of the social, political, economic, and religious factors that affected that role.

Numerous musical examples of Black music genres and excerpts from the compositions of Black composers are presented. Recordings are suggested so that the reader may hear how each Black music genre and selected composer sound. In addition to a complete discography of each Black composer's recorded compositions, an up-to-date listing of *all* of their compositions is included in this study. Many photographs are also included, permitting the reader to identify with the artists being discussed.

Finally, Black music and its relationship with Black dance is examined in detail. The research identifies the roots of Afro-American dance and also gives insight into the manner in which the contemporary dances of Black youth have often been manipulated by the recording industry.

I owe a debt of gratitude to Dr. Lewis B. Hilton, who gave me excellent direction while doing the original research that formed the basis for this book. His constant encouragement, advice, and adherence to a standard of excellence shall never be forgotten.

Two sources must be cited because they made available to me my initial contact with written sources about American Black music. Both pointed in the direction that this study would take. Harold Courlander's *Negro Folk Music, U.S.A.* and Eileen Southern's *The Music of Black Americans: A History* have been invaluable.

Finally, credit must be given to my wife, Ethelyn, for the patience she has shown while this project came to fruition. It was her constant encouragement that helped make it possible.

Tilford Brooks

introduction

Why Study Black Music?

A Black subculture exists within American society. It has exerted an enormous amount of influence on American music. Yet until recently, even though music composed and performed by Blacks had made such a great impression, little was known about it.

Those who should have been aware of the total American musical scene—including researchers, teachers, composers, and performers—frequently were ignorant about many aspects of Black music.

One might ask, What is Black music? Does it include only those musical forms such as spirituals, blues, and jazz, which are indigenous to the Black ethnic group? If a Black musician composes music in the European tradition, is this also Black music?

There are those who are of the opinion that music written by Blacks in the European tradition is simply an imitation of the music of White composers, that Black music must be restricted to those musical forms that are Black in origin. There are others who contend that the Black musician who writes music in the European tradition brings to that music a set of unique experiences that are manifested in his music; that regardless of the tradition in which the music is written, it is Black music providing it was written by a Black person who has lived the Black experience; and that even though it may not be written in one of the traditional Black music

1

forms, this music is intuitively Black because of the cultural environment in which it was created.

There will be no attempt in this book to define Black music other than in its simplest meaning. For our purposes here, the term "Black music" will refer to all music that is indigenous to Blacks or composed by Blacks. Ideological questions as to what music is Black and what is not will not be considered here.

Another question one might ask is why Black music has not been given serious study until recently. One answer is that those persons who were inclined to believe that Blacks were inferior also tended to believe that Black music was inferior. On the other hand, there were liberal citizens who were in the vanguard of changing social attitudes It would seem that this was the most logical group to champion the cause of Black music. It became quite obvious, however, that the attitudes of this group did not permit it to come to grips with social conditions as they actually existed. When emphasis was being placed on the study of Black culture, this group could not adjust their attitudes accordingly. Consequently, it was these same liberals who felt that Black music should not be isolated for serious study.

Although White America was greatly responsible for the absence of the serious study of Black music, guilt in this matter must be shared by Black America as well. As alluded to earlier, Blacks failed, for whatever reasons, to seriously study the music indigenous to their ethnic group. As an example, for years many Blacks ignored the spiritual because they looked on it as a relic and reminder of slavery. They failed to take into account its inherent beauty or to view it as a symbol of determination and fortitude. They allowed their own prejudices to perpetuate the neglect of both Black folk music forms and music composed by Black musicians.[1]

To compound the problem, some educators at Black colleges were interested in creating an awareness of Bach, Beethoven, and Brahms among their students[2] while ignoring most music forms[2] indigenous to Blacks.[3] They seemed even less aware of the importance of such individual

---

[1]There was an additional problem faced by Black and White composers alike, but more so by Black composers. Most composers have to lecture or teach at colleges in order to earn a living. Until recently, college teaching jobs were unavailable to most Black composers, and those who did enter the teaching profession did so at small, obscure, impecunious Black colleges. Since many of these colleges did not have orchestras, some composers turned to composing for college choirs, never to return to the orchestral medium again.

[2]The one Black music form that Black colleges did not ignore was the spiritual. This music, initially performed by the Fisk Jubilee Singers of Fisk University, became an integral part of the repertoire of many Black college choirs, including those of Hampton Institute and Tuskegee Institute.

[3]In all fairness, it must be pointed out that one reason that Blacks were being trained only in the music of European composers was the desire of Black educators to prepare their students to compete with White musicians on an equal basis in the composing and performing of music in the European tradition.

artists as the late Duke Ellington, Ornette Coleman, or Ray Charles.[4] In their efforts to assimilate the culture of White American society, these educators relinquished one of their most precious possessions—their cultural heritage.

In many ways, Black music *is* unique and is out of the mainstream of Western music. This should surprise no one, for when a society is segregated, it is destined to develop its own culture. When a group lives in isolation, it is nearly impossible to assimilate completely the culture of the dominant society. But because Black culture is different from that of White society does not in any way make it inferior. Black music, which is one facet of the culture, is no exception. And the uniqueness and originality that it possesses are its essence.

Antonín Dvořák, the famous Bohemian composer who left his native land to become director of the National Conservatory of Music in New York during the early 1890s, recognized the worth of Black music and advocated its employment in the development of nationalism in American music.

> . . . the future music of this country must be founded upon what are called Negro melodies. This must be the real foundation of any serious and original school of composition to be developed in the United States.
>
>   They are pathetic, tender, passionate, melancholy, solemn, religious, bold, merry, gay or what you will. It is music that suits itself to any mood or purpose. There is nothing in the whole range of composition that cannot be supplied with themes from this source.[5]

The point to be made here is not that the music of this country should be founded on Black music, but rather that Black music was recognized as being vital for a viable American music by no less a musical mind than Dvořák.

It is imperative that knowledge about Black music be made available to all of our students, since it is an essential aspect of American culture. Blacks have been deprived of the knowledge of their cultural history because White society has pretended for the most part that it never existed. When it has been acknowledged, it has often been deemed inferior and consequently not worth knowing since it has been judged primarily by a European standard. When the worth and importance of Black music are finally recognized, it will be seen that Whites as well as Blacks have been culturally deprived by being unaware of this unique culture.

When the contributions of Black musicians to American music are

[4]This situation began to change slowly approximately ten years ago when some Black colleges began to recognize jazz as a legitimate art form worthy of serious study. Among this group are Howard University, Southern University, and Texas Southern University.

[5]Antonín Dvořák, "Real Values of Negro Melodies," *New York Herald*, May 21, 1893.

examined closely, all doubt as to whether Black music should be studied is erased. Slave musicians were utilized to produce music for both the civic and social life of southern communities. Minstrelsy, although it became a caricature of the Black man, was born of Black music produced by slaves on the plantation for the entertainment of their masters. Ragtime's most outstanding composer, Scott Joplin, was Black, as was one of the first composers of jazz, Ferdinand "Jelly Roll" Morton. The originators of "swing," that style of jazz that was performed by White bands of the thirties, were the Black arrangers Fletcher Henderson and Don Redman. Bebop was originated by Blacks in the early forties because of the desire to create a new musical style free of White commercialism. Miles Davis was the catalyst in the creation of cool jazz, and rock and roll developed from the Black style known as rhythm and blues.

The jazz and ragtime idioms have been utilized quite extensively in the compositions of White composers from the European tradition. Among them are Claude Debussy, Darius Milhaud, Igor Stravinsky, Aaron Copland, Erik Satie, Ernst Krenek, Randall Thompson, and Maurice Ravel.

On the other hand, there have been Black composers whose music is largely in the European tradition. Among this group are Nathaniel Dett, Clarence Cameron White, William Dawson, William Grant Still, Howard Swanson, Hale Smith, Thomas J. Anderson, and Olly Wilson. These outstanding musicians have been involved in composing all kinds of music, from electronic to multifarious, from piano sonatas to symphonies, and from musical comedies to operas. The only restrictions on the kinds of music composed by Black musicians are those imposed by the musicians themselves, who have the ability and expertise to compose in all forms and media.

Black Americans are insisting that they be given the opportunity to become aware of their cultural heritage. They want to know their cultural roots and to develop an awareness of their cultural history. In addition, it is important that White Americans be made aware of the cultural heritage of the Black minority so that they may realize how greatly Blacks have contributed to American society through their industry, genius, and culture.

It is time that all of our educational institutions, from the primary grades through graduate school, fulfill their responsibility of teaching *all* of our citizens about *all* of our citizens.[6]

[6]It is gratefully acknowledged that the ideas expressed in this chapter have been strongly influenced by the thinking of Dominique-René deLerma. For a more detailed exposition of why Black music should be studied, read his chapter, "Some Curricular and Philosophical Challenges in Black Music," in *Black Music in Our Culture*, ed. Dominique-René deLerma (Kent, Ohio: Kent State University Press, 1970), pp. 25–34.

chapter one

Black Music and Its Roots

While the music of Black Americans is a unique facet of American culture, many of its attributes are not peculiar to the United States. Because of common roots in the music of West Africa, American Black music bears strong resemblance in many ways to the music of other Black people of the New World. When American Black music is examined, the evidence points overwhelmingly to African musical survivals as having contributed to its uniqueness.

African musical survivals have persisted in American Black music despite certain factors that have tended to discourage them. By contrast, in Central and South America and the Caribbean islands, three factors—one societal, one musical, and one religious—helped to produce a favorable climate for the survival of African musical characteristics.

In North America, Blacks found no favorable ground for the cultivation of African musical tradition because of the attitude of White society toward Blacks. Since the slaves were regarded as inferior, their cultural background was ignored. Blacks were supposedly humanized through inducing them to adopt behavior patterns befitting an inferior caste. Consequently, North American Blacks soon learned to be ashamed of their African heritage. By contrast, the attitudes of the White population toward Blacks and toward African culture in Latin America was conducive to the survival of African rhythms in the music of these Blacks. This is partially because of extensive intermarriage between Europeans and Africans in the slave areas of South America, which helped foster a feeling of equality among Blacks in this area. On the other hand, so many of the Africans were constantly at war with the Whites that they were simply left alone.

The folk music of Spain and Portugal, the European powers dominant in Latin America during the slaving period, was somewhat similar to African music and built upon a more complex rhythmic foundation than the music of Northern Europe. Perhaps their music was more complex rhythmically because of the conquest of Spain in the Middle Ages by the Moors of North Africa. The slaves of North America, on the other hand, were exposed to the music of the White population in which rhythm was subordinate to melody. The music of slave owners in the United States did not lend itself so readily to a fusion with the African musical style. African music contained mixed meters and offbeat accents, while the music of the slave owners of North America contained only one time signature in each song in which the rhythm of the melody coincides with the pulse of the meter.

Richard Waterman describes the contrast between the opportunities for religious syncretization offered in Roman Catholic countries with those in the United States:

> . . . the unassimilable nature of the ideas presented to the slaves by the Protestant creeds of the United States is striking. Most of those who preached to the slaves were either Methodists or Baptists, and their faiths offered few concepts which the Negroes, in the light of their training in African religions, could grasp. The hierarchical polytheism of Africa had to be repudiated almost entirely before any part of the new religious dogma could be accepted. But accepted it was, and with the loss of their gods the slaves had no reason to retain the music and the rhythms associated with them.[1]

In Latin America, the situation was quite different:

> In these Roman Catholic countries and in the Caribbeans, the Negroes, by identifying their gods with the saints of the Church, were able to retain much of the structure of the African hierarchy of supernatural beings. With their gods they retained, of course, much of the technique and the paraphernalia associated with African religious worship. Prominent in this connection were drums and rhythms.[2]

While it is obvious that African slaves in the United States were given little opportunity to retain their African musical style, certain factors did operate to keep alive the African concept of rhythm. The anthropologists Melville Herskovits and Richard Waterman contend that the musical atti-

---

[1]Richard A. Waterman, "'Hot' Rhythm in Negro Music," *Journal of the American Musicological Society* (January 1948), p. 29.

[2]*Ibid.*, p. 27.

Among the most famous dance companies to blend European and African influences, the Alvin Ailey dance troup is pictured here at the finale of Alvin Ailey's masterpiece "Revelations." (Photo courtesy Columbia Artist Management.)

tudes, values, and appreciations of Blacks are established at the subconscious level and are learned through imitation rather than actually taught. For the most part, their conception of rhythm has withstood change induced from without, even though there were forces strong enough to cause great modifications in the features of those aspects of African culture that are more overt and consciously maintained.

White society has maintained a favorable attitude toward Black dancing from times of slavery to the present, which has helped to perpetuate Black dance rhythms. Black dance evolved along lines similar to Black music. Its source is likewise a blend of European and African traditions in an American environment. At the risk of oversimplification, it can be said that, in general, it was the European influences that contributed its elegance while African influences gave it its rhythmic impetus. Those slaves with the ability to dance were often given preferential treatment and prestige in proportion to their virtuosity as dancers. It could be said that a similar situation prevailed for many years following the end of slavery.[3]

[3]Dancing as a Black art form seems to have passed into disfavor among White society in recent years. One of the last Black solo dancers to receive the acclaim of White America was Bill "Bojangles" Robinson (1869–1949). One of the last Black dancing groups to enjoy similar success was the Four Step Brothers (1928–1960s). On the other hand, there seems to be an upsurge of White interest in Black artists dancing in modern dance forms and ballet. The Black dancers Bill Frank and Alvin Ailey, among others, are gaining increasing recognition in this idiom.

In the music itself, certain channels have remained open to varying degrees. In some regions of the United States, either African drums or substitutes for them in the form of overturned baskets or pans persisted all through the period of slavery. Religious songs learned from Whites were soon given the rhythmic treatment peculiar to Black music. Such devices as hand-clapping and foot-stomping in lieu of drumming and the use of offbeat accents in the African musical style became common.

Improvisation, one of the most prominent characteristics of American Black music, is common in the music of West Africa. This trait, found especially in songs of derision or allusion in this country, is used in similar songs in West Africa. In many of the tribes, there are professional *griots** with great facility in improvisation and caustic tongues who often collect tribute from tribal members for what they withhold as well as for what they say.

While the predominance of the human voice is common to most folk music, the manner in which it is employed in American Black music is directly related to the music of West Africa. In both musics, a variety of vocal timbre is found, ranging from falsetto tones to a raucous vocal quality. The call-and-response pattern, so much a part of the Black spiritual and work song, is a survival of West African musical practices. Even the so-called "blue notes," so widely used in the music of American Blacks, are of West African origin. As each of these characteristics of American Black music is discussed in detail, it will become obvious that they are all survivals of music indigenous to West Africa.

People of African descent in various parts of the New World have shown marked differences in degree of acculturation, as have Blacks of various socioeconomic strata within a given area. While many scholars recognize these differences in speech, religious practices, family life, and music, there is no general agreement as to why they exist.

Some scholars attribute these differences not to survivals of African culture but rather to incomplete acculturation, due in part to isolation. Other scholars contend that traces of African culture can be discovered in nearly every phase of Black life in the Western Hemisphere.

E. Franklin Frazier[4] and many other sociologists subscribed to the former belief and denied the survival of any Africanisms. It was Frazier's contention that because of cricumstances, the slaves had to acquire a new language, adopt new work habits, and take over the folkways of their new environment. Consequently, their children, who knew only the American environment, soon forgot the few memories of their native land that had been passed on to them, and developed motivations and kinds of behavior

---

Griot is a French term for a professional musician of West Africa.

[4]E. Franklin Frazier, *The Negro Family in the United States* (Chicago: University of Chicago Press, 1948), p. 15.

Rural southern Black women frequently wore kerchiefs on their heads, an Africanism female slaves brought to the New World. (Photo courtesy Special Collections Division, Tulane University Library.)

in conformity with the New World. As a result, the habits and customs that characterized the life of their forebears in Africa disappeared.[5]

The chief advocates of the survival of Africanism in the New World are anthropologists, of whom Melville J. Herskovits was one of the leading spokesmen. Herskovits and others have documented conclusively that such survivals do exist in social organization, religion, language, and the fine arts.

> The habit of carrying burdens on the head, so widespread in tropical countries, is favored in West Africa and the West Indies. To what extent it has survived in the United States cannot be said, but that the practice has had an important influence on walking style is apparent. . . . The ways in which southern rural Negro women habitually carry their infants . . . corresponds exactly to one manner in which infants are transported in West Africa . . . [a baby is strapped to her back]. The other method, still commonly to be seen . . . is to use one arm to hold the child as it straddles the hip of its carrier. . . . Concerning the wearing of headkerchiefs in the United States, another Africanism, . . . [it] was common enough so that it came to be accepted as an integral part of the conventional portrait of the Negro "mammy." . .[6]

[5]Later, Frazier modified his thinking on the subject of African survivals in this country. But while he came to agree that there are some survivals in the Black subculture, he disagreed as to the extent of these survivals.

[6]Melville J. Herskovits, *The Myth of the Negro Past* (New York: Harper and Brothers, 1941), pp. 146–49.

It is evident that African survivals are more widespread than at first believed.

In agreement with Herskovits is Harold Courlander, who writes:

It is difficult to imagine that huge numbers of African exiles, gathered together in a new setting, would forget everything they knew and become a vacuum into which the attributes of another culture could be poured at will. In the ordinary course of adjustment, the African and his descendants absorbed and learned from the dominant culture in which they found themselves. Those attributes of the master culture which were essential to their survival, or which were congenial to their past learning, were taken over most quickly, while they clung to those aspects of African life for which they found no satisfactory substitutes.[7]

Black music in the United States "could have come into being only in the United States, where elements of specific cultures were brought together under conditions that were not exactly duplicated anywhere else."[8] Courlander amplified the above statement by adding:

European and African elements mingled to produce one result in the Spanish islands of the Caribbean, another in the English islands, a third in the French islands. The result was still different in Brazil and Venezuela.[9]

The music of Blacks in the United States preserved its African traits partly because music was not really suppressed to a great degree. Although the drums were viewed with suspicion and subdued, the slaves' music was largely tolerated by the dominant culture and generally encouraged. The music of Blacks was not only valued as entertainment by the masters but also as a means of increasing the work production of the slaves. Consequently, some of its characteristics were incorporated into the musical idiom of the dominant culture. Therefore, the retention of African musical traits among the slaves was enhanced because of the milieu in which the slaves functioned.

Black music in the United States has both general and special characteristics that distinguish it from the music of pure European or Anglo-American origin. The manner in which effects are achieved and in the exploration of instruments and the human voice are peculiar to Black music. And it is significantly different in the literary sense—the specialized qualities of its imagery and the nature of the ideas with which the images deal.

The characteristics of Black music that will be discussed below apply only to those Black music forms indigenous to the American Black. They

[7]Harold Courlander, *Negro Folk Music, U.S.A.* (New York: Columbia University Press, 1963), 3–4.

[8]*Ibid.*, p. 1–2.

[9]*Ibid.*

include spirituals, work songs, field hollers, blues, ragtime, jazz, gospel songs, rhythm and blues, rock and roll, and soul music. A critical examination of the Black tradition reveals a number of distinguishing characteristics.

RHYTHMIC CHARACTER

One of the most characteristic qualities of Black music in the New World is its rhythm. Music in the European tradition and the music of Blacks in the United States, Latin America, and Africa are all characterized by a regularity of pulse. Regularity of pulse indicates a scheme of regularly recurring accents that underlies the particular rhythm of a melody or harmonic progression, accents that are regularly spaced in time even though they may not be continually expressed.

Regularity of pulse acts as a framework in which an essential component of American Black music, a variety of uneven rhythms, is achieved. The music of Blacks may be contrasted with music in the older European tradition by stating that the former makes use of uneven rhythm with a regular tempo while the latter employs even rhythm with accelerandos, ritards, and different tempi. It must be pointed out that this rhythmic difference is due in part to the fact that a great deal of American Black music is used for dancing while much music in the European tradition is not.

While both African and American Black music contain an absolute regularity of pulse, the character of the rhythm of the two musics shows marked differences. African music is frequently polymetric, in that one drummer may appear to play in $\frac{4}{4}$, a second in $\frac{3}{4}$, and others in still other meters. This mixture of meters is usually maintained throughout each piece. Although such cross-rhythms are common in American Black music, they do not usually persist consistently throughout the length of each musical entity.

Although it is true that cross-rhythms appear in both African music and American Black music in varying degrees, the approach to these rhythms is vastly different in each. To explain the complexity of African rhythms as being simply polymetric is insufficient. It is true that in African music there can be a series of rhythmic motifs of ever-changing time-length that can only be intelligibly set down in a series of bars of continually changing value, such as $\frac{3}{8}$, $\frac{4}{4}$, and so on. Its time is irregular, being a mixture of duple and triple time. The African approach to rhythm is largely additive.

On the other hand, the rhythmic structure of American Black music and music in the European tradition is based on a divisive system. For example, $\frac{2}{4}$ exists as a basic pattern before it is divided into one accented and one less accented beats.

A. M. Jones[10] has explained the additive principle as it relates to African music. This music is built up from a small basic time unit whose speed is constant for all instruments right through a piece even though polyrhythm is evident.

> When the African plays 3 against 2 in polyrhythm what he sometimes does is to set up this relationship permanently right through a piece of music or a main section of it. This is apparently a denial of our insistence on the constancy of the basic unit of time. For if you play permanently two rhythms 3 against 2 what you are really doing is employing two basic time-units. For example:

EXAMPLE 1.1   Two basic time units

But this is not the only way to exploit 3 against 2. There is another way, and it is this which the African usually employs.

EXAMPLE 1.2   One basic time unit

> Both voices are still in the relationship of 3 to 2 (3 bars of the top line to 2 of the bottom), but this time it is the top line which is going quicker. Now if, as before, the top line represents the basic time-units, the bottom line is going *slower*. When this happens, the basic time-unit is not *apparently* forsaken by any instrument, for in this case the slower time is a definite compound of the basic time-units: whereas the top line takes them two at a time, the bottom line takes three at a time. This makes an enormous difference to the sound of a piece of music, for 3 against 2 played in this form by Africans produces no audible clash of basic time at all.

Therefore, the point to be made is that while American Black music is akin to African music in its polyrhythmic complexity, its approach to cross-rhythms is divisive in nature rather than additive, and thus in this respect, contrary to popular opinion, is similar to music in the European tradition. While melodic rhythmic syncopation in American Black music is usually far more complex than that found in music in the European tradition, they approach syncopation in a similar, divisive manner.

---

[10]A. M. Jones, *Studies in African Music*, Vol. I (London: Oxford University Press, 1959), p. 102–3.

A second characteristic of the rhythm of American Black music is its syncopation. A rhythm having stresses that do not agree with the normal metric stresses is said to be syncopated. There is a peculiar relationship between the steady pulse of rhythm against what may be complex beat patterns by a drummer against the rhythm of the melody. While the accents in melodies of pre-twentieth-century European music tend to fall on either the upbeat or downbeat, melodic accents in American Black music may occur at various other points. It may occur (1) by rhythmic anticipation:

EXAMPLE 1.3   Rhythmic anticipation

(2) by rhythmic suspension:

EXAMPLE 1.4   Rhythmic suspension

(3) by an indicated stress on an unaccented beat or on a subdivision of the beat:

EXAMPLE 1.5   Stress on unaccented beat

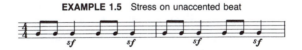

(4) by having a rest on the beat and sound on a subdivision of the beat:

EXAMPLE 1.6   Sound on subdivision of beat

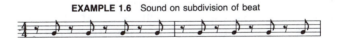

Many jazz performers have found that the European system of notation does not lend itself to jazz expression and that the more strictly one adheres to the precise note values, the more mechanical, the more "square," a performance becomes. In some cases (but not all) a quarter note should be sounded for as short a period of time as an eighth note.

EXAMPLE 1.7   Articulation of eighth and quarter notes

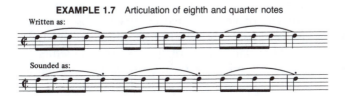

Dotted half notes may be sustained three beats, but sometimes a written dotted half note may be given only two and one-half or three and one-half beats.

EXAMPLE 1.8   Articulation of dotted half note

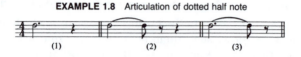

(1)   (2)   (3)

Notes within a phrase may receive different dynamic stress even though one dynamic marking may be indicated for an entire phrase.

EXAMPLE 1.9   Different dynamic stress in a phrase

Basically, the music of the jazz ensemble is a problem in rhythm. The drummer creates jazz patterns on drums that the horns use to project melody and harmony. Certain articulations, however, are vital to the expression of these patterns.

While syncopation in American Black music is usually far more complex than that found in music in the European idiom, both approach syncopation in a similar, divisive manner. On the other hand, the African is not concerned that the inherent stresses of the melody agree with the regularly recurring rhythm of the metrical background. African melody is free to pursue its own course, with its own accents originating from its form. When the accents of the melody and the pulse of the meter (background rhythm) separate, the rhythm of the melody coincides with multiples of the basic beat. Thus, it becomes additive.

Another form of syncopation occurs within the percussive elements. For example, in $\frac{4}{4}$ meter we are conditioned to expect the accent to fall on the first and third beats of each measure. In American Black music, it is common to place the melodic accents on one and three, and the percussion accents on two and four. Due in part to the use of polyrhythms, there may be variation within the pattern; the melodic accents may fall on two or four, and the percussion accents on one or three.

A further characteristic of American Black rhythm is the manner in which rhythmic patterns are performed with variations in timbre and tone. To an even greater extent, African percussion is used to produce melodic and timbral patterns of considerable complexity. A majority of African instruments are percussive, but each is designed to produce a different pitch or timbre. The many kinds of drums are supplemented by rattles, iron gongs, calabashes, and sticks. Other instruments, such as the marimba, the musical bow, and the sansa (said by some ethnomusicologists to be the predecessor of the marimba), combine rhythmic and melodic functions but give more support to the rhythms than to the melodies.

Music in the pre-twentieth-century European tradition does employ tuned kettledrums and a variety of other tuned percussion instruments, but their melodic and rhythmic function is very restricted in comparison to the role of African percussion. Of course this is partly because music in the European tradition is usually notated while African music is basically an improvisatory music. The specific pitches as well as the rhythm is notated.

American Black music utilizes the melodic and timbral functions of percussion instruments less extensively than African music, but more extensively than music in the older European tradition. Variations in timbre are employed in many Black churches through hand-clapping, foot-stomping, and tambourine playing. The jazz drummer utilizes varying timbre and tone by augmenting his snare drum and bass drum with tuned tomtoms and cymbals, woodblocks and cowbells, and by varying the manner in which he strikes the snare drum head.

The rhythm section of a jazz band consists not only of drums, but also of piano, guitar, and string bass. Since the latter three are tuned instruments, they have a tonal as well as a percussive function; they thus provide a further illustration of the importance of tonal and timbre lines in the basic rhythmic patterns of American Black music.

CALL-AND-RESPONSE PATTERNS

The call-and-response pattern is one of the readily recognized characteristics of some American Black music. In Black music there seems to be a natural tendency toward two-part singing, with the first part being that of the leader and the second that of the group. Other variants of the pattern include solo answered by solo and group answered by group.

Similar patterns may be found in music in the European tradition. One such pattern is responsorial psalmody, which consists of a plainsong chant sung by a soloist alternately with a chorus. In the United States, there developed the common practice of "lining out" psalms or hymns, in which, because all of the members of the congregation did not possess hymnals or could not read, the leader sang each line and the congregation repeated it.

The African pattern of call and response differs from both the European and American patterns in that the leader's part and the responsive part may overlap when the leader starts a new phrase before the congregation has quite finished. Although some authorities regard this as accidental, it seems definitely intentional, if for no other reason than the consistency with which it occurs.

MODE, SCALE, AND HARMONY

American Black music—whether work songs, religious songs, or jazz—contains partially flatted third and seventh scale degrees (E is the third degree and B the seventh in the key of C major). The aberration of these tones, being microtonal, results in their not coinciding with any diatonic scale or mode.

EXAMPLE 1.10   Diatonic scale with blue notes

Many students of Black music have attempted to explain these flatted tones within the framework of major or minor modes. It is the contention of some that when the diatonic major scale contains flatted third and seventh steps, it becomes a "blues scale." Others are of the opinion that while blues scale may be a reasonable term, it is not a correct one since this scale is not a special ten-tone scale. The ten-tone scale is the major diatonic scale with the microtonally lowered third and seventh steps added. It would be more proper to refer to this scale as major-minor, or, more simply, bimodal.

One important characteristic of this music has been largely overlooked. In Black music, singers attack the third and seventh tones and the octave in an endless variety of ways—swoops, slurs, smears, glides—in an effort to employ every sound of which the human voice is capable. It is also typical for the instrumentalists to attempt to imitate these vocal techniques by producing these characteristic nuances and tonal ambiguities. (Just the opposite is true of music in the European tradition in which the singer's goal is largely to imitate the sound of instruments.) Various wind and string instruments can bend tones and thereby give a reasonable imitation of the vocal effects found in Black music. Such imitation is also practiced on the piano. The tones on the piano are fixed and cannot be manipulated in any way; however, the major third and the major seventh must be lowered a full half step if they are to be lowered at all. In order to compensate for this rigidity, tone clusters that are "blue" in quality are employed; the flat and natural keys of the third and seventh steps of the scale are sounded simultaneously in an attempt to imitate microtonal lowering of the pitch.

Elaborate theories have claimed that the superimposition of African pentatonic scales on European diatonic scales resulted in two uncertain tonal areas, thus causing the so-called "blue tones." In fact, however, there are a variety of tones in African, Afro-Haitian, Afro-Cuban, and American Black music that do not conform to notes in our tempered scale. These tones cannot be explained as happening by chance for they have apparently been occurring in Black music for several hundred years. Neither can they be explained as alterations of tones of the European diatonic scale. What has not been taken into account with both theories is that the musicians who employ these tones often are fine musicians capable of minutely distinguishing one tone from another. These tones are, for the most part, incidentally conceived rather than being conceived by chance. They are components of a tradition that has its roots in West Africa, not in Western Europe.

African music tends to emphasize pentatonicism. American Black music not only employs the pentatonic scale (in the key of C:CDEGA) but also variants of this scale such as the diatonic major scale lacking either its fourth or its seventh (or, put another way, the pentatonic scale plus an additional note, either the perfect fourth or the major seventh). Several other scales are found in American Black music. These include the major scale with flatted seventh, the minor scale with raised sixth, the minor without the sixth, and the minor with raised seventh. It has been suggested that these scales are survivals of scales brought from Africa. To the contrary, it is improbable that African scales fit perfectly into the European notational system, but rather that the above-mentioned scales are the equal-tempered scales that they most nearly approach. That scales indigenous to West Africa before there had been Western influence would fit into the European notational system seems highly unlikely.

The term "harmony," as it was used in Europe in the eighteenth and nineteenth centuries, means the structure, functions, and relationships of chords. A chord is considered three or more different notes sounded simultaneously, though it may be represented by only two notes with a third implied. Consequently, harmony can be considered to be any simultaneity of tones. In a large amount of American Black folk music, its harmonies are partially the result of polyphony. This polyphony may arise from the overlapping of leader and chorus lines in the call-and-response patterns. While voice overlapping of this type is most often heard in the church, it is also employed in secular singing. It seems that in the Black vocal tradition, polyphony is preferred to a melody with harmonized accompaniment in the traditional sense. It also appears that varied rhythmic, tonal, and melodic interest are featured at the expense of traditional harmonic interest.

As stated earlier, harmony is usually considered any simultaneity of tones. While this is not harmony in the traditional sense, there can also be a simultaneity of rhythms. Such is the circumstance in a considerable amount of American Black folk music. Quite often, layers of cross-rhythms are utilized, resulting in a counterpoint of rhythms. This simultaneity of rhythms is found in Black music everywhere.

While the blue notes performed on instruments are considered an imitation of vocal style, the lowered third and seventh tones are often used harmonically as well as melodically. These tones can often be found in jazz chords. When these tones are used harmonically, there exists more nearly a bimodal scale (both major and minor) because these tones are lowered a full one-half step. In addition to chords containing the blue notes, many other kinds of altered chords are employed in jazz.

VARIETY OF TIMBRE

A great variety of timbre pervades all of American Black music, whether it be vocal or instrumental. In pure vocal music differences in the qualities of sound employed by various voices can be found. In instrumental ensembles, a variety of instruments possessing widely different timbres is employed. By comparison, music in the older European tradition does not put as much emphasis on variety of timbre.

Harold Courlander[11] has described how various singing conventions are employed in Black music to produce a wide variety of sound quality. While some of these effects are not peculiar to American Black music, they are generally not found in other American music. One of these conventions is the use of falsetto, sometimes for a note or two, on occasion for whole phrases or entire songs. Falsetto is also used quite extensively in African singing.

In various kinds of Black folk music the singer may employ humming, moaning, and groaning. On occasion, the moaning is given another dimension by being done in falsetto.

A third characteristic quality heard particularly in Black religious singing is the softening of various final consonants to produce a desired aural effect. For instance, final r's and l's may be converted into n's and m's producing a musical sound resembling humming. Often, "hammer" is sung as "hummun," "father" as "fathum," "angel" as "angun," and "steel" as "steem." This technique is a musical device not usually employed in conversational speech.

Portamento—sliding or gliding from one tone to the next—is extensively used in American Black music, both vocal and instrumental. Singers attack and release notes in this music through the use of swoops, slurs, smears, and glides, all of which are forms of portamento. It is quite easy to perform slides on the trombone because of the manner in which the instrument is constructed.[12] While it is much more difficult to perform portamento on the trumpet and clarinet, it can be done if there is complete coordination of embouchure, breath, and fingering.

A final example of characteristic vocal timbre found in both the African and American Black traditions is the foggy, rough, or raucous singing

---

[11]Harold Courlander, *Negro Folk Music, U.S.A.* (New York: Columbia University Press, 1963), pp. 24–26.

[12]This effect is often incorrectly called *glissando*. Since glissando is a rapid scale, it is a very difficult effect to produce on the trombone; a simple movement of the slide produces not a rapid scale, but a continuous change of pitch.

voice. There is no apparent striving for the "smooth" and "sweet" qualities so highly regarded in the European idiom.

Just as instruments imitate the voice in intonation, they also imitate the quality of its timbre. In Black instrumental music, a variety of techniques is employed to produce a wide range of timbre. In New Orleans jazz, as an example, there are three distinctive tone colors—clarinet, trumpet, and trombone—to distinguish its heterophonic lines. In jazz of the 20s and 30s, performers on these instruments made use of such special instrumental effects as the growl, produced by simultaneously blowing and humming into the instrument; the shake, produced either by an exaggerated hand vibrato or by jaw vibrato; lipping, in which the pitch is controlled by stiffening or slackening the lip muscles; fluttering, produced by vibrating the tongue against the upper alveolar ridge of the mouth (the bony ridge behind the teeth); and the use of muting devices such as hats and bathroom plungers. The practice of varying instrumental timbres has its roots in the music of West and Central Africa, where buzzing and other vibrating effects are intentionally produced on African horns and trumpets.

In jazz of the late 20s and 30s, the various combinations of instruments employed gave rise to a greater variety of timbre. Some of the instrumental combinations employed in jazz include a solo instrument, either open or muted, played against a background by similar instruments or by other instruments of the orchestra in varying combinations; and groups of instruments of the orchestra employed against each other in varying combinations. Often, the background instruments employ sustained chords, riffs,[13] or fill-ins.

In light of the instances cited, it becomes obvious that this characteristic quality of varying timbre is used extensively in both the vocal and instrumental forms of American Black music.

HETEROPHONY

The texture of American Black music is predominantly horizontal rather than vertical. When music in the European tradition is written in a horizontal texture, it is said to be contrapuntal or polyphonic. Neither term accurately describes the distinctive texture of much American Black music. Since in this music each voice or instrument frequently performs simultaneous variations on the same melodic line, a more appropriate term is *heterophonic*.

In Black church singing, for instance, it is common for the congregation to sing in unison or at the octave. At times, a departure from the melody by certain members of the congregation may result in intervals that

[13]The riff is a relatively short phrase that is repeated.

approximate seconds, thirds, fourths, or fifths. Heterophony is also one of the principal characteristics of New Orleans-style jazz. It is the result of combining two instrumental parts, one of which is not a truly independent part but rather a slightly altered version of the other part.

In practice, heterophony is the result of improvisation. Improvised and semi-improvised harmonization, as exemplified by heterophony, are basic to the Black tradition. On the other hand, the type of premeditated harmonizations employed in some forms of Black music are latter-day developments shared with music in the European tradition. The various kinds of American Black music that have been conceived in the style of Black music but transcribed in European notation are usually written within the framework of European harmony, and they tend to lose their heterophonic characteristics as a result.

IMPROVISATION AND THEME-WITH-VARIATIONS FORM

Aside from rhythmic complexity, improvisation is the most salient characteristic of American Black music. Improvisation had been an integral part of performance during the Middle Ages, Renaissance, and Baroque periods of music in Western Europe. After the time of J. S. Bach, however, the art of improvisation, as an essential part of performance practice, declined. This is not to imply that improvising stopped after Bach, for it was the test of musical talent into the beginning of the nineteenth century. It did, however, become a special rather than a customary part of musical performance, a display of technical prowess used to complement the notated compositions performed by artists at concerts. Undoubtedly, European notation and the desire for repeated performances contributed greatly to the decline of improvisation as an integral part of music in the European tradition.[14] It must be pointed out that in the last few years there has been a renaissance in improvisation on the part of European and American composers.

Improvisation is utilized extensively in Black folk songs, and it is an essential element especially in songs that employ the call-and-response pattern. In a spiritual or work song, the leader has license to improvise on the melody in his call, while the response usually repeats its basic melodic line without change. Songs of West Africa, as was mentioned above, are performed in the same manner.

[14]It is interesting to note the difference in performances of popular songs by Black and White singers. In many instances, the White singer will sing the melodic line of the song as written, without change, from beginning to end. On the other hand, the Black singer may sing the first chorus as written (though most often not), but will be sure to improvise on the melodic line while singing additional choruses.

In work songs and songs of derision or allusion, the singer has great latitude in improvising the words as well. In some songs, the words may be changed with each performance while the melodic line remains constant; in others, both the words and melodic line may be improvised simultaneously. Improvisation of words is common in the music of Blacks not only in the United States but also in Central and South America and West Africa.

Improvisation has been an important part of jazz since its inception around the turn of this century. A false impression exists among the listening public that the jazz soloist who improvises is creating new material spontaneously. In fact, however, when a jazz musician improvises, he calls on a reservoir of material gained through years of listening, absorbing, analyzing, and imitating the work of performers before him, his contemporaries, and his own work. He modifies and adapts melodic fragments, rhythmic patterns, and entire phrases to his own conception. When this is adroitly done, the performance not only seems to be spontaneous, but the material appears to be that of the performer. The outstanding soloist knows when to use his own material and, above all, how to make the performance sound spontaneous.

Another form of improvisation common in American Black music is collective improvisation, such as that found in New Orleans jazz, where each performer is limited by the necessities of the ensemble and has a specific part to play in the total sound. In the New Orleans ensemble, the cornet provides the melodic lead, and the clarinet embroiders the cornet line heterophonically, while the trombone improvises more on the harmony than the melody. Thus, the type of improvisation that each instrument of the ensemble will play is quite clearly defined.

A natural way to extend a melody is to follow it with a variation on itself, then a second variation, and so on. Exactly the same principle is involved when a performer improvises on a melodic line or theme.

Whatever else it may be, improvisation is variation. The theme may be a melodic subject, a harmonic progression, or a rhythmic pattern; it may consist of any of these singly, or in any combination. Since improvisation is such an important part of American Black music, it follows that the most typical form of Black music is the theme with variations.

PREDOMINANCE OF HUMAN
VOICE AND PERCUSSION

Because American Black music lays great stress on complex rhythm patterns, it is to be expected that percussion plays an important part in performance. As stated earlier, in vocal music, even though no percussion instruments are employed, the hands and feet are used in a percussive manner. Thigh-patting was used to accompany old-time social dances such as the Juba. Hand-clapping, thigh-slapping, and foot-stomping are employed in children's ring games, playparty songs, and certain types of religious songs. It is apparent that these musical devices are of African derivation.

Of course the percussive element has been a fixture in jazz since its inception. The central role of rhythm is manifested through a great variety of "traps" (woodblock, tom-tom, cowbell, bass drum, snare drum, cymbal, etc.) played by the drummer in the jazz band. The rhythm section (piano, string bass, guitar, and drums), although melodic to a great extent, is primarily percussive in its function.

Since the human voice is the primary vehicle for melody in most folk musics, it is not surprising to find that it also predominates in American Black folk music. The voice occupies a position of such importance that it even influences the manner in which many instruments employed in this music are played; the variations in timbre and the inflections of pitch that a jazz musician produces on his instrument are modeled on vocal technique. In jazz, the voice may be used as an instrument in the *scat* vocal (singing using nonsense syllables). At other times, the melody is shared by the vocalist and an instrument; the vocalist may stop in the middle of a line and let the instrument complete it, or the vocalist's line may be answered by an instrument in lieu of the actual words.

INSTRUMENTATION

Although instruments employed in American Black music are largely of the simpler kind, this does not necessarily imply that they are primitive. Some of these instruments may be variations of instruments with a sophisticated history. Many appear in well-developed forms, others in forms that are elemental. Nevertheless, it must be clearly understood that the use of simple instruments does not necessarily mean that music is elemental. As an example, the wood block is primitive in a historical sense but is used in symphony orchestras extensively.[15]

Most Black street bands used orthodox European instruments. Makeshift groups, however, used all kinds of instrumental devices, including "frying pans, lard tins, a washboard, a washtub bass, a harmonica, a kazoo, a guitar, and clacking sticks or bones."[16] While these instruments may appear to be substitutes for the real thing, certain specific sound qualities were demanded of each.

[15]Harold Courlander, *Negro Folk Music, U.S.A.* (New York: Columbia University Press, 1963), p. 205.

[16]*Ibid.*, p. 206

One of the instruments found in American Black music is the wash-tub bass. This instrument, also known as "gutbucket" or simply "tub," provides the bass line. It consists of an inverted washtub to which an upright broomstick is attached. A cord is strung between the upper end of the stick and the washtub. Sound is produced by plucking or slapping the string; by changing the position of the stick, the tautness of the cord varied, thus producing different pitches. The progenitor of the washtub bass is believed to be the earth bow, an instrument found in West and Central Africa and in the Black communities of the West Indies.[17]

A historical study of the washtub bass in Black music makes it apparent that its function is parallel to that of the string bass in jazz. Both instruments are played in the same manner, and both take the bass part in the ensemble. While plucking the string bass is not a new technique, its use as an instrument that is not normally bowed is foreign to the European tradition.

Scraped instruments, which are found in Black cultures of the New World, are probably of African origin, although these kinds of instruments have been known to develop in other cultures.[18] Various forms of the scraper are found in several Black New World cultures. The *guiro,* a notched gourd that is scraped with a piece of wire or bamboo, is found in Cuba; a metal object such as a nail is drawn across the teeth of a saw in the Bahamas; a kitchen grater or piece of perforated sheet metal scraped with a wire is common in Haiti; and a scraping tool drawn over the teeth of the jawbone of a donkey is used throughout the Caribbean and in parts of the United States. But the most widely used scraped instrument in the United States is the ordinary washboard. The washboard performer scrapes the metal surface with a wire, a thimble, a nail, or a bare finger. By manipulating the fingernail and soft part of the finger, the performer is able to produce variations both in timbre and articulation.[19] It can be assumed that the availability of the washboard made it easily transferable into a musical instrument because of the heritage of African scraping instruments. This instrument was often used by jazz bands of the twenties and may still be heard in some "rhythm and blues" bands recorded as late as the forties.

Steel frying pans were used extensively by the street bands of New Orleans and other southern cities as percussive devices. While their connection with percussion devices that preceded them in the African tradition is not immediately obvious, it is not too difficult to detect that this modern hardware is employed within the framework of that tradition. Frying pans and other common metal objects used as gongs or bells are not

[17]*Ibid.*
[18]Scraped instruments were also common in ancient Mexico, for example.
[19]*Ibid.,* p. 207.

recent additions to Black music of this country but were used in the New Orleans street bands of the late nineteenth century. Metal percussion is important in much of the music of West Africa as well as in African cultures of the Caribbean and the South American mainland. In each of these Black cultures, forged iron bells—used singly, in pairs, and in threes—"have been commonly used as an element of percussion accompaniment to singing."[20]

In the United States, metal percussion was continuously used in various musical activities. Although the availability of the frying pan may have played an important part in its use as a musical instrument, it can be considered a descendant of earlier instruments rather than a makeshift device. Although the pitch of the pans is not precise, they are nevertheless used as pitched instruments (just as the African musician uses his bells), often two or three in combination with other instruments.

European cymbals and triangle are two other kinds of metal percussion devices that were used extensively by both the small street bands and the large brass bands that were a part of the Black musical scene in cities throughout the South and North in the second half of the nineteenth century. The sounds produced by these instruments were very compatible with the music of these groups. Their sounds closely approximated that of the African bell and were effective as bell substitutes. Because the cymbals and triangle produced tones of longer duration than the African bell, however, they were employed as a part of the overall sound rather than for a rhythmic background pulse or a figure embroidering upon basic drum patterns.[21]

The drum is usually regarded as the nucleus of West African instrumentation. One of the functions of music in the culture of West Africa is as an element in the worship of gods. Since worship is an organized event, the only music performed is that traditionally associated with the given occasion. Thus, music associated with worship is narrowly restricted.

The drum is disproportionately significant in the music of the various Black cultures of the New World as it is in West Africa. While the slaves were able to retain much of their African religious structure in Roman Catholic countries of the New World, such was not the case in White Protestant North America. The slaves were forced to repudiate their gods, and therefore had no reason to retain the music associated with them. Also, drums were outlawed for fear of rebellion among the slaves. The situation of the African slaves in the United States, then, was not one that afforded

---

[20]*Ibid.*, p. 208.
[21]*Ibid.*, p. 211.

them much opportunity to retain their African musical style and the percussion instruments associated with it.

"African drums and drumming were familiar in the New Orleans area . . . [a Roman Catholic society] . . . late in the nineteenth century"[22] where batteries of drums were used for accompaniment to dance. Although groups of drums such as these are no longer found in the United States, the African drum battery does survive in the practice of the jazz drummer. This one-man percussion battery utilizes tuned tom-toms, woodblocks, and cowbells in addition to the European snare drum, bass drum, and cymbals.

There are numerous accounts of the tambourine being played by slaves during the social and civic functions of White communities in the eighteenth and nineteenth centuries. They became extremely popular in this century among religious groups of the Sanctified sect. Although the tambourine is of Near Eastern origin (it was introduced into Europe in the thirteenth century as a result of the Crusades), it has become an integral part of Afro-American instrumentation.

Probably the best known of American Black instruments is the banjo. It has a body like a tambourine (that is, a parchment stretched over a circular frame on one side only), a bridge, and a long neck with several strings. It is played with a plectrum or with the fingers.

Since no precise equivalent of the instrument is known either in Europe or in Africa, it is extremely difficult, if not impossible, to ascertain its exact history. Several theories have been advanced as to the origin of the banjo, but none has been authenticated. One theory considers the banjo to be an adaptation of the West African calabash banjo, the *bania* of Seregambia, Africa.[23] In another theory, the banjo is thought to be a Black adaptation of the medieval *Pandore* (written at the close of the eighteenth century as *Banjore*).[24] A third theory speculates that the banjo's name was derived from an African instrument, the *Bandju*. The tribes of the Congo utilized this primitive stringed instrument, which consisted of a shallow wooden tray, over which strings were stretched, with a short handle. As large numbers of American Blacks came from the hinterlands of Western Africa, it may be that they gave their native title to the instrument that served their same purpose in the New World. (The banjo was also known as "bonja" up until about 1830.) It was thought by some to have been picked up in Africa by Blacks from Arabian traders who played the Arabian rebab and other

[22]*Ibid.*, p. 211.

[23]Hope Stoddard, *From These Came Music* (New York: Harper and Row Publishers, 1952), p. 65.

[24]Francis W. Galpin, *European Musical Instruments* (New York: E. P. Dutton and Company, Inc., 1937), p. 102.

similar stringed instruments.[25] In this country, the banjo was formerly also known as the "African banjo"; when the steel banjo was created, its makers ceased calling it by this name.

Bone or wood clappers have been a part of Black music in this country since the early days of slavery. At one time, they were made from the sunbleached rib bones of sheep or oxen. Other clappers were made of two flat sticks of wood, about five inches in length. During the twentieth century, pairs of spoons have been widely used as clappers. The performer holds a pair in each hand, one between the index and middle fingers, the other between the middle and fourth fingers. They are clicked together by the use of the wrist and thumb; by skillfully manipulating them, the performer can produce a continuous staccato, brittle, clacking sound, with rhythmic variations as desired.

PERSISTENT MOODS IN LYRICS AND MUSIC

Although there are composers of program music who think music is denotative, it is this author's belief that music is an abstract, non-denotative art, which still may be experienced as representing a certain mood or sentiment whose musical expression has been standardized within a culture. Continued association of certain elements in music with certain images plays a considerable role in the musical definition of mood.

Musical elements are experienced time and time again in conjunction with texts, programs, or extramusical experiences that either designate the mood directly or imply it. The idea that music may be "happy" or "sad" applies as equally to American Black music as to any other music. Many spirituals are examples of the former, while many blues typify the latter. Although spirituals have been called "sorrow songs," a preponderance of these songs can be seen to exude elation, joy, and hope when properly understood. Many blues lament a love affair gone wrong or some similar event of a sad nature, while other blues songs express a kind of joy. (A person who has never lived the "Black experience" may find it difficult to perceive either mood while listening to these songs.)

Eroticism and satire are two more moods often evoked by the words of Black songs wherever the African tradition has persisted: Africa itself, the West Indies, South America, and the United States.

American Black music, however—especially jazz, blues, and rock and roll—generally implies a physical activity, primarily dance. Black dance music is sometimes regarded by non-Blacks as being erotic in nature, a

---

[25]H. G. Schwartz, *The Story of Musical Instruments* (Elkhart, Indiana: Conn Band Instrument Division, 1938), p. 295.

mood that it often evokes because of a lusty, "low down," "gutbucket bar-room" quality.

The blues often contain sexual double meanings and metaphors. An example is the following:

> I come home last night about half past ten,
> I tried to get the key in the lock and couldn't get it in,
> 'Cause she done changed, well she done changed the lock on the door.[26]

Custard Pie Blues contains an erotic metaphor:

> I'm going to tell you something baby,
> Ain't going to tell you no lies,
> I want some of that custard pie.
> You got to give me some of it, (three times)
> Before you give it all away.[27]

In many rhythm-and-blues songs, the lyrics are earthy and direct in their meaning without any of the hypocrisy found in many White American popular songs. Examples of pop songs that have sexual connotations but are hypocritical in their approach are *You Took Advantage of Me, Heat Wave,* and *All of Me.*

Satire, which is familiar in West Indian Calypso music, is also common in American Black music. Satire was used to ridicule Whites during the period of slavery. The slaves were able to do this without suffering recriminations because it was supposedly all done in fun.

Satire was not reserved only for Whites, however; it was directed at Blacks as well. The song *Old Lady Sally Want to Jump-ty Jump*[28] ridicules a lady who is no longer young and cavorts in an inappropriate manner in order to get a man; it ends with a bit of unrelated ridicule directed at a preacher:

> Old Lady Sally want to jump-ty jump
> Jump-ty jump, jump-ty jump,
> Old Lady Sally want to jump-ty jump,
> And Old Lady Sally want to bow.

> Throw that hook in the middle of the pond,
> Catch that girl with the red dress on,
> Go, gal, ain't you shame? Shamed of what?
> Wearin' your dress in the latest style.

---

[26]Courlander, *Negro Folk Music,* p. 131.
[27]*Ibid.,* p. 129.
[28]*Ibid.,* pp. 153–54.

Many fishes in the brook,
Papa caught 'em with a hook,
Mama fried 'em in a pan,
Baby eat 'em like a man.

Preacher in the pulpit
Preachin' like a man,
Tryin' to get to Heaven on a 'lectric fan.
Do your best, Papa Daddy, do your best.

FUNCTIONALITY

Music in the Black culture of West Africa, unlike the "art music" of Europe, is not a separate, autonomous social domain. African music has no separate, abstract function, but rather is an aspect of social, political, economic, and religious life. American Black music, although it is often performed for its own sake as musical entertainment, is also frequently used in conjunction with some other activity. Cries, calls, work songs, and sea chanteys are associated with work; early New Orleans jazz was associated with marching; spirituals, anthems, shouts, and gospel songs are associated with worship; and rhythm and blues, rock and roll, and soul music are associated with dance. Obviously, this sort of functionality is not peculiar to American Black music, for most folk musics are functional to a great degree. The separation of functional and nonfunctional music seems peculiar to Western music and has had its effect on Black music.

DANCE

American Black dance is inextricably related to the dance of West Africa. It is the opinion of Herskovits that African dance was carried over into the New World to a greater degree than almost any other trait of African culture.

American Black dance can be mostly divided into two categories, the traditional and the popular, though there is an ambiguous area between the two that defies categorization. Traditional Black dances consist of (1) those dances that were an integral part of Black culture in this country, whether derived from African or European sources or a fusion of both; and (2) those dances that have been preserved and handed on by an unselfconscious process. On the other hand, the popular dance, although it may contain steps or motifs extracted out of Black tradition, is a synthetic, contrived, short-lived dance form tailored for widespread popular appeal.

New Orleans occupies a special position in the history of Black dance because of its unique social structure. New Orleans Blacks were divided into two classes. There were the Creoles of Color, of French or Spanish and African descent, who devoted themselves to European culture and dance. Their children were sometimes sent to Paris to be educated, and they danced quadrilles at country balls. At the same time, a large number of slaves lived on big plantations, a setting in which African dance had a good chance to survive. These slaves also enjoyed African dances at Congo Square in the heart of New Orleans.

There are accounts of many dances being seen performed by the slaves in Congo Square. Among them were "the Juba, the Bamboula, the Counjaille, the Babouille, the Cata or Chacta, the Voodoo, the Congo, and the Calinda." While they are now extinct in the United States, it is interesting to note that "all of these dances were then, and are to this day, well-known in the West Indies."[29]

> The name Voodoo (more properly Vodoun or Vodun) was particularly well-known in the Caribbean islands on which had been settled African slaves from the region of Dahomey. In a generic sense, it referred to all Dahomean cult activities; a Vodun dance was any dance related to Dahomean cult worship, and therefore, . . . does not refer . . . to any one specific dance.[30]

In the predominantly British-Protestant environment in other sections of the country, the majority of Blacks had less direct contact with Whites. Thus the blending of African and European elements of the dance was much slower. As the dance evolved, however, many of the "African elements became more formal and diluted [while] the British-European elements [tended to become] more fluid and rhythmic."[31]

By the time easily recognizable African forms had seemingly disappeared, Blacks were producing dances and music in a new style. It must be emphasized, however, that a number of elements or motifs characteristic of African dancing, such as the shimmy, the crawl, the shuffle, the strut, and the jump, remained an integral part of American Black dancing. Other surviving elements of African dance are its improvisatory quality and a powerful, propulsive rhythm that may appear in the singing, the stamping, the clapping, and the dancing all at one time.

The Buzzard Lope, a dance once known throughout the South, has almost disappeared. It may have been similar to the African buzzard dance (the buzzard is common to both Africa and the South, and the dance is a close imitation of this bird). In the United States, this dance was part of a danced story with a running commentary in which the turkey buzzard quite realistically goes about eating a dead cow.

The Giouba, which became known as the Juba in the United States,

---

[29]*Ibid.*, p. 190.

[30]*Ibid.*, p. 191.

[31]Marshall and Jean Stearns, *Jazz Dance* (New York: Macmillan Co., 1968), p. 24.

lost most of its African characteristics before taking on new movements, some of which outlived the original and survived in popular dance.

One hybridized but recognizable survival from the African circle dance is the Ring Shout. The Baptist Church prohibited all drumming and dancing, which eliminated most African religious rites. But since most religious groups, taking their cue from the Baptists, defined dancing as involving the crossing of the legs, the Ring Shout, which employed clapping and stamping instead of drumming, and a shuffle step in which the legs did not cross, was considered acceptable.

Many of the changes that have taken place in African dance in this country have been caused by the British-European tradition. As time goes on, however, the overall direction is one of Black dance exerting an increasingly strong influence on American popular dance as a whole. This is the antithesis of the usual pattern described by anthropologists, in which the culture of a dominant group consumes the culture of a weaker group, which may or may not be in the minority.

Like music, dance is functional in African culture and plays a part in the religious, political, social, and economic structure of that culture. Consequently, music and dance are closely correlated, both being fundamental elements in the aesthetic expression of the people of West Africa.

Although to a lesser degree, a similar situation exists in the Black subculture of this country. Where there is music, there is dance, and vice versa. One does not, and seemingly cannot, exist without the other. They are so interrelated, that the one seems to gain its substance for persistence and survival from the other.

As this discussion has shown, the forms, styles, techniques, and instruments indigenous to Black music have been influenced by two traditions, one African and the other European. This mixture, which has taken place in the social milieu of the United States, has produced a music that is not only unique, but that could have come into being only in this country.

chapter two

Black Music Forms Before 1900

By far the most considerable and important body of non-European music in the United States is the rich and varied expressions of Blacks.

Music peculiar to the American Black has often been said to be in the "American Black idiom." The American Black idiom is that body of unique individual and collective musical expressions that has been established as the particular way Blacks prefer to perform music and is their natural and characteristic musical language. It must be pointed out, however, that all music written by the American Black cannot be said to be in the American Black idiom. There are certain qualities that characterize this body of music. These characteristics were discussed in chapter one. This music is frequently written not only by Blacks, but also by Whites.

Black music forms may be categorized into two groups and two periods of development. Those forms that developed before 1900 are folk music forms that were not originally notated and were usually not composed by one individual. On the other hand, those forms that originated around and after 1900 are notated[1] and composed, usually by one indi-

---

[1]The exception is New Orleans jazz, which is a non-notated, improvised music. This music, however, was developed via the marching band, which did utilize notated music. See chapter three.

vidual. This chapter will examine the kinds of Black music that originated before 1900; the next chapter will deal with those forms that developed in this century.

SPIRITUALS

Perhaps it is of some importance to clarify and define the kinds of songs that are included in that large body of Black religious music commonly referred to as "spirituals." Three types of songs are usually included in this corpus of religious music, these being known as *spirituals, jubilees,* and *shouts,* though it is often difficult to distinguish one from another with any degree of precision.

Black religious songs that possessed a lyrical quality and expressed a wide range of emotions, such as elation, hope, and sorrow, were called spirituals. The term "spiritual" was used because of the relationship between this type of song and the "holy spirit." The jubilee was often an exuberant song that was said to come from the heart of the individual as opposed to the "holy spirit," causing him to sing to God of his happiness. The shout could be either of the other forms, when it was used as a dance song.

Since it is often difficult to distinguish one of these forms from the others, and because these terms tend to be used interchangeably, at the risk of oversimplification, all these religious songs will be referred to as spirituals.

There has been a great amount of discussion as to the origin of the Black spiritual. George Pullen Jackson[2] and Newman I. White[3] contend that the spiritual was originally the same as the camp-meeting song and spiritual song sung by Whites. Guy Johnson and Howard W. Odum[4] also believed that the Blacks borrowed from the Whites. On the other hand, writers such as John Lovell, Jr., Henry Edward Krehbiel, James Weldon Johnson, and Alain Locke are of the opinion that the Black spiritual is rooted in Africa.[5]

[2]For a thorough discussion of the theory that the Black spiritual resulted from the imitation of White spirituals, see George Pullen Jackson, *White and Negro Spirituals* (New York: J. J. Augustin, 1943), the most authoritative work with this point of view.

[3]Newman I. White, *American Negro Folk-Songs* (Hatboro, Pennsylvania: Folklore Associates, Inc., 1965).

[4]Howard W. Odum and Guy B. Johnson, *The Negro and His Songs* (Hatboro, Pennsylvania: Folklore Associates, Inc., 1964).

[5]The most authoritative book on the Black spiritual is John Lovell, Jr., *Black Song: The Forge and the Flame* (New York: Macmillan Co., 1972); but see also Henry Edward Krehbiel, *Afro-American Folksongs* (New York: Frederick Ungar Publishing Co., 1962); James Weldon Johnson and J. Rosamond Johnson, *The Book of American Negro Spirituals* (New York: The Viking Press, 1925); and Alain Locke, *The Negro and His Music* (Port Washington, N.Y.: Kennikat Press, 1968).

Of course it is unreasonable to assume that, under the conditions of the kind of life experienced by Blacks in the South both during slavery and after emancipation, the Blacks could have departed completely from the African musical tradition. Blacks lived in a society in which separation of the races was at least the custom if not always the law. The separation of the races minimized outside musical influences and perpetuated the survival of African musical characteristics. The experiences of the African in the New World milieu did not drive out of existence the musical tradition that he brought with him from Africa.

Jackson and his followers have either overlooked or disregarded unmistakable evidence that refutes their position that the White spiritual is the progenitor of the Black spiritual.[6] In the first place, very few Blacks were permitted to attend camp meetings, since the typical slaveowner simply did not permit his slaves to attend religious services. In addition, when Blacks did attend these meetings, the usual pattern was to keep them separated from the Whites. Consequently, the Blacks had little opportunity to learn from Whites the hundreds of spirituals that they sang at camp meetings.[7]

While there is solid evidence that Black and White spirituals coexisted, there is absolutely no proof of the preexistence of the White spiritual. The African slaves came from a strong tradition of vigorous singing and continued to sing once they were brought to these shores, the major change being in the language used. Consequently, the spiritual was established by the end of the seventeenth century.[8] The camp meeting tradition, which produced the White spiritual, did not get started until the beginning of the nineteenth century, and the White spiritual came into being some time later.

It is interesting to note the findings of Mieczyslaw Kolinski[9] in a comparison of Black spiritual songs and the songs of Western Africa. He concluded that thirty-six of the spirituals examined are identical to some songs of Western Africa or resemble them closely. Fifty other spirituals were discovered to have formal structures identical to those of certain West African songs. As an example, *No More Auction Block* is musically almost the same as one of the Ashanti songs of Ghana.

This is not to imply that Black spirituals are entirely African in nature; without a doubt there have been European musical influences on this song form. The preponderance of evidence, however, points toward the Black spiritual being primarily rooted in the African musical tradition.

[6]See John Lovell, *Black Song: The Forge and the Flame*, chapter 6, pp. 24–70.

[7]*Ibid.*, pp. 81–83.

[8]*Ibid.*, p. 77.

[9]"Return of the Native," *Bulletin D'Information No. 3, Premier Festival Culturel Panafricain* (Algeria, May 1969), cited in *American Musical Digest* (October 1969), pp. 31–32.

The question then arises as to how that portion of this body of religious songs that originated with the Blacks was "composed." As mentioned earlier, there is considerable evidence that a large portion of Black spirituals were not imitations of, or influenced by, White hymns or spirituals. This body of Black music probably originated from two sources. One source of origin consisted of the melodies indigenous to Africa. It is not illogical to assume that some of the African melodies brought to these shores by slaves did survive the cultural transition and were used as models for Black spirituals. The second source involves the spontaneous creation by talented individuals. A frequent source of song material was a single line taken from a preacher's sermon. The Black preacher, using the reciting-tone[10] kind of delivery, often established a call-and-response pattern between himself and the congregation,[11] frequently reiterating a single line over a period of time. At the end of the sermon, this material was often used as the basis of a song; if this song was repeated at a later date, it could become a part of the service of the Black church.

The texts of Black spirituals embody a number of themes projecting the Christian concepts of faith, love, and humility, with considerable emphasis on salvation. Another group of texts deals with events and stories from the Old and New Testaments. So many Biblical events have been treated in spiritual texts that, if they were placed in chronological order, they would be almost equivalent to an alternative version of the Bible.

Often these Biblical events were recast in a dramatic form. In an effort to enhance the drama, other subject matter was drawn either from the Bible or from any aspect of contemporary life that seemed suitable and useful. As an example, there are interpolations from the New Testament into the Old Testament, and vice versa. Few Black spirituals project mystical or abstract philosophical concepts; rather, most of them tend to be concerned with particular events, episodes, stories, and revelations.

Black spirituals are marked by an economy of statement, employing very few words to tell an entire Biblical story in dramatic fashion. Certain standard images are used over and over again. Two examples are Elijah's chariot and its modern counterpart, the train, which represents more modern transportation to the same ultimate destination for those who have found salvation. Other standard images include the wheel of Ezekiel and the gospel shoes.[12]

Interchange of texts and melodies was frequent, with the words of spirituals being set to several different tunes. In instances where the text

[10]The "reciting tone" is a manner of declamatory speech or chant performed largely on a single fixed pitch.

[11]Examples of the kinds of preaching that were common in the Black church can be heard on the recording *Negro Religious Songs and Services* (Library of Congress AAFS-L10).

[12]Courlander, *Negro Folk Music*, pp. 39–41.

and the melody were in different meters, syllables were either extended (often over many beats) or contracted to fit the meter of the tune.

There were also various practices of combining the texts of two or more spirituals. Favorite refrain phrases were often associated with stanzas to which they had little or no apparent relationship. This patching together of texts stems from the fact that stanzas often were not standardized as to order and often did not belong strictly to any particular song. The nonstandardization of song verse was a result of a tradition in which individuals were singled out because they possessed certain musical talents. On the other hand, because the song leader was required to possess a good memory for, and facility with, both words and tunes, as well as the ability to improvise with taste, these skills contributed to the interchanging of texts between religious songs.

The content of these songs is closely related to their form, for song form is determined to a great extent by the way in which stanza and refrain are put together.[13] Some of the songs are constructed in a simple, short-phrase, call-and-response form. An example is "What You Going t'Do When the Lamp Burns Down?"·

(leader)	Oh, poor sinner,
(chorus)	Now is your time,
(leader)	Oh, poor sinner,
(chorus)	Now is your time,
(leader)	Oh, poor sinner,
(chorus)	Now is your time,
	What you going to do
	when your lamp burns down?

(leader)	Oh the lamp burns down
	and you cannot see,
(chorus)	What you going to do
	when your lamp burns down?

(leader)	That salvation flows-a
	both full and free;
(chorus)	What you going to do
	when your lamp burns down?

(Repeat section A and end.)

---

[13]George Robinson Ricks, *Some Aspects of the Religious Music of the United States Negro: An Ethnomusicological Study with Special Emphasis on the Gospel Tradition* (New York: Arno Press, 1977).

Other songs place emphasis on the choral response with longer phrases.[14] *Lord, Until I Reach My Home* is an example of this form:

(chorus)   Until I reach my home,
           Until I reach my home,
           I never 'spect to give the journey over,
           Until I reach my home.
           (Repeat)
(leader)   Old Satan's mighty busy,
           He follows my night and day,
           And ev'ry time I go to pray,
           I find him in my way.
           (Repeat the chorus.)

Still another type combines the short-phrase call-and-response pattern with a long-phrase choral refrain that dominates the song.[15] *I am Seeking for a City* illustrates this form:

(leader)   I am seeking for a city
(chorus)   Hallelujah,
           I am seeking for a city
           Hallelujah,
(leader)   For a city into the heaven
(chorus)   Hallelujah.
           For a city into the heaven, Hallelujah.
           Lord, I don't feel noways tired,
           Oh, glory, Hallelujah;
           I hope to shout glory when this world is on fire,
           Oh, glory, Hallelujah.

Irrespective of the types involved, a number of variations were possible through the repetition of various parts of a song. Sections of a song could also be extended at the discretion of the leader or by local tradition.

Modes

The melodic style of the Black spiritual is simple. Among the scales are the major, natural minor, mixed major and minor, pentatonic, hexatonic (lacking either the fourth or the seventh tone), major with both raised and lowered seventh tone, major with lowered seventh tone, minor with lowered seventh tone, and minor with raised seventh tone.

Many writers, including W. E. B. DuBois[16] have termed the spirituals

[14]*Ibid.*, p. 37.
[15]*Ibid.*
[16]William E. B. DuBois, *Soul of Black Folk* (Chicago: A. C. McClurg, 1903), pp. 250–64.

"sorrow songs" because they are a product of the period of slavery (not because they are sad). The popular conception is that the minor mode is the best indicator of sorrow and suffering; and therefore, most spirituals were thought to be in this mode. In fact, most Black spirituals are in the major mode. The major and minor modes are not unqualified expressions of happiness and sorrow.

Although the frequent departures from the major scale listed above are all significant, perhaps the most striking occur in those songs that are in the minor mode. It is common practice to raise the seventh tone in minor one semitone because of harmonic considerations. In addition, the sixth tone is usually raised when ascending to avoid the interval of an augmented second (three semitones) between the sixth and seventh tones of the minor scale. In many of the Black spirituals in the minor mode, the sixth tone (the avoided fourth in major) is omitted entirely, and in others, it is raised without disturbing the seventh tone. Thus, some of the spirituals in minor with a major sixth are without the leading tone. Some Black spirituals utilize scales identical to those of the medieval church modes, among them the Dorian and Mixolydian modes.

The departures from the major and minor scales listed above are in many instances only approximations of the tones as they are sung; the European notational system is inadequate to represent many of these tones in their true pitch.

The examples below show the various scales and modes utilized in the spiritual, each accompanied by a spiritual in the appropriate mode.

EXAMPLE 2.1 Major scale: *Murm'ring Word*

EXAMPLE 2.2 Natural minor scale: *My Soul's Been Anchored In De Lord* (also Aeolian scale).

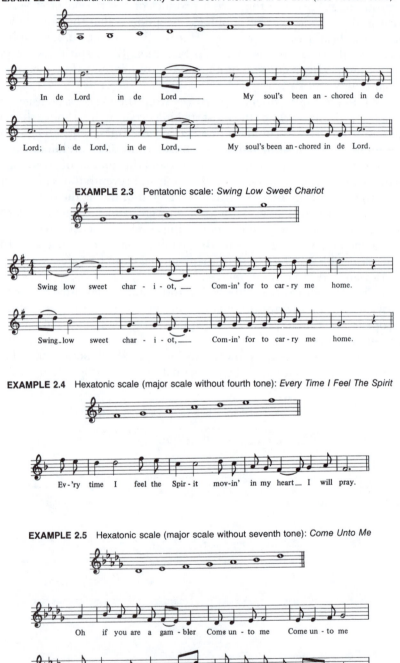

EXAMPLE 2.3 Pentatonic scale: *Swing Low Sweet Chariot*

EXAMPLE 2.4 Hexatonic scale (major scale without fourth tone): *Every Time I Feel The Spirit*

EXAMPLE 2.5 Hexatonic scale (major scale without seventh tone): *Come Unto Me*

Come un - to me   Come un - to me an' be saved.

EXAMPLE 2.6 Major scale with both raised and lowered seventh tone: *Roll, Jordan, Roll*

Roll, Jor - dan, roll,   Roll, Jor - dan, roll,   I

want to go to heav'n when I die to hear Jor - dan roll.

EXAMPLE 2.7 Major scale with lowered seventh tone (transposed Mixolydian mode): *A Great Camp Meetin'*

Oh, walk to - ged - der, chil - dren Don't you get a - wea - ry,

Walk to - ged - der, chil - dren Don't you get wea - ry walk to - ged - der chil - dren

Don't you get a - wea - ry, Dere's a great camp meet - in' in de prom - ised land.

Gwine to mourn an' neb - ber tire _____ mourn an' neb - ber tire

mourn an' neb - ber tire; ___ Dere's a great camp meet - in' in the prom - ised land.

EXAMPLE 2.8 Minor scale without sixth tone: *Nobody Knows the Trouble I See*

No - bod - y knows the trou - ble I see Lord No - bod - y knows the

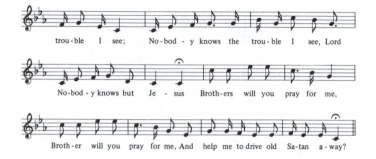

trou-ble I see; No-bod-y knows the trou-ble I see, Lord

No-bod-y knows but Je - sus Broth-ers will you pray for me,

Broth-er will you pray for me, And help me to drive old Sa-tan a-way?

EXAMPLE 2.9 Minor scale with raised sixth tone (transposed Dorian mode): *You May Bury Me in de Eas'*

You may bur-y me in de Eas' You may bur-y me in de Wes', But I'll

hear de trum-pet soun'___ in dat mourn - in'.

EXAMPLE 2.10 Minor scale with raised seventh tone: *Baptizing Hymn*

Free - ly___ go march-ing a-long, Down in-to the wa - ter

Free - ly___ go march-ing a-long, Like Zi-on's sons_ and daugh-ters.

EXAMPLE 2.11 Mixed major and minor scale: *Nummer Me One*

Num-mer me___ one,___ Num-mer me___ one

Num-mer me___ one, I'm goin' to the judge-ment bar.

EXAMPLE 2.12 Dorian mode: *Run to Jesus*

Run to Je - sus; shun the dan - ger; I
don't ex - pect to stay much long - er here.___

EXAMPLE 2.13 Mixolydian mode: *No Condemnation in My Soul*

I feel all right___ no con - dem - na - tion. Feel all right___
no con - dem - na - tion, Well I feel all right____
no con - dem - na - tion No con - dem - na - tion in mah soul.

The spiritual was brought to the attention of American society in two ways. The Fisk Jubilee Singers, of Fisk University in Nashville, Tennessee, included the Black spiritual in their concert repertoire as early as 1871.[17] They made extensive concert tours in the United States commencing in that year and in Europe beginning in 1873.

The Black composer Harry Thacker Burleigh (1866–1949) was the first to arrange Black spirituals as solo art songs for the concert stage. Burleigh, born in Erie, Pennsylvania, did not begin to study music seriously until the age of twenty-six, when he was awarded a scholarship to the National Conservatory of Music in New York. It was during Burleigh's second year at the conservatory that he had the privilege of meeting Antonín Dvořák, who had come to this country to serve as director of this institution. Burleigh was a constant visitor in the Dvořák home, where he found time to copy manuscripts and to sing spirituals at Dvořák's request.

Even though Burleigh served in several capacities simultaneously, such as baritone soloist of Saint George's Episcopal Church and Temple

---

[17]The Fisk Jubilee Singers will be discussed in detail in chapter four.

Harry Thacker Burleigh, first arranger of Black spirituals as solo art songs for the concert stage. (Photo courtesy the New York Public Library, Schomburg Collection of Negro Literature.)

Emanu-El, he still found time to concertize extensively. He became a widely traveled concert artist, performing in the United States and Europe.

Although Burleigh was the first Black man to acquire a national reputation as a composer, arranger, and singer, the extent of his works has never been common knowledge. While he is best known for his solo arrangements of Black spirituals, especially that of *Deep River* in 1916, he had previously composed nearly one hundred songs, including three song cycles.

Through the efforts of Burleigh, the spiritual was elevated to the status of an art song, and it came to be included in the concert repertoire of many singers. Before Burleigh began arranging spirituals, they had been performed mainly by vocal quartets and choral groups; through his work, they became available to some of the great voices of the twentieth century.

The impact that the Black spiritual has had on American music has been great. Its influence has been felt in music in the European tradition, beginning with Dvořák's journey to this country in the 1890s and in the beginnings of jazz in the same decade. Although America was late in discovering the worth of this indigenous music, its value was realized before it became extinct, with the result that it has been largely preserved for posterity.

WORK SONG

The work song was a part of African culture long before Blacks came to America, and it remained an integral part of Black culture long after their arrival in the New World. Thus, the work song was present in the culture of the slaves earlier than any other form of music. Because it retained the greatest number of Africanisms, the work song forms a strong link between pure West African music and the music of the slaves.

The work song took on unique qualities in America for a number of reasons. While the practice of singing to accompany one's labor is indigenous to West Africa, it is obvious that working one's own field in his own land is quite different from forced labor in a foreign land. Thus, the references in the songs accompanying the work changed radically. In addition, White masters suppressed references to the gods and religions of West Africa, not only because they thought all African religious customs were barbarous, but because they feared that too-constant evocation of the African gods could mean that the slaves were planning to leave the plantation as soon as they could. For similar reasons, the use of drums was also prevented, since drums could be used to incite revolt as well as to accompany dancers.

Consequently, the work song, as it took its new shape in America, was stripped of all pure African ritual and found a new cultural reference. This was most difficult to do within the African-language songs themselves, however. The diversity of African labor—such as fishing, weaving, and hunting—which was the source of this kind of song, was replaced quite suddenly by unvarying, grinding toil that consisted mainly of cultivating the fields of the White master. As a result, those songs associated with the

The work song was used to accompany the slaves cultivating fields of various crops, in this case, sugar cane. (Photo courtesy Special Collections Division, Tulane University Library.)

various African labors lost their pertinence. Courlander commented:

> It is not only in group singing that the American Negro work gang shows similarities with African tradition, but in the patterns of group working as well. Throughout large parts of West and Central Africa, formal and informal labor groups for mutual assistance are commonly observed, and the tradition has survived strongly in Haiti, Jamaica, and other West Indian islands. Even where the institutionalized aspects of gang work have been altered in Africa, as in the instance where men gather to work for pay, the old patterns of work have nevertheless continued. The rhythmic use of tools, the sense of community, and responsive singing have remained significant elements in those patterns.[18]

The work song lent itself to gang labor, for in this setting, its prime function was to enhance the ability of the men to work.

> The substance of the gang songs ranges from the ribald to the devout, from the humorous to the sad, from the gentle to the biting, and from the tolerant to the unforgiving. The meanings can be personal or impersonal. The statement can be direct, tangent, or metaphoric. As throughout Negro singing generally, there is an incidence of social criticism, ridicule, gossip, and protest. The men may sing of the work they are doing, women, heroic events, places they have been, good lives or lives gone wrong, preachers and gang bosses, the hard lot of the Negro, or salvation.[19]

They may express a variety of transient moods about the relationship of the gang worker to his work, his fellow laborers, and his employers.

A singing leader was necessary if the work song was to serve its function of keeping the men in a working spirit. It was imperative that the leader have a feel for the work being done and an understanding of the men with whom he was working. A capable singing leader sensed "what kind of song . . . [was] . . . needed at a given time."[20]

The structural patterns of the work song are varied in the relationship of the leader and chorus.[21] In one type, the leader and the chorus sing the melody in unison except for occasional harmonies in seconds, thirds, fifths, and octaves. When sung in octaves, the upper voice may be falsetto.

EXAMPLE 2.14 *Go Down, Old Hannah*

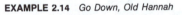

In another type, each line sung by the leader is different and is repeated by the chorus.

---

[18]Courlander, *Negro Folk Music,* pp. 91–92.

[19]*Ibid.,* p. 89.

[20]*Ibid.,* p. 90.

[21]The structural patterns discussed here are adapted from Courlander, *Negro Folk Music, U.S.A.,* pp. 92–94.

EXAMPLE 2.15 *Lost John*

(leader)	And I heard a little boy
(chorus)	And I heard a little boy
(leader)	Didn't see no one
(chorus)	Didn't see no one
(leader)	It was old Lost John
(chorus)	It was old Lost John
(leader)	He said he was long gone
(chorus)	He said he was long gone
(leader)	Like a turkey through the corn
(chorus)	Like a turkey through the corn
(leader)	With his long clothes on
(chorus)	With his long clothes on
(leader)	Had a heel in front
(chorus)	Had a heel in front
(leader)	And a heel behind
(chorus)	And a heel behind

Some work songs are structured so that the leader repeats each line of text with a varied melody. In between, there is an alternating response sung by the chorus.

EXAMPLE 2.16 *Chopping in the New Ground*

In another variant, each solo line sung by the leader is different, and each is followed by a fixed choral response.

EXAMPLE 2.17 *We Need Another Witness*

There are also work songs in which each solo line is sung twice by the leader. After each line there is a fixed choral response in the text.

EXAMPLE 2.18 *Hammer Ring*

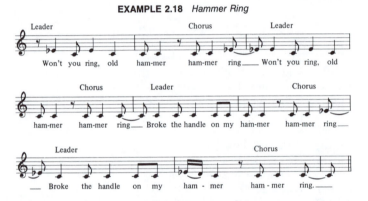

Another variation is one in which the leader sings a solo line that has one or more repetitions. The chorus picks up the last phrase or word of each line and then sings a response.

EXAMPLE 2.19 *Rosie*

Since many combinations of the above patterns are employed, the variations become seemingly endless.

EXAMPLE 2.20 *Mighty Bright Light*

It was a might-y bright light_ that was shin - ing down_ It was a
might - y bright light_ that was shin - ing down_ It was a
might - y bright light_ that was shin - ing down_ Oh, a
might - y bright light that was shin - ing down._

A number of the forms mentioned above[22] were also found in the work songs of the English-speaking islands of the Caribbean and Haiti.

While work songs were heard mainly on the railroads and in prison camps in the recent past, group singing was commonplace in planting, harvesting, and other agricultural operations only a generation or two ago.

Another form of work song, the "chantey" or "shanty" has been known to exist for years, but the failure to associate it with the Black man has been because he is rarely connected with sea life. Most of these songs have been found in South Carolina, New Orleans, and coastal Alabama.

It was customary for a ship to set out to sea with a starboard watch of Blacks and a port watch of Whites, while the work song leader was usually Black. This kind of crew became known as a "chequered crew."

The construction of the chantey is closely related to the songs associated with the labors of Blacks on land, and the method of singing it is practically the same as that followed by land workers. These songs were extemporized at sea by the chanteyman, who led the singing, and the words and melody were in the vernacular of the seafaring man.

There are several theories as to the origin of the name "chantey" or "shanty." Although it is thought by many that the name was not used before 1869, this kind of folk song of the sea was known before that date. *The Sailor's Song Book,* which was published in 1842, contained many chantey-type songs. Subsequently, a number of sailor song anthologies

[22]Examples 2.14 and 2.18 may be heard on *Negro Worksongs and Calls,* ed. B. A. Botkin (Library of Congress AAFS-L8); Examples 2.15, 2.16, 2.17, and 2.20 are available on *Negro Prison Camp Worksongs,* ed. Harold Courlander (Ethnic Folkways Library FE 4475); Example 2.19 may be heard on *Afro-American Spirituals, Worksongs, and Ballads,* ed. Alan Lomax (Library of Congress AAFS-L3). All examples are used by permission.

The "chantey" is a work song associated with sea life; in this scene, Blacks are shown working on a dock as stevedores loading cotton. (Photo courtesy Special Collections Division, Tulane University Library.)

have appeared. (The word "chantey" or "shanty" is generally thought to have been derived from the French word *chanter,* which means "to sing.")

The chantey is primarily a manner and style of singing. The amount of European or West African influence on any one chantey depended pretty much on who was singing it at the time, but as a type of work song, the sea chantey furnishes an example of an early blending of Euro-African musical qualities. Some of the most popular of the chanteys that originated in Alabama and South Carolina have religious texts and have some of the same emotional religious qualities as are found in the spiritual.

The tie between work and music in the Black tradition has practically disappeared in most sections of the United States. The sea chantey and the work song were very much a part of American Black culture.

CRIES, CALLS, AND HOLLERS

Cries, calls, and hollers, so important to the tradition of the rural Blacks of the South, are also common in the Caribbean area and in West Africa, where this elemental melodic form originated. Widely used during the days of slavery, these forms are fast disappearing.

It is exceedingly difficult to distinguish the call from the cry or the

Slaves were frequently separated over large geographic areas (in this case, a rice field), making cries, calls, and hollers a functional part of their existence. (Photo courtesy Special Collections Division, Tulane University Library.)

holler, and, in fact. it would appear that all three terms are synonymous. Each geographical section of the South seems to give its own name to the genre: "cornfield holler," "cotton field holler," "whoop," "water call," and "field call," to list a few.

Calls were as functional in this country as they were in Africa. During slavery days, the plantation laborers were not permitted to mingle at will with friends on nearby plantations. But men and women working together over a wide stretch of fields could maintain social contact throughout the workday by calling back and forth and singing songs together. Sometimes responses would be sung from different parts of the field. Often an individual would sing to the others and they would assist as he improvised and developed his theme.

Courlander made the following comments in regard to field calls:

There were calls to communicate messages of all kinds—to bring people in from the fields, to summon them to work, to attract the attention of a girl in the distance, to signal hunting dogs, or simply to make one's presence known. There were still others, more aptly described as cries, that were simply a form of self-expression, a vocalization of some emotion.[23]

[23]Courlander, *Negro Folk Music*, p. 81.

The field hand did not have to coordinate his singing with that of his companion; he could sing at his own speed, though other workers might pick up his call.

> A man working under the hot sun might give voice to such a cry on impulse, directing it to the world, or to the fields around him, or perhaps to himself.[24]

> The cry does not have to have a theme, or to fit into any kind of formal structure, or to conform to normal concepts of musical propriety. It is often completely free music in which every sound, line, and phrase is exploited for itself in any fashion that appeals to the crier. It may be short and sharp, with an abrupt end, or . . . it can waver, thin out, and gently disappear into the air. It may consist of a single musical statement or a series of statements, and may reflect any one of a number of moods—homesickness, loneliness, lovesickness, contentment, exuberance.[25]

Later calls approximate a song style. The following example, which gives reference to "jungle," means that Rufus has been in prison or some other kind of trouble.[26]

EXAMPLE 2.21   *Hey Rufus* (greeting call)[27]

It is difficult to describe the embellishments employed in singing a holler. A typical example is the cornfield holler that follows. In singing this particular holler, the singer utilizes portamenti and falsetto. The notes with

[24]*Ibid.*

[25]*Ibid.*, 82.

[26]*Ibid.*, 85.

[27]This greeting call may be heard on *Negro Folk Music of Alabama,* Vol. 1, ed. Harold Courlander (Ethnic Folkways Library FE 4417). Used by permission.

crosses for noteheads are sung with a catch in the voice like a descending yodel.

EXAMPLE 2.22   Arwhoolie (cornfield holler)[28]

The ornamentation and free rhythms heard in field calls may also be heard in spirituals, blues, and solo work songs.

While field calls, cries, and hollers were indigenous to the rural areas of the South, the cities had calls of their own. In almost any large city of the South, one might hear the calls of food vendors, junk peddlers, and the like.[29] In the North, many service and merchandise peddlers advertised their wares in a similar fashion. Even today, city peddlers of watermelons, eggs, corn, and other produce can be heard each summer selling their wares from trucks by using various calls.

Although this music is almost totally extinct in its original rural setting, it was an antecedent of a musical form that is very contemporary—the blues.

THE BLUES

The blues was one of the most distinctive song forms to evolve out of the American social and cultural milieu of the last century. It is not only a musical expression, but also a social expression. It is a reflection of the isolation of the Black in American society, who, forced to live outside of the dominant culture, developed his own culture and found within the difficulties and pain of his experiences the materials for a rich and vital music.

Since the blues was a part of the oral tradition of Black music, and because there are no written accounts of its early history, the exact time of its inception is obscure.

It has been theorized that the blues developed as early as the middle of the nineteenth century. It is known that the blues became the music of itinerant Black men. The majority of Blacks in the South, however, did not gain mobility until after the slaves were emancipated. It was subsequent to

[28]This holler can be heard on the record album *Negro Work Songs and Calls*, ed. B. A. Botkin (Library of Congress AAFS-L8). Transcribed by permission.

[29]Street calls of vendors are contained on the record album *The Music of New Orleans*, ed. Samuel Charters (Folkways Records FA 2461, Vol. 1).

this acquired mobility that the travelling Black musician incorporated the blues into his repertoire.

With emancipation, Blacks were promised freedom of the kind enjoyed by other Americans. The failure of Blacks to gain true freedom created the psychological milieu in which the blues was developed.

According to another theory, the blues form was not generally known throughout the South much before 1900. The blues developed in many different areas of the South almost simultaneously. By the time New Orleans-style jazz had developed (just before the twentieth century), the blues form was not only already established but had been incorporated into this jazz medium.

As with any music form, development was gradual and took place over a long period of time. The blues as an entity, however, came into being sometime around the beginning of the last quarter of the nineteenth century.

Work songs, spirituals, and field hollers, all with African roots, played a crucial role in the creation of the blues form. With the work song, the individual is a part of the group in the act of performing labor. This Black music form has a regular beat and utilizes call-and-response patterns. The blues has retained the work song's function to the extent that the group can identify with the plight of the blues singer. Those musical characteristics common to the work song are a part of the blues because of the force of the Black ethnic group's common heritage.

Many spirituals are all but identical, harmonically and melodically, with the blues. The spiritual *Nobody's Fault But Mine* is very similar to the eight-bar blues, and *Precious Lord, Hold My Hand* bears a close resemblance to the sixteen-bar blues form. *St. James' Infirmary* is closely related to the spiritual *Hold On, Keep Your Hands On the Plow*. Without a doubt, the blues has an affinity to the spiritual. The blues was also influenced by English popular ballads and Protestant hymns, whose conventional harmonic progressions were to become part of the blues structure.

The holler is perhaps the most important single element in the blues, partly by virtue of the intensity of its personal expression. The subjects of loneliness and hardship pervade both genres, and strong melodic similarities can also be found. Although the influences on the blues are complex, the holler, freely structured and modal in character, is also perhaps its major musical progenitor. At times, it is difficult to distinguish a field holler from an archaic blues form.[30] For a long time the two intertwined uncertainly, with the field holler readily apparent in the singing of country blues men. The nineteenth-century blues was, like the holler, freely struc-

[30]Listen to the recording *Negro Blues and Hollers*, ed. Marshall Stearns (Library of Congress AFS-L59).

tured; the contemporary blues structure did not come into being until the twentieth century.

Blues have been said to be statements of loneliness, despair, unhappy love affairs, pessimism, and the like. As a form of expression, however, the blues are more than a statement of personal misery. The blues song may be said to be an expression of criticism or complaint that serves as a relief from the troubles being experienced by the singer.

Blues Form

Historically, the blues structure has been a varied one. Prior to the twentieth century, its length depended on the number of measures required by the singer to complete his statement and could consist of eleven, fifteen, nineteen, or any number of measures. Certain blues were done in such a free style as to fall into no clear-cut bar pattern at all. In either instance, the main consideration of the blues singer was that his song should sound "right" to him.

In the twentieth century, two factors have contributed to the stabilization of the blues form. The practice of notating the blues, begun by W. C. Handy with his first published blues in 1912,[31] helped to freeze the blues into a twelve-bar form. The recording of blues songs, begun in 1920,[32] tended to standardize their length, owing to the fixed amount of time available on one side of a 78 r.p.m. record.

The twentieth-century blues usually falls into a twelve-bar pattern in $\frac{4}{4}$ meter, divided into three sections with the overall rhyme scheme of AAB. Occasionally this basic stanza unit is contracted to eight bars or expanded to sixteen, but most recorded, notated blues are based upon this twelve-bar sequence.

Harmonically, the twelve-bar blues follows a simple chord pattern. The first four bars are usually based upon the chord of the tonic; the next two bars are based on the chord of the subdominant; the next two bars are then based on the tonic chord again; the following two bars are based on the dominant chord; and the last two bars return to the tonic chord.

EXAMPLE 2.23 Twelve-bar blues chord structure

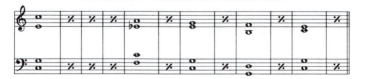

[31]The song *Memphis Blues,* though published in 1912, was written in 1909 as a political song entitled *Mister Crump.* W. C. Handy is discussed later in this chapter.

[32]The song *Crazy Blues* was recorded in 1920 by Mamie Smith. Although the song was not really a blues, it started the blues craze of the twenties.

There are variant harmonic formulae to the twelve-bar blues form.

The contracted eight-bar form of the blues may be based on the following chord progression:

EXAMPLE 2.24   Eight-bar blues chord structure

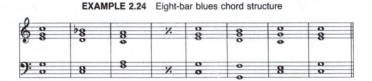

The sixteen-bar blues forms may have a harmonic foundation consisting of the following chord progressions:

EXAMPLE 2.25   Sixteen-bar blues chord structure

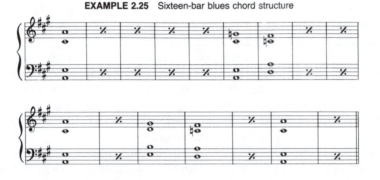

The twelve-bar blues form, which is based on the tonic, subdominant, and dominant harmonies, is influenced by the simple chord progression of the twelve-bar English popular ballads and the frequent tonic-dominant harmony of the Protestant hymns. Although it is difficult to designate the single most important influence on the harmonic structure of the blues, it is probably the vernacular European tradition.

Many early blues singers used open guitar tunings[33] and often made only the most superficial effort to follow the chord progressions of the conventional twelve-bar blues form. But they usually sang the harmonic progressions, even if they did not alter the accompaniment figures. Other blues singers merely employed a drone, over which the blues were sung. When harmony was used, it was done so without any consistent plan.

The blues, in its original form, consisted of singing over a steady, percussive rhythm. The lines were of variable lengths determined by the chosen text. In addition, there were pauses of varying lengths that were

[33]The guitar is tuned in this manner to an open chord. The open E tuning was usually E-B-e-g-b-e', a minor tuning, but it was played with one finger on the third string, raising the g to the major g-sharp. The open G tuning was generally D-G-d-g-b-d'. The open D tuning was D-A-d-f#-a-d'.

determined by the length of time it took the singer to think of another phrase.

In this early style, the singer did not need a prearranged series of chords as long as he performed by himself. When the blues became a group performance, however, some preconceived plan was needed in order for everyone to not only start and stop together, but to make harmonic changes at the same time.

The text of the twelve-bar form employs a three-line stanza, of which the second line is a restatement of the first, and the third line is a contrasting statement. It is unusual for the blues stanza to consist of three different lines of text instead of two or four. This lyric form is quite rare in English literature and may have originated with the American Black.

An example of blues verse in the twelve-bar form contains a three-line stanza.

> Make your bed up higher, and turn your lamp way low.
> Make your bed up higher, turn your lamp way low.
> I'm gonna hug and kiss you, ain't coming here no more.

All blues melody is antiphonal in structure. Each four-measure phrase will often have a melody that is a little more than two measures in length. Consequently, the accompanying instruments may use the remaining length of the phrase for improvisation. The instruments function as antiphonal answers to the voice in those measures in which they are featured.

Some blues employ a four-line stanza in which the second and fourth lines rhyme, while others contain a six-line stanza in which the fourth and sixth lines rhyme.

The blues melody is derived from the chord structure, but it has a tonal concept of its own in that the third, seventh, and sometimes the fifth tones are microtonally lowered. These characteristic "blue notes" are of course common to many Black music forms. Since these tones always resolve to a note that lies about one-half-tone lower, there is a strong tendency in the blues toward a descending melodic line.

Most blues melodies utilize either the lower or upper half of the regular eight-note scale. Each of these groups comprise a tetrachord. Taking into account the "blue note" contained in each tetrachord, there are actually five tones in each group.

EXAMPLE 2.26 Lower tetrachordal grouping

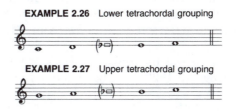

EXAMPLE 2.27 Upper tetrachordal grouping

Bessie Smith, prototype of the blues singer.
(Photo courtesy Duncan P. Schiedt Collection.)

Bessie Smith's *You've Been a Good Ole Wagon* is an example of a blues song in which the notes of the lower tetrachord are used for the melody. *Cold in Hand Blues,* also sung by Bessie Smith, employs the notes of the upper tetrachord in forming the melodic line.[34]

The blues singer uses all of the vocal devices indigenous to the Black singing style. These include blue notes, portamenti, falsetto, moaning, and groaning.

The blues was established in some of its variant forms quite early and more or less simultaneously throughout the South. The blues has also gone through a number of phases and naturally evolved into many types during its history. The first phase of the blues as an established form was the *archaic* or *country blues*. This style, which is indigenous to the Mississippi Delta, is characterized by nonstandardized forms, unamplified guitar, and spoken introductions and endings. Also utilized are ostinato patterns in the guitar accompaniment, bottlenecks used on the frets of the guitar, and rough, growling tones with the falsetto voice used for contrast or emotional emphasis. Some of the adherents of this style were Son House, Robert Johnson, Blind Lemon Jefferson, Lightin' Hopkins, Brownie McGhee, and Sonny Terry.

The second phase was the *classic* or *city blues*. This style, which came into existence during the 1920s, can be characterized by its standardized

[34]Listen to *You've Been a Good Ole Wagon* and *Cold in Hand Blues* by Bessie Smith on *The Bessie Smith Story* (Columbia, CL 855/8).

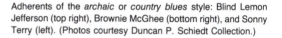

Adherents of the *archaic* or *country blues* style: Blind Lemon Jefferson (top right), Brownie McGhee (bottom right), and Sonny Terry (left). (Photos courtesy Duncan P. Schiedt Collection.)

Female singers dominated the second phase, *classic* or *city blues*. Pictured are Ma Rainey (top), ıda Cox (bottom right), and Alberta Hunter (bottom left). (Photos courtesy Duncan P. Schiedt Collection.)

form with regular beginnings and endings, and two or more instruments in the accompaniment—sometimes up to seven. This blues style, which lasted until about the middle 1930s, was dominated by female singers—Bessie Smith, Ma Rainey, Bertha "Chippie" Hill, Hociel Thomas, Ida Cox, Alberta Hunter, and Sippie Wallace, among others.

The third phase is the *contemporary blues.* Saxophones and electric guitars are added to the accompaniment and the music is notated and arranged. In addition, the vocal line tends to be sung in a shouting style and is often accompanied by a *riff*—a short, repeated melodic phrase coordinated with the blues chord pattern. Some of the practitioners of this style include Jimmy Rushing, Joe Turner, Walter Brown, Jimmy Witherspoon, Louis Jordan, Amos Milburn, T-Bone Walker, Albert King, B. B. King, Gatemouth Moore, and Charles Brown.

W. C. Handy.   Although the blues came into being around the last quarter of the nineteenth century, William Christopher Handy (1873–1958) was one of the first musicians to notate a blues composition. The son of a minister, Handy was born in Florence, Alabama. He had a varied career in music. After having organ lessons as a boy, he began to play with the local Black brass band, sang with local quartets, and eventually played with a Black dance orchestra. Later he taught school, worked as an itinerant musician, played cornet at the Chicago Fair in 1893, and worked as a cornetist and arranger with the Mahara Minstrels. In

W. C. Handy, one of the first musicians to notate the blues. (Photo courtesy Fisk University Library's Special Collection.)

1903, he organized the first of several bands to give concerts and play for dances. He established a music publishing company in 1907 with a young singer, Harry Pace.

It was not until 1909 that Handy wrote his first blue composition. The song, *Mr. Crump,* was written for a mayoral candidate, Edward H. Crump, running on a reform ticket. To gain the Black vote for Crump, Handy wrote this campaign song in a style that would appeal to Blacks. The song was an instant success and may have been decisive in Crump's election. Later, Handy rewrote the song as a piano composition, changed the name to *The Memphis Blues,* and published it in 1912. In 1912, the Theron Bennett Company of New York purchased all the rights to the tune for fifty dollars. With the addition of lyrics by George A. Norton Bennett, *The Memphis Blues* was republished and became a tremendous success. The blues had become a part of Tin Pan Alley.

Two years later, Handy, in an attempt to capitalize on the growing fame of *The Memphis Blues*—which had brought him so little financially— wrote the world-famous *St. Louis Blues.* It was published in 1914 by the Pace and Handy Music Company in Memphis, Tennessee. Among other Handy blues compositions are *Jogo Blues* (1913), *Joe Turner Blues* (1915), and a collection, *Blues: An Anthology* (1926).

BLACK CREOLE MUSIC

To better understand Black Creole music, it is important to understand what a Black Creole is and what significance this has in relation to his music.

The term "Creole" derives from the Spanish word, *criollo,* meaning "native to the place," and signifies birth in a foreign land. A child born in Spain of Spanish parents is a Spaniard, while a child born in a foreign land of Spanish parents is called a *criollo.* The Spaniards consistently applied this term to all of their offspring born in foreign territories of the New World in which the Spaniards settled—South America, Central America, Mexico, the West Indies, and the Southern part of the United States.

The French settlers of Louisiana substituted the term *Creole* for *criollo;* therefore, the first generations of offspring of the French in the New World were known as Creoles. Later, when there was intermarriage between the French and the Spanish in Louisiana, the term Creole included the descendants of this union.

Still later, there were offspring from the intermixing of French and Spanish settlers with other natives of Louisiana, most of whom were of African ancestry. In turn, this group of progeny were labeled Creoles. Thus, the term was applied first to the White inhabitants of Louisiana and then to those of mixed blood, regardless of their comparative Whiteness or Blackness.

Those Creoles who were an admixture of French and/or Spanish and African ancestry were of various skin colors. A Creole who had seven parts White blood and one part Black was known as an octoroon; three parts White and one part Black blood, a quadroon; half White blood and half Black, a mulatto; three parts Black blood and one part White, giffon; and seven parts Black blood and one part White blood, a Black Creole. It was the Black Creoles who produced the music that will be discussed here.

Creole songs, which are such an important part of Creole music, were conceived in a language that developed from the French language of the ruling class, a dialect or patois that also became known as Creole. It is still in use today in parts of Louisiana.

The free-born Creoles of mixed French and/or Spanish and African ancestry, the *Gens de Couleur* as they were known, lived in an environment that contained two powerful influences serving to encourage their musical talent. One of these was the opera. Grand opera, which was performed in New Orleans from 1837 on, was given regularly, several performances a week, throughout the season by troupes of singers from France. The other influence was that of French folk music, brought by their French ancestors to the New World.

The Black Creole slaves, the servant class, were deprived of these influences. They did not understand the French language in which both the opera and the French folk songs were sung. Even if this group had possessed a knowledge of French, however, opera probably would not have been a perceptible influence simply because slaves were not permitted to attend operatic performances.

The Creole slaves created songs to fit their language—most characteristically, love songs, lullabies, and satirical songs. Under the influence of unique environmental conditions, they created a folk music different from any other. The three elements that influenced it—the Spanish, the French, and the African—made this a unique genre.

The Creole songs probably originated in much the same manner as Black spirituals. Probably, some individual—who by reason of his poetic and musical ingenuity was looked up to by the group as a leader—feeling an urge brought on by some event or personal experience, began one strain of a song. The fascinations of the melody and rhythm perhaps attracted others present and produced a spontaneous response. By constant repetition, a new song came into the repertoire of the Black Creoles. Occasionally, a song was composed by someone who possessed some musical training; in most instances, however, the songs were the spontaneous expression of the illiterate Black Creoles.

In a comparison of Black Creole songs with Black spirituals, in only one respect are they alike: Since both were the creation of a partly African people, the rhythmic element is distinctive and prominent in both. However, they differ in every other way. There is a vast difference in the environment within which each kind of music appeared: Protestant America on one hand, and Catholic French America on the other. This resulted in differences both in the language of the songs and in their subjects.

In the case of language, the Afro-American slaves used a corrupted form of English, while the Creole slave made an entirely new language of his own. Creole is similar to, and yet different from, Parisian French, so that a Frenchman who had not lived in Louisiana might have difficulty understanding it.

The second difference, the subject matter chosen for the songs, is as interesting as the first. Many of the songs of Black Americans were deeply religious. This may be due in part to the constant, terrible oppression that they experienced and in part to the influence of the congregational singing of hymns in the Protestant Church.

With the Black Creoles, the situation was quite different. Even though slavery itself is always harsh, the Latin-Catholic nationalities always seem to have shown considerably more human regard for slaves under their domination, or at least they seem not to have regarded slaves as subhuman. Therefore, the songs of these Creoles, instead of being documentaries of sorrow and grief, told of romance for the most part, which reflects a direct Latin influence. In addition, the Catholic Church, unlike the Protestant churches, exerted little or no influence on the music of the Creole slaves, inasmuch as the service was for the most part in Latin, and the music consisted of Gregorian chant and solemn Masses.

Creole songs, like most folk songs, are simple in melodic and harmonic character. Most often they are sung in unison, in contrast to the heterophony found in Black spirituals. Because of the strong Franco-Spanish influence, melody is more important to the Black Creole than harmony. The rhythm, which reflects African influence, is also of considerable importance. Still, in many of these songs, the words seem more significant than any other component.

The phrases of Black Creole songs are usually short, and usually there is melodic, harmonic, and rhythmic contrast between the phrases and periods. Most songs are predominantly major in mode, and a variety of forms are employed.

One example of a romantic Creole song is *Pov' piti Lolotte,* which is well known among Creoles in the West Indies as well as in Louisiana.[35] This love song is concerned with a fellow who grieves for the girl he loves since she is heartbroken because her female rival has been given an embroi-

---

[35]The melody of this song, slightly varied, is now widely known as *Skip to my Lou.*

dered petticoat that came from some wealthy gentleman. He has been unable to become the object of her affection.

EXAMPLE 2.28 *Pov' piti Lolotte*[36]

Pov' pi - ti Lo - lotte a mouin Pov' pi - ti Lo - lotte a mouin,

Li ga - gnin bo - bo, bo - bo, Li ga - gnin dou - le

Pov' pi - ti Lo - lotte a mouin, Pov' pi - ti Lo - lotte a mouin,

Li ga - guin bo - bo, bo - bo Li ga - guin dou - le.

Dansé, Conni, Conné is a Creole folk lullaby in which baby is gaily danced up and down, possible in his last moment of play before the sandman comes.

EXAMPLE 2.29 *Dansé, Conni, Conné*[37]

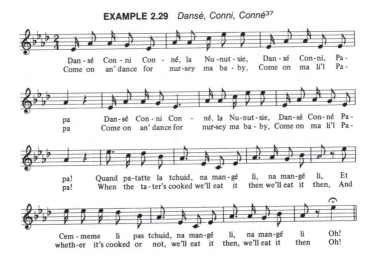

Dan - sé Con - ni Con - né, la Nu - nut - sie, Dan - sé Con - ni, Pa -
Come on an' dance for nur - sey ma ba - by, Come on ma li'l Pa -

pa Dan - sé Con - ni Con - né, la Nu - nut - sie, Dan - sé Con - né Pa -
pa Come on an' dance for nur - sey ma ba - by, Come on ma li'l Pa -

pa! Quand pa - tatte la tchuid, na man - gé li, na man - gé li, Et
pa! When the ta - ter's cooked we'll eat it then we'll eat it then, And

Cem - meme li pas tchuid, na man - gé li, na man - gé li Oh!
wheth - er it's cooked or not, we'll eat it then, we'll eat it then Oh!

Satire, as employed by Black Creoles, was probably a survival of a primitive practice brought to the New World by their ancestors from Africa. An example of this kind of biting humor is *Marie-Clémence*, which was sung to harass a woman who sold cheap cooked food.

[36]Example 2.28 is used by permission. From Henry E. Krehbiel, *Afro-American Folksongs* (New York: Frederick Ungar Publishing Co.), p. 136.

[37]From Camille Nickerson, arr., *Five Creole Songs*. Used by permission.

EXAMPLE 2.30 *Marie-Clémence*[38]

Ma - rie Clé - mence mau - di,   La mo - ri fritt li man - di

Col - lier-choux li   mau - di,   Toutt bag-gäle li   mau - di

Ma - rie Clé-mence   mau - di,   La - mo - ri fritt li   mau - di

Col - lier-choux li   mau - di,   Toutt bag-gäle li   mau - di   Aïe! ___

Loqué moin, loqué moin,   loqué moin!   Moin Ké ne - yé   co   moin,

Moin Ké né - yé   co   moin   En - bas qouðs pile   ouôche - là!

The songs of the Black Creoles of Louisiana are a unique and distant genre, bearing some similarities to the music of Afro-Americans, yet different in many other ways. The character of this music reflects the influences of the French and the Spanish along with the African. This blending of three cultures has produced a music quite different from any other music found on the North American mainland.

The pre-1900 forms that are indigenous to the American Black are a unique folk music peculiar to the United States. What is more important, however, is that from these forms evolved a twentieth-century music that has had a profound effect on not only American composers and music, but also on European composers and music in the European tradition.

This "music of the soil"—the spiritual, the work song, the field holler, the blues—influenced not only ragtime, gospel songs, and that musical entity called "rhythm and blues," but also the many jazz styles of the twentieth century, considered by many to be America's most original musical product.

Thus, Black music evolved from a non-notated music, handed down from generation to generation by word of mouth, to a notated, composed music that has in turn been influenced and westernized to some degree by the European musical tradition.

[38]Used by permission of Frederick Ungar Publishing Co., New York.

chapter three

Black Music Forms After 1900

A considerable body of American Black music came into being around or after the beginning of the twentieth century. Interestingly enough, all of this music, with the exception of New Orleans jazz, is notated. This was the first step, among many, in which this music was imbued with principles of Western music. American Black music, however, still maintained enough African characteristics to retain its particular character. This music is still a unique facet of the American arts. This uniqueness has continued to remain in the music because of the social milieu in which it took place.

RAGTIME

Ragtime, essentially a piano music that flourished for about twenty years, from 1896 to 1917, was an immediate forerunner of New Orleans jazz. Ragtime is not just an older name for jazz; it was one of the influencing factors on this art form. Both ran a parallel course until ragtime virtually died out after the end of the First World War.

This new music was exposed to the public through a series of worlds fairs: the World's Columbian Exposition at Chicago in 1893; the Trans-

Mississippi at Omaha in 1899; the Pan-American at Buffalo in 1901; and the Louisiana Purchase at St. Louis in 1904.

The advent of ragtime on the American musical scene was timely. Because this country had experienced a long depression from 1893 to 1898, it was a welcome relief from riots, hunger marches, and threats of revolution. This new music, along with the cakewalk,[1] a popular dance of American Black origin, was like a fresh start for the country.

It is not known when the name "ragtime" was first applied to this kind of music. A newspaper writer in Chicago, whose identity has been forgotten, is credited as the first to use the name "ragtime" in print in early 1897. Although there were earlier songs that had sections that were "ragged,"[2] the first published instrumental number completely in ragtime and so entitled was published in 1897. This composition, written by a White man, W. H. Krell, was entitled *Mississippi Rag*. The first rag published by a Black man was Tom Turpin's *Harlem Rag*, also in 1897. The first recorded use of the word "ragtime" in a title was in 1898 when a Black Detroit composer named Fred Stone had a song published that was entitled *Ma Ragtime Baby*.

Published compositions had ragtime strains in them long before the first recorded use of the word itself. One reason for this is that the *coon song*,[3] a product of minstrelsy, is an imitation of the Black man's singing. Black singing is sometimes characterized by ragtime rhythm.

In the next few years following the publication of the first instrumental rag, two Black composers, Tom Turpin and Scott Joplin, produced rags that incorporated certain characteristics that governed the style throughout its history. Among these were the familiar multi-theme structure, key change, and the familiar rhythm of two strong beats per measure underlying simple syncopation. Their early rags are among the best known and most often played. Turpin's *Harlem Rag* and *St. Louis Rag,* Joplin's *Maple Leaf Rag* and *The Entertainer,* and the Joplin-James Scott collaboration *Sunflower Slow Drag* established the basic ragtime style.

These two great pioneers were followed by other outstanding Black ragtime composers and performers, such as Louis Chauvin, Arthur Marshall, Scott Hayden, Tony Jackson, and Ferdinand "Jelly Roll" Morton; and later, Artie Matthews, Charley Thompson, and Robert Hampton.

Ragtime is Black dance music. It is based on Black dance melodies

---

[1]This dance was originally performed on plantations by slave couples. A cake was awarded to the pair who danced with the proudest, high-kicking steps. Eventually, this dance became a part of minstrelsy and was accompanied by syncopated music that was later called ragtime.

[2]The term "ragged" denotes the use of such rhythms as ♫ ♩ and various kinds of syncopations against a regular rhythmic bass, as well as an irregular ("ragged") melodic line.

[3]While the term "coon" is scarcely less opprobrious today than "nigger," the word was merely one of a whole variety of designations for the Black man used during this period and much earlier.

and is intended as accompaniment for dancing. Its basic rhythm is that of the two-step or cakewalk. The dance origins of ragtime are the primary source of the complex rhythms found in this music, in particular its syncopation.

Ragtime is distinguished from many other musics by its use of syncopation. Unlike most European music, it is often syncopated from start to finish. This device is used in music in the European tradition but less often than in ragtime. If syncopation is used for an extended period of time, the syncopated beat may soon acquire the character of the unsyncopated beat. Ragtime solved this problem by maintaining both a syncopated and an unsyncopated beat at the same time.

In its simplest form, the rhythm of ragtime consists of accents on the weak and normally unaccented second and fourth beats of the measure in the pianist's right hand against a precise and regularly accented bass in the left hand. In further amplification of the role of syncopation in ragtime, the left hand plays simple harmonies largely based on the primary triads in "downbeat-upbeat" style, which may have been taken from the minstrel banjo. The downbeats are usually single bass notes, octaves, or tenths, and the upbeats are usually chords. The right hand is free to embellish the chord basis set by the left hand with runs and arpeggios and much syncopation.

Ragtime is a highly sectionalized music; its structure consists of either three-part or four-part forms in contrast to the single forms of the thirty-two-bar song or the blues. The most common ragtime form consists of an AABBACCDD design. (Occasionally the repeat of A following the B strain is eliminated.) An example is the *Maple Leaf Rag* of Scott Joplin, whose form is as follows:

Key:	Sections A, and B: A flat
	Section C: D flat
	Section D: A flat
Form:	
	Section A twice—32 bars
Section I	Section B twice—32 bars
(ternary)	Section A once—16 bars
Section II	Section C twice—32 bars
(binary)	Section D twice—32 bars

EXAMPLE 3.1 *Maple Leaf Rag*

 Section A:

Section B:

Section A:

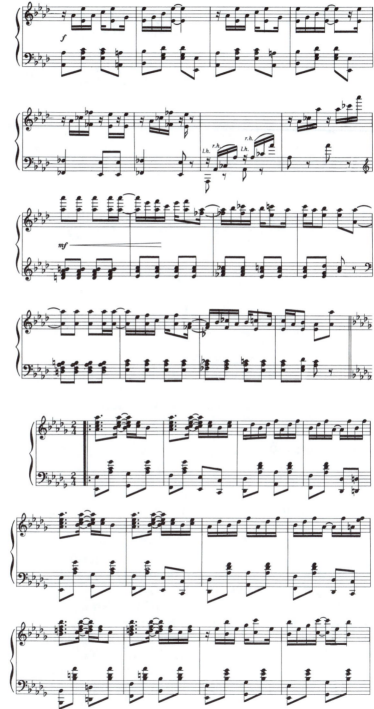

Section C:

Section D:

It is thought by some writers that the rag has a thematic scheme similar to the quadrille, a French dance popular in New Orleans during the nineteenth century. The quadrille has a five-part, sectionalized form like the typical rag; however, the meter of this fashionable dance shifts from $\frac{6}{8}$ to $\frac{2}{4}$ alternately, while the rag remains in $\frac{2}{4}$ or $\frac{4}{4}$ meter throughout. The quadrille may have had some influence on the rag, since, for instance, Jelly Roll Morton is known to have modeled his *Tiger Rag* after a quadrille whose name is unknown. But the evidence overwhelmingly points to the march as the formal progenitor of ragtime despite the difficulty in finding exact schematic correspondence between the two forms. Both rag and march are in duple meter. In fact, many of the early ragtime compositions were called "marches" and Joplin often marked his rags "tempo di marcia" or "in slow march time." There are other indicators of the influence of the march on ragtime. This syncopated music developed in the Midwest where marches have always been very popular. The structure of rags resembles that of the march in that many rags modulate to the subdominant key in the C section just as the march does in its comparable Trio section. Finally, the John Philip Sousa band "ragged" many marches (that is, performed them in ragtime rhythms) at the turn of the century. The sum total of the evidence suggests very strongly that there was substantial march influence on ragtime.

The march was exerting an influence on another Black music form that was developing around the same time as ragtime, New Orleans jazz. It seems unlikely that this influence would be evident in one kind of music and not in another when both were developing at the same time and in the same region. However, ragtime, a contemporary of early jazz, was isolated from it to some extent and is a separate body of music. Although it exerted some influence on jazz, there is an essential difference between the two.

Jazz is essentially an improvised music. The process of improvisation consists of expanding on a given theme and its harmony. Thus, the starting point is the theme and the chords that accompany that theme; the end product depends entirely on the improvisor.

On the other hand, ragtime is composed music, and it is intended to stand alone. The composer did not write a melody and then set about arranging it within the context of a given harmonic structure. It is in this sense that ragtime is closer to music in the European tradition than is jazz.

It is probably true that the ragtime pianist did indulge in some form of improvisation, however. This is evident in the recordings of *Maple Leaf Rag* by Jelly Roll Morton and Eubie Blake.[4]

The development of the rhythmic complexity of ragtime music is associated with certain geographical areas in the United States. The parent style has been labeled "Sedalia," after the Missouri town in which Scott Joplin began to gain fame. He specified that his rags should be played slowly. The result is a plodding music with heavy syncopation in the right hand while the left hand produced an "oom-pah" effect typical of the march. Yet the overall structure and the melodic lines are generally considered excellent. A number of piano rolls of Joplin's compositions, recorded in 1907, give an idea as to his style of playing ragtime. These rolls re-

---

[4]*They All Played the Maple Leaf Rag* (Herwin Records 401) includes recordings by Jelly Roll Morton and Eubie Blake. Both Morton and Blake took liberties with the melody both pitchwise and rhythmically. While jazz had matured and may have influenced their playing style by the time these recordings were made (1939 and 1969 respectively), each played this tune as he remembered playing it around the turn of the century. If each recording is a true replication of their ragtime style at that time, then ragtime was improvised to a limited degree, the difference being that the melody of each section of a ragtime composition was improvised slightly as opposed to a single melody in jazz being the focal point of freer improvisation.

produce his actual performances and are made to be played by the old-fashioned Pianola.[5]

EXAMPLE 3.2   *Frog Legs Rag*[6]

The next step in the development of rhythmic complexity in ragtime takes its name from the city that is often referred to as the birthplace of ragtime, St. Louis. The St. Louis style consisted of rags being played with new life and zest. The manner of performance displayed a vigor and brilliance not found in the placid two-beat style of Turpin and Joplin. While using increased tempos, the performers of rags in the St. Louis style tended to dispense with the heavy march two-beat of the left hand, playing instead four evenly accented left-hand notes in the same time interval. The disappearance of the accents on the first and third beats in the left hand made for a more flowing rhythm. In this style, it is frequently difficult to see where the syncopation lies, for it often depends as much on the style of the performer as it does on the notation. The St. Louis style can be illustrated by an excerpt from James Scott's *Frog Legs Rag*.

The third step in ragtime's rhythmic development is associated with New Orleans and Ferdinand "Jelly Roll" Morton. New Orleans rags differed from other rags in musical form as well as in spirit for three reasons. First, the melodic line and the harmony have a romantic quality derived from both the classic and the folk music of France, Spain, and Italy. Second, the rhythm is more strongly accented and less restrained than that of

[5]This is an instrument that was manufactured both in its original form as an instrument external to the pianoforte, and in the later form in the pianola-piano in which the playing mechanism is incorporated in the body of the pianoforte. The later development of the pianola was known as the "Duo-art Piano." Rudi Blesh and Harriet Janis, in *They All Played Ragtime* (New York: Oak Publications, 1966), state the following description of the pianola: The pianola . . . was a portable mechanism in a cabinet that one moved up to a piano. It included the tracker bar for the player roll. Bellows actuated by four pumps operated the hammers, which moved up and down. The operator sat in front of this mechanism to work it, and in turn its hammers, functioning like fingers, hit the keys of the piano, from which the music emerged in a chain reaction from operator to cabinet to piano. The mechanism had a sixty-five-note spread . . . p. 232.

[6]*Frog Legs Rag* by James Scott, 1906.

the classic ragtime of the Joplin school. Finally, there is a tendency toward the use of two or more intertwined melodies, instead of classic ragtime's single treble melody over an accompanying bass. The bass line tends to become melodic, producing a kind of counterpoint. It is interesting to note that this added melodic figuration is apparently derived from two sources, the European operatic tradition and the singing tradition of West Africa.

The New Orleans ragtimer also used the rolling or walking (two-beat) bass in his music. The regular-metered ragtime bass reacted with the off-beat treble to set up polyrhythms of a more complex structure. These running basses introduced a countermelody to the treble; so that in typical New Orleans ragtime passages of this sort, there is not just melody and accompaniment but two concurrent melodies. These various qualities developed to their zenith in the ragtime-jazz piano of Jelly Roll Morton. New Orleans ragtime style with its "ragging" bass line is illustrated by excerpts from Morton's *Frog-i-more Rag*. The figure ① is used to indicate the walking or rolling bass, while the figure ② is used to indicate the melodic-type bass.

EXAMPLE 3.3 *Frog-i-more Rag*[7]

[7]*Frog-i-more Rag* by Ferdinand "Jelly-Roll" Morton, © 1918 Fred Morton, © Renewed 1946 Edwin H. Morris & Company, A Division of MPL Communications, Inc. International Copyright Secured. All Rights Reserved. Used By Permission.

The fourth and last step in its rhythmic development is best represented by the music played in New York City's Harlem. This music, called "rent-party piano" or simply Harlem piano style, was not generally recognized as ragtime because of the lateness of its discovery by White society— after 1920—even though it emerged simultaneously with the ragtime found in other areas.

Harlem-style ragtime utilized a new rhythm and a faster tempo, which came from Black church singing and had its roots in the old ring-shouts. "Slow-drag" ragtime (Joplin or Sedalia style), which was considered out of date, was replaced by the brilliant, fast techniques of the old Black church ring-shouts, which utilized the ragtime bass but in which the traditional trio was generally omitted. A kind of rhythmic fervor was in evidence. The shout utilized one intricate theme after another and interrupted the "stride" with complex broken bass rhythms. It depended on a constant building up of tension and excitement to a sudden, staccato ending. This style of ragtime reached its peak in the compositions and performances of Luckeyeth "Luckey" Roberts, James P. Johnson, Willie "The Lion" Smith, Thomas "Fats" Waller, Eubie Blake, and many other lesser-known artists. An example of the Harlem rent-party style is *The Carolina Shout* by James P. Johnson.

EXAMPLE 3.4 *The Carolina Shout*[8]

The term "classical" has been used several times in this section to denote a specific quality of ragtime. The term is applied to those rags that serve as a standard or model. It is used in the sense that the syncopated music referred to is highly developed along ragtime's own proper lines and is performed in a very artistic manner. The term has no reference to music of the Classic period in the European tradition. It was applied to piano ragtime early in the twentieth century and was a commonly accepted term by 1912 or 1913.

Three interrelated factors contributed to the demise of ragtime as a piano style: (1) the commercialism of Tin Pan Alley, (2) ragtime's failure to

Harlem-style ragtime represents the fourth stage in the development of this musical form. Its proponents included Luckeyeth "Luckey" Roberts (top left), James P. Johnson (top right), Willie "The Lion" Smith (middle left), Thomas "Fats" Waller (middle right), and Eubie Blake (bottom). (Photos courtesy Duncan P. Schiedt Collection.)

continue to develop, and (3) the fact that it was transformed and devoured by jazz.

The irony of ragtime's vast success is that the commercial tunesmiths of Tin Pan Alley did their best to garner every dollar possible from imitations of this stylized, composed music of folk origins, and in doing so, ruined the very music from which they were reaping huge profits. Because the complex cross-rhythms found in ragtime could not be played by the general public, a simplified form that could be played by anyone who could read music was circulated in the form of sheet music and sold tremendously from coast to coast.

This music was also distributed on pianola rolls. Most piano roll companies employed a pianist who could "rag" any tune for issue on a piano roll, the end result being a product characterized by a monotonous sameness. By 1900, Tin Pan Alley took over this art form of Black folk origin, and the success of ragtime and its diluted and derivative forms was overwhelming. It soon developed into a national fad, making hits of instruction books such as Christensen's *Instruction Book for Ragtime Piano Playing* and songs like Irvin Berlin's *Alexander's Ragtime Band.* (Both writers, like most of Tin Pan Alley during this period, were White.)

Ragtime became a featured part of latter-day minstrelsy, vaudeville, cabaret, and cafe. The light classics were often ragged to insure popular appeal. Even John Philip Sousa, on European tours beginning in 1900, featured such ragged numbers as *At a Georgia Camp Meeting* and *Hunky Dory,* neither of which was originally a ragtime composition.

Because the merit of a piece of music and the level of commercial success that it achieves have nothing in common, sheet music sales cannot be used to judge the value of a ragtime composition. While a real masterpiece like *Maple Leaf Rag* was a national hit, so were many pieces that have since been judged to be inferior. Conversely, many great ragtime compositions may have remained virtually unknown.

If any art form is to remain viable, it must continue to develop. But ragtime became a stereotyped, highly imitative kind of popular music. It was able to incorporate a greater fusion of European and African musical elements than any music before it. But ragtime began with such a great preponderance of formal European characteristics that, even though it absorbed more and more of the African rhythmic complexity, it was never able to go the rest of the way and incorporate the bittersweet mood of the blues. So ragtime remained cheerful, pianistic in concept, and predominantly European.

As ragtime became more popular, development ceased, perhaps because of the difficulty of the music itself. The public could not play the real thing, so publishers could not make money issuing it. Consequently, there was no financial need to continue its development.

The advent of jazz proved more destructive. The rougher syncopation and more flexible harmonies of jazz moved in and absorbed the younger musicians, in whose hands ragtime was so transformed as to lose its identity.

As stated earlier, jazz, as an improvised music, is essentially different from the composed music of ragtime. In order for jazz to adapt ragtime to the requirements of improvisation, it was necessary to change its form. In ragtime, there are usually four themes, each as important as the others. Such a structure is not suitable for improvisation because the problem arises as to which melody will be used as the basis for improvisation. There-fore, a gradual alteration took place, with the final theme assuming greater importance and the earlier themes reduced in number and influence. Eventually the opening melodies served as verse, while the last one became the central part of the composition that the musicians explored with all the improvisatory ideas at their command.

In all fairness, it must be added that perhaps this form and style of piano music were not destined for a long life. Perhaps ragtime's greatest weakness, and that which led to its demise, was its monotonous similarity of sound.

The position of Blacks in American society determined the status of ragtime music for a considerable part of its early history. It was developed and heard in the White underworld, which contributed to the rejection of ragtime by many elements of society that would have been likely to accept it had they been able to consider the music apart from its unfavorable environment.

Scott Joplin.   Scott Joplin (1868–1917), was accorded the title "King of Ragtime" and was generally acknowledged as the most influential com-poser in this field. Joplin, born into a musical family, became interested in

Scott Joplin, the "King of Ragtime." (Photo courtesy Duncan P. Schiedt Collection.)

the piano at the age of seven and received formal musical training on this instrument at the age of eleven. In his early teens, he became an itinerant pianist, travelling all over Texas, Louisiana, and the Mississippi Valley. Not only did he gain considerable playing experience, but he also heard many self-taught musicians and singers and a tremendous amount of Black folk music.

Joplin's travels brought him to St. Louis in 1885 and he made this wide-open river town the hub of his musical activities. After playing St. Louis and nearby towns in Missouri and Illinois, Joplin went to Chicago in 1893 to perform at the World's Columbian Exposition. In 1894 he went to Sedalia, Missouri to live and there began to write music for the first time.

The first two compositions by Joplin were published in Syracuse, New York in 1895. They were *A Picture of Her Face* and *Please Say You Will*, two typically Victorian songs with conventional harmonies and sentimental lyrics. The next three published compositions were piano solos entitled *The Great Crush Collision March, Combination March,* and *Harmony Waltz.* None of these compositions foreshadowed the ragtime style that was to become so fashionable a few years later.

After an absence of two years because of his tours, Joplin returned to Sedalia in 1896. He entered the George Smith College for Negroes, taking advanced courses in harmony and composition. During this period Joplin continued to develop his piano skill, worked seriously at composition, and organized his own orchestra, which featured his compositions.

In 1898, with the ragtime craze sweeping the country, Joplin was able to find a publisher for one of his compositions in this musical idiom. His *Original Rags* was published in March 1899, by Carl Hoffman of Kansas City, Missouri. Later that same year, John Stillwell Stark, a White music publisher, heard Joplin playing a new rag at the Maple Leaf Club in Sedalia, liked it, and bought it for fifty dollars and royalties to the composer. *Maple Leaf Rag,* which was published later that same year, not only set high standards for future ragtime compositions in the classic style, but incorporated certain characteristics that were to remain standard for this style throughout its history. Among these were the familiar multi-theme structure, key change, and two-beat rhythm underlying simple syncopation. Because *Maple Leaf Rag* was a tremendous financial and artistic success, Joplin and Stark collaborated on the composition and publication of a number of ragtime masterpieces. Joplin became the leading ragtime composer, and Stark was the leading ragtime publisher in the country.

Two important figures in ragtime music, Arthur Marshall (1881–1956) and Scott Hayden (1882–1915), were protégés of Joplin. As he did with the gifted youth in any town in which he remained for a period of time, Joplin began to teach these youths when he returned to Sedalia in 1896. Out of this came some outstanding ragtime music. Joplin collaborated with Hayden in writing four rags: *Sunflower Slow Drag* (1901), *Some-*

Arthur Marshall, protegé of Joplin, at piano; G. Tom Ireland (l.); and Bob Darch at the Sedalia Centennial Celebration, 1960. (Photo courtesy Trebor Tichenor.)

thing Doing (1903), *Felicity Rag* (1911), and *Kismet Rag* (1913). Joplin joined Marshall in composing two rags: *Swipesy Cake Walk* (1900), and *Lily Queen* (1907).

In 1900, Joplin moved to St. Louis where he continued to compose many rags and also to devote some time to teaching. In 1902, Stark published four of Joplin's rags: *A Breeze from Alabama, Elite Syncopation, The Strenuous Life,* and *The Entertainer.* In addition, two other compositions, *Cleophia Two-Step* and *March Majestic,* were published during the same year.

Joplin also revived *The Rag-Time Dance,* an earlier effort in extended form. This composition was conceived as a folk ballet with narrative soloist and choreography based on popular dances of this period, such as the cakewalk and the slow drag. The narrator sang such verses as:

> Let me see you do the "rag time dance,"
> Turn left and do the "cake walk prance,"
> Turn the other way and do the "slow drag"—
>
> Now take your lady to the World's Fair
> And do the "rag time dance."[9]

[9]Rudi Blesh and Harriet Janis, *They All Played Ragtime* (New York: Oak Publications, 1966), p. 69.

The entire work required more than twenty minutes to perform. This composition is significant because it indicates Joplin's ability to think in terms of extended ragtime instrumental forms.

Continuing his interest in the extended ragtime forms, Joplin composed and produced, in St. Louis, a ragtime opera, *A Guest of Honor,* in 1903. The manuscript has since been lost. While public reaction was favorable, the opera was never published as a complete work.

In 1906, Joplin continued to compose rags and also recorded a number of piano rolls of his own compositions. In this same year he set out on a series of vaudeville tours that lasted until 1909 when he finally settled in New York.

In 1908 Joplin published an instruction book on ragtime for the advanced student, *The School of Ragtime—Six Exercises for Piano.*

In New York, Joplin began to teach again and entered the experimental period of his career as a composer of rags. Although syncopation remained an essential part of his style, it seems to have been toned down considerably. His phrasing became longer and his harmonies more complex. His modulations became more extensive, and foreign keys were occasionally established within the sixteen-bar framework.

Specifically, three main features of the new style are readily apparent. First, there is increased freedom in the left hand. In his earlier rags, Joplin relied on the "oom-pah" left-hand pattern very strongly. During his later period, the left hand assumes a more independent character, carrying melodic passages and delineating harmonies more specifically. An excellent contrast between the earlier role of the left hand and its new emphasis is provided in the opening bars of *Maple Leaf Rag* (1899) and *Euphonic Sounds* (1909). In the former, the left hand contains the usual oom-pah effect; in *Euphonic Sounds,* it is largely absent. It must be pointed out that Joplin did not dispense with the oom-pah effect entirely; in fact, in the

EXAMPLE 3.5 *Maple Leaf Rag*

EXAMPLE 3.6 *Euphonic Sounds*

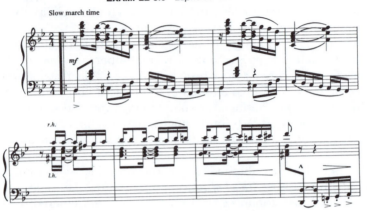

majority of his late rags he retained it. Nevertheless, he did utilize the new bass line enough to indicate that he was experimenting in this vein.

Another feature of Joplin's experimentation during this period is his attempt to maintain rhythmic momentum implicitly rather than explicitly. One procedure normally used to maintain rhythmic momentum is to notate the melodic voice so that it syncopates the third note of an eight-note pattern (or its equivalent).[10] This kind of pattern tends to give rhythmic impetus to the melodic line. Joplin manages to avoid doing this in two of his rags during this period: the first two strains of *Euphonic Sounds* and the last strain of *Magnetic Rag*. When syncopation occurs, it is not as obvious. Excerpts from the first two strains of *Euphonic Sounds* are as follows:

EXAMPLE 3.7 First theme, *Euphonic Sounds*

EXAMPLE 3.8 Second theme, *Euphonic Sounds*[11]

[10]See Example 4.5.

[11]*Euphonic Sounds* by Scott Joplin. Copyright © 1909 by Mills Music, Inc. Copyright renewed. All rights reserved. Used by permission.

Last, but by no means least significant, Joplin reveals in two of his rags of this period an increased concern with structure. Joplin was instrumental in establishing the early form of the piano rag, a form that can be represented as AABBACCDD. *Euphonic Rag*, however, was cast in cyclical form and is a complete rondo: AABBAACCAA. While there are other rags of this period by Joplin that employ the cyclical principle, they are not authentic rondos. Among them are *Kismet* and *Magnetic Rag*, in which the first theme is stated only at the beginning and the end.

Joplin's change of rag form is directly opposed to the transformation of this form brought about by jazz pianists. Jazz sought one theme as a center for improvisation and weakened the sense of larger form exhibited by ragtime. Joplin's efforts were apparently attempts to strengthen this sense of form.

In general, the various ideas with which Joplin was working were not sufficiently synthesized into a unified style. These experimentations were short-lived. They were not incorporated in his compositions over a long period of time. His further development of the ragtime idiom may have been thwarted by his efforts in the composition of opera.

While Joplin experimented with ragtime rhythm and form, he became increasingly obsessed with writing and producing his second opera. Publishers were reluctant to publish this work because there was little likelihood of financial success. Finally, in 1911, Joplin published the piano version of his opera *Treemonisha*—230 pages—at his own expense.

The opera, in three acts, employs eleven soloists. There are twenty-seven musical numbers, including an overture and a prelude to Act III. Unlike Joplin's earlier work *Guest of Honor*, *Treemonisha* is not called a ragtime opera. This work was Joplin's last effort to create a ragtime classicism that could compare with the best of European music.

Hoping to attract a backer, Joplin, with the help of Sam Patterson, trained the cast and organized a single performance, which was given in Harlem in 1915 without scenery, lighting, costumes, or an orchestra. Joplin played the accompaniment on the piano. The performance was not well received by the Harlem public, a crushing blow from which Joplin never recovered. His mind, which had shown considerable strain as early as 1911, began to falter. He began to experience periods of dark depression at an accelerated rate. Finally, his mind gave way completely. On April 11, 1917, Scott Joplin died insane.

When the news of Joplin's death reached John Stark in St. Louis, he wrote a two-line obituary that reflected the significance of this Black man: "Scott Joplin is dead. A homeless itinerant, he left his mark on American music."

JAZZ

Jazz, from its inception, has developed into several distinct styles. Each will be discussed separately.

New Orleans Jazz

Not only is it impossible to establish the exact beginnings of jazz as a distinct, self-contained music, it is just as impossible to ascertain the one geographical place in which jazz began, for early jazz, in both its essential and its peripheral manifestations, sprang up in many parts of the United States, not only in New Orleans.

Another erroneous generalization is that all music played by Black musicians in New Orleans or elsewhere in this period was jazz. Some of the music was jazz; some of it contained elements that eventually became essential ingredients of jazz; and some of it was simply not jazz at all. A great part of this music was borderline music that was on the verge of becoming jazz. This early music was multifaceted, and its character depended not only on its geographical location but on its audience. Where the audience was White or composed of middle-class Blacks, the more authentic forms of jazz were not heard.

It is possible however, to ascertain the birthplace of one style of jazz. New Orleans-style jazz was born in the city of New Orleans, and how it came into being has been largely substantiated. This music could have developed only in New Orleans; in no other city in the United States were the conditions and the environment of New Orleans duplicated.

New Orleans was founded about 1718 as a colony of France, and was ceded to Spain in 1762. Spain ceded Louisiana back to France in 1800. The Louisiana Territory, of which New Orleans was a part, was sold to the United States by France in 1803. This city, which had been under three flags in less than one hundred years, had become a multiracial center of many cultures from diverse parts of the world. Not only were there the French, the Spanish, and the Americans, but successive waves of immigration gave New Orleans a large Italian population. And from Africa came the slaves. Thus, New Orleans was a city with cultural traditions very different from those found elsewhere in the United States. One reflection of this cultural difference was the existence of the class known as Creoles of Color.

Provisions of the Louisiana "black code" of 1724 permitted the manumission, or individual emancipation, of slaves by their masters. Children shared the status of their mothers, and when a White Creole died, he frequently provided in his will that his African or part-African mistress would be set free. In addition, White gentlemen continued to take "colored" mistresses. Both situations helped to create a class of Creoles of Color with French and Spanish as well as African blood in their veins. As free men and women, many colored Creoles became wealthy landowners or prosperous small businessmen who sent their children to France for an education. Hence, New Orleans society was divided into three strata: The Whites formed the upper class; the middle stratum was made up of the Creoles of Color; and the Black slaves formed the lowest echelon.

The Black slaves were permitted to carry on their African music and dancing in a large open field at Rampart and Orleans Streets called Congo Square. Favorite dances of the slaves were the Calinda (a variation of which was also used in Voodoo ceremonies) and the Bamboula, both of which were primarily based on primitive dances of Africa.

Elements of the West African musical influence found at Congo Square contributed to the birth of jazz. Two factors aided this evolution: the tremendous popularity of the military band and the gradual adoption of European instruments by Blacks.

The military band had reached its peak in popularity in France under Napoleon. As a former colony of France, New Orleans followed the French tradition in bands very closely and became famous for them. Bands were utilized to furnish music for almost every occasion—parades, picnics, riverboat excursions, concerts, dances, and funerals.

Prior to the Civil War, there were several bands in both the North and South that were composed of free Blacks. Two of these bands were led by Frank Johnson (1792–1844) and James Hemmenway (1820–49). Many of these Black musicians acquired their training and instruments during the war of 1812. These bands played march music in an excellent manner, but in the European tradition, with very little African influence in evidence. It was not until after the Civil War that the field slave had an opportunity to become a part of this kind of musical activity. Numerous bands disbanded in New Orleans immediately after the Civil War. Their instruments, having been pawned by these former soldiers, were plentiful and cheap, offering an excellent opportunity for the emancipated slaves to secure them.

These former slaves formed their own street bands and participated in various kinds of parades on many occasions. These groups played the standard march tunes in a self-taught style that exhibited a considerable amount of West African influence.

The preeminence and frequency of Black bands in New Orleans was due not only to the close ties with France and the general popularity of bands, but also to the existence of secret Black societies that gave these bands employment on a wide range of occasions. Out of this cultural milieu came the beginnings of jazz, not in the 1890s but shortly after emancipation.

The emancipation of the slaves had ramifications that put the Creoles of Color in a tenuous position. On the one hand, from the time Louisiana became a part of the United States, there was a great influx into New Orleans of Southern Whites with different ideas about color and race. After the Civil War, there was an influx of ex-slaves from nearby sugar and cotton plantations. The Creoles of Color were beginning to find themselves caught in the middle.

In 1874 the White League was organized for a two-fold purpose: to throw out the Yankee carpetbaggers and to keep the Black man "in his place." As segregation and prejudice grew, the colored Creoles found themselves more and more in the Black world. Bit by bit, they were pushed out of any job a White man could use.

The downtown, upper crust Creole taste in music did not embrace the style of early jazz. These Creoles cultivated a taste for the European classics, and for this purpose organized the Philharmonic Society, which was composed of trained musicians under the direction of men such as Constantin Deberque and Richard Lambert. By the 1880s, this stratum of New Orleans society had its own society bands as well. These bands played in a smoothly harmonized, arranged style foreign to the improvisational roots of jazz. Eventually, and against their will, these Creoles of Color moved uptown to play music with their darker colleagues. They could play European instruments correctly and they could read music, but they could not play jazz at first.

As the Creoles of Color began to lose their position in New Orleans society, more of them began to enter jazz and to help shape the classic form of this idiom. Some of these outstanding musicians were Lorenzo Tio, Alphonse Picou, George and Achille Baquet, Sidney Bechet, Edward "Kid" Ory, Honore Dutrey, Emanuel Perez, Buddy and Joseph Petit, Ferdinand "Jelly Roll" Morton, and many others.

When the Creoles of Color migrated uptown to join the ex-slaves, there was a meeting of two musical traditions. The Creoles brought with them a highly sophisticated European musical tradition, ranging from opera to folk songs of French and Spanish influence. On the other hand, the ex-slaves came from a musical tradition more obviously rooted in Africa and anchored in emotion, out of which had developed the work song, spiritual, field holler, and blues.

There were many outstanding bands and musicians active in New Orleans music. One of the earliest bandleaders was a cornetist named Claiborne Williams who led the St. Joseph Brass Band. This band, popular in the 1880s, played not only for parades but also for cotillions for those Blacks who wanted to imitate White dances. Another popular band during this period was the "sweet"[12] band of John Robichaux. When his own group was not booked to perform, he was active as a member of the outstanding Excelsior Band. Also important during the 1880s was the Imperial Band.

In the 1890s, there were the Peerless, Indian, Columbus, Diamond Stone, and Onward Brass Bands, all of which had reed instruments and were excellent. The greatest band of them all during this period, however, was Charles "Buddy" Bolden's (1868–1931) Ragtime Band, a group that set the style in New Orleans. His band also fixed the New Orleans jazz instrumentation of one or two cornets, clarinet, trombone, bass, guitar or banjo, and drums. Bolden himself was a very gifted cornetist.

[12]The term "sweet" is used to indicate a smooth, arranged, "legitimate" style of playing.

Early jazz was used mainly in the streets of New Orleans for parades and funerals. (Photo courtesy Special Collections Division, Tulane University Library.)

Other outstanding bands were the great Olympia Band of 1900–11, featuring the excellent cornetist Freddie Keppard; the Eagle Band, which included Keppard, Bunk Johnson, and other excellent New Orleans musicians; and the Superior and Magnolia Bands.

During its very early period, jazz was used mainly in the streets for parades and funerals. The bands played slow, mournful dirges all the way to the cemetery while the horse carriages and the mourners followed. After the actual interment had taken place and the procession was filing away from the cemetery gates, the band would break into a syncopated rendition of some song such as *Oh, Didn't He Ramble*.

The typical small string bands, sometimes referred to as sweet bands, had played for Black dancing in New Orleans since long before 1890. In these groups, there were various combinations of violin, guitar, mandolin, string bass, and occasionally piano. The kinds of music played were French quadrilles, waltzes, Creole and popular song arrangements, and light classic and operatic overtures. The style of these groups was less raucous and sweeter than the brass bands. During those years the function and repertory of the street brass band and the indoor string band were kept separate.

Sometime around 1890, the brass band began to be used for dancing. It is not known at what kind of occasion this first came about, whether during Carnival time, at a Sunday band concert in one of the parks up-town, or in some large hall rented for the purpose of dancing. At any rate, social dancing became the rage, and dance halls sprang up downtown and uptown.

This newfound activity placed greater demands on the musicians. A richer, more organized, and more developed music than that of the marching bands was needed, since social dancing demanded not only variety but pieces more generally appropriate to the activity and the mood of the occasion.

Because of the size and noisiness of these dancing affairs, there was a need for a strong and rhythmic music. This led not only to an expansion of the bands, but also to changes in the structure of the music itself. Its repertory was enriched by the inclusion and transformation of French and Italian music of several kinds, as well as by Creole and popular songs. As an example, New Orleans had a strong tradition of French and Italian opera dating from as early as the first quarter of the nineteenth century. Operatic arias were whistled and sung on the street just as popular songs are performed today. Some of the feeling, if not the actual melodies, was incorporated into this early jazz.

The second French element in the classic jazz of New Orleans is found in the dances that were popular in the last part of the nineteenth century. Polkas, mazurkas, schottisches, waltzes, and other kinds of dances sometimes were contained in the five-section dance group known as the quadrille. Many of these already had been converted into ragtime; now jazz took them over and transformed them completely.

Meanwhile, the string bands diminished in popularity, although they still played in saloons and at small social functions. Still later, from 1897 to 1917, they were employed in the better class of bordellos where the loud brass band was taboo.

New Orleans jazz has been said to be a product of Storyville, that district in New Orleans that was set aside for prostitution. Storyville, which came into being through the efforts of Alderman Story for the purpose of containing prostitution within one section of the city, lasted from 1897 until 1917 when it was closed by order of the War Department in Washington, D.C. This was the first and last attempt for many years to license prostitution in an American city—a Catholic city—following the practice of many Catholic cities in Europe, most notably Paris.

While Storyville catered to this new jazz and provided employment for perhaps two hundred musicians, most of these players performed in the cabarets and gambling places of the district and not in the bordellos as had been generally thought. Only singers, solo pianists (such as Jelly Roll Morton), and smaller combinations including string trios, were employed in the brothels since the larger brass bands were too loud for these houses.

Both before the establishment of the Storyville district in 1897 and during its heyday, there was a much clearer distinction between bands than afterwards. In the 1880s and 1890s, most of the bands were marching bands that paraded for occasions such as funerals and special celebrations and provided a sort of dance music when the celebrations called for dancing. The dance bands of the kind that had an influence on New Orleans jazz were relatively few in this period.

New Orleans jazz is more directly connected with military band music of the late nineteenth century than with any other source. The standard New Orleans instrumentation and its function have their foundation in the trio section of the band march, in which the melody is characteristically carried by the cornets or trumpets against a countermelody in the low brasses and a florid embellishment in the high woodwinds.

Although the influence of the marching band was directly responsible for the manner of performing New Orleans jazz, the players came to the marching band with a rich background of West African culture. They had heard and made music at dances, picnics, parties, weddings, and funerals. They had sung work songs and love songs and had danced jigs, quadrilles, and stomps. In addition, they had heard the folk tunes of Scotland, Ireland, and England, the art songs of Spain and Italy, and the melodies of French arias, as well as the tunes of minstrel shows. Combine all of this with the spiritual of the plantation, the blues, and ragtime, and it becomes readily apparent that the music played by the Storyville bands and their immediate successors emerged from these diverse sources.

Instrumentation. The New Orleans style is distinctively an instrumental style performed on three or four wind instruments, with a combination of other instruments carrying out a rhythmic function: piano, tuba, drums, and guitar or banjo.

The primary difference between pure New Orleans jazz and some later imitations is that the latter consists of music written out in an arrangement while New Orleans jazz is spontaneous collective improvisation.

The cornet is the most important melodic instrument. By adhering closely to the melodic line, even on those occasions when he has a solo, the cornetist permits the clarinetist and trombonist to conceive their parts so that they seldom coincide with the cornet or with one another on the same note.

The jazz clarinet's tone, especially in the high register, enables it to penetrate the sound mass of the brass and rhythm section. Because the instrument is fluent and highly agile, the clarinetist fills in his own phrases between the lead notes, utilizing rapid runs, protracted, piercing single notes, and short, staccato, repeated ones. This marvelous New Orleans technique is based on the French woodwind tradition, brought into jazz by the Creoles of Color, who received formal training in the classical style.

The New Orleans clarinet players also employed much portamento.

On the other hand, the growl (fluttertongue) effect and other "dirty" tones were seldom used because only the pure tone of the clarinet could pierce through the powerful tones of the other instruments.

The baritone and alto horns in the early jazz band contributed a kind of polyphonic and melodic element as well as polyrhythmic variety. When these instruments dropped out in the formation of the classic[13] jazz band, their composite functions devolved upon the trombone and this led directly to the development of the trombone style known as "tailgate."[14]

In the "tailgate" style, the trombonist set up a countermelody against the melodic line as played by the cornet. His part was the freest and most inventive of the three voices, and consequently perhaps the most difficult. The trombonist had to fill in the bass or harmony when needed, add rhythmic, expressive phrases, and penetrate the ensemble with sharp, loud tones as well as portamento.

During the early period of jazz, the snare and bass drums and tuba composed the rhythm section. The rhythm section of the classic jazz band, however, included guitar or banjo, drums, string bass or tuba, and piano. It was the function of these instruments to maintain a steady, unaccented $\frac{4}{4}$ meter and occasionally to emphasize the harmonic rhythm while varying the accents within a measure.

The tuba or string bass (a nonmilitary instrument) supplied the rhythmic bass line; the drums produced the strong, purely rhythmic background; and the banjo or guitar (also a nonmilitary instrument) gave additional rhythmic-harmonic support. The piano played a similar role, but it was not easily transportable for open-air functions and was only used when jazz was played indoors for dancing. When playing as a part of the rhythm section, the pianist underlined the metrical beat, the left hand playing single notes on the accents so as to double the bass line, and the right hand playing chords, usually on all four beats, doubling the banjo or guitar part.

The texture found in New Orleans jazz is more closely allied to heterophony than polyphony. As described earlier, heterophony results when two voices or parts are combined, one of which is not a truly independent voice but rather a slightly altered version of the other. Polyphony is the result of combining two independent voices or parts. Below, a tune is treated first heterophonically and then polyphonically to contrast the two styles.

---

[13]The term "classic" is applied to New Orleans-style jazz commencing around the turn of the twentieth century.

[14]Advertising by hand-wagons came in during this period. The bands were seated in the huge horse-drawn vehicles and roamed all over town playing their music. The trombonist was relegated to the lowered tailgate, where his plunging slide could not bruise another player. From this custom, the term "tailgate" trombone was derived and is still used to denote this New Orleans style.

EXAMPLE 3.9 Heterophony[15]

EXAMPLE 3.10 Polyphony[16]

The forms that are characteristic of classic New Orleans jazz are the blues, stomps, rags, and marches. None of these forms is structurally fixed. As an example, the blues chorus, although twelve bars in length, may be preceded or followed by interludes or transitions in four-, eight-, or sixteen-bar sections. When the melodic and harmonic materials in these latter sections are similar to the chorus material, it is often difficult to determine exactly where one section begins and another ends. New Orleans jazzmen may have improvised simply on the traditional blues harmonies on occasion, but more often they worked with specific blues pieces. These songs may contain eight-, twelve-, or sixteen-bar verses. The verses were not only often repeated but sometimes returned to after a number of repetitions of the chorus, giving the impression of a modified ternary structure.

Except for the characteristic stomp section, stomp pieces are found in a variety of forms. Excluding introductions, endings, and interludes, stomps are usually constructed in sections of eight or sixteen bars with individual sections occasionally repeated with variations. The general plan is usually AABBCC, with the C section comprising the stomp itself. At times there is a return to the beginning (*da capo*) that arbitrarily goes on to the end of any of the sections.

The rhythmic pattern of the stomp may take any one of three forms.

EXAMPLE 3.11 Rhythmic patterns of the stomp

[15]Leroy Ostransky, *The Anatomy of Jazz* (Seattle: University of Washington Press, 1960), p. 162.

[16]*Ibid.*

Rags, as discussed earlier in this chapter, are sectional forms with each section having its own melody. The New Orleans march may consist of one strain of sixteen bars repeated over and over, or it may exhibit the same form as marches in the European tradition: introduction, repeated first strain, repeated second strain, sometimes a transition, and trio.

The New Orleans ensemble produced a number of varying textures. They range from the heaviest texture, which consists of several melodic lines being played simultaneously, to the lightest, the solo "break" unaccompanied. Intermediate textures include heterophony performed by all instruments; a homophonic texture; a solo instrument accompanied by the other instruments in a polyphonic, heterophonic, or homophonic texture; and a solo instrument accompanied by the rhythm section.

In New Orleans-style jazz, the tonality is firmly maintained within each melodic line. While the principal mode is major, there is frequent interchange of the major and minor third scale degrees. The major and minor seventh scale degrees are also used frequently. The minor seventh occurs most frequently as the secondary dominant of the subdominant (V7 of IV).

The harmonic foundation of New Orleans jazz is the same as that of the marches from which it evolved. The primary triads—tonic, subdominant, and dominant (I, IV, V)—provide the harmonic basis for each composition; the secondary triads—supertonic, mediant, and submediant (II, III, VI)—and the augmented triad are used less frequently. Diminished-seventh chords are fairly common and secondary dominants enjoy wide usage. The most often-used secondary dominant is the V7 of IV; a favorite harmonic progression of this style is the series of consecutive secondary dominants: V7 of II, V7 of V, V, V^7, I (or in jazz terminology, in the key of C: A7, D7, G7, C).

EXAMPLE 3.12   Progression of secondary dominants

V7 of II   V7 of V V^7 I
   A7   D7   G7   C

The standard blues progression is employed widely: three bars of I, one of V7 of IV, two of IV7♭, two of I, two of V7, and two of I (or in jazz terminology, in the key of C: three bars of C, one of C7, two of F7, two of C, two of G7, and two of C; the V7 [G7] is added to the last measure when the chorus continues into another chorus).

New Orleans jazz utilizes collective improvisation as opposed to solo improvisation, which will be discussed later in this chapter. The variations stay fairly close to the original melody and employ added arpeggios and scalelike figures, passing and auxiliary notes and anticipations, and variations of tone quality. Many special instrumental effects are used, including the growl, the shake, lipping tones higher or lower, and fluttertonguing.[17]

EXAMPLE 3.13   Collective improvisation, *Easy Living* [8]

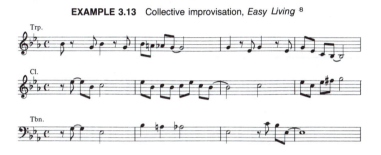

The most frequent rhythms of New Orleans-style jazz are the dotted eighth note followed by the sixteenth ♩♪ , and syncopated patterns that place the accent on the second half of either beat of the measure. There is also a frequent, almost infinitesimal delay or anticipation of melodic voices above the regular pulse of the more percussive instruments.

Jazz has often been accused of being destructive of morals. The Black church, with its moralistic attitude, joined White American society in a character assassination of one of America's few original folk forms because of its historical associations. As we have seen, jazz originally thrived in Storyville, the red light district of New Orleans. Later, after Storyville was closed down in 1917, it became associated in Chicago with an underworld that included the speakeasy and the gangster. Perhaps the most important reason for White American society's negative attitude toward jazz was the notion that jazz was "nigger" music created by Blacks and performed, at its best, by Blacks.

It seems that rock music has replaced jazz as the music for dancing. This may be due in part to the fact that jazz is no longer functional, that it is difficult music to dance to. Rather, jazz has become a highly intellectualized, esoteric music. Because of its heavy, driving beat, rock has filled the void.

The Jazz Composer.   The role of the composer in jazz has often been misunderstood. Because of its improvisatory nature, most solo performers in jazz can be considered composers since they are in effect composing

[17]See chapter one for a discussion of these special instrumental effects. Also in chapter one is a discussion of how notation is used as merely a guide in written jazz.

[18]*Easy Living.* by Leo Robin and Ralph Rainger. Copyright © 1937 by Famous Music Corporation. Copyright © renewed 1964 by Famous Music Corporation. Used by permission.

spontaneously. They are composers only in this very general sense, however, as their composing is not only intimately related to, but is largely determined by, their role as performers. Even a composed jazz piece very often is based on a tune with a standard chord progression and form like that of the twelve-bar blues, for example. This kind of composition is in a different category from music in the European tradition, and has actually played a very minor role in the development of jazz.

The basic stylistic and conceptual advances in jazz have been determined by its great instrumentalist-improvisers, not by its great composers. The composers are not the men the performer emulates on his instrument, for it is impossible for a performer on one instrument, such as the trumpet or saxophone, to imitate the collage of sound emanating from an orchestra performing a composition in the musical style of Count Basie, for example. In addition, many composers are either not virtuoso musicians or they perform in such an unorthodox manner as to make it extremely difficult for a performer to emulate their style. The best that can be hoped for is mere imitation. An outstanding example of such a composer is Thelonious Monk. Monk has very limited piano technique when compared to the great jazz virtuosos such as Art Tatum. While his limited technique is quite adequate to convey his musical ideas as a soloist, his style is so unorthodox that it would be difficult for a performer to emulate him. Among others in this category are Ornette Coleman, Sun Ra, and Lester Bowie.

While jazz has produced few composers in the strictest sense of that term, several of those composers have been significant in the history of jazz. These composers have written works that are not merely tunes based on standard chord progressions and forms; rather, they are original multi-thematic structures that embody a definite, detailed compositional conception. And while the results of their efforts may have had little influence on jazz styles, the compositions of these composers have remained of great interest to jazz musicians.

Jelly Roll Morton.　Although New Orleans-style jazz is a non-notated music based on collective improvisation, it was from this performance style that jazz's first composer emerged—Jelly Roll Morton (1885–1941).

Ferdinand "Jelly Roll" Morton, a pianist active in ragtime as well as jazz was perhaps the first genuine jazz composer. Born in New Orleans, Morton composed his first blues, *New Orleans Blues*, at the age of seventeen. It became popular among the city's various bands.

At nineteen, Morton became restless and decided to use jazz as a means of escape from the Jim Crow and Creole prejudice of New Orleans. After 1904 he was constantly on the move, using his native city only as a base of operations. It was Morton's desire to write a tune in each of the cities he visited. Consequently, in 1905, while in Mobile, Morton wrote

Ferdinand "Jelly Roll" Morton, perhaps the first genuine jazz composer. (Photo courtesy New Orleans Jazz Museum.)

Alabama Bound. It was also in Mobile that Morton wrote his famous *King Porter Stomp*,[19] named after a close friend of Morton's, Porter King.

Morton is acknowledged not only as the first jazz composer, but as the first musician to write down a jazz arrangement in musical notation. His arrangement of his tune *Jelly Roll Blues* was made in St. Louis and published in Chicago in 1915, probably the first such publication of its kind.

Beginning in July, 1923, Morton recorded for the Gennett Company, chiefly as a piano soloist. It was during this period that he recorded some of his best compositions, including *King Porter Stomp, New Orleans Joys (New Orleans Blues), Grandpa's Spells, Kansas City Stomp, Wolverine Blues,* and *The Pearls.* The following year he recorded *Shreveport Stomp* and *Original Jelly Roll Blues.*[20] The five solo sides that resulted from two recording sessions are among Morton's most characteristic original melodies. Four of the

---

[19]*King Porter Stomp* is of great importance in the development of jazz. Fletcher Henderson used it in the repertory of his band, and Benny Goodman, for whom Henderson arranged music, used this tune as a theme for a number of years.

[20]Morton also participated in the first racially mixed recording date; with the New Orleans Rhythm Kings, a White group, he recorded *Mr. Jelly Lord, Milenberg Joys,* and *London Blues.*

compositions were recorded later in orchestral versions. A comparison of the piano and orchestral versions reveals how the solo rendition anticipates the group performance. The tempos are identical, the thematic arrangement is similar, and passages in the solo performance are found to be equally orchestral in the later version.

In September of 1926, Jelly Roll Morton and his Red Hot Peppers began recording a series of compositions for the Victor Company that established him without a doubt as one of the most creative figures in the history of jazz. Many critics regarded these recording sessions, which lasted until 1928, as the best prepared and most carefully rehearsed jazz records ever.

The final highlight in Morton's life was his marathon recording session for the folklore archives of the Library of Congress in which he recorded his version of the history of jazz.

Morton's best arrangements, when carefully examined, are found to be not mere orchestrations, but carefully organized structures in which all the details of instrumentation, timbral relationship, and rhythmic and harmonic counterpoint are realized as integral compositional elements. He gave to jazz a more linear concept, as opposed to the vertical, harmonic emphasis of ragtime and other musical forms. This change was important, for without it there could be no jazz. The employment of this concept made possible the forward momentum of rhythm, an essential element of swing. Had his music been structured vertically, it would not have had the rhythmic impetus so necessary for a "swinging" feeling. Morton's use of his right hand eliminated the strict repetitions and imitations of ragtime and substituted instead variational procedures.

In Morton's compositions, he contrasted the final rocking stomp with a delicate and quiet preceding section derived from the old ragtime trio section. By retaining this aspect of ragtime, Morton gave variety to his compositions.

While the schematic framework and syncopated rhythms of ragtime were important elements of Morton's compositional style, the blues played an equally important role. Involved were two sets of opposites. Ragtime was based on strict repetition of phrases and was basically an unimprovised music, whereas the blues was essentially an improvised music that contained no exact repetition.

Morton used the riff as a secondary line or idea and wove it into the fabric of a solo improvisation. The riff was used not as motivic variation, but because it provided an alternative melodic variant for a given harmonic context. This device was used as another means of providing contrast and variety. Another device used almost obsessively by Morton as a means of providing contrast and variety was the "break."[21] Morton is probably one

---

[21]The break is a short passage, usually unaccompanied, interpolated by a performer or performers between ensemble sections.

of the few musicians to make it a principle. Not only did his performances contain many breaks, but they are often written directly into his compositions. The actual notation of the break as a part of the fabric of a composition was the kind of step only a composer would take.

Morton used melodic bass writing in his compositions. He had played trombone occasionally as a youth, and consequently trombonelike figures permeate his music.

EXAMPLE 3.14 Trombone-like bass line, from *Frog-i-more Rag*[22]

Jelly Roll Morton continued to experiment in musical form in an effort to provide the greatest possible variety in musical content. He combined two principal ideas: the two- or three-part form with its modulations and interludes inherited from ragtime, and the concept of perpetual variation. Within a single composition are found individual structural elements that produce further levels of variety and contrast. They include solos, countermelodies, polyphony, harmony, and stop-time rhythm.

At the height of his career, Morton had little influence on his contemporaries or successors. The thirty-two-bar popular song became an important form in jazz during the twenties. While other major jazz artists succumbed to the influence of this form and placed it in their repertories, Morton refused to do so. Consequently, his music represents the end of a particular phase of jazz.

The Roots of Swing

It has become popular to capsulize the development of jazz into three major geographic locations and correlated chronological periods. New Orleans is usually considered to have been the center of jazz activity during the first two decades of this century; Chicago was in the limelight during the twenties; and New York is associated with the twenties, thirties and subsequent periods. While there is some factual basis for this neat categorization, it is dangerously oversimplified. Many strands of jazz history from different areas of the country are greatly intertwined, resulting in an exceedingly complex pattern of social and musical cross-references within a surprisingly broad geographic area.

The New Orleans style of jazz has been discussed in the previous section of this chapter. The so-called "Chicago style" was predominantly a White jazz style, and is therefore largely beyond the scope of this study. There were Black influences in Chicago, however, which will be discussed because of their effect on the swing style of the thirties. The New York period, including the advent of the big bands and the swing phase of jazz, will also be discussed. There was a parallel development of big bands in the Southwest during this period, with Kansas City as the focal point. This phase of jazz history has been ignored by many jazz historians but will be dealt with here.

Since swing, the jazz style of the mid-thirties, was dominated by White bands (although there were also excellent Black swing orchestras), this section will be concerned primarily with the antecedents of swing, whose major contributors were Black.

Chicago.   With the closing of Storyville in New Orleans, many jazz musicians left the city in search of opportunities for work. Some worked on the excursion boats operating up and down the Mississippi River, while others settled in Chicago. It was in Chicago, in 1923, that New Orleans-style jazz reached its peak as an art form, through the performances of King Oliver and his Creole Jazz Band. As mentioned earlier, this jazz style consisted of collective improvisation in a non-notated form.

While New Orleans jazz was rising to great heights and influencing musicians throughout various sections of the country, another event was about to take place that was to have a great impact on future jazz. Jelly Roll Morton stopped in St. Louis briefly in 1912 and here apparently made the first arrangement of one of his piano compositions. As mentioned earlier, this arrangement of his *Jelly Roll Blues* was published in Chicago in 1915,

King Oliver's Creole Jazz Band (Oliver fourth from left), with Louis Armstrong (second from right). (Photo courtesy New Orleans Jazz Museum.)

which probably makes it the first jazz orchestration ever published. So it was during this period that jazz became a notated music for the first time.

When Storyville was closed in 1917, the musicians headed north in search of work, finding the way prepared by the earlier spread of ragtime. During the next five years or so, Chicago took the place of New Orleans as the nation's jazz center. Joseph "King" Oliver's Creole Jazz Band was the toast of that northern metropolis. Oliver's group was the epitome of the New Orleans style at its peak. In 1923, the year of the culmination of the New Orleans style, the personnel of the band included Louis Armstrong on cornet.

Louis Armstrong.   Louis Armstrong (1900–71), perhaps the most influential figure in all of jazz,[23] came to Chicago in 1922 to join King Oliver's Creole Jazz Band. It was in this context that the seed was germinated that was to change the total jazz concept. Performing in the New Orleans style, Armstrong and Oliver executed duet breaks (on cornets). Beyond any doubt, the popularity of their breaks and the excitement they generated were strong contributing factors in eventually expanding the solo break into the full-fledged solo.[24] Thus, jazz began to move from collective improvisation to solo improvisation.

It was when Armstrong joined Fletcher Henderson's orchestra in New York in 1924 that he emerged as a soloist. The Henderson orchestra, which emphasized soloists and arrangements, gave Armstrong the freedom to develop a mature style and not be encumbered by the restrictions and limitations encountered in Oliver's band. In this context, Armstrong was able to experiment and refine the personal ingredients that were to become his mature style.

In November 1925, Armstrong left Henderson's orchestra and returned to Chicago. There he played with the orchestras of Erskine Tate and Carroll Dickerson. Tate's ten-piece orchestra was the best large group in Chicago and in many respects was Henderson's counterpart. Since his repertory also included light classics such as the *Blue Danube Waltz,* all of Tate's musicians were required to read music. Dickerson's band, also ten pieces, embraced the new "arranged" style that tended to be commercial and polished.

While the engagements with the Tate and Dickerson orchestras were important in helping to develop the mature Armstrong solo style, the most

[23]Although Armstrong was very influential during the twenties, he became more commercial commencing with the thirties. Consequently, his stature as a musician diminished to some degree among his peers.

[24]Solo improvisation, while not new to New Orleans-style jazz, had been used primarily as a contrast or interlude between polyphonic sections. Even in the so-called polyphonic sections, however, one instrument tended to dominate the texture.

Louis Armstrong, perhaps the most influential figure in all of jazz. (Photo courtesy New Orleans Jazz Museum.)

important events of these years were his famous Hot Five and Hot Seven recordings, made between 1925 and 1929. This long-term recording project has been recognized as one of the most remarkable in the history of jazz.

The two groups never performed as a unit outside the recording studios. This was the beginning of a practice that has since become common.

On the first recording date in November 1925, the group played in a slightly modified New Orleans style. While the group no longer practiced only collective improvisation, their style had not yet fully crystalized into one with a solo concept of improvisation.

In the initial group that Armstrong organized to record for Okeh records, there were neither drums nor string bass. Lil Hardin on piano and Johnny St. Cyr on banjo laid down such a solid beat that neither of the aforementioned instruments was missed. The new emphasis on solos was inevitable because Armstrong and clarinetist Johnny Dodds were two of the greatest solo improvisors to perform in the same group. In Kid Ory, the group had the best trombonist of his time. The Hot Five contained excellent musicians who were able to grasp the concept of solo improvisation.

As Armstrong moved further away from the New Orleans style, his maturity as a soloist began to emerge. As a result, the performance style of the group began to change. The ensembles were often written out in a thinner harmonic style. When there were fully improvised sections, they were no longer in the typical New Orleans style, since the clarinet and trombone were given secondary melodic lines that played under Armstrong's lead. In addition, solos were much more numerous. Each of these changes were innovative and were to have an impact on the future development of jazz.

West End Blues, recorded in June 1928, is the outstanding number on this record date and perhaps on any record date in which Louis Armstrong has taken part. His introductory free-tempo cadenza was for a time one of the most widely imitated of all jazz solos and had implications for all jazz. This performance was outstanding in that it combined two concepts—the use of the opening break, which had seldom been used up to this time, and the extended stop-time chorus[25]—into a cadenza that is apparently free in tempo. Yet in spite of this apparent freedom of tempo, the introduction is definitely in double-time (that is, twice the speed of the main tempo of the piece).

EXAMPLE 3.15   Introduction to *West End Blues*[26]

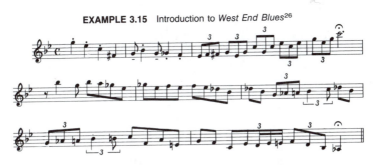

The years of the Hot Five and Hot Seven represented a peak of activity in which Armstrong became one of jazz's greatest innovators. More than any other individual, he changed the concept of jazz from that of a collectively improvised music to one centered on solo improvisation, and in so doing created one of the salient characteristics of swing.

New York.   Many of the musicians who became associated with jazz history in New York did not play jazz at all. Most musicians in this area were still playing one of the vast number of popular styles developing at that time. The music ranged from pure ragtime to light classics. During the immediate pre-World War I period, jazz was but one of the many competing music forms for popular consumption.

---

[25]Stop-time is a type of discontinuous rhythm that was originally used to accompany tap dancers, and was extended to accompany singers and instrumentalists. In jazz, it generally involves playing on only the first beat in every two measures.

[26]*West End Blues*, words and music by Clarence Williams and Joe Oliver. © Copyright 1928, 1947 by MCA Music, A Division of MCA Inc., New York, N.Y. Copyright renewed. Used by permission. All rights reserved.

James Reese Europe (conducting) dominated the earliest stages of jazz as it was developing in New York. (Photo courtesy New York Public Library, Schomburg Collection of Negro Literature.)

The man who dominated the decade prior to the advent of Fletcher Henderson and Duke Ellington in the twenties was James Reese Europe (1881–1919). Europe, who was born in Alabama, completed his education and musical training in Washington, D.C. He came to New York in 1904, attracted by the possibilities for obtaining employment with one of the Black musical companies. Europe was able to gain the position of musical director for the Cole-Johnson production of *The Shoo-Fly Regiment* in 1906 and remained with the company for three years; he then became musical director of the musical *Mr. Lode of Kole* for one more season.

In 1910, Europe organized the Clef Club with the purpose of protecting the interests of Black musicians and was appointed conductor of the club's orchestra. By 1914 the Clef Club orchestra had become so popular that a concert was given in Carnegie Hall, the first orchestra playing "popular" music to do so. The huge orchestra consisted of forty-seven mandolins, twenty-seven harp-guitars, eleven banjos, eight violins, one saxophone, one tuba, thirteen cellos, two clarinets, two baritone horns, eight trombones, seven cornets, one pair of kettle drums, two string basses, and ten pianos.

Europe also had a small orchestra—usually having six or seven members (one or two violins, cornet, clarinet, piano, mandolin, and drums)—for society dances where his syncopated music became the rage among the social set. He became associated with the popular ballroom-dance team of Irene and Vernon Castle, and together they enjoyed overwhelming success. The Castles and Europe collaborated in devising the fox trot and many other popular steps that came to be identified with the Jazz Age (the twenties). Although Europe's group was not playing jazz, but a syncopated kind of music developed out of ragtime, he became the most important transitional figure in the prehistory of jazz on the East Coast.

The orchestra of Fletcher Henderson (1898–1952) was the most influential jazz group in New York for many years. His group was really the first of the "big bands" of jazz.

In 1923, Henderson and his group auditioned for and got the job at the exclusive Club Alabam on Forty-fourth Street. The group that he brought into the club was to have a profound effect on the makeup of the jazz orchestra. Henderson's group only contained two more men than the eight associated with the New Orleans-style jazz groups, but he changed the entire concept of the jazz orchestra. The two additional men were saxophonists, and he exchanged the clarinet for another saxophone. Thus, for the first time there was a true reed section, one of the fundamentals of big-band jazz. Later, the trumpet section was increased to three, and the trombones to two, while the rhythm section was increased to four players.

The band's alto saxophone player was Don Redman (1900–64) a child prodigy who had been educated at Storer College in West Virginia, the Boston Conservatory of Music, and the Detroit Conservatory of Music. Redman, who was able to play most wind instruments, joined Billy Paige's Broadway Syncopators as player and arranger before becoming a member of the Henderson orchestra.

The Fletcher Henderson Orchestra (at Roseland, 1928) was the most influential jazz group in New York for many years. (Photo courtesy Duncan P. Schiedt Collection.)

Don Redman, alto saxophonist and arranger of jazz specialties for the Fletcher Henderson group. (Photo courtesy Duncan P. Schiedt Collection.)

Up to the time that Redman became a member of Henderson's group, most of the music played was stock arrangements.[27] Redman began to arrange jazz specialties for the band. Redman incorporated some unique ideas into his arrangements. He used the saxophones as a section just as most of the arrangers of this period were doing, but with one important difference: Instead of simply harmonizing the melody for the section, Redman would write passages in an often complex improvisatory style and harmonize them for the entire section to play as a group. He often divided the melodic line between the brass instruments and the saxophones, with one section beginning a phrase and the other ending it.

Early in his arranging career, Redman instituted the practice of having the saxophones give a melodic statement in harmony against a background of sudden interjections by the brass. And as a culmination of what was to be the major ingredient of the swing style, he was able to achieve a fusion of individual solos with arranged section work that sounded improvised and spontaneous.

During the twenties, Paul Whiteman was playing a kind of music that he called "symphonic jazz." In 1925, his publicist announced that no longer was improvisation an important component of jazz. He also stated that the Paul Whiteman orchestra played from scores as do the members of any musical organization, and that these scores displayed outstanding part writing and a variety of tonal timbre.

Both Fletcher Henderson and Don Redman demonstrated without a

---

[27]A stock arrangement is music arranged by a professional arranger and published for use by any band.

doubt that Paul Whiteman's publicist was completely wrong. They were able to combine outstanding arrangements with improvised jazz in such a manner that the notated and improvised sections flowed together smoothly without a break in musical character. Redman was able to create in his written arrangements the same feeling of spontaneity that was exhibited by Henderson's soloists. In Redman's arrangements, the improvised solo became an integral part of the whole score, and improvisation remained the cornerstone of his concept of jazz.

William McKinney, a drummer who had organized a band in 1921, decided in 1927 to become a full-time business manager for the group and sent for Don Redman to come to Detroit as the orchestra's musical director. The group, known as McKinney's Cotton Pickers, became one of the outstanding jazz groups of this period under Redman's direction.

Because of the void left by Redman's departure, Henderson began to write for his band. Gradually, Henderson grew more familiar with arranging techniques; his style reached maturity by 1932. Like Redman, Henderson was able to write arrangements in which the brass and reed sections produced an illusion of spontaneity equal in many ways to that of the improvised solos.

In 1934, the Benny Goodman orchestra was featured on a program of the National Broadcasting Company called "Let's Dance." The Goodman band was an instant success. The formula that Goodman employed included an emphasis on orchestration while leaving room for instrumental solos.

McKinney's Cotton Pickers Orchestra, directed by Don Redman, was centered in Detroit. (Photo courtesy Duncan P. Schiedt Collection.)

In 1935, Henderson was temporarily without a band for the first time in a dozen years. It was at this juncture that he became chief arranger for Benny Goodman. Goodman had realized that for big bands to achieve success in the swing era, they must play distinctive arrangements. He proceeded to acquire arrangements from Black arrangers such as Horace Henderson (Fletcher's brother), Edgar Sampson, Benny Carter, and Jimmy Mundy, as well as Fletcher Henderson. The enthusiasm of Goodman and his players for Henderson's arrangements in particular had much to do with the band's success.

During the thirties, when bands such as Goodman's, Artie Shaw's, Tommy Dorsey's, and several other White groups were reaping huge financial rewards (in 1937 the Goodman band earned $350,000, with each player receiving about $10,000), there were several Black bands that were great artistic successes but were able to earn very little money because of the attitude of White society. With the exception of the Duke Ellington and Count Basie bands, Black bands found it extremely difficult to survive. Bands led by Earl Hines, Don Redman, Chick Webb, Andy Kirk, and Jimmie Lunceford contributed a driving swing music to the jazz idiom but unfortunately realized only modest financial rewards.

Despite the recognition Goodman has received (both artistic and financial) for his matchless musicianship, his influence on jazz has been relatively small. He was, however, one of the first White bandleaders to hire Black musicians (Lionel Hampton, Charlie Christian, and Teddy Wilson). He refused to become interested in the various jazz styles that began to manifest themselves in the forties and fifties and went into semiretirement.

Duke Ellington.   Edward Kennedy "Duke" Ellington (1899–1974), pianist, arranger, and composer, exerted a tremendous influence on jazz. Ellington, born in Washington D.C., began playing professionally in his hometown while still a teen-age ragtime pianist. He wrote his first composition, *Soda Fountain Rag,* at the age of fourteen. He demonstrated talent in both music and art, but decided in favor of music. By 1919, Ellington was supplying small bands for dances and parties. Two members of his small band, saxophonist Otto "Toby" Hardwick and drummer Sonny Greer, both became fixtures with Ellington's New York-based orchestra for many years. Most Washington orchestras played in a style that was very commercial and were generally led by well-known ragtime pianists. Most of the musicians in these groups consisted primarily of reading or "legitimate" musicians.

In 1922, Duke, Hardwick, and Greer came to New York to join the Wilbur Sweatman Orchestra, which played production-type theater dates and acts. After working sporadically in New York, Ellington returned to Washington. During his short stay in New York, Duke wrote the music for the ill-fated musical show, *Chocolate Kiddies,* of 1924. While the show never

Edward Kennedy "Duke" Ellington and his orchestra exerted tremendous influence on jazz. (Photo courtesy Duncan P. Schiedt Collection.)

reached Broadway, it enjoyed an extremely successful two-year run in Berlin.

The second trip to New York in 1923 met with better results. Under the leadership of banjoist Elmer Snowden, the group was able to find employment and was finally engaged to play at the Hollywood Club. It was there that Ellington took over the leadership of the group and began to mold it into a first-rate (now ten-member) orchestra.

Ellington had little formal training other than piano lessons. He had long discussions about compositional techniques with composer Will Marion Cook and composer-arranger Will Vodery. His piano style came under the influence of the leading ragtime pianists of that time—Willie "The Lion" Smith, James P. Johnson, Luckeyeth "Lucky" Roberts and Thomas "Fats" Waller. The influence of this Harlem piano style characterized all of Ellington's early orchestral work. There exist examples of fairly literal transcriptions of his piano playing, such as *Washington Wobble*. By contrast, Jelly Roll Morton took a given piece for piano and made an orchestration to fit the requirements of the instruments for which he was writing. Ellington's pianistic approach to orchestration, however, had far-reaching consequences in relation to the voicing of the instruments in his orchestra. Just as the Eastern school of jazz pianists—the "stride" school—had a largely orchestral conception of piano sound, Ellington had his band directly imitate his piano.

In the early 1920s there were several Black orchestras that played "symphonic jazz" in an attempt to emulate the big White bands like that of Paul Whiteman. By contrast, in the middle and late twenties the big White orchestras attempted to acquire the style of the Eastern Black bands that reflected the spread of the New Orleans jazz style. Largely through the initial efforts of trumpeter James "Bubber" Miley (1903–32), the Duke Ellington orchestra was able to transcend the Eastern style of symphonic jazz in the late twenties and early thirties. Miley introduced a rougher sound into the band through the use of a growling style. Miley taught this style of playing to Joseph "Tricky Sam" Nanton (1904–48), and together they developed the band's famous "jungle" effects through their use of the growl and plunger.

In late 1927, a crucial event in Ellington's career took place. King Oliver turned down an offer to play at a night club called the Cotton Club, and Ellington's orchestra got the job in his place. Not only did this job mean steady employment for his band, but most importantly, it offered Ellington an opportunity to write music for floor shows and production numbers. There was a steady need for new background music for the constantly changing acts at the Cotton Club. This requirement enabled Ellington to experiment and investigate composition (rather than arranging) as a medium of expression. Ellington developed into one of America's foremost composers while working for five years at the Cotton Club.

Except for hints of orchestration and harmony that he acquired from Will Vodery (1885–1951), chief arranger for the Ziegfeld Follies, Ellington developed his ideas with almost no borrowing from outside his specific field. (It has been alleged by some writers that Ellington was influenced by the music of Ravel and Delius. The truth of the matter is that Ellington never heard of or was interested in hearing these composers until after his style had matured years later.)

Ellington applied to his orchestrations the voice-leading that he used on piano. He did not think contrapuntally, but utilized parallel blocks of sound in such a way that the lack of occasional contrapuntal relief is not noticeable. Another aspect of Ellington's voice-leading is the manner in which he scored the baritone saxophone. During this period in jazz, it had become popular to use parallel ninth chords in introductions and bridges[28] of various tunes. Instead of giving the baritone saxophone the root of the chord, as was the common practice, Ellington had the saxophonist play the

---

[28]Bridge is the name given to the third eight-bar section in a thirty-two-bar song form; also called the *channel.*

seventh tone just below the root. He avoided duplication of pitches by keeping the baritone saxophone away from the bass line and by giving him important notes within the chord that determine the quality of that chord.

While most bands of the period ended each number with full ensemble (sometimes collectively improvised), Ellington began to end each tune with a short reprise of the theme, which did not contain collective improvisation, a pattern he used extensively for years to come.

Another characteristic of Ellington's music is his use of phrase-lengths that are not based on either the thirty-two-bar song form or the various blues forms. In *Birmingham Breakdown*, the main theme is a twenty-bar phrase that consists of a succession of similar two- and four-bar segments. This composition paved the way for the five-bar phrases of *Creole Rhapsody* and the ten- and fourteen-bar phrases of *Reminiscin' in Tempo*. These compositions in turn led to the larger extended works of Ellington.

Many of Ellington's arrangements were a collective process in which many of his sidemen would contribute musical ideas, often altering a composition in some way. In 1939, Billy Strayhorn (1915–67), a pianist and composer, joined the Ellington orchestra as an arranger and developed a style over the years that combined so well with Ellington's that it became difficult to ascertain who was responsible for a specific arrangement or composition.

The kinds of compositions written by Ellington can be placed into several categories. Among them are ballads that became very popular with the general public, dance numbers, "mood" compositions, production numbers, and compositions written for specific occasions. In the thirties, he became known for a long series of popular song successes. Among them were *Mood Indigo, Solitude, Sophisticated Lady, In a Sentimental Mood, I Let a Song Go Out of My Heart,* and *I Got It Bad and That Ain't Good.* It is interesting to note that Ellington also wrote the lyrics to most of his songs, and by 1970 he had written more than 2,000 compositions.

Ellington made his first film, *Check and Double Check*, in 1930 and in 1933 came the first of several European tours. In 1943, he began his annual Carnegie Hall concerts and presented in the inaugural program his first composition in extended form, *Black, Brown and Beige*, subtitled *A Tone Parallel to the History of the Negro in America.* It is a lengthy piece in three movements, employing materials invented in the spirit of work songs, blues, and spirituals.

This was the beginning of a new period in his career. Ellington was one of the first jazz composers to compose in a concert context. Between 1943 and 1950, he included at least one composition in extended form in each of his annual concerts at Carnegie Hall. Among the best known are *New World a-Coming, Deep South Suite, Such Sweet Thunder, A Drum Is a Woman,* and *Far East Suite.*

Suite Thursday (1960) is the first long work in which Ellington directly

"Duke" Ellington receiving an honorary doctorate at Washington University in St. Louis, Missouri, just one of his many achievements and
honors. (Photo courtesy Herb Weitman, Washington University Photographic Service.)

undertook to integrate the various sections of a suite by having his opening section state the various melodies and motives that the later sections develop.

In 1963, Ellington wrote the music for a show, *My People,* which was performed at Chicago in celebration of the "Century of Negro Progress Exposition" (1863–1963). He had previously written one musical comedy, *Beggar's Holiday* (1946). Ellington started an opera, *Boola,* which was not completed.

Although Ellington was not the first to carry jazz into the church, his sacred jazz concerts, beginning in 1965, contributed greatly to this growing movement and added a new dimension to his musical career. His first concert was given at New York's Fifth Avenue Presbyterian Church on December 26, 1965. Some of the works were composed especially for this occasion, while others had been composed earlier. The opening piece, *In the Beginning God,* employs full orchestra, choir, and solo voice. Then follow the gospel and spiritual songs *Tell Me It's the Truth* and *Come Sunday; The Lord's Prayer;* a saxophone version of *Come Sunday;* two more spirituals, *Will You Be There* and *Ain't But the One;* a piano solo, *New World a-Coming;* and the finale, *David Danced Before the Lord with All His Might,* for orchestra and tap dancer.

On his seventieth birthday, April 29, 1969, Ellington was presented the nation's highest civilian honor, the Presidential Medal of Freedom, by President Nixon. Although recommended for the Pulitzer Prize for his long-term achievements by an advisory committee, the trustees of Columbia University, who control the award, refused to accept the recommendation. Despite occasional examples of such shortsightedness, it is evident that Ellington is one of the outstanding musicians in the history of American music, regardless of idiom.

Kansas City and the Southwest.   The orchestras of the Southwest provided much of the musical entertainment for this region of the country. In doing so, they became self-sufficient, which contributed greatly to the development of regional stylistic characteristics.

Interest in jazz did not become a reality in this area until the twenties (Chicago and New York had become involved much earlier). There have been efforts on the part of some jazz historians to link this delayed interest in jazz with the closing of Storyville in 1917. It is true that many of the Storyville musicians were forced to look for work elsewhere and that the Southwest was nearby. There is no evidence, however, that the better musicians of New Orleans infiltrated this area.

The delayed emergence of jazz in the Southwest, and particularly Kansas and Missouri, occurred because this area possessed an indigenous popular music of its own: ragtime. During the period when bands in Chicago and New York were making the transition from ragtime to jazz, the bands and orchestras in the Southwest continued playing ragtime, though in a commercialized form.

Bennie Moten.   Many bands contributed to the development of stylistic characteristics peculiar to the Southwest, but the band that undoubtedly exerted the most influence was the band of Bennie Moten (1894–1935). Moten's band, based in Kansas City, had a repertory around 1920 that consisted of ragtime pieces and "sweet" popular songs. By 1923, his group had expanded to six players and was the most popular band in Kansas City.

It was the Okeh Record Company that started the blues craze with the recording of *Crazy Blues* by Mamie Smith in 1920. In an effort to satisfy the insatiable appetite of the record-buying public for more blues material and also to compete with the Columbia and Paramount record companies, Moten's band was engaged to record some twenty sides in 1923 and 1924, half of them blues.

Moten's band was blues-oriented simply because the blues had always had strong roots in the Southwest. Many of the best-known early itinerant blues singers were born and reared in Oklahoma, Arkansas, and Texas. These country blues were not in competition with ragtime as played by the bands and orchestras of this area because the blues idiom was primarily the product of the individual performer, while ragtime was a result of group activity. Because the blues was performed by individual singers and musicians on crude instruments, it had existed at a separate social, cultural, and musical level from that of orchestras, which performed for dancing. After the blues became popular with the general public, the larger bands of the

The Moten Band (c. 1931) contributed substantially to the stylistic development of jazz in the Southwest. (Photo courtesy Duncan P. Schiedt Collection.)

The Count Basie Orchestra, still fundamentally a swing band, continues to be popular even today. (Photo courtesy Duncan P. Schiedt Collection.)

Southwest performed this music more consistently than orchestras anywhere else. From these roots developed a way of playing jazz that eventually superseded the New Orleans, Chicago, and New York styles.

Moten's band as well as other groups of the Southwest began to develop riffs in their blues numbers.[29] It was not long before this device became a fundamental jazz orchestral technique.

EXAMPLE 3.16   Riff based on twelve-bar blues structure

It was the Moten band of 1932 that epitomized the swinging, blues-oriented style identified with Kansas City. The brass-and-reed riff choruses were utilized in such a manner as to allow each successive riff chorus to build upon its predecessor. The use of this device encouraged a driving, rhythmic style.

Moten's band formed the nucleus of the William "Count" Basie (b. 1904) band after Moten's death in 1935. The Basie group finally reached New York and has consistently been an outstanding orchestra since its debut there in 1937.

From three different areas of the country—Chicago, New York, and the Southwest—came the musical elements that were the basis for the swing style of the thirties. It was unfortunate that the Black practitioners of this style were for the most part not given the artistic and financial recognition due them. Instead, this music was commercialized, polished, and diluted by White musicians to the point of becoming artistically self-defeating. Eventually, these musicians lost the favor of their audiences by continuing to employ overused techniques and devices. Black musicians, becoming disenchanted, began to explore new musical horizons in quest of a more meaningful music.

Bebop

The changes that took place in jazz during the early forties were both revolutionary and evolutionary in nature. They were revolutionary be-

[29]Another band of the Southwest that exemplified the blues tradition was the group led by Jesse Stone, a well-trained musician, composer, and arranger. Stone's Blues Serenaders were probably more blues-oriented than even Moten's group, the premier band of this region.

cause they transformed the music completely, retaining only the concept of solo improvisation. These changes were evolutionary, however, in that they were the result of gradual development.

There was resentment among many Black musicians because of the way White musicians in the thirties had "stolen" their music. There was also dissatisfaction with the static condition of jazz at the end of the swing era as exemplified by White bands. The latter reason was probably the chief stimulus for change. Creative artists usually expand their craft in order to excite the imagination, and so it was with jazz.

Swing had featured the virtuoso musician. Most big band arrangements during this period opened with a plain, direct statement of the theme in orchestrated form, and then turned the melody over to improvised solo choruses. Jazz had broken away from the traditional collective improvisation and had become a music that featured the individual performer.

Black bands of the swing period, such as Jimmy Lunceford, Chick Webb, Erskine Hawkins, Cab Calloway, Andy Kirk, Count Basie, and Duke Ellington, continued to maintain the basic emotional ingredients of jazz even though its outward shape had been changed. These bands offered a hot, direct approach to the music, an emotional excitement closely allied with their rhythmic drive, and they injected tremendous fire into the ensemble work. In essence, Black bands cannot be held responsible for the dissatisfaction that had grown among jazz musicians in the late thirties. The success of the Count Basie orchestra—still fundamentally a swing band—up to the present time indicates that the inertia of the late thirties resulted not from the Black bands but from an outside influence.

In the opinion of Blacks, an inertness had pervaded swing as a result of commercialism and the distorting effect of Tin Pan Alley. When the swing movement was in the hands of Black musicians, it was comparatively safe from commercial dilution because of the color bar and the prevalent attitude of White society toward Black performers. Once Goodman, Shaw, and other White bandleaders began to feature a kind of swing in their style, however, the commercial music market began to infiltrate and dilute that very style. These bands quickly established a bond with the field of popular dance music. The section work became too smooth in texture; the fire and emotionalism that were such an important part of Black swing music almost died out; and the soloists, while possessing great technique, seemed to lack feeling for the music they were playing. Goodman is mentioned here not as an offender against the Black conception of swing (he used the arrangements of Fletcher Henderson and other great Black arrangers), but because he began the chain reaction that caused swing to become a part of the commercial field.[30]

---

[30] A comparison of performance styles between Black and White bands of the swing era can be made by listening to the recordings of *One O'Clock Jump* by the Count Basie and Harry James orchestras.

Because the swing movement had degenerated, it became obvious that jazz must either seek a revolutionary solution or struggle vainly against Tin Pan Alley. Ironically, the financial success of Goodman and other White bands had undermined the already limited field of the Black swing bands of this period. Those Black bands that did not modify their jazz style to compete with the White bands suffered heavily, and many were forced to disband. Only Ellington and Basie were able to survive without a modification in style. When the new style finally arrived, as with every previous form of progress in jazz, it was brought about by Black musicians.

The Bebop Pioneers.   By 1939, the seeds of change were germinating. The musical strands that were to crystalize into a new music came from five principal, divergent sources. They were Lester Young, tenor saxophonist with the Count Basie orchestra; Jimmy Blanton, a young string bassist with the Duke Ellington band; Clyde Hart, pianist, who at one time played with the Lionel Hampton orchestra; Roy Eldridge, trumpeter, who played with many big bands, including the Gene Krupa orchestra; and Charlie Christian, a young guitarist with the Benny Goodman orchestra.

With the exception of Christian, and Lester Young to some degree, these men did not become actively involved in the new music for one reason or another. But their natural solo styles pointed the way to a fresh approach for jazz expression. It was through them that the stylistic limitations of the swing period were broken down.

Lester Young took an active part in the preliminary stages of the movement and then disassociated himself from it. Eldridge simply did not embrace the modern style when it finally emerged. Jimmy Blanton and Clyde Hart might have contributed further, but their careers were shortened by death. Christian, who was also fated to die before the movement reached maturity, was the catalyst who helped a younger generation of jazz musicians to master the technique of this new music. Subsequently, the movement matured in the hands of Charlie "Yardbird" Parker and John Birks "Dizzy" Gillespie.

The first instrumentalist to exhibit tendencies to break away from the accepted swing approach was Lester Young (1909–59). While Young was an innovator, he was not attempting to forge a new school of jazz, but simply to produce a style that was his personal approach to swing. His playing style was characterized by a soft tone, devoid of vibrato, and an exploring style of phrasing as opposed to the direct, attacking phrases of his saxophonist contemporaries. Young played with a relaxed (almost lagging) and subtle style.

Roy Eldridge (b. 1911) was similar to Young in that he was concerned with personal creation and improvement rather than attempting to achieve a wholly new style. Eldridge was representative of the virtuoso musician of the swing period and embraced technique as an important facet of his style. From his horn came the first attempt at adding complexity to the long,

The Bebop Pioneers: Jimmy Blanton (with Ivy Anderson, vocalist) (top left), the Lester Young Band, with Clyde Hart on piano (bottom left), Roy Eldridge (top right), and Charlie Christian (on guitar) with the Benny Goodman Orchestra (bottom right). (Photos courtesy Duncan P. Schiedt Collection.)

simple lines and decisive phrases of the traditional trumpet solo style, which culminated in the mature style of Dizzy Gillespie. In Eldridge's style, phrasing became more flexible as the longer, flowing lines were interspersed with short, staccato runs.

Among pianists, Clyde Hart (1910–45) was the first to influence the new music, and did so in two ways, by contributing both to its general harmonic development and to the modern piano solo style. While a member of the Lionel Hampton small group in the late thirties, he exhibited a tendency to improvise over the chord sequence instead of the melody,

After the death of Charlie Christian, alto saxophonist Charlie Parker (left) and trumpeter Dizzy GIllespie (bottom) emerged as the most important influences on bebop. (Photos courtesy Duncan P. Schiedt Collection.)

Lester Young, the first instrumentalist to attempt breaking away from the swing approach.
(Photo courtesy Duncan P. Schiedt Collection.)

applying subtle variations to the basically simple harmonic patterns[31] in a manner different from anything that had been done before. Instead of employing the left hand to maintain a steady rhythm, this function was allowed to be taken over by the string bass. The harmonies were then played in block chords (using both hands at once) in irregular rhythmic patterns. During a piano solo, Hart's left hand was free to imply the chord changes and punctuate the improvising of the right hand. Thus, the pianist had more latitude to broaden the range of harmonic deviations from the single harmonic patterns of a given composition.

The string bass had been used traditionally as a supplementary element in the rhythm section and occasionally to perform short solos. It was not until Jimmy Blanton (1921–42), bassist with the Duke Ellington orchestra, projected his presence in American jazz that the function of this instrument changed. Through his playing it was demonstrated that an instrument previously employed purely for rhythmic purposes also could be used as a solo voice. His playing also indicated that the rhythm could be remolded to conform to the phrasing of the front-line soloists. This new flexibility in permitting the rhythm section to work more closely with the melody instruments was an important step. Although Blanton died at the age of twenty-two, he contributed greatly to American jazz during the short span of two years.

Guitarist Charlie Christian (1919–42), who died only a few months

---

[31]Improvising over a chord sequence is discussed later in this section.

before Blanton, joined Benny Goodman's orchestra in mid-1939, and commenced to change the concept of playing the guitar. He broke away from the traditional full chordal style of providing a steady rhythmic pulse by utilizing the guitar as a front-line instrument that doubled the unison ensemble phrases. Although Christian did not introduce the amplified guitar to jazz, he was the first guitarist to realize its full potential. Earlier attempts to use this modified instrument had been made by Eddie Durham of the Count Basie band and Floyd Smith of the Andy Kirk orchestra. It was Durham, whom Christian heard with the Count Basie orchestra in 1937, who motivated him to get a guitar. Up to that time, he was a pianist.

The method Christian used in playing the amplified guitar made the unamplified instrument obsolete. The unamplified guitar had been used in jazz primarily as a rhythm instrument; on occasion it had been used as a timid and hard-to-hear solo instrument playing either chorded or single-string passages. Christian used the guitar as if it were a horn, creating long, flowing lines by use of the single-string technique and because he could sustain notes due to the amplification of the instrument. With the guitar now able to hold its own with the other instruments, Christian employed it not only in a solo role, but as an additional melodic line in the ensemble instead of merely as a chordal instrument in the rhythm section.

Young, Eldridge, Hart, Blanton, and Christian were all transitional figures between swing and the new movement either by choice or because death cut short their musical careers. Young and Eldridge were the only two of this group who had the choice as to what path their careers would take. It was Christian, although he was on the New York musical scene for a very brief time, who was the unifying force in bringing together the various individualistic musical strands that propelled jazz into a new period of development.

Harry Minton, a former saxophonist and the first Black delegate to be elected to Local 802, the New York branch of the American Federation of Musicians, opened a club for musicians in the Hotel Cecil in Harlem. It was his desire to make available to all musicians a place where they could meet and discuss musical ideas and play without restrictions. Bandleader Teddy Hill, who had just returned from a tour because of financial difficulties, was made manager. Almost every night, musicians would gather and hold informal jam sessions.[32] Because of Minton's policy, the public had no influence over what was played at these sessions. Each performer was free to improvise for the satisfaction of his artistic standards. Consequently, Minton's Playhouse, as it was called, became the proving ground for progressive jazz musicians.

---

[32]A jam session is an informal gathering of musicians for the purpose of unrestricted solo improvisation. It began as a spontaneous after-hours diversion for jazz musicians who felt musically constrained during professional engagements.

Drummer Kenny Clarke took a small group from the disbanded Teddy Hill Orchestra to form the nucleus for all-night jam sessions at the Hotel Cecil in Harlem. The saxophonist (left) is the jazz great, Coleman Hawkins. (Photos courtesy Duncan P. Schiedt Collection.)

Drummer Kenny Clarke took a small group from the disbanded Teddy Hill orchestra to form the nucleus for the all-night sessions in early 1940. Charlie Christian, playing with Benny Goodman at the Pennsylvania Hotel in New York, would join the sessions at the Harlem club with his guitar and amplifier once the hotel set had ended. Lester Young was leading a group that included Clyde Hart on piano, at a club called Kelly's Stable. They would often stop by Minton's for the sessions. When Duke Ellington and his orchestra were performing in New York, Jimmy Blanton often joined the group at Minton's. Other performers who gathered around Christian were pianists Thelonious Monk, Bud Powell, Kenny Kersey, and Tadd Dameron; trumpeters Joe Guy, Benny Harris, and Dizzy Gillespie; saxophonist Charlie Parker; bassist Oscar Pettiford; and Denzil Best (who was still experimenting with piano and trumpet and had not yet started playing drums).

Sometimes these sessions would convene instead at Monroe's Uptown House, another Harlem club. But in either location, the playing of the soloists was always explorative. Significantly, a salient feature of the swing era, the solo, was the focus of exploration in these new developments. All the new ideas that were developed here came from the solo choruses.

It was Christian who pointed the way toward the development of a new jazz style. Not only was he the most important influence in the reshaping of the melodic line, the elevation of the guitar to a front-line instrument, and the manner in which the rhythm section performed in coordination with the modern front-line soloists, but he based improvisation on the harmonic structure rather than on a melodic source.

Many of Christian's adherents in the Minton sessions had given no thought to the development of a cohesive jazz form; they looked on these sessions as a means of exploring new solo devices for their personal satisfaction.

Upon Christian's death from tuberculosis in the spring of 1942, the Minton group was left without a leader. His death, however, spurred many of the participants to search for a collective form commencing from the point where Christian had left off. The small group unison-ensemble was the first step. The group played the theme in unison. In turn, the jam sessions became the setting for a contrived experiment with form. The ensemble played the melody in unison, followed by a series of solos, which in turn were followed by the melody in unison. Thelonious Monk and Tadd Dameron soon made attempts at serious jazz compositions that uti-

Thelonious Monk developed the theories of Clyde Hart and moved the piano closer to the front line of instrumentation. (Photo courtesy CBS Records.)

lized the various devices that came to the fore in the explorative jam sessions at Minton's. These attempts were followed by efforts to score the themes using the instrumentation of the group.

As the new music evolved, the function of each of the components of the rhythm section and the front-line instruments was changed from what they were in swing. During the swing era, the rhythm section usually played four beats to each bar, with all instruments of this group following parallel, unchanging lines. Christian had changed the entire concept and made the section more flexible in its effect. The new concept centered around the string bass as the anchor of the main rhythmic pattern. With the bass supplying a steady beat, the drummer was free to be more flexible. Kenny Clarke, for instance, used an incessant dinning of the cymbal that made possible a fluid quality in his approach to the rhythm. He was then free to introduce cross-rhythms, punctuation, and variations to the customary $\frac{4}{4}$ pattern; bass drum accents and rim shots[33] were used to punctuate the melodic line. In addition, the drummer worked out simple patterns to conform with the thematic structures produced by the front-line instruments.

Thelonious Monk, house pianist at Minton's, was developing the theories of Clyde Hart with a considerable degree of success. The left hand was used to construct the harmonic framework of the composition while also punctuating the improvised phrases produced by the right hand. Monk also began to employ fill-in chords for the gaps in the melodic line. This insured a degree of continuity in the improvisations of the front-line instruments. By doing so, Monk moved his instrument closer to the front line.

The guitar was permitted the greatest flexibility of all the instruments. In the hands of Christian, it would merge with the rhythm section on one occasion and become a front-line instrument on another. Its improvised solos possessed the phrasing qualities of the saxophones; by being amplified, it could follow any front-line instrument without a loss of drive or volume.

Among the front-line instruments associated with this movement, a single saxophone replaced the reed section of the big band, and a single trumpet replaced the brass section of that era. In effect, the unison-ensemble was a return to the small-group concept that had been associated with New Orleans jazz.

After Christian's death, it was trumpeter Dizzy Gillespie (b. 1917) and alto saxophonist Charlie Parker (1920–55) who emerged as the most important individual influences in the progress of this new jazz.

[33]A rim shot is executed by placing the head of the drumstick on the drum head with the other end across the rim of the drum and striking that stick with the other, producing a loud, staccato sound.

The general public was not aware of this new music until 1944 because the musicians' union had instituted a recording ban against the record companies. Swing audiences, outside of the two clubs in Harlem where the music was gradually being developed, were unaware of its existence. In 1944 and 1945, after the recording ban was lifted, Parker and Gillespie made the first recordings of this music; in addition, they received their first jobs in clubs along 52nd Street. Almost immediately the new music was given a name. The term was onomatopoetic. A feature of the new solos was to end a phrase with two short notes on the downbeat; these notes may have suggested the word "bebop."

EXAMPLE 3.17   Possible origin of the term "bebop"

At first, bebop was not accepted by the general public and many musicians. When it did become accepted, the world of swing disappeared rapidly. However, the demise of swing was related to other factors as well, including the amusement tax on admissions to dance halls.

Parker was perhaps the most important improvising mind in modern jazz. In all probability, no one soloist will ever again dominate the modern jazz field as he did. His style was characterized by a unique tone that was deemed hard and harsh by many, a dexterity of fingering that had no precedent among alto saxophonists in the earlier years of jazz, and a great wealth of musical ideas. Because of its strong affinity with blues, Parker's style was powerfully emotional.

Gillespie is the antithesis of Parker. He is a practical musician who has a sense of organization. It was he who changed the Minton concept of the unison-ensemble to a large group in the late forties. Gillespie's style was originally fashioned after the playing of Roy Eldridge; once he found his own conception of jazz, however, he discarded the swing influence. His style is characterized by a pure tone and a facility of execution.

Tadd Dameron (1917–65), a pianist-arranger and intimate of Monk, helped move bebop out of the small band into the larger ensemble. As an arranger, Dameron was concerned with adapting the new musical ideas of the Minton group in order to create a new big-band sound and was the first to do so.[34]

In an effort to break cleanly with all facets of swing, the pioneer jazzmen based their improvisations almost entirely on the harmonic foundation. They often constructed new compositions upon the harmonies of

---

[34]Billy Eckstine, the singer, formed a band in 1944 that was perhaps the first big band to move in the direction of incorporating bebop. Gillespie and Parker were members of the original group. However, Gillespie's band of the late forties was the first big band with a mature bebop style. Dameron wrote for both groups.

already-familiar popular songs such as *I Got Rhythm, What Is This Thing Called Love?, Whispering,* and *How High the Moon.*

In the new style, there was increased use of passing notes in melodic improvisation. By adding the sixth, seventh, ninth, eleventh, or thirteenth to a chord, with all their inflections and enharmonic versions, any note could become a part of the chord and available for improvisation:

EXAMPLE 3.18 Chord structures with inflections

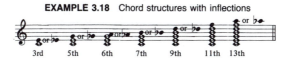

It is a common practice in bebop, as in other modern music idioms, for non-chord tones such as sevenths and ninths to remain unresolved at the end of a phrase.

EXAMPLE 3.19 Unresolved ninth tone[35]

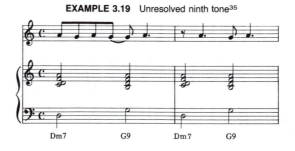

The melodic treatment of the lowered (flatted) fifth became very unpredictable. Sometimes it was resolved as expected; at other times, it escaped the expected resolution by way of a leap. These leaps gave bebop its unpredictable character:

EXAMPLE 3.20 Lowered fifth resolved[36]

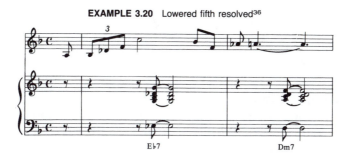

[35]*Satin Doll,* by Duke Ellington. © 1958, Tempo Music Publishers, Inc., New York. Used by permission.

[36]*A Night in Tunisia,* by "Dizzy" Gillespie and Frank Paparelli. © copyright 1944, 1947, 1949 by MCA Music, A Division of MCA Inc., New York, N.Y. Copyright renewed. Used by permission. All rights reserved.

EXAMPLE 3.21   Lowered fifth unresolved

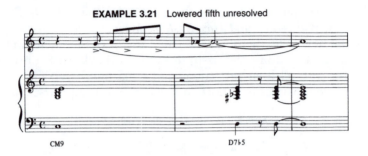

Bebop did not generally employ square phrases of even length. Not only did bebop phrases vary in length, but they were frequently at odds with the natural phrasing of the song upon which they were built. Both Parker and Gillespie refused to be hemmed in by the original construction of a melody. They cut through bar lines and other divisions of a tune to express the phrasing that seemed most suitable to them for the melodic line being produced:

EXAMPLE 3.22   Irregular phrasing[37]

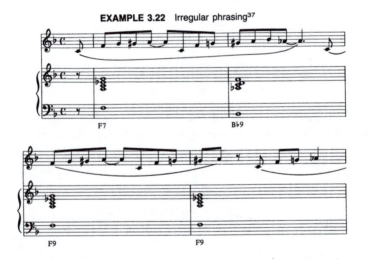

It became common in this new music to replace the existing harmonic patterns of popular tunes with substitute chords, which in essence became a new harmonic structure. When the original chords were replaced by new ones, a new thematic line was often superimposed on them:

---

[37]*Straight, No Chaser*, by Thelonious Monk. Copyright owner, Thelonious Music, a Division of Bar Thel Music Corp., New York. Used by permission.

[38]*I've Got Rhythm*, by George Gershwin. © 1930 (Renewed) New World Music Corporation. All Rights Reserved. Used by permission of Warner Bros. Music.

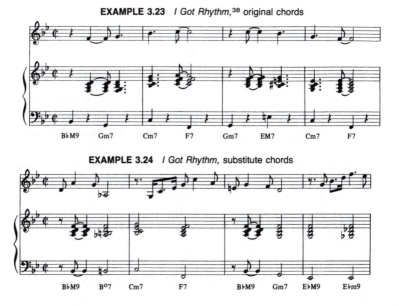

EXAMPLE 3.23 *I Got Rhythm,*[38] original chords

EXAMPLE 3.24 *I Got Rhythm,* substitute chords

Another example of chord substitution occurs in the twelve-bar blues.

EXAMPLE 3.25 Original twelve-bar blues structure

EXAMPLE 3.26 Twelve-bar blues structure with substitute chords

The changes that took place in the music of the early forties were quite radical to those ears that had been accustomed to the sounds of swing. This has been the case, however, when any great style change has taken place in jazz. When the New Orleans style of jazz evolved into swing, there was a similar "strangeness" of sound.

It must be remembered that if jazz is to remain a viable force in American culture, creativity must be free to exert itself and its practitioners must be allowed to expand their craft.

Presently, jazz has become so intellectual and esoteric that it has lost teenagers as consumers of this idiom. Whereas jazz was once a medium by which people danced, it has become a music for listening purposes only, and consequently, may have lost some of its appeal to young audiences.

Cool Jazz

Since jazz's inception around the beginning of the twentieth century, one of the essential aspects of its growth has been the continuous bond of action and reaction. In its early stages, jazz was a music based on collective improvisation by a small ensemble. Reaction set in immediately prior to the swing era, changing the concept of jazz to one based on solo improvisation. Then came a complete change in direction that was evolved by the men who developed bebop. After the musicians involved with bop had established a fiery, frenetic norm for their music, reaction once again set in. As so often happens when change takes place, the swing of the pendulum went back beyond not only the frenzy of bop, but also beyond the outgoing emotionalism of the Black bands of the swing era. The resulting music was played in such an understated manner that subsequently it became known as "cool jazz."

Miles Davis. The Black trumpeter Miles Davis (b. 1926) is frequently cited as the epitome of the cool style because his tone is devoid of vibrato and because of the deliberate, carefully stated nature of his playing. To cite Davis as being the innovator of cool jazz, however, would not only be unfair to the other musicians associated with him in this movement, but also

Miles Davis, the epitome of the cool style, with Dizzy Gillespie. (Photo courtesy Duncan P. Schiedt Collection.)

inaccurate. It would be more appropriate to classify him as the catalyst in bringing about the development of this new style. He was the unifying force that brought together several musicians of similar stylistic inclinations who contributed to this new approach in jazz.

There were two sources that influenced the development of cool jazz—one Black and the other White. The first of these was the tenor saxophonist Lester Young, whose roots were anchored in swing. His solo style, described in the previous section, became the trademark of all tenor saxophonists of the cool jazz school. The other major influence was the orchestra of Claude Thornhill (1909–65), an arranger who formed his own band in 1939. Thornhill's sound, which became characteristic of his group during the forties, was placid and sonorous and was based on the use of horns with no vibrato in their tones.

Initially, Thornhill attempted to produce a sound that approximated that of the French horns through a blending of the trombones and wood-winds and by having the trumpets and trombones play into derbies.[39] In 1941, he went one step further by adding French horns to the band. The horn timbre gave the overall sound of the band an even more somber effect. Later, during the mid-forties, Thornhill increased this effect by adding a tuba. This instrument was common to early jazz groups but had been used rarely since the late 1920s. Thornhill, however, used this instrument in a different manner from the way it was used in early jazz. Instead of using the tuba simply as a component of the rhythm section, he wove it into the textural fabric of the band's sound.

It was Davis' desire to achieve a unique orchestral effect that would transcend the confines of the unison-ensemble that was so characteristic of bebop. Impressed with the Thornhill sound, Davis gathered around him a group of musicians with the idea of emulating that sound within the context of a small group. Included in the group were Gil Evans (former arranger with the Thornhill band), Gerry Mulligan, John Lewis, John Benson Brooks, Johnny Carisi, and George Russell. The overall Thornhill sound was uppermost in Davis' mind, but there were other considerations as well. One of his objectives was to expand the limited form to which ensemble playing had been reduced, which consisted almost entirely of solos sandwiched between unison passages. Davis wanted a medium-sized group, capable of supporting soloists with scored backgrounds in the same fashion as was being done by full orchestras. This required a new ensemble sound of contrasting section voicings within the front line.

The final composition of the band was determined by several other important requirements. Davis desired a front line that possessed a rich,

---

[39]The derby is one of many muting devices used by performers on brass instruments in jazz. Its use evolved from the use of the derby hat for this purpose. Subsequently, a device made of metal or a hard fiber material was manufactured in the shape of a derby for the specific purpose of muting a brass instrument.

full sound of considerable depth, subdued in its unison voicings but capable of producing contrapuntal designs within the arrangements. The baritone saxophone, French horn, and tuba would increase the pitch range, giving the ensemble a range of approximately three and a half octaves.

As a result, in 1948 Davis built his group as a miniature of the Thornhill band. It included French horn, tuba, trumpet, trombone, alto and baritone saxophones, piano, bass, and drums. This was the smallest number of instruments that could still produce the Thornhill sound as well as all the harmonies that the Thornhill band used.

While Davis' group emulated the sound of the Thornhill orchestra, it reflected the subtle approach originally advocated by Lester Young. As with Young, the sound was relaxed, yet the relaxation of this group was the inevitable outcome of the instrumental design being used.

The Davis group was a racially integrated one. The White musicians, who came chiefly from the Thornhill band, included Gerry Mulligan on baritone saxophone, John Barber on tuba, bassist Joe Shulman, and alto saxophonist Lee Konitz. Shortly afterwards, Sandy Siegelstein left the Thornhill orchestra to become a member of this unique group. The arrangers for the group included Gerry Mulligan, Gil Evans, Bud Powell, Cleo Henry, Johnny Carisi, John Lewis, and Davis himself.

The Davis nonet had a short-lived existence. It played a two-week engagement at the Royal Roost and Clique (later to become Birdland) clubs in New York. No records were made by the group during this period because another recording ban had been imposed by the American Federation of Musicians, which lasted through almost all of 1948. As soon as the recording ban was lifted, record companies were on the lookout for exceptional groups. The nonet reassembled in Capital Records' studios in mid-December, 1948 for the first of three sessions that were to stretch out over a period of fourteen months.[40] Although their initial impact was slight, the records that came out of these sessions were to have a profound effect on the development of jazz in the fifties.

Cool jazz became the style of a predominantly White, West Coast school of musicians. Among the few Black musicians involved in West Coast jazz were tenor saxophonist Wardell Gray, bassist Curtis Counce, pianist Hampton Hawes, and drummer Chico Hamilton.

John Lewis and the Modern Jazz Quartet. John Lewis (b. 1920) was involved with Davis both in the planning and as a pianist in the nonet group. He is one of the few genuine composers of jazz and one of the most successful. Lewis is thoroughly grounded in the use of classical composi-

---

[40]The recordings produced by Davis' nonet are available on *Miles Davis: Birth of the Cool* (Capitol TT 1974).

tional devices and has incorporated several classical forms into his work, among them the fugue, toccata, and concerto grosso. The Modern Jazz Quartet, of which he was musical director and pianist during its more than twenty years of existence, included many of his original compositions in its repertory. In fact, several of Lewis' compositions have become part of the growing number of modern jazz standards[41] that are interpreted by many groups.

John Aaron Lewis was born in La Grange, Illinois but was reared in Albuquerque, New Mexico. He was born into a very musical environment. His father played piano and violin, and his mother studied voice with the daughter of Schumann-Heink. Lewis began studying the violin and piano when he was seven and continued these studies throughout his youth. He entered the University of New Mexico and majored in anthropology. After serving in the army from 1942 to 1945, Lewis went to New York for further study at the Manhattan School of Music. He earned bachelor's and master's degrees there and later taught at the same school. He also became a member of the Dizzy Gillespie big band (1946–47) as pianist and arranger. It was during this period that Lewis composed his first work in extended form, *Toccata for Trumpet and Orchestra.* He then played with several jazz groups, such as those of Illinois Jacquet, Lester Young, and Charlie Parker. He was also an important contributor, as composer-arranger-performer, to the Miles Davis recordings in 1949–50.

The date of inception of the Modern Jazz Quartet is rather nebulous. Some of its members were active in the rhythm section of Dizzy Gillespie's orchestra (1946–48); Milt Jackson, Kenny Clarke, and Lewis, along with Al Jackson on bass and Chano Pozo on bongos, made some recordings in 1948 for the Sensation label. The real beginning of the Quartet came in August 1951 when Jackson, Lewis, Ray Brown, and Clarke assembled for a recording session as the Milt Jackson Quartet for Dizzy Gillespie's Dee Gee records. Following this session, three of the performers expressed a desire to continue playing as a group. Percy Heath became the bassist in place of Ray Brown, and a cooperative group was formed with no single man as the leader. Soon thereafter, however, John Lewis became musical director through mutual agreement.

The first recording by this group was made in 1953. One of Lewis' originals was a Bach-like fugue, *Vendome,* and it indicated the kinds of musical forms that appealed to this group—most importantly, collective improvisation within a variety of traditional European forms.

In 1957 Lewis became director of the Music Inn School of Jazz, an annual three-week workshop course. The sessions incorporated roundta-

---

[41]The term "standard" is used to denote familiar, well-established popular songs or instrumental compositions used by jazz musicians as a basis for improvisation.

ble discussions by musicians and the late Marshall Stearns, along with practical experience in writing for large and small groups, playing with both
types of groups, and lessons in the jazz techniques of various instruments.

Lewis also became involved with Gunther Schuller, the founder of the
Modern Jazz Society (later the Jazz and Classical Music Society). The
"Third Stream" can be said to have had its origins in this group. Third
Stream music, a term coined by Schuller, consists of the fusion of jazz (one
stream) with music in the European tradition (second stream) to produce a
compound of the two musics (third stream). (Actually, this was just the
latest in a long line of attempts to effect a fusion of jazz and classical music.)
Lewis formed Orchestra U.S.A. for the express purpose of performing
contemporary music of all kinds, including jazz.

Among its ventures into Third Stream music, the Modern Jazz
Quartet recorded two albums. One album pairs the group with the Beaux
Arts String Quartet, and the other with the Stuttgart Symphony. Lewis
contributed the composition *Sketch* to the former album and an arrangement of *God Rest Ye Merry Gentlemen* to the latter.

Well-known works by Lewis include *Fontessa* (1956); a suite, *Three
Little Feelings* (1956), for brass ensemble; and the film score *Sait-on Jamais*
(*One Never Knows*), released in the United States as *No Sun in Venice* (1957).
Among his outstanding jazz fugues are *Concorde, Vendome,* and *Versailles.*
His *Three Windows,* from the score *Sait-on Jamais,* is based on a triple fugue.
Other film scores by Lewis include *Odds Against Tomorrow* (1959), *Exposure*
(1959), and *A Milanese Story* (1962). He also composed a ballet score for the
San Francisco Ballet Company, *Original Sin* (1961).

Besides his musical leadership of perhaps the best small ensemble in
jazz history, Lewis has made an important contribution to the synthesis that
modern jazz has achieved in its second decade.

Hard Bop

As stated earlier, the history of jazz is filled with actions and reactions.
Cool jazz of the early fifties was a reaction to the bebop movement. However, in its use of superficial effects for their own sake, the cool musicians
often drained the music of the vitality that had been one of its essential
components. These effects included an apparent improvisational style that
was contrived, having been worked out beforehand; a very relaxed tempo
that lacked a "swinging" beat; and the use of an "airy" tonal quality that was
the essence of sublimity.

Emotionalism had been an integral part of jazz from its inception to
the advent of the cool style. This emotional element had always been present probably because jazz was played as a music for dancing. After World
War II, however, jazz became increasingly cerebral in an attempt to trans-
form itself into music for listeners only. Some of the most obvious dance

East Coast proponents of hard bop: Art Blakey (top right) and Horace Silver (bottom left). (Photos courtesy Jack Whittemore and BLue Note Records, respectively.)

rhythms disappeared or were subdued, to the point where the music lost what many believed to be essential jazz qualities. The musicians of the cool school proceeded to eliminate or subdue the aforementioned qualities and, in the minds of many musicians, became excessive in changing the stylistic character of this music.

There began a movement on the East Coast to restore the old vitality. This Eastern style has been labeled "hard bop" (also, at first, "funky"[42]) as opposed to the West Coast school whose style has often been called "soft

---

[42]The term "funky" is originally an Anglo-Saxon word that had an Afro-American meaning of "smelly."

bop." The founder of this movement or style was the pianist and composer Horace Silver (b. 1928), musical director of Art Blakey's Jazz Messengers in 1954. Silver attempted to rediscover in the blues and in contemporary Black gospel music important qualities that, in his opinion, jazz had lost in the early fifties.

The music of the Black church had been allied to jazz since its earliest days in New Orleans when the jazz treatment of hymns was a common part of New Orleans jazz. In addition, the music of the Black church was shaped from the same sources that provided the basic ingredients for jazz. As jazz became more and more sophisticated and lost contact with its sources, the association between church music and jazz all but disappeared, especially from the forties on.

When the jazz musician sought to "return to the roots," jazz and church music were united again. This time, however, the prime association was with modern gospel song, a highly emotional style of singing that, in turn, was influenced by earlier jazz and the blues. Consequently, when the gospel influence was joined to a reawakened feeling for blues, the resultant music was highly volatile and emotional. The music produced by the combination of these two influences possessed a quality described as "dirtiness" or "funk" in jazz music jargon. Horace Silver has described "funkiness" as a sort of lowdown blues feeling.

Other descriptive terms used in this kind of jazz were "wail," "groove," "swing," "blow," "back-home," "cook," and "lowdown." Interestingly enough, almost all of these terms imply highly emotional and uninhibited expression, and several of them had often been applied to the jazz of the thirties.

It was not too long after the funky style of jazz arrived in the mid-fifties that it became, through simplifications, a commercial commodity called "soul jazz." Genuine jazzmen have always communicated a strong emotional side to their playing that might be termed soul. With the Black church as the starting point, this term was gradually translated from an objective to a noun—soulful to soul.

Unfortunately, the "soul" title presented record producers and advertisers with a sales slogan. Many of them seized the chance to turn this new trend to their financial advantage and began presenting many diverse stylists under the banner of soul. Not only was this kind of misrepresentation misleading to the public, but it complicated what was in fact a straightforward musical outlook. It was not long before soul jazz had lost its appeal.

Silver's music, though it encourages "finger-snapping and head-shaking," is actually carefully designed and rehearsed, with deliberate craftsmanship in evidence. Harmonically, his music belongs to the modern jazz idiom; but because of its intense emotionalism, his group sounds like a hybrid form of a bebop combo and a small blues band from Kansas City.

Silver's compositions were motivated to some extent by a desire to get away from the similarity of pattern that had proven a sufficient framework for the bop musicians. He started including little interludes, similar to short introductions for each soloist, to relieve the monotony.

Silver also made extremely effective use of the limited instrumentation at his disposal. For the horns he wrote riff patterns and rhythms as accompaniment material, thus treating them as substitutes for the saxophone or brass sections of the big bands of the thirties.[43]

Another device used by Silver was to take a traditional two-bar riff and expand it into an eight-bar theme. He continually strived to break through the cliches of thirty-two-bar popular song forms and their eight-bar substructures, for instance, by interpolating phrases of six bars in pieces of thirty-eight bars (16/6/16).

It was through Horace Silver—and such other musicians as drummer Art Blakey, pianists Bobby Timmons and Les McCann, and the late alto saxophonist Julian "Cannonball" Adderley—that jazz returned to its roots and recaptured the vitality and emotionalism that had disappeared in the early fifties. While this movement has been called regressive, self-conscious, monotonous, and even contrived, this "return to roots" brought back to jazz the emotional element that is such a fundamental facet of this idiom.

Free Form Jazz

The emphasis on "soul" became a strong factor in the jazz of the late fifties. But the projection of this quality grew into a fad that retained only the most superficial aspects of the viable music on which it was based. A part of the flood of emotionalism that welled up in jazz following the recovery of its blues roots was drained off by the exploitation of "soul jazz." At the same time, this emotionalism was providing a foundation for a group of musicians who were establishing an important new approach to jazz.

At the center of this approach were three musicians—Sonny Rollins, Miles Davis, and John Coltrane.

Sonny Rollins. Sonny Rollins (b. 1930) was originally a part of the hard bop school. While his improvisation contained a great emotional element, however, he was more directly concerned with shape and structure than most of his hard bop colleagues. Rollins' efforts were focused on achieving the greatest possible freedom within a disciplined and logical structure.

The role of the soul movement in jazz history was short-lived; because the work of the musicians associated with this movement was of a narrow

[43]Listen to the album *Horace Silver Quintet: Blowin' the Blues Away* (Blue Note 4017). The jazz tune entitled *Sister Sadie* is especially representative of his style.

compass, soul jazz produced few valid new directions. The improvisations of Rollins were of far more significance. He extended the harmonic range of the jazz solo and enlarged on the rhythmic concept of Charlie Parker. With Rollins, for instance, the "middle eight" bars of the thirty-two bar song form could become a ten-bar sequence.

Rollins did as much as any single musician to change the direction of jazz in this period. It was during the mid-fifties that he accomplished his stylistic breakthrough, and it presaged the great change toward the harmonic and rhythmic liberties of the next ten years. The breakthrough consisted of his utilizing thematic improvisation in a very strict sense. Up to this time, most performers departed completely from a given theme and improvised freely on a chord structure. The trend sparked by Rollins was to bring thematic (or motivic) and structural unity into improvisation. Some performers now accomplish this by combining composition and improvisation in the manner of the Modern Jazz Quartet; others, like Rollins, accomplish the same ends solely by means of extemporization.

Rollins is as imaginative rhythmically as melodically. His remarkable use of polyrhythm enables him to reshape completely the accepted measure-by-measure patterns of the thirty-two-bar chorus. He runs the gamut of extremes, from almost a whole chorus of nonsyncopated quarter notes to asymmetrical groupings of five and seven or other syncopated rhythms, which are extremely difficult to notate.

Rollins' vivid imagination has led him to emulate techniques not indigenous to his instrument. An example of this takes place in *Way Out West*,[44] where, returning from his second solo, Rollins imitates Shelly Manne's closing snare-drum roll on the saxophone.

Sonny Rollins broadened the harmonic and melodic language of jazz by employing seemingly endless variants and permutations of a given motive.[45] Through his efforts, jazz began to become much freer in its scope.

Miles Davis.   It is remarkable that during the time of his great public success, Miles Davis had the personal conviction that permitted him to move in the direction of change rather than to maintain his status quo. Davis, the catalyst in the development of cool jazz in 1948, has continued to explore and develop his talent.[46] This is unusual—virtually unique—in a music where many instrumentalists have been able to sustain and refine the achievements of their twenties and early thirties, but few have been able to continue at a high pitch of creativity.

[44]From the album *Way Out West* (Contemporary 3530).

[45]An excellent example of Rollins' thematic improvisation is *Blue 7*, a cut from the album *Saxophone Colossus* (Prestige 7326).

[46]Davis is now involved with combining electronic instruments with jazz.

Miles Davis, catalyst in the development of cool jazz, continued developing his talents in the direction of free form jazz during the 1950s. (Photo courtesy Duncan P. Schiedt Collection.)

In 1959, Davis recorded an album entitled *Kind of Blue*,[47] one of the most provocative events in jazz since the forties. Most of the tunes were new to the musicians and were presented to them for the first time when they arrived for the recording session. Most of the improvisation was done using points of departure that jazzmen had only rarely undertaken before—most importantly, modal improvisation. For example, in the tune *So What*, the improviser uses the Dorian mode for sixteen measures, then moves up a half-step for eight measures, then back down a half-step for the final eight measures. (The Dorian mode approximates very closely the blues scale; in the Dorian, however, the third and seventh degrees are fixed a semitone above the second and sixth degrees, whereas in the blues scale these degrees sometimes appear as in the major scale or only slightly flatted.) In *Flamenco Sketches*, five different scales are used, the soloist improvising on each of them in turn.

By utilizing the modal approach to improvisation, Davis virtually reversed the course of modern jazz and the techniques that had occupied its players since the early 1940s. It was during the bebop period that improvisation shifted from being melodic-oriented to a harmonic-based technique. Davis was thus shifting the emphasis from complex chords and fancy harmonic substitutions to just a chord or two. Divorcing his improvisations from the chord sequence gave him more freedom to become inventive melodically. When a composition is based on a set harmonic progression, once the harmonic sequence has been completed there is

[47]Columbia 1355.

nothing for the improviser to do but repeat what he has just improvised with variations. Because the modal approach is based on scales rather than chords, the improviser is less concerned about harmonic progressions. Davis thus laid the groundwork for the development of both John Coltrane and, to a lesser degree, the more extreme, more melodic Ornette Coleman.

The album *Kind of Blue* was influential both in and of itself, and because it paralleled other independently conceived events in jazz. However, for awhile it seemed a rather isolated event for Davis himself, more immediately important to John Coltrane's development than Davis'. During the next few years, Davis' repertory consisted primarily of ballads and standards.[48] Then, beginning in 1965, Davis returned to the jazz principles he had employed six years earlier, and he began to build a repertory of original, instrumentally conceived jazz compositions of unusual and imaginative structures. Once again, Davis was in the forefront of change.

John Coltrane.   John Coltrane (1926–67) brought to jazz a rich and varied background gained through his experiences as a member of various rhythm-and-blues groups. His style contained a high emotional content with undiluted power, as if always at full pitch. His opening bars were as full of passion as those ending an improvisational section.

Coltrane did not attract attention in the jazz world until he joined the Miles Davis quintet in 1955, having spent a decade in which he was known as a capable, but in no way extraordinary, saxophonist. From that point onward, he had many followers and imitators; there are still musicians who show the influence of Coltrane's playing at almost every period of his career.

Initially, Coltrane was thought of as a hard bop player as opposed to a cool performer. But his early uniqueness rested on the fact that he was a vertical player (that is, oriented toward arpeggiated harmonies and harmonic leaps) in the same mold as Coleman Hawkins, rather than a primarily linear improviser who, like most of his contemporaries, emulated Lester Young. Thus, he was moving somewhat counter to the direction that jazz saxophone had been taking since the mid-forties.

Coltrane returned to the Davis group in 1958. During this period his playing was marked by very long phrases at extremely rapid tempos, an effect characterized as "sheets of sounds." Whereas Charlie Parker utilized an eighth-note pattern as the basis of his improvisation, it often appeared that, in an effort to get all the notes played in an allotted space of time, Coltrane was reaching for a sixteenth-note pattern. When he desired to play a certain number of harmonies in a given time and the number did not

---

[48]In American vernacular usage, a *ballad* is a romantic popular song, usually in slow or medium tempo, most often thirty-two bars long. A *standard* is a tune that has become a jazz classic.

John Coltrane, saxophonist, brought to jazz a much greater freedom of improvisation within a formalized structure. (Photo courtesy Duncan P. Schiedt Collection.)

work out in metrically even values, he would put his notes into uneven groups like fives and sevens in order to get them all performed on time.

Another aspect of Coltrane's skill that has aroused a considerable amount of controversy is his use of harmonics. He was able to play two notes at the same time, a technique that has found increasing acceptance among woodwind performers.

After participating in the Miles Davis album *Kind of Blue,* in which there were modal pieces with few harmonic challenges, Coltrane set out on his own. In his first album, he recorded *Naima,*[49] which consists of a series of sophisticated harmonic progressions over an E-flat pedal tone, with a B-flat pedal in the bridge, and allows the soloist to take either the progressions or the pedal tone as the basis for improvisation.

My Favorite Things represents another effort to secure melodic freedom. This popular song had built in the same sort of things he had been working on: very little chordal motion and folk-like simplicity. It was also very similar to the modal approach that Coltrane had embraced. This recording became a best seller.

Two extended performances from 1961 represent a turning point in Coltrane's improvisational style. On *Impressions* and *Chasin' the Trane,* his improvising became more horizontal and linear than previously. The for-

[49]*Naima* is on the album *Giant Steps* (Atlantic 1311).

mer utilizes the same modes and song form Davis used on *So What*; the latter uses reiterated phrases or motives that are not used sequentially or developed to any degree.

Coltrane's *Ascension*,[50] one of his most daring recordings, is a thirty-eight-minute performance directly indebted to Ornette Coleman. The performance sometimes screams and shrieks, and at other times, soars and sings.

In his explorations and experimentations, Coltrane was able to bring to jazz a much greater freedom of improvisation within a formalized structure. However, an even less confining form seemed to be the goal of the most thoroughgoing individualist that jazz produced in the late fifties.

The modal experiments by Davis and Coltrane and the thematic improvisations of Rollins gave jazz the means to become much more free in structure and form. The time was right for the emergence of musicians who could extend this idea in their own personal ways.

Ornette Coleman.   Ornette Coleman (b. 1930) was one of these, though he was not the first to attempt free form in jazz. Lennie Tristano, blind pianist and teacher, had attempted to achieve an unpremeditated group music, but his music lacked emotional content. Charles Mingus, string bass player and leader, was involved in similar efforts; in his "extended form" a soloist may spontaneously extend a piece by turning any of its chords into a pedal tone for as long as he wishes to explore it.

Coleman's approach has always seemed more natural and alive. He is very aware of the genuine roots of jazz because of his experience as a member of several rhythm-and-blues bands. It is highly possible that Coleman's contributions to jazz will become as important as those of Morton, Armstrong, and Parker.

It might seem strange that the music of a performer of Coleman's magnitude should need justification, but his music continues to evoke much criticism as well as favorable reaction. John Lewis has called Coleman the only really new thing in jazz since the mid-forties. Classical composer and critic Virgil Thomson, going back even farther, has said Coleman was the first new thing he had heard in jazz since Louis Armstrong. Leonard Bernstein has called him a genius. Other critics have opposed Coleman's music, including pianist Andre Previn and trumpeters Dizzy Gillespie and Maynard Ferguson. Ferguson went so far as to accuse him of having bad intonation and bad technique.

The basis of Coleman's approach is freedom from the limitations imposed by adhering to a given key, given harmonic progressions, or a given rhythm. It is Coleman's conviction that it is wrong to regard the

[50]*My Favorite Things* (Atlantic 1361); *Impressions* (Impulse A-42); *Chasin' the Trane* (Impulse A-10); and *Ascension* (Impulse A-95).

Ornette Coleman, one of the most controversial figures in all of jazz. (Photo courtesy CBS Records.)

European sense of pitch as absolute. This radical idea is completely unacceptable to certain critics who claim that it places his work outside the jazz idiom.

In 1958, Coleman made his first recordings for the Contemporary Record Company. The impact of these recording sessions was felt throughout the jazz world. In 1959 he came to New York, preceded by the high praise of musicians who had heard him. He played a white plastic alto saxophone, first out of economic necessity, and then because he liked the sound he was able to produce.

Coleman's style of free melodic improvisation is not based on the outline of a succession of chords, as in earlier jazz, but on a harmonic pedal point or "drone." From that one tonal center, the soloist must produce an interesting melodic line.

Coleman's mode of playing is a natural development in a jazz that was dominated by men like Coltrane who were making incredible efforts to extend jazz improvisation without completely abandoning the harmonic framework. Coleman rejected any enforced adherence to the harmonic structure. The themes that he produced are used as the basis for free extemporization, but the harmonies of these themes do not in any way direct his solos. Rather than having set chord progressions limit the scope of his improvisation, Coleman preferred to have the harmonic pattern follow his own melodic invention.

At times, Coleman performs entire passages made up of completely unrelated melodic statements. More often, however, he elaborates on each

idea before passing to the next. A two- and three-bar phrase may be paraphrased and extemporized throughout the next twelve or fourteen measures before another idea is presented. Since there is no true harmonic
base, each adaptation resembles the original phrase only in its general
design.

Coleman's approach to the use of sounds and chords seems to reflect
the predominance of the human voice in Black music from its inception. It
is Coleman's belief that there are some intervals that tend to project the
human quality if they are played at the right pitch, and that a performer is
capable of producing this quality of sound if he is actually hearing and
trying to express the warmth of the human voice. He also insists that since
several different chord progressions can fit the same melody, musicians
who perform his compositions should perform each improvisation on the
melodic line to different chord progressions.

Quincy Jones, a Black arranger, prophesied that Coleman would
eliminate the piano from his future groups to enhance the aleatory, or
"chance," character of the music by removing its set chordal structure.
Since there was no need for the harmonic progressions to be played for the
other instruments to follow, Coleman did in fact dispense with using the
piano in his group. The piano-less group, which had been an innovation of
Gerry Mulligan's back in the early fifties, was possible because the piano
was no longer a necessary component of the rhythm section. This change
enhanced the concept of free improvisation.

The role of the rhythm section in Coleman's group is almost opposite
that of previous jazz styles. In previous styles, the soloist followed the
rhythmic patterns set by the drummer and bass player, whereas in free
form jazz, the rhythm section attempts to follow the soloist. In fact, it is
Coleman's desire that the drummer play a kind of percussive part within
the music rather than merely "accompany" it.

In free form jazz, of which Coleman's style is representative, the beat
is seldom explicitly stated. Instead, the rhythm section produces continually shifting, overlapping and sometimes conflicting layers of rhythm.

It is Coleman's preference that the bassist should play independent
lines against the lines of the soloist but should not be concerned with
choosing the best notes of each chord to perform with the soloist. Instead,
he should just play within the range of his instrument that corresponds to
the range of the soloist; that is, if the soloist is playing in the high register,
then the bassist should play within that register on his instrument.

Coleman feels that intonation is a matter of context and expression. It
is his belief that a performer can play sharp or flat in tune and that a D in a
context of joy should not sound like a D representing sadness. Further-
more, split tones, harmonics, tense upper-register cries, and gutteral low-
register sounds may all be used expressively.

Many of Coleman's compositions have programmatic titles that attempt to convey a mood: for example, *Lonely Woman, Congeniality,* and

Peace.[51] He often employs a tonal center. In contrast to his usual quartet recordings (alto saxophone, trumpet, bass, and drums), Coleman's most ambitious one is entitled *Free Jazz,*[52] which utilizes two quartets of the aforementioned instrumentation. This work was recorded in one uninter-rupted thirty-six-and-a-half-minute session. The only patterns followed in this continuous free improvisation by the double quartet were a series of brief ensemble themes spaced so as to introduce each soloist in turn. The remainder of the recording consists of unpremeditated, sometimes collec-tive, improvising.

Within two years, Coleman's work had a profound effect on the two most influential saxophonists of the fifties—John Coltrane and, indirectly, Sonny Rollins. Coltrane readily admitted that Coleman showed him how to extend the range of his improvisations, and Rollins also embraced many of Coleman's improvisational principles.

Jazz/Rock Fusion

In the last ten years, Miles Davis has embraced yet another kind of jazz, a new form that is often called "electric jazz" (because of the wide use of electronic instruments), or "jazz/rock fusion," or simply "fusion music."

In 1964 Davis formed a group of younger musicians that included drummer Tony Williams, bassist Ron Carter, pianist Herbie Hancock, and saxophonist Wayne Shorter. Each of these musicians became an important figure in the fusion music of the seventies.

Davis and his group recorded the albums *Miles in the Sky* and *Filles de Kilimanjaro* in 1968. In the former, there was a hint of rock and the first use of the electric piano by Herbie Hancock. In the latter, there is the use of quasi-rock rhythms with a heavy beat at times. The next year, the Davis group recorded *In a Silent Way,* an album that utilized a number of electric instruments, including two or three electric pianos. John McLaughlin, a guitarist more closely associated with rock than jazz, was one of the musi-cians involved in this recording. *In a Silent Way* pointed in the direction that Davis was to take. In 1970 the album *Bitches Brew* was recorded. This rock-oriented recording utilized a full complement of electronic instruments and again featured the guitar of John McLaughlin. Other albums that followed in this style included *Miles at the Fillmore, Jack Johnson, Big Fun,* and *Live-Evil.*[53] Once again, Davis had changed the course of jazz.

Miles Davis' explorative, innovative approach to jazz has enabled him to continually serve as a dynamic influence on other jazz performers. At

---

[51]*Peace, Lonely Woman,* and *Congeniality* are on the album *The Shape of Jazz to Come* (Atlantic 1317).

[52]Atlantic 1367.

[53]*Miles in the Sky* (Columbia PC-9628); *Filles de Kilimanjaro* (Columbia PC-9750); *In a Silent Way* (Columbia PC-9875); *Bitches Brew* (Columbia PG-26); *Miles at the Fillmore* (Columbia PG-30038); *Jack Johnson* (Columbia PC-30455); *Big Fun* (Columbia PG-32866); and *Live-Evil* (Columbia G-30924).

Miles Davis, an important figure in both cool and free form jazz, continues to influence the jazz world with his abilities in fusion music. (Photo courtesy CBS Records.)

Herbie Hancock, pianist, played with Miles Davis during the late 1960s and continues to exert influence on fusion music. (Photo courtesy CBS Records.)

times, this influence has come to bear long range effects, but it also has come about because of the close associations other musicians have had with Davis. Herbie Hancock, who was a member of Davis' group when he began experimenting with jazz/rock fusion, later formed a group called the Head-hunters. One of the group's initial releases included a remake of an original composition Hancock recorded in the early sixties—*Watermelon Man*. The second recording was made with electric and African instruments.[54]

Other jazz/rock fusion groups include Weather Report, which included Joe Zawinul on electric piano and Wayne Shorter on reeds, and Donald Byrd and the Blackbirds, a group that was formed at Howard University with college students and that has since gained a reputation as one of the outstanding jazz/rock fusion groups.

RHYTHM AND BLUES, ROCK
AND ROLL, AND SOUL

When a young man named Elvis Presley made television appearances on the Tommy Dorsey and Ed Sullivan shows in the fall of 1955, many people heard rock-and-roll music for the first time. To them, this was the beginning of the rock-and-roll era. To others, the rock-and-roll era began somewhat earlier, during the latter part of 1954, when they saw and heard Bill Haley and his Comets perform *Rock Around the Clock* in the motion picture *Blackboard Jungle*.

The truth of the matter is that while both of the above-mentioned White artists helped rock and roll gain national prominence, the real origin of rock antedates both Elvis Presley and Bill Haley. In fact, the history of rock is largely synonymous with the development of rhythm and blues since the early part of 1954.[55]

In the spring of 1954, a group of young Black singers called The Chords recorded some songs for Atlantic Records, among them a song called *Sh-Boom*.[56] All five singers of this group were given credit for composing the song because it was written, as many rock selections have since been written, in the recording studio. Because there was some doubt about how saleable the song would be, it was released on a subsidiary label of Atlantic—Cat Records—created especially for the occasion. By July of

---

[54]Herbie Hancock, *Head Hunters* (Columbia KC-32731).

[55]The term "rock-and-roll" was reputedly coined in 1951 by a New York disc jockey named Alan Freed. Freed, who came to New York from Cleveland, worked for radio station WINS and later for WABC and pioneered the raucous, rapid-fire style of announcing that still tends to be characteristic of rock programming. He worked primarily with rhythm-and-blues records, which were aimed primarily at the segregated Black market. Freed supposedly derived the term "rock-and-roll" from an old blues, *My Baby Rocks Me With a Steady Roll*.

[56]*Sh-Boom* is available on *History of Rhythm and Blues*, Vol. 2 (Atlantic SD-8162).

1954, the record had generated enough sales across the country to break into the national *Billboard* chart of best-selling popular songs,[57] and after only three weeks on the charts it reached the top ten. While it was not the first rhythm-and-blues record of that year to make the chart (the Crows recording of *Gee* had already done so), it was the first to reach the top ten.

An indication of the impact this record had on the national audience lies in the number and variety of "cover"[58] versions that were made of *Sh-Boom*. The largest-selling cover was issued by the Crew Cuts, a White vocal group from Canada. It was released during the week in which the Chords' version reached the pop charts, and it reached the top ten itself just one week later. *Sh-Boom* was also covered by Billy Williams on Coral Records and by Sy Oliver on Bell, both of whom were pop-oriented. In addition, the cover made by Bobby Williamson even penetrated the country-and-western market. *Sh-Boom* reached England's top-twenty chart by the fall of 1954, and Stan Freeberg used it as the basis for one of his successful parodies of popular culture in the same year.

Sh-Boom was indicative of the future of pop music in several respects. It was studio-composed. It had a big rhythmic beat, which was characteristic of rhythm and blues. It touched on a theme that was to become central in teenage songs—dissatisfaction with the world as it is and the yearning for a better world: "Life can be a dream, sh-boom, sh-boom." And last, though it was initially recorded by Blacks for the segregated Black market, it had its greatest success in cover versions by White singers.

Chuck Berry. To single out any Black performer as being the most significant in the early rock-and-roll idiom is almost certain to do an injustice to the many others who have made great contributions in this phase of Black music. Therefore, at the risk of omitting many artists who have made an impact on this idiom, it is this writer's opinion that the most influential Black performer in early rock and roll was Charles "Chuck" Berry.

Berry's influence is completely distinct from that of many other Black performers in this idiom, just as his musical style is different. In fact, his musical style was a harbinger of the era that was dominated by White rock performers.

Chuck Berry's first recording was the up-tempo (fast) *Maybelline* in 1955, a recording that went on to become that rarity in the music business, a *Billboard* Triple Crown: number one on the rhythm-and-blues, country-and-western, and pop charts.

---

[57]The term *popular* is a generic term referring to a mass market while the term *pop* is simply an abbreviation and refers to the music that appeals to that mass market.

[58]A *cover* is a copy by one artist of a song previously recorded by another. The extent to which records by Black artists were covered by Whites will be discussed later in this chapter.

Because of the success of *Maybelline*, Berry began to work major theaters, night clubs, arenas, and auditoriums with prominent rhythm-and-blues shows on tour. His greatest impact on the music industry came via the medium of films, however. He appeared in such rock films as *Rock, Rock, Rock*, and *Go Johnny Go*, singing his hit tunes *Johnny B. Goode, Little Queenie*, and *Memphis, Tennessee*.[59]

Berry's style did not change over a long period of time. His lyrics were relevant to youth because they were about the realities of youth: cars, girls, school.

Unlike most rhythm-and-blues artists, Berry does not use the saxophone as an accompanying instrument. While he does use the piano and drums, his music is characterized by his piercing electric guitar. In his songs, Berry repeatedly uses an identical introductory phrase on the guitar, or a slight variation of it. He also utilizes similar guitar melodies and combinations as part of the internal structure of each song. In addition, the guitar frequently penetrates the lyrics and responds to one or two lines of a given verse. This union of voice and guitar accounts equally for the total impact of the sound.

Despite thumping rhythmic backgrounds, Berry's vocal style is not Black rhythm and blues but has a White rock-and-roll quality about it. Accordingly, it is not surprising that the White rock-and-roll group The Beach Boys adapted the melody of Berry's *Sweet Little Sixteen* for one of their early hits, *Surfin' USA*. To White groups and their followers, the Chuck Berry sound was more easily imitated and managed than that of contemporary blues singers such as Muddy Waters or Howlin' Wolf. Country star Buck Owens made a top best-seller of Berry's tune *Johnny B. Goode*, a success that suggests that Berry's style also embodies elements of country-and-western music. Although none of this is intended to minimize Chuck Berry's formidable contribution to the rock scene, it is noteworthy and socially significant that his impact and influence stem from the "whiteness" in his vocal style.

In contrast to popular ballad singers, Chuck Berry wrote both words and music of nearly all of the songs he recorded. During the 1950s, this practice gradually became common among rock-and-roll artists, and it marked a major difference between rock and roll and the other musical styles that made up the pop field.

The Chuck Berry influence was strongly felt when the English sound hit this country in 1964. An integral part of the English sound came from Chuck Berry's music; English groups like the Beatles, the Rolling Stones, and the Animals all admitted the influence of Chuck Berry on their styles.

---

[59]Most of the songs mentioned in this section, including *Maybelline, Johnny B. Goode, Memphis, Tennessee, Rock and Roll Music*, and *Roll Over Beethoven*, can be found on Chess Records (LPS 1514D), *Chuck Berry's Golden Decade*.

The Beatles recorded two of his songs, *Rock and Roll Music* and *Roll Over Beethoven*.

The urbanization of Black folk music transformed country and classic blues into rhythm and blues. Several other factors were also important in molding its musical style. They included the electrical amplification of the guitar, organ, and bass; the demise of big bands, both Black and White; and the emergence of numerous small record companies catering to the Black market.

Although rhythm and blues contained a vocal line, it was primarily music for dancing and not for listening or entertaining. Hence, words were frequently employed and manipulated for their rhythmic properties alone, often consisting of nonsense syllables.

Rhythm and blues utilized the same characteristic beat employed by Black bands of the swing era. White bands like Benny Goodman and Tommy Dorsey made use of a four-to-the-bar pattern with accents evenly distributed on the four beats.

EXAMPLE 3.27   Accents evenly distributed

By contrast, Black bands such as that of Jimmie Lunceford put extra stress on the second and fourth beats of a measure, which superimposed a two-beat feeling on the four beats. It was this afterbeat stress that rhythm and blues acquired.

EXAMPLE 3.28   Accents on second and fourth beats

By the mid-fifties, a syncopated variant of eight-to-the-bar, common in boogie-woogie, became a characteristic not only of rhythm and blues, but also of early rock and roll. Instead of spacing the eighth notes evenly, the offbeats were shortened while the stress on them was lightened.

EXAMPLE 3.29   Syncopated eight-to-the-bar pattern

Along with the appearance of this kind of rhythmic base is found the genesis of the shuffle or stomp style so characteristic of the early hits of artists like "Little Richard" Penniman (*Tutti Frutti*), Chuck Berry (*Maybelline*), and Fats Domino (*Blueberry Hill*).

Rhythm and blues was the vehicle by which the twelve-to-the-bar rhythm—consisting of four groups of eighth-note triplets, in which the first note of each set is accented—was projected as a rhythmic force in popular music.

EXAMPLE 3.30 Twelve-to-the-bar rhythmic pattern

This sound was a part of early rock and roll, especially as played by the piano in the upper register. Fats Domino's *Blueberry Hill* and the Platters' *The Great Pretender* are examples of this rhythmic style.

In later rock and roll, this pattern is modified by omitting the middle note of each set of eighth-note triplets.

EXAMPLE 3.31 Modified twelve-to-the-bar rhythmic pattern

The development of the electric bass in the mid-fifties contributed greatly to the use of these rhythms. It had been the role of the conventional string bass to underline either (1) the downbeats, (2) the afterbeats, or, as in swing, (3) all four beats.

EXAMPLE 3.32 Various bass lines employed

The electric bass guitar, which was perfected by the Fender company and is generally known as the *Fender bass* even though other companies now manufacture it, has gained a position of prominence in contemporary music. Its reduced size increased the melodic possibilities of this instrument while its electrical amplification gave a more powerful bass line to both Black and White rock.

The direct influences on rock and roll from the Black music tradition are: (1) rhythmic characteristics; (2) emphasis on percussive sound qualities; (3) call-and-response pattern; (4) characteristic vocal elements (shout, growl, falsetto); (5) blue notes; and (6) gospel chord progressions.

Before 1954, popular music consisted of three fields: rhythm and blues, pop, and country and western. With the emergence of rock and roll, the distinction among these three became increasingly fluid, and an integration of their previously separate musical characteristics took place. Rock and roll was an amalgamation of these three musical styles. Rhythm and blues contributed the beat (there was more significance in the "rhythm" of rhythm and blues than in its "blues"); country and western donated the prominent guitar; and pop music offered, at least to early rock, its idealized subject matter—images such as angels, Paradise, weddings, eternal love, and heaven (in Black rock, the lyrics tended to be more earthy). Without question, the most important of these contributions was that of rhythm and blues.

What happened to *Sh-Boom* happened again and again to other songs throughout 1954 and later. The usual pattern involved an unknown rhythm-and-blues song, by an unknown group, on an unknown label; when this song broke into the pop charts, it would be covered by pop versions. Among the many songs from the rhythm-and-blues field that were covered by White artists were the Moonglows' *Sincerely,* covered by the McGuire Sisters; Joe Turner's *Shake, Rattle and Roll,* by Bill Haley and the Comets; Etta James' *Dance With Me, Henry* and LaVern Baker's *Tweedle-Dee,* by Georgia Gibbs; Nappy Brown's *Piddily Patter Patter,* by Patti Page; the Penguins' *Earth Angel,* by the Crew Cuts; Fats Domino's *Ain't That A Shame,* the El Dorados' *At My Front Door,* and Little Richard's *Tutti Frutti,* all covered by Pat Boone; Fats Domino's *I'm Walkin',* by Rick Nelson, and his *Boll Weevil,* by Teresa Brewer; Ivory Joe Hunter's *A Tear Fell* and Sam Cooke's *You Send Me,* also by Teresa Brewer; Ray Charles' *I've Got a Woman,* by Jo Stafford with the title changed to *I've Got a Sweetie;* The Cardinals' *Wheel of Fortune,* by Kay Starr; Gene and Eunice's *Ko Ko Mo (I Love You So),* by Perry Como; and Boyd Bennett's *Seventeen,* by the Fontaine Sisters. There were many other examples.

The White pop covers of these early rock-and-roll songs tended to outsell the originals for two reasons. First, since it was the major record companies that generally sponsored the artist who did the cover material, their promotional and distribution facilities were much greater than those of the independent companies. Second, because this new music sounded strange and foreign to a majority of listeners, the pop-style imitations were able to modify its strangeness, making it more palatable to the White audience.

The integration of pop music and rhythm and blues took place on decidedly White terms. There were efforts by Whites, for instance, to censor the lyrics of certain rhythm-and-blues songs; as a consequence, rhythm and blues tended to suffer from a loss of cultural identity.

Chronologically parallel to the rock-and-roll movement was the evolution of the popular folk trend between 1958 and 1963. As the folk movement developed, it embraced the social cause of Blacks, exhibiting a deep commitment to the cause of freedom and equality regardless of race. The popular folk movement, however, was stylistically White, more so in fact than rock and roll. Consequently, there was an exclusion of Black artists from this folk form.

There was also an absence of Black artists from the era of the early sixties when English rock was so popular in this country. Groups such as the Beatles and the Rolling Stones repeatedly acknowledged the strong influence of rhythm and blues on their music, leading to a revival of some interest in Black artists among White audiences in England and the United States. The truth of the matter is that interest in Black artists on the part of White audiences never had materialized in the past because the social attitudes of White audiences and recording-company executives tended to govern the policies of record companies. It was not until very popular White groups such as the Beatles and Rolling Stones sanctioned the music of Black artists that White audiences began to embrace the music of Blacks to a limited degree. It is much more accurate to state that Black artists in the rhythm-and-blues field were "discovered" by White audiences in both countries for the first time. This initial contact with Black artists and their music came about slowly and was never as widespread as the Black contribution to rock actually deserved.

Rock and roll in the sixties contained numerous signs of a growing sophistication and was fast becoming irrelevant to the Black man because it presupposed cultural values with which he was neither familiar nor sympathetic. During this same period, Blacks were concerned with defining their own culture in its broadest terms.

A symbol of the Blacks' effort to achieve cultural definition was the emergence of the term "soul" during the latter half of the 1960s. In the Black ghetto, singers were referred to as "soul brothers" and "soul sisters." Radio stations proclaimed the "soul sound." The term was used increasingly to designate an entire field of Black music, music that spoke of and to the Black condition.

This kind of music actually became nationally popular and commercially successful. For the first time, the music of Blacks was accepted on the Blacks' terms and was not censored or modified to suit the musical taste of White audiences.

A precise, objective meaning of the word "soul" in terms of music is almost impossible to isolate, since its use depends upon personal responses. Soul is the manifestation of the bittersweet Black experience and/or Black lifestyle. Accordingly, it emerged in the sixties not only as a concept of Black identity but also of Black musical expressiveness. Black music gives the Black artist the vehicle by which he can express that profound, quasi-religious feeling.

The kinds of records that were best-sellers in the Black community from about 1965 on give every indication that soul is more a general feeling than a particular musical style. These songs ranged stylistically from the traditional blues of Albert King to the polished renditions of the Fifth

Dimension, and from the "authentic" sound of the late Otis Redding to the commercial jazz of the Ramsey Lewis Trio.

At the risk of oversimplification, the performers of soul music may be divided into two groups, one Black and the other White. The Black performers, singers and players, produce a music that is in the gospel-blues tradition. The White performers in this idiom attempt to imitate the Black soul sound. Sometimes they are successful. On other occasions, the music produced is a poor imitation. Representative performers of this group were the Righteous Brothers, the Paul Butterfield Blues Band, and Blood, Sweat and Tears.

Stylistically, soul as performed by Blacks can be further divided into two subcategories. In one soul style, it appears that a conscious effort has been made to make the performing groups popular among White audiences as well as in the Black community. The record company most representative of this approach is Motown Records. Under the direction of Berry Gordy, Jr., this completely Black-controlled company has become a major power in the record industry. Motown provided much of the foundation for soul music as it is generally known today by producing a gospel- and blues-derived style.

The decision by Motown to broaden the appeal of its recording artists may have been influenced by the phenomenal success of the Supremes, who helped to define and "Whiten" the Motown sound. While these women had a feeling for gospel harmony and a vibrant beat, their overall sound had only a tint of "Blackness," perhaps just enough to make them sound different from White singers and appeal to White audiences.[60]

The Motown sound is an admixture of rhythm and blues with pop. It uses gospel rhythms and harmonies, a pronounced afterbeat, and a tempo suitable for dances such as the Boogaloo, the Frug, the Mashed Potato, and the Watusi.[61] These Black ingredients were diluted and polished, especially through the use of strings; on many recordings of the Supremes and other groups, violins have been added through superimposition (overdubbing) in an effort to give their recordings a wider audience.

---

[60]It is extremely difficult to verbalize the characteristics of "White" or "Black" music when discussing the idioms of rhythm and blues, rock and roll, and soul music. Whether the performer is Black or White, the end product evolved from common roots—that great reservoir of Black music in general, and the rhythm-and-blues idiom immediately prior to 1954 in particular.

The White performer generally interprets the music by following somewhat more nearly the written notation, as opposed to the practice of the Black singer. Black singers often alter the melody and lyrics to achieve a more expressive reflection of their feelings. This is done in part through the use of vocal devices such as falsetto, slides, portamenti, and glissandi. Improvisation, embellishment of the melodic line, uninhibited shouting, erotic frenzy, and earthy lyrics are all characteristics of Black popular music. Generally speaking, it may be said that the performer in Black music is a creator while his counterpart in White music is an interpreter.

[61]See the section of this chapter on gospel music, where its harmonic and rhythmic characteristics are described fully.

Some of the outstanding performers involved in recordings for Motown Records were Smokey Robinson and the Miracles, Martha Reeves and the Vandellas, the Four Tops, the Temptations, Stevie Wonder, the Jackson Five, and Marvin Gaye.

The second subcategory of soul music was designed principally for the Black community and is much more earthy and raucous. The record companies most representative of this soul style were Stax Records and its subsidiary, Volt Records, neither of which is still in existence. The name Stax was formed by combining the first two letters of the surnames of its White owners, Jim Stewart and his sister Estelle Axton. It was an integrated enterprise, with a Black executive vice-president, Al Bell, and an integrated studio band.

The chief architect of this style was the late Otis Redding. His unique phrasing enabled Redding to cut across ethnic and cultural lines and appeal to both Black and White audiences. Although he made records for less than five years, in that brief period his impact was so great that, two months before his death in 1967, the English trade paper *Melody Maker* named him the World's No. 1 Male Vocalist, a title that had been monopolized during the preceding decade by Elvis Presley.[62] Some of the other performers involved in recording for Stax Records were Carla Thomas, Rufus Thomas, Sam and Dave, Albert King, Johnnie Taylor, The Emotions, and Eddie Floyd.

A second record company, Atlantic Records, superseded Stax Records as the primary representative of this earthy, unpolished approach to soul music. Although Atlantic eventually made a great contribution to the development of soul, in its early years it seemed to be moving in a pseudo-White direction. Commencing in 1958, Atlantic Records became the first company to use violins on rhythm-and-blues records.[63] They also made use of written arrangements and studio musicians, major departures from rhythm-and-blues recording practices up to that time.

After Atlantic became associated with Stax/Volt as distributor it relinquished the sophisticated rhythm-and-blues sound to companies like Motown Records and acquired a more Black, earthy, gospel-like quality. One of the artists who was instrumental in changing Atlantic's image was the singer Aretha Franklin.

Some of the many artists associated with Atlantic were Wilson Pickett, Solomon Burke, Percy Sledge, Arthur Conley, Archie Bell and the Drells, Barbara Lynn, the late King Curtis, Don Convay, Barbara Lewis, and Joe Tex.

Richard Penniman, popularly known as Little Richard, popularized a new element in rhythm and blues—gospel frenzy—that became the ear-

---

[62]A record album that demonstrates the unique Otis Redding style is *The Dock of the Bay* (Volt Records S-419).

[63]*History of Rhythm and Blues, 1947–60*, 4 records (Atlantic S 8161–8164); *History of Rhythm and Blues, 1961–67*, 4 records (Atlantic S8193–8194, S 8208–8209).

mark of Black music in the soul era. In 1955 his *Tutti Frutti* became a sensational hit and was the forerunner of a memorable list of up-tempo, shuffle tunes. By 1956, Little Richard had no fewer than four shouters that climbed to number one on the rhythm-and-blues charts. He continued his amazing streak of best-selling songs and records in 1957. In the fourth year of his dynamic rise, 1958, he had one big hit and then stopped recording. He had become interested in religion and decided to give up all performing.

After returning to the music world as a performer in 1963, Little Richard found a lack of interest in his singing style, which indicated that the rock scene had become too White-oriented to accept his combination of scat sounds and suggestive words. Once the trend turned toward more Blackness in rock-and-roll music, Little Richard was once again temporarily in great demand, this time by White audiences.

Stylistically, Little Richard is the predecessor of contemporary soul music, as his style is anchored in gospel rather than the blues. Almost every important practitioner of soul got his start in the Black church and derives hyperactive and intensely emotional qualities from this gospel source. In essence, this is Little Richard's style. Most of his records are fast-tempo shouts with a boogie shuffle.

The influence of Penniman's style ranges far and wide. In the mid-fifties, he exerted great influence on Elvis Presley, who recorded many of his songs. The Beatles were also influenced by him and recorded several of his songs, with Paul McCartney often actually singing in Little Richard's gospel-rooted style.

Perhaps the artist on whom Little Richard exerted the greatest influence was Otis Redding. Redding, who like Penniman was also a Macon, Georgia resident, was constantly aware of the Little Richard sound as he grew up in this Georgia town. From him, Otis derived his driving style, which was to become an important part of the raw soul style.

Little Richard, the epitome of flashy performers, sold more than thirty million records in less than two years.[64] As stated earlier, he was a predecessor of soul music and was a direct influence on current soul singers. Since his reentry into the popular music field in 1963, however, he has exerted very little influence on this idiom.

One of the facets of rock and roll since the late 1950s is the phenomenon of a whole series of dance fads. When rock first came into being, the prevailing dance was the jitterbug, a jazz dancing style held over from the 1940s. In the mid-fifties, Elvis Presley changed the American dancing style by adding greater eroticism to these dances. While Presley was the popularizer of the new style because of his national exposure on television

---

[64]Two albums of hit songs by Little Richard have been reissued: *Here's Little Richard* (Specialty 2100), and *Greatest Hits* (Okeh 14121).

and personal appearance tours, he was not its originator. It was instead the rhythm-and-blues singer Bo Diddley (Ellis McDaniel) who originated the swivelling hip motion copied by Presley. The first dance to originate in the rock-and-roll era was the Bop, which was greatly influenced by Presley's antics.

By the time rock and roll was three years old, it had revolutionized dancing styles. The jitterbug survived for more than a decade, but rock-and-roll dances changed overnight. In several instances, these dances were inspired by records in which the lyrics provided directions for their performance. Although each dance was characterized by specialized movements, new dances were invented so quickly that no particular style became standard.

The most important general feature of these dances was the lack of contact between partners. Partners casually faced one another and each was unrestricted in his interpretation of the music through the dance. While there was physical separation between the partners, the music served as a basic framework of the dance within which each dancer improvised.

Among the dances invented during the 1950s and 1960s were the Harlem shuffle, the Limbo, the Swim, the Fly, the Wiggle Bobble, the Duck, the Boobaloo, the Shingaling, the Funky Broadway, the Bristol Stomp, the Cool Jerk, the Freddie, the Fish, the Mashed Potato, the Watusi, the Loco-Motion, the Twist, the Madison, the Hitch Hike, the Popeye, the Frug, the Jerk, the Surfer Stomp, the Monkey, the Boston Monkey, the Shake, the Temptation Walk, the Pony, the Skate, the Bounce, the Philly Jerk, the Batman, the Gully Gully, the Waddle, the Walk, the Stomp, the Dip, the Shotgun, the Yolk, the College Yolk, the Chicken, the Funky Chicken, the Sex Machine, the Ghetto, the Football, the Funky Football, the Push and Pull, the Thing, and the Popcorn. In the seventies, there were dances such as the Bump, the Electric Twist, the Break Down, the Flintstone, the Dog, the Yoke, the Four Corners, the Guitar, the Rock, the Worm, the Swan, the Hustle, the Bus Stop, the Loose Booty, and the Robot. The list of dances given is not all-inclusive, but it is representative. Most of these dances were originated by Blacks. To the casual observer, these dances may have looked very much alike; but to the dancer, each one incorporates subtle changes and refinements.

Commercialism finally engulfed the rock-and-roll idiom to such a degree that performers were actually inventing dances through their lyrics in an effort to sell records. This, in part, accounts for the great turnover in currently popular dances. In essence, the dance was controlled by the performer rather than by the people.

Another example of the extent to which commercialism had pervaded not only the rock-and-roll movement, but the entire record industry was the revelation in 1959 through congressional hearings that executives of the record industry were paying disc jockeys to play records released by the executives' own companies. Thus, the recording industry was dictating public taste in music just as performers were dictating public taste concerning dance. This scandal and practice, which linked the record and broadcasting industries together, was popularly known as "payola."

While it becomes very difficult at times to distinguish among rhythm and blues, rock and roll, and soul music, simply because all three idioms are so closely interrelated by their common roots, they can generally be distinguished on the basis of performing style between Black and White musicians. At its inception, rock and roll was primarily Black music. As it was taken up more and more by White performers, however, it lost some of its Black character in order to make it more palatable to White audiences. At the same time, it must be pointed out that the White properties incorporated into this music did have a great influence on Black audiences as well.

So authentic rhythm and blues remained neglected and isolated for a long time, appreciated and participated in by Blacks only. Beginning with the middle sixties, "soul" music, became nationally popular and commercially successful. This latest movement in popular music has been designated by many as a rhythm and blues revival. To call this new movement a "revival" is incorrect for two reasons. Rhythm and blues had never lost popularity with Black performers or the Black community. It has continued to be a dynamic force in Black music. On the other hand, this musical style was never popular with White audiences. Therefore, it is impossible to revive an interest that never existed in the first place. In essence, commencing with the mid-sixties, rhythm and blues, of which soul music is but one component, began being discovered and listened to by White audiences for the first time.

GOSPEL SONGS

The gospel tradition was greatly influenced by the older styles of Black religious music, but its development is inextricably related to the split of Holiness groups from the orthodox Black churches. The "Holiness" or "Sanctified" groups are so-called because they emphasize living a perfect life, free from sin. The primary characteristics that differentiate them from the orthodox Black church include emphasis on healing, sanctification resulting in gifts of prophesy, speaking in unknown tongues, healing powers, and shouting and using various musical instruments within their services. The free expression of religious and musical behavior common among rural Southern Blacks began to assert itself among the Holiness groups and was further developed in an urban setting.

The Church of God in Christ of the Holiness sect was the primary influence on the emerging gospel tradition. All of these groups, however, including the Sanctified and Pentecostal sects, contributed to its development. Their innovations included the use of drums, tambourines, triangles, and guitars (the innovative use of instruments was not permitted in the orthodox Black church), an emphasis on rhythm, and a freedom of expression both in singing and dance.

The first published Black gospel songs that included both words and music were those written by Reverend C. Albert Tindley, a Methodist minister, from 1899 to 1906. (F. A. Clark was the Black arranger responsible for the written parts.) Most of his compositions were gospel songs in the conventional sense—that is, tabernacle[65] and revival songs that leaned heavily on Black spirituals. His songs were published in Baptist hymnals along with those of White composers. One widely-used song book classifies Tindley's *Stand By Me* as a spiritual; his *Nothing Between* is the same kind of song. Another of Tindley's songs, *I Do, Don't You* was sung at the National Baptist Convention in Chicago in 1921, where the response of the audience was tremendous.

The various Holiness groups used Tindley's songs as models and began to create a repertory of religious songs characterized by free interpolation on the part of the congregation and rhythmic instrumental accompaniment. Because the use of piano, guitar, and drums was regarded by orthodox Black churches as a sinful attempt to bring ragtime and blues into the church, this musical style tended to remain within the Holiness groups.

Thomas Dorsey.   Although C. A. Tindley is rightfully credited with originating this musical genre, the person who has exerted more influence on the gospel tradition than any other is Thomas A. "Georgia Tom" Dorsey (b. 1899). Composer, publisher, performer, teacher, choir director, and organizer, Dorsey has been involved with gospel music since he joined the Pilgrim Baptist Church of Chicago in 1921. Here he began a career in religious music that has made him world-renowned, even though his own church was slow in accepting his songs.

Dorsey's first successful songs were greatly influenced by the songs of Tindley. The earliest of these, *If I Don't Get There,* was published in the popular *Gospel Pearl Song Book.* The second, *We Will Meet Him in the Sweet By and By,* was included in the special edition of the *National Baptist Hymnal.* While both of these songs have the Dorsey touch of swing and bounce, they are standard tabernacle songs and contain little of the special quality that marks his more mature style.

Thomas Dorsey had previously enjoyed a career as a member of a band called the Whispering Syncopators and as piano accompanist for Ma Rainey, the foremost blues singer of her era. He also wrote her theme song,

---

[65]Tabernacle songs have texts that usually focus on a single theme. Each theme is emphasized through repetitions of individual phrases with a chorus following each stanza. The texts deal with such themes as individual conversion and assurance of salvation and heaven.

The Stormy Sea Blues, which became a popular hit. In addition, he wrote *Tight Like That* for blues singer Tampa Red, and he arranged music for the Brunswick and Vocalion recording companies.

In 1928, Dorsey began to change the style of his gospel songs, emphasizing the beat and adding blues riffs to his music. These songs sold much faster than his earlier songs. The melodies of Dorsey's mature songs came to be written as simply as possible in order to give maximum latitude to the soloist and accompanist for improvisation and individual interpretation. (The "soul-singing" style found in gospel music has a great similarity to that found in blues singing.)

Dorsey's success in the gospel music field was due not only to his ability as a songwriter, but also because he changed the format of published religious songs. Prior to this time, gospel songs were circulated by their composers on small sheets that contained only the words, while the melodies had to be learned from those who knew them. Dorsey reproduced both words and music on single sheets, which could be purchased for fifteen cents per copy.

Dorsey's contribution to this new music extended beyond publication and composition. He expended a great amount of energy in his promotional efforts to make gospel music acceptable to the orthodox Black churches. During those lean years, Dorsey also trained and accompanied scores of singers, among them Mahalia Jackson, Sally Martin, Clara Ward, and Roberta Martin.

Gospel music was banned by most of the orthodox churches, but it gradually gained acceptance after it was endorsed by the National Baptist

Thomas A. "Georgia Tom" Dorsey has exerted more influence on the gospel tradition than any other. (Photo courtesy Duncan P. Schiedt Collection.)

Mahalia Jackson, prototype of the gospel singer. (Photo courtesy Duncan P. Schiedt Collection.)

Convention in Chicago in 1930. In order to gain further respect for this new music, Dorsey created the National Convention of Gospel Choirs and Choruses, Inc. in Chicago in 1932, starting with a nucleus of some two hundred persons. Gospel music did gain respect, and its success can be measured by the success of Dorsey's songs. He has written more than four hundred and fifty songs, of which the most famous, *Precious Lord Take My Hand,* has been published in twenty-six languages and released on recordings in most European countries. In this country, Dorsey's songs have been sung and recorded by scores of White performers, among them Red Foley, The Voices of Walter Shuman, Eddie Arnold, Tennessee Ernie Ford, Morton Downey, Elvis Presley, and Fred Waring.

Gospel Style

The most prevalent opinion as to what constitutes gospel music is that it consists simply of the introduction of jazz rhythms and blues singing into religious music. It must be pointed out that secular and religious Black folk music are merely facets of a single musical culture. As in many other Black music forms, ornamental melodic devices such as swoops, slurs, smears, and glides, all of which are forms of portamento, are fundamental characteristics of the performance of gospel songs. In addition, the lead singer utilizes improvised patterns of vocal embellishment. Several of these patterns are: (1) alternating notes a minor second apart; (2) alternating notes a major second apart; (3) use of notes forming patterns of thirds and fourths; and (4) combinations of the above patterns.

EXAMPLE 3.33   Improvised patterns of vocal embellishment[66]

The nature of these melismatic passages is essentially melodic, but some of the tones used are foreign to the underlying harmonic structure. In the above musical examples, some tones (marked Au) are auxiliary tones and others (marked Ap) are appoggiaturas.

Syncopation is a prominent feature in the performance of gospel songs. Points of rhythmic stress, durational values of tones, and individual phrases in the melodic line vary. The strongest pulse, which usually occurs on the first beat of each measure, is not placed with any regularity in gospel songs as is usually done in church music in the Western tradition. This is because gospel songs employ a free, fluid rhythm.

Harmonic usage found in the gospel style includes (1) six-four chords in series, (2) incomplete chords due to the doubling of tones, or (3) the dropping out of a voice, and (4) supertonic harmony as a substitute for subdominant harmony in the cadence.

EXAMPLE 3.34   Harmonic usage in the gospel style[67]

[66]George Ricks, *Some Aspects of the Religious Music of the United States Negro: An Ethnomusicological Study with Special Emphasis on the Gospel Tradition* (New York: Arno Press, 1977), p. 296–97.

[67]Ricks, *Religious Music of the Negro.* p. 302.

The basic chords of the tonal system are employed, but harmonic usage common in the gospel style is usually avoided in the traditional hymns of the White church.

The accompanying instruments most commonly used in gospel music are the piano and organ, either together or separately. Sometimes they are supplemented by other instruments, such as the tambourine, saxophone, or trombone. There are three techniques of keyboard accompaniment found in gospel music. They are (1) an overlapping call-and-response pattern, (2) a pattern in which the basic beat is established in the bass in octave patterns while the right hand improvises octave and chord patterns, and (3) a pattern in which the inner tones move against stationary tones in the upper and lower positions.

EXAMPLE 3.35   Three techniques of accompaniment on keyboard instruments[68]

[68]Ricks, *Religious Music of the Negro*, pp. 304–5.

The instrumental accompaniment in this style also contains secondary dominants that are often avoided in Western church music.

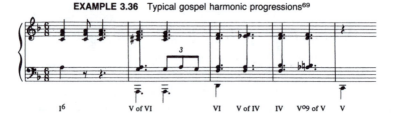

EXAMPLE 3.36   Typical gospel harmonic progressions[69]

The affinity of jazz and gospel music for each other has made it possible for many gifted Black singers who received their basic musical training in religious music, as performers in church choirs or smaller singing groups, to enter the jazz or popular fields with ease. Among those who have made the conversion are the late Dinah Washington, a former gospel singer in Chicago; Billy Williams, formerly with the Golden Gate quartet; the late Sam Cooke, formerly with the Soul Stirrers; Ray Charles, formerly of the Five Blind Boys; Sarah Vaughan, formerly a member of a Baptist choir in Newark, New Jersey; the late Nat "King" Cole, who formerly sang and played in his father's church in Chicago; Aretha Franklin, who formerly sang in her father's church in Detroit; Della Reese, formerly a performer with Mahalia Jackson who had her own gospel group; Dionne Warwick, formerly with the Gospelaires; and Lou Rawls, who formerly sang with the Pilgrim Travelers of Chicago. In addition, many of the Black rock-and-roll quartets began as gospel singing groups.

Gospel music is also closely related and similar in some ways to the older spiritual style. Gospel songs share two major characteristics with this older form of religious music. In the first place, both are emotionally inspired. Second, both are subject to individual interpretation in performance. Because free melodic, rhythmic, and harmonic interpretation are important facets of gospel music, inventiveness is a primary consideration for gospel composers and performers. Songwriters, working with a full expectation of improvisation by the performer, write the music as simply as possible, giving the performers ample opportunity for improvisation. An example of how a melodic line is embellished by a solo singer is given below, where the written melody of *What a Friend We Have in Jesus* is compared with a version sung by a gospel singer.

EXAMPLE 3.37   *What a Friend We Have in Jesus*[70]

[69]Ricks, *Religious Music of the Negro*, p. 306.
[70]Ricks, *Religious Music of the Negro*, p. 309.

The performance of most choral gospel songs is based on the overlapping leader-chorus, call-and-response pattern.

Thus, gospel music, that phenomenon of the twentieth century, spawned by the Holiness groups and rebuffed by the orthodox Black church, has become known throughout the world. In the process, its influence has transcended religious bounds and has affected popular music as well.

chapter four

The Black Musician in American Society

While Blacks in general have been compelled to endure an inferior status in American society, Black musicians have enjoyed the high esteem of a portion of this same society from early slavery times to the present. In spite of almost insuperable odds, they have been able to make outstanding contributions in the field of music. But although Black musicians have been held in high esteem by fellow White musicians, they have often failed to receive due recognition and financial rewards from society at large.

BLACK MUSICIANS PRIOR TO 1865

In 1619, with the purchase of twenty Blacks from the captain of a Dutch frigate by the settlers of Virginia, there began the importation of human beings to America against their wills that was not to stop until two hundred years later.

Virginia finally resorted to slavery only after exhausting every possibility in an effort to solve her labor problems. Indian slavery was a dismal failure, while White servants were found to be unsatisfactory both because there was not an adequate supply of them and because indentured servants

164

had to be replaced every few years as their period of service expired. While a specified period of service applied also to Indian and Black servants in the beginning, this problem was resolved by making Blacks the victims of perpetual servitude.

In the early decades of slavery, it was justified on religious grounds; in theory, when the slave was converted to Christianity, his period of servitude ended. The system was justified as an effective means of bringing the heathen slave under the influence of the Christian religion. But the effect of this doctrine would have been to destroy the system it rationalized since Blacks who readily embraced Christianity would have become entitled to their freedom. Therefore, it became necessary, in the latter part of the seventeenth century, to shift the basis of slavery from religion to race.

When the plantation, with its peculiar traditions and culture, became a way of life in certain parts of the South, it became a social as well as an industrial and political organization in which the lives of slaves and masters were intertwined in a web of social relationships. It was under such conditions that the culture of the Whites was transmitted to the Blacks and vice versa.

The extent of the acculturation process depended on the extent of contact between Whites and slaves. On larger plantations, this contact was limited to the overseer. On smaller plantations with fewer slaves, however, contact between the slave and the master and his family was much more extensive. It was in this milieu that the acculturation process began.

The Slave Musician

The eighteenth-century slave was rapidly assimilating the culture of America where there were extensive contacts between the races. The Blacks were learning to read and write the language prevalent among their masters. As an example, in New Orleans many Blacks learned French, the language of the ruling class. In addition, many slaves became skilled artisans. There is a considerable amount of evidence of the musicianship of the slave and of the use made of it in the social and civic life of each community.

Eighteenth-century advertisements for runaway slaves often indicate that they were able to play musical instruments. Some examples are:

Whereas Cambridge, a Negro Man belonging to James Oliver of Boston doth absent himself sometimes from his Master: said Negro plays well upon a flute, and not so well on a violin. This is to desire all Masters and Heads of Families not to suffer said Negro to come to their Houses to teach their Prentices or Servants to play, nor on any other Accounts. (*Boston Evening Post*, October 24, 1743.)

Run-away from Capt. Joseph Hale of Newbury, a Negro Man, named Cato, the 6th instant, about 22 years of Age, short and small, speaks good English and can read and write, . . . took with him a Violin and can play thereon. (*Boston Gazette*, July 9, 1745.)

Run-away from his Master Eleazer Tying, Esq., at Dunstable, on the 26th May past, a Negro Man Servant call'd Robin, almost of the Complexion of an Indian, . . . talks good English, can read and write, and plays on the Fiddle; . . . (*New York Gazette*, July 18, 1748.)

Run-away on the Monday the 7th of June, a likely mulatto man named Francis, of a middle stature; he is about 25 years old, . . . He can write a pretty good hand. (*Portsmouth Chronicle*, July 10, 1790.)

On the 25th ultimo, from the subscriber, living near Culpepper Courthouse, a Negro Man named Jack, about 30 years old, 5 feet 10 or 11 inches high, very muscular, full faced, wide nostrils, large eyes, a down look, speaks slowly and wore his hair cued, . . . He is artful can both read and write and is a good fiddler. (*Virginia Herald*, January 21, 1800.)[1]

The second half of the seventeenth century saw the emergence of the second generation of Virginia-born and English-speaking Blacks. Planters decided that by this time the slaves had become sufficiently "civilized" to serve in the mansion as well as in the field, and from then on Black servants directed and ran plantation houses.

Colonial planters had brought with them from England a love for entertaining. Slaves were frequently sent to the inns to extend to all who frequented them the hospitality of the plantation house.

For their music, the colonists imported from Europe their favorite instruments, which house slaves were permitted to play. Among these instruments were the fife, the violin, and the chalumeau.

As an example, Sy Gilliat, body servant to Lord Botetourt, was official fiddler at state balls. Gilliat was described as wearing:

. . . an embroidered silk coat and vest of faded lilac, silk stockings, terminating in shoes decorated with large buckles . . . and a powdered brown wig. His wardrobe consisted of fifty suites, and his manners were as courtly as his dress.[2]

Sy Gilliat's assistant was London Brigs, who was said to play the flute and clarinet[3] with equal facility. When they played their music, "sometimes a

---

[1](Anon.) "18th Century Slave Advertisements," *Journal of Negro History* I (April 1916), pp. 163–81. Used by permission.

[2]From *The Negro in Virginia*. Copyrighted, permission by Hastings House, Publishers.

[3]The instrument was probably the chalumeau. The European clarinet evolved from the chalumeau and was developed by Johann Christoff Denner of Nurnberg, Germany in the last decade of the seventeenth century. The name "clarinet" was not mentioned before 1732 in Johann Gottfried Walther's *Musicalisches Lexicon*.

'congo'[4] was danced and when the music grew fast and furious, a jig would wind up the evening."[5]

The role that slave musicians played in the social and civic life of the White community has also been documented in the travel accounts of foreigners and visitors from the North. Nicholas Cresswell, for instance, tells in his travel journal of the Black music he encountered at a ball for Whites that he attended.[6] In 1806, Thomas Ashe observed a band of Blacks playing instruments in a Virginia inn. He describes the music as sounding "Ethiopian" and reports that the Whites danced in a manner appropriate to the kind of music being played.[7]

Augustus Longstreet's description of a Black tambourinist and other musicians playing at a White ball in the 1830s is also illuminating. The tambourinist produced an effect called a "rattle snake note" with his middle finger.[8] "The musicians were all blacks, neatly dressed. The band consisted of three performers on the violin, one on the clarinet, one on the tambourine and one on the triangle."[9]

A Black band playing for square dancing by Whites is reported in an account by Caroline Gilman, who describes how they played on violins, clarinets, tambourines, triangles, and bass drum, and how they shouted above the din of the music in Negro dialect.[10]

J. S. Buckingham described a musical occasion in White Sulphur Springs, Virginia, in 1839.

> . . . the orchestra was filled by negro musicians; the bands being almost always formed of coloured people. Every door and window at which, if unoccupied, fresh air might have come in, was crowded by the negro servants of the visitors.[11]

---

[4]While this dance is identified with Blacks, it is quite possible that a dance of the same name but with somewhat different steps was performed by the ruling class.

[5]*The Negro in Virginia*, p. 36.

[6]Nicholas Cresswell, *The Journal of Nicholas Cresswell, 1775–1777* (New York: The Dial Press, 1924), p. 53.

[7]Thomas Ashe, *Travels in America, performed in 1806 for the purpose of exploring the rivers Alleghany, Monongahela, Ohio and Mississippi, and ascertaining the produce and condition of their banks and vicinity* (Newburyport, Mass.: E. Sawyer and Co., 1808), p. 315.

[8]A "rattle snake note," or "thumb roll," is a roll executed by moistening the thumb and rubbing it on the skin around the edges of the instrument, causing the jingles to vibrate.

[9]Augustus Longstreet, "The Ball," *Georgia Scenes, Charscters, Incidents, etc. in the First Half Century of the Republic* (New York: Harper and Brothers, 1840), p. 167.

[10]Caroline Gilman, *Recollections of a Southern Matron* (New York: Harper and Brothers, 1837), p. 76.

[11]James Silk Buckingham, *The Slave States of America*, Vol. II (London: Fisher, Son, and Co., 1842), p. 336.

Charles Dickens described witnessing two Black musicians entertaining White patrons in a New York saloon in 1842, one playing fiddle while the other played tambourine.[12]

B. I. Wiley cites the role of the Black body servants of soldiers in the Union Army.

> . . . a few of the body servants were sometimes called on to act as musicians for the units to which their masters were attached. Josephus Blake, servant of General John B. Gordon, said that he and two other servants provided the music to which Gordon's regiment marched. One played the fife and one beat the drum.[13]

These accounts, limited as they are, illustrate the point that Black musicians were actively engaged in the social and civic life of the community.

The Free Black Musician During Slavery

While millions of Blacks were in slavery in many sections of the New World, there were many free Blacks who were befriended and encouraged by the Whites in their communities to gain an education and participate in the arts. Many of these Blacks were gifted, trained musicians, composers and performers of outstanding ability whose compositions and performances were acclaimed in America and around the world.

Although slavery was widely practiced in the New World, there had been some free Blacks during the entire colonial period. While most Blacks were brought to the New World as slaves, many came as indentured servants and became free upon the expiration of their terms of service. Others had secured their freedom before the institution of slavery had fully developed. Many slaves, with the cooperation of their masters, were able to hire themselves out as free laborers; when they had earned enough money by this means, they were able to buy their freedom. Still others secured their freedom by simply running away.

The free Black population, however, increased from five principal sources: 1) children born of free colored persons; 2) mulatto children born of free colored mothers; 3) mulatto children born of white servants or free women; 4) children of free Negro and Indian parentage; and 5) slaves who were set free.[14] A considerable portion of the increase in the free Black population occurred simply because births outnumbered deaths.

[12]Charles Dickens, *American Notes for General Circulation* (Paris: Baudry's European Library, 1842), Chapter 6.

[13]Bell Irvin Wiley, *Southern Negroes, 1861–1865* (New Haven: Yale University Press, 1938), p. 136.

[14]John H. Russell, *The Free Negro in Virginia: 1619–1865* (1913). (Baltimore: The John Hopkins Press), pp. 40–41, cited by E. Franklin Frazier, *The Negro in the United States* (New York: The Macmillan Company, 1957), p. 59.

The chief means by which the free Black class was increased was through manumission. Slaves gained their freedom through both public and private action. A Virginia will dated 1645 is the earliest known document of this kind. One of the earliest examples of public action in freeing slaves occurred in 1770 when the legislature of Virginia conferred freedom upon a slave for discovering a conspiracy of Blacks who planned to levy war in the colony.

Many slaves were able to gain their freedom through the benevolence of free Blacks. During the last quarter of the eighteenth century, slave owners in Virginia possessed unrestricted powers to free their slaves. Frequently, free Blacks brought slave friends or relatives from a White master when they were up for sale and then liberated them. To prevent this, a law was passed that required any slave manumitted after May 1, 1806, to leave the state within the space of twelve months, the penalty for not doing so being forfeiture of freedom. Free Blacks continued to purchase their relatives and friends but held them as slaves, refusing to assist in their banishment from the state by executing a deed or will of manumission.

The amount and kind of social relationship that existed between the free Blacks and the Whites were important determining factors in the degree of acculturation of Blacks. In particular, the kind of music and musical activity developed by free Blacks reflected the extent to which they had assimilated the music and culture of the White man. As a result, there were wide variations in the kinds of music and styles of performance absorbed from White culture.

There were also wide variations in the character of the institutions of free Blacks and in their standards of behavior, which were closely related to the extent of their social isolation and to their economic status. Many free Blacks were able to overcome this isolation and assimilate White cultural values through formal education because of certain economic advantages. A few free Blacks were educated in Europe, but most attained White cultural values not through formal education but because either they or their ancestors had lived in close association with Whites, and White patterns of behavior had become incorporated into their family traditions. With each passing generation, prestige values among free Blacks were based more and more on White values, which in turn had a great effect on their musical values, styles, and activities.

While most communities denied free Blacks any extensive social contact with Whites, New Orleans was an exception to this fact. The free Blacks of New Orleans, because they were largely of mulatto origin, constituted a separate or intermediate stratum in the community. The origin of this group is due primarily to the association between Spanish and French settlers and Black and Indian women because of a scarcity of White women. This free mulatto population was later augmented by thousands of well-to-do and cultured mulatto refugees from Haiti in 1809 and 1810.

An important source of social mixing was the quadroon balls, which males of mulatto origin were not permitted to attend. Only the quadroon women, accompanied by their mothers or female chaperons, were permitted at the balls, which were patronized by White men. The quadroons were either young women whom White men were keeping as concubines or those who were eligible for such relations. Free mulatto men could gain admittance only in their capacity as musicians; consequently, many of them became professional musicians.

Most of the mulattoes identified with Whites through blood and culture; and therefore, they set themselves apart from slaves and free Blacks. They were not only proud of their racial heritage but also believed that their "cultural achievements" exceeded those of their Black counterparts.

While free Black musicians of outstanding ability were to be found in many cities (for instance, Philadelphia), especially during the nineteenth century, New Orleans produced a disproportionately large number of notable Black musicians. The music of free Blacks of New Orleans reflects not only the assimilation of White culture, but also the kind of training received by many Blacks in the conservatories of Paris.[15]

The free Blacks of New Orleans were able to send their sons to France for musical training because of their secure economic position. As an indication of their affluence, in 1860 the amount of property owned by them amounted to about fifteen million dollars.

The Chevalier de Saint-Georges.   There is some evidence concerning the kind of music written by free Blacks who were trained in the Parisian conservatories. The most notable example is the music of Joseph Boulogne Chevalier de Saint-Georges (1739–99). Saint-Georges, though not born in New Orleans but in Basse-Terre, Guadeloupe, was a mulatto who received his musical education in Paris. He was a violin pupil of Leclair and studied composition with Gossec.

Saint-Georges wrote numerous compositions. Among them are six string quartets, fifteen concertos for violin, one concerto for bassoon, four operas, one sonata for harp, six sonatas for violin, three sonatas for harpsichord or fortepiano, three symphonies, and eleven symphonies concertantes. Additional works include various romances, airs, duos, etc.

The string quartets by Saint-Georges generally have only two movements, a sonata-allegro and a minuet or rondo, utilized by many contemporary eighteenth-century composers, including Johann Christian Bach and Francois Gossec. His quartets are written in a clear, flowing style.

---

[15]The nineteenth century was the period of the great popularity of Blackface minstrelsy practiced by Whites. As a consequence, many free Blacks felt a compulsion to give the lie to the characterization of the Black man that these minstrels were popularizing in England as well as in the United States. By embracing the music of the cultured White man, the Blacks set out to prove that they were capable of producing all kinds of music.

EXAMPLE 4.1   Beginning of rondo, first quarter, Op. 1, No. 1[16]

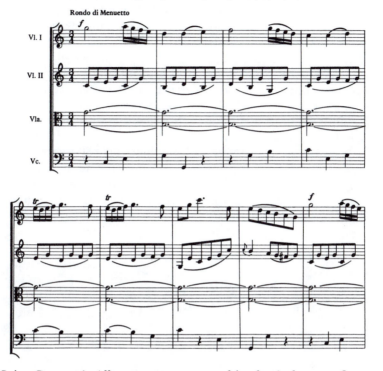

Saint-Georges's *Allegros* are constructed in classical sonata form upon two themes, the exposition ending in the dominant. Following the development, the thematic material is recapitulated in the tonic key.

The composer's concertos are in three movements: *Allegro, Adagio* or *Largo,* and, generally, *Rondeau.* His themes, in their inflections and cadences, at times recall those of Gluck.

EXAMPLE 4.2   Beginning of Andante, concerto[17]

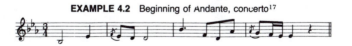

There are nine surviving *symphonies concertantes* by Saint-Georges, two others having disappeared. These are concerto-like works written for two principal violins and orchestra.

Of the nine sonatas known to have been composed by Saint-Georges, three are called sonatas for harpsichord or fortepiano "with violin accom-

---

[16]Lionel de la Laurencie, "The Chevalier de Saint-Georges," trans. Frederick H. Martens, *Musical Quarterly* V, 1 (January 1919), p. 82. Examples 4.1 and 4.2 used by permission.
[17]*Ibid.,* p. 83.

paniment." In these sonatas, the violin does not actually play a secondary role as an accompanying instrument but collaborates on fairly equal terms throughout. Six are violin sonatas. The sonatas are in two movements: an initial *Allegro* followed by a Minuet or *Rondo*. The *Allegro* movements, like those of the string quartets, are constructed in sonata form.

Saint-Georges was among the most brilliant of French *virtuosi* on the violin. His technical skill included particularly the ability to play chordal passages at a rapid tempo and shift quickly from the extreme upper register of the instrument to the lower register with no difficulty.

Even though most of the music that was composed and performed by free Black musicians from New Orleans between 1800 and 1865 is no longer available, a sufficient quantity is still extant. The surviving music is very similar to that of contemporary White composers, indicating that the free Black composer of New Orleans was imitative and tended to use little of his Black heritage.

EXAMPLE 4.3   Lucien Lambert, *Au Clair De La Lune*[18]

LUCIEN LAMBERT, Op. 30.

[18]James Monroe Trotter, *Music and Some Highly Musical People* (Boston: Lee and Shepard, 1878), pp. 69–77.

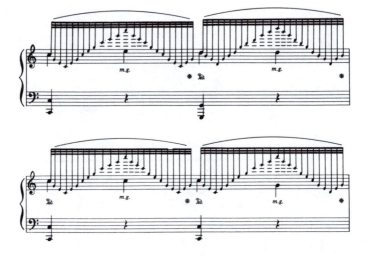

The economic status of free Blacks was not the same in all sections of the country. In the North, their economic status was less favorable than in the South because of the competition of White labor. In addition, northern Blacks were frequently the objects of violence on the part of White workers, especially during periods of economic depression.

In spite of these almost intolerable conditions, free Blacks were able to become accomplished musicians and composers. Some received excellent press notices not only in this country but also abroad. In fact, several of these performers gave command performances before English royalty.

Noteworthy among Black performers from the North were Thomas J. Bowers, tenor; Elizabeth Taylor Greenfield, soprano; John T. Douglas, violinist; Benjamin J. Janey, tenor; J. M. Holland, guitarist; Marie Selika, coloratura soprano; and Peter P. O'Fake, violinist. Among accomplished performers from the South were Richard Lambert, conductor; his sons, Lucien, John, and Sidney Lambert, instrumentalists; Maurice J. B. Doublet, violinist; McDonald Repanti, pianist; Henry Corbin, violinist; Thomas Green "Blind Tom" Bethune, pianist; Eugene Convertie, pianist; and Constantin Deberque, conductor.

BLACK MUSICIANS
AFTER THE CIVIL WAR

For two centuries White Northerners and Southerners had subscribed to the view that Blacks were of a permanently inferior type. Since slavery had been concentrated in the Southern states, Southerners had based their defense of the institution along lines of Black inferiority.

In their effort to keep the slaves in their place, Southern slaveholders found their task complicated by the presence of several hundred thousand Blacks who were not slaves. To make sure that they did not become a threat to the slave regime, free Blacks were denied the full rights and privileges of citizens. For these Blacks, there was no equality in the courts, no right to assemble, no freedom of mov   it without restrictions, and no free education.

Outside the South, free Blacks fared only slightly better. While opportunities for Blacks to secure an education increased in the nineteenth century, most schools were segregated. There were also many instances of the segregation of Blacks by White denominations in the churches. In addition, many acts of violence were perpetrated against the Blacks in many cities, among which were Detroit; Portsmouth, Ohio; Philadelphia; and Utica, Palmyra, and New York City, New York.

Following the close of the Civil War, the former slaves simply augmented the class of free Blacks. Whites attempted to apply to the former slaves the identical principles and practices that had been used against free Blacks before the war.

The Black Musician and Minstrelsy

Minstrelsy, which originated among the Blacks as entertainment for White masters on the slave plantations of the South, came to the White American stage as an invidious imitation of Blacks by White actors. Minstrelsy perpetuated the image of the Black man as a shuffling, loud-laughing, dancing, continuously grinning buffoon.

Although minstrelsy was of Black origin and born of Black music, the Black performer did not participate in the commercial minstrel show to any great extent until after the Civil War. Even then, because of the unchanged attitudes of Whites, the liberation of the Black performer from the public conception of his role was still a long way off. Consequently, these Black performers imitated the performances of White minstrels during the preceding twenty-five years, including blacking their faces.

When the Black musician came into prominence in minstrelsy, it was as part of all-Black minstrel companies. The first successful group of this kind was the Georgia Minstrels, which was organized in 1865 by George B. Hicks. This company, with many changes of personnel, was reorganized on three different occasions, with changes in name. After the first reorganization, it was known until 1878 as Callender's Georgia Minstrels. It was then bought by Jack Haverly and became known as Haverly's European Minstrels. Finally, in 1882, this company was reorganized as Callender's Consolidated Minstrels. Three European tours were undertaken—in 1876, 1880, and 1882—that made them world-famous. Although the company is said to have included outstanding managers, comedians, and dancers, the musicians are of prime importance here. At the height of its success, around 1876, the Georgia Minstrels consisted of twenty-one performers, most of them trained musicians. They performed music of the concert repertoire in concert halls and attracted the cultivated musical public. Whenever it was possible to combine serious music with the stereotype of minstrelsy in their programs, it was done. In fact, this company was recognized for its contrast with the purely slapstick performances of other companies.

Other large and famous Black minstrel companies of the 1890s included the Hicks and Sawyer Minstrels, the Richards and Pringle Minstrels, and the McCabe and Young Minstrels.

As indicated earlier, although there were a few Black minstrel performers on the American stage before the Civil War, there was still active prejudice against Blacks as stage performers long after the war had ended. This was partly because of the personal attitudes of White theater owners against the hiring of Black performers and partly because of their reluctance to hire Black actors for fear of driving White patrons away from the theater.

James A. Bland.   There were many Black songwriters of this period who used the minstrel show merely as a vehicle to get their songs before the public. Among them was James Bland (1854–1911), the foremost Black composer of minstrel songs.

Bland, born in Flushing, New York, moved with his family to Washington, D.C. He became a page in the House of Representatives and later attended Howard University. After teaching himself to play the banjo, Bland spent many hours composing and singing his songs to his own accompaniment. Often he was invited to perform at the parties of Washington notables and before members of several private clubs.

Bland had long dreamed of a career on the stage as a minstrel. When he sought a job, however, he was turned down because he was Black. He eventually left college to join Haverly's European Minstrels. On tours with this group, Bland introduced many of his songs, for which he had written both the lyrics and the melodies. They were an immediate success. His first songs are the ones for which he is best remembered: *Carry Me Back to Old Virginny* (1878), *Oh, Dem Golden Slippers* (1879), *In the Evening by the Moonlight* (1879), and *Hand Me Down My Walking Cane* (1880). Many of Bland's other songs were appropriated and presented as their own by other minstrel players.

In 1881 Bland toured England with the Haverly troupe and was such a success that he decided to stay. Dispensing with the blackface makeup he had worn as a minstrel, Bland toured the music halls and theaters of England and the Continent as a singer and banjoist. Germany especially enjoyed Bland's performances. He played His Majesty's Theater in Lon-

James A. Bland, the foremost Black composer of minstrel songs. (Photo courtesy Fisk University Library's Special Collections.)

don and was called for command performances before Queen Victoria and the Prince of Wales.

Bland enjoyed a highly successful career in England. Consequently, he was able to give help to young performers attempting to get a start in show business. When he returned to the United States in 1901, his money was gone. He worked for awhile in a clerical job in Washington and then made one last attempt to resume his career by appearing in the musical, *The Sporting Girl.* He then moved to Philadelphia where he died. Bland was buried in an unmarked grave in a Black cemetery in Marion, Pennsylvania.

In 1939 the American Society of Composers, Authors, and Publishers (ASCAP) located Bland's grave and erected a headstone identifying him as the prolific composer of almost seven hundred songs. (The Library of Congress lists only fifty-three of them.) One, *Carry Me Back to Old Virginny,* was adopted in 1940 as the official song of the state of Virginia. Before its adoption, the song was commonly accepted as the work of White composer Stephen Foster.

Black Musical Comedy

Developments in Black minstrelsy in the years of its peak success had strong implications for the American musical stage. Black musicians and performers, as so often has been the case in American musical history, played an important role in bringing about these changes.

Black musical comedy had its inception in 1890 when Sam T. Jack, a White producer, conceived the idea of a Black show that would glorify

Black girls. Jack recruited Sam Lucas, Fred Piper, Billy Jackson, and Irving Jones, all well-known minstrel performers, and a chorus of sixteen beautiful Black girls and opened *The Creole Show*. This was the first show to give prominence to Black girls and to use up-to-date songs and jokes, though it was still cast in the traditional minstrel pattern. It enjoyed a run near Broadway for four or five successful seasons.

The second effort of a similar kind was *The Octoroons*, produced by John W. Isham, another White producer. This show departed more from the minstrel format than its predecessor by having a thin thread of a story and by using Black women in starring roles as well as in chorus numbers.

Isham then produced *Oriental America*, the first all-Black show to play Broadway and the first to make a definite break with a minstrel traditions. The show concluded with a medley of operatic selections, and thus demanded good singers as well as clever comedians. The stage was now set for genuine Black musical comedy written and produced by Blacks.

Will Marion Cook.   Will Marion Cook (1869–1944) played a significant role in establishing Black musical comedy on Broadway. His efforts in this direction culminated with his production of *Clorindy, the Origin of the Cakewalk* in 1898 at the Casino Roof Garden. The show, with music by Cook and lyrics by Paul Laurence Dunbar, created a sensation on Broadway.

Will Marion Cook played an important role in establishing Black musical comedy on Broadway. (Photo courtesy New York Public Library, Schomburg Collection of Negro Literature.)

Cook was well-prepared for the role he was to play in the production of Black musical comedy. He studied violin at Oberlin Conservatory, attended the Hochschule in Berlin for three years where he studied with the renowned violinist Joseph Joachim, and then did further work at the National Conservatory of Music in New York, studying harmony and counterpoint with John White and composition with Dvořák.

Cook was the chief composer for a succession of musical comedies following *Clorindy*. Most of them featured the celebrated vaudeville team of George Walker and Bert Williams and their theatrical company. Among the librettists and lyricists for these productions were Dunbar, James Weldon Johnson, Alex Rogers, Jesse Shipp, and Harry Smith, and songwriters J. Leubrie Hill and James Vaughn. His first three attempts after *Clorindy*—*Jes Lak White Folks* (to his own libretto, 1899), *The Casino Girl* (1900), and *The Policy Players* (1900)—were not as successful. Thereafter came three hits: *In Dahomey* (1902), a satire on the American Colonization Society's movement to take Blacks back to Africa; *In Abyssinia* (1906), again set in Africa, with a huge cast including live camels; and *In Bandana Land* (1907), a spoof on Black life in the South. *In Dahomey* opened in Times Square on Broadway, the first Black musical comedy to do so.

Two later musical comedies by Cook were *In Darkeydom* (1914) and *The Cannibal King*, which was never produced. His shows contained songs that became very popular both with theatergoers and the nation at large. In addition, his early shows helped to popularize the cakewalk, which became the dance craze of the United States and Europe for several years. Among the songs that became popular were *Who Dat Say Chicken in Dis Crowd?*, *That's How the Cakewalk's Done, Emancipation Day, Darktown's Out Tonight*, and *Swing Along*.

In 1912, Cook published *A Collection of Negro Songs*, which included *Rain Song, Exhortation—A Negro Sermon, My Lady*, and *Wid de Moon, Moon, Moon*. Cook collaborated with his son Mercer to write a Black folk opera, *St. Louis Woman*, in 1929. It was based on Black life along the Mississippi in the 1890s.

J. Rosamond Johnson.   Another Black composer active in musical comedy was J. Rosamond Johnson (1873–1954). Johnson, the brother of the novelist, playwright, and poet James Weldon Johnson, was born in Jacksonville, Florida. Educated at the New England Conservatory, Johnson was also a stage performer, having performed in Oriental America on the vaudeville circuit. In addition, he collaborated with his brother to write songs, including *Lift Every Voice and Sing* (1901), often referred to as the "Negro National Anthem."

Another of Johnson's collaborators was William Cole (1863–1911), singer, actor, dancer, writer, and stage manager. Cole is also known for presenting the first all-Black, full-length musical comedy, *A Trip to Coon*

J. Rosamond Johnson was another Black composer active in musical comedy. (Photo courtesy New York Public Library, Schomburg Collection of Negro Literature.)

Town (1898), which was also the first show to be written, organized, produced, and managed by Blacks. It broke away from the minstrel tradition by having a genuine plot involving some character development, as well as songs, dances, and pretty girls.

The collaboration of the Johnson brothers and Cole resulted in the writing of show tunes and popular songs. In 1903 *The Evolution of Ragtime,* subtitled "a musical suite of six songs tracing and illustrating Negro music," was produced. Among their most impressive shows were *The Shoo-Fly Regiment* (1906) and *The Red Moon* (1908), written in the mainstream Broadway style without minstrel comedy scenes.

The Johnson brothers and Cole were signed by Joseph W. Stein and Company to a three-year contract. Believed to be the first contract between Black songwriters and a Tin Pan Alley publisher, it included guaranteed monthly payments. Many singers and performers used their songs. For Anna Held, they wrote *The Maiden with the Dreamy Eyes;* for Lillian Russell, *The Maid of Timbuctu;* for Bert Williams, *My Castle on the Nile;* for Marie Cahill, *The Congo Love Song* and *Under the Bamboo Tree;* for Fay Templeton, *Fishing;* for George Primrose, *Didn't He Ramble;* and for Klaw and Erlanger productions, *The Sleeping Beauty* and *Humpty Dumpty.* Johnson wrote only one more musical show, *Mr. Lode of Kole* (1909).

Johnson published two collections, *Shout Songs* (1936) and *Rolling Along in Song* (1937), and he collaborated with his brother on two others, *The Book of American Negro Spirituals* (1925) and *The Second Book of Negro Spirituals* (1926). His best-known choral work is *Walk Together Children,* for chorus and orchestra. In the latter years of his remarkable career, which brought him equal popularity in England, he played in *Porgy and Bess,* *Mamba's Daughters,* and *Cabin in the Sky.*

Gussie Davis

The success of the Johnson-Cole team in Tin Pan Alley followed that of Gussie L. Davis (1863–99). Davis was born in Dayton, Ohio. He first worked as a Pullman porter and later took a job as a janitor at the Cincinnati Conservatory of Music. This job put Davis in close contact with music, and he soon learned musical notation. Davis wrote over three hundred songs and was one of the most popular songwriters during the 1890s.

Davis' initial songs were published by a small printer in Cincinnati. Among them were *'Neath the Maples Long Ago* (1886), *In a Lighthouse by the Sea* (1886), *Wait Till the Tide Comes In* (1887), and *The Hermit* (1888), which were all fairly successful. Having come to New York in 1890, Davis began publishing songs with the Edward B. Marks firm. His first song to become popular was *The Fatal Wedding* (1893), an elaborate composition with a *maestoso* introduction including excerpts from Mendelssohn's *Wedding March* and chime effects. Beyond question, his most successful composition was *In the Baggage Coach Ahead* (1896). The actual incident on which the song was based took place on a train on which Davis worked as a porter. It proved to be a sensation, becoming extremely popular all over the country. Other songs included *Picture 84* (1894), *Parted at the Altar* (1895), *Down in Poverty Row* (1895), *Beyond Recall* (1896), *If I Could Only Blot Out the Past* (1896), *When I Do de Hoochy Koochy in de Sky* (1896), *Get on Your Sneak Shoes, Children* (1898), and *My Creole Sue* (1898).

Black College Musical Groups

The Black spiritual, contemporary of the comic "jig-song and dance," was contrary to the stock conception of Black character and status and therefore was ignored by most Whites. A further cause of White ignorance was that in many instances Black congregations did not allow Whites to witness, much less transcribe, their melodies; they simply refused to sing. But indifference to the Black spiritual, for whatever reason, was not confined to Whites. There were many Blacks of this period, especially the educated, who attempted to ignore the spiritual as though it no longer existed. Some Blacks found the lyrics to certain spirituals objectionable; others felt the institution of slavery had been so degrading to them and their ancestors that they preferred having nothing to do with anything that reminded them of the past.

Fisk University was established in 1866 at Nashville, Tennessee for the purpose of aiding in the education of newly freed slaves. During its early years, Fisk struggled to stay in existence. Not only did it have to contend with the general antipathy of Southern Whites toward the idea of

The Fisk Jubilee Singers "rediscovered" the spiritual and brought it new respectability. (Photo courtesy Fisk University Archives.)

educating the Blacks, but the Ku Klux Klan was actually burning schools established for Blacks and murdering and intimidating persons associated with the movement for Black schools.

George L. White, one of several northern White army officers assigned to the school after the war to aid in the education of these Blacks, formed a group of singers at the school. Its purpose was to perform classical music at Fisk, in Nashville, and in neighboring towns. At White's request, the group ended each rehearsal with a spiritual.

After the Fisk singers, initially known as the Nashville Students, had developed into a first-rate musical group, it was decided to take them on tour in 1871 for the purpose of raising funds for the struggling school. In the beginning, the tour did not go well, as very few turned out to hear them. After reaching Oberlin, Ohio, where the group was to sing for a religious meeting, White decided they should sing some spirituals, though many of the singers were reluctant to do so for fear that the listeners would laugh at them. Their performance of *Steal Away* captivated the audience, and they were an instant success. During the remainder of the tour, people turned out by the thousands to see and hear the Jubilee Singers, as they were now called. Because of the success of the tour, the group was able to raise $150,000 and save the school. In succeeding years, the group toured Europe and England and gave command performances for kings and queens.

As a result of the "rediscovery" of the spiritual by the Fisk Jubilee Singers and their audiences, the slave songs gained respectability and acceptance from Blacks and Whites alike and some of the most characteristic products of Black music were salvaged.

In 1874, Hampton Institute of Hampton, Virginia, sent a group of singers north to raise money for their school. Soon afterwards, Tuskegee Institute of Tuskegee, Alabama, and other Black colleges sent their choirs on similar tours. These groups not only raised much badly-needed money for their respective institutions but also made contributions to the promotion of Black music. These schools have continued to sponsor outstanding singing groups up to the present time, though their musical emphasis has shifted away from the spiritual and the repertoire has expanded to include all kinds of music.

The Black Musician and the European Concert Tradition

While the Black musician was becoming a vital force in minstrelsy for the first time in the period following the Civil War and college musical groups were helping to promote Black music by including the Black spiritual in their concert repertoire, many Black musicians were still very active as composers and performers of music in the European tradition. While a few Blacks continued to go abroad for musical training, many were now receiving their musical education in the conservatories of this country.

Among the Black musicians who were significant as concert performers in the nineteenth century were Anna Madah and Emma Louise Hyers, soprano and contralto respectively; Wallace King, tenor; John Lucca, bass-baritone; Nellie E. Brown, soprano; Flora Batson, soprano; Madame Marie Selika (née Mary Smith), soprano; Frederick P. White, pianist; William H. Bush, organist; M. Hamilton Hodges, baritone; Sidney Woodward, tenor; and Rachel Walker, soprano.

More Black performers were able to excel on the concert stage as singers than as instrumentalists. There are two probable reasons for this. First, a concert instrumentalist must usually have started training at an early age with a competent teacher and an excellent instrument. Because of social and economic reasons, most blacks did not have the advantage of an early start. Second, it was natural for Blacks to excel as singers because of their long and important singing tradition, which pervaded all aspects of the religious, social, and domestic life of most Blacks.

BLACK MUSICIANS IN THE TWENTIETH CENTURY

During the nineteenth century, in an effort to assimilate the White culture, many Black musicians imitated White music, intent on proving that they were capable of producing all kinds of music. With the advent of the twentieth century, this situation reversed itself to some degree. It was now the White musician's turn to imitate Black music. While such efforts at imitation were highly complimentary to the Black musician's ability, American society refused to accord these same Black musicians the recognition due them. Thus, as will be documented, the Black musician's aspirations have continually been frustrated in the twentieth century.

The same kinds of social attitudes that were prevalent in the middle of the nineteenth century continued to prevail during the twentieth century. We have seen how, in minstrelsy before the Civil War, Whites imitated Blacks by the use of Black-type songs and Black caricature, yet barred Blacks from the American stage. This was to be the model for a common sequence of events.

The Black Musician in Jazz, Blues, and Popular Music

Paul Whiteman, the White bandleader, made jazz semirespectable by giving a jazz concert in 1924 at Aeolian Hall, New York City, a stronghold of European symphonic music. This was perhaps Whiteman's major contribution to the development of jazz.

In the 1930s, White swing bands received lucrative hotel engagements and enjoyed huge financial success. By contrast, all-Black bands were forced to play "one-nighters" (performing in a different town each night) with poor eating and sleeping accommodations and low pay. A further paradox is that many of the White bands of this period owed much of their success to Black arrangers, such as Fletcher Henderson, Don Redman, Sylvester Oliver, and others.

William Grant Still, the distinguished Black composer, enjoyed a career as an arranger for many jazz bands before turning to the composition of symphonic music, and he described the role of the Black arranger as follows:

> Some of the "unsung heroes" of popular music . . . are the arrangers, many of them colored. They are paid for their work, and sometimes get public credit for it. I am told, however, that very few bandleaders will not succumb to temptation and place their own names on an arranger's work—or a composer's—if they think they can get away with it.[19]

In discussing further the plagiarism of music arranged and composed by Black musicians, Still relates,

> Years after I had left New York, I heard some of my arrangements over the radio, parading under the pseudonym then being used by the man who had

[19]William Grant Still, "The Men Behind American Music," *The Crisis* 51, No. 1 (January 1944), pp. 12–13.

employed me as an arranger over a long period of time. I had naturally been paid for every arrangement, but there was certainly no agreement that in accepting such payment I was selling my identity as arranger. No financial remuneration can pay a man amply for anonymity. On a subsequent radio program I heard an announcer say that this same former employer of mine had *originated* a style of orchestration that has since been widely copied in American music when, as far as I knew, he has never made an orchestration in his life and had depended on me even to select many of the compositions to be orchestrated.[20]

The exploitation of the Black musician through his music did not end with the demise of swing. In the late 1940s, Miles Davis' style of "cool" jazz was adopted by a group of West Coast musicians who were predominantly White. The musicians in this group became known as the West Coast School of jazz and enjoyed nationwide popularity among jazz buffs. While this group of White musicians was highly successful, Miles Davis, the Black originator of the style, was merely receiving recognition by other musicians and not by the American public.

Many Black jazz musicians, seeing no change in the attitudes of Whites toward them as performers, decided to go to Europe to perform and live. There they received the acclaim and recognition that always seemed to escape them in this country.

Even in the blues, a form indigenous to Black culture, American society has failed to give the Black musician the recognition and the accompanying financial rewards he so richly deserves. Many White artists are often given lucrative recording contracts by the major record companies even though they have demonstrated only so-so ability in this idiom. The Animals, the Rolling Stones, Janis Joplin, and a number of groups performed out-and-out blues numbers taken from records by Jimmy Reed and Howling Wolf. The Rolling Stones still include blues like Robert Johnson's *Love in Vain* among their offerings. Other blues performers who are White include Johnny Winter (who supposedly received a $600,000 contract before he recorded a note); John Fahey; Jo-Ann Kelly (British); Eric Clapton; The Cream; Blood, Sweat and Tears; Paul Butterfield Blues Band; Canned Heat; and the Righteous Brothers. On the other hand, Black performers such as Albert King, an undisputed master of the blues, have generally been denied lucrative recording contracts.

When rock and roll was a commodity performed by Black musicians for Blacks only, it was called "rhythm and blues." Around the middle of the 1950s, when White performers began to imitate this kind of music, record companies immediately began to promote these White artists to the nation at large. But despite discrimination on the part of the record companies, several Black artists have been able to attain considerable wealth and fame, among them James Brown, Diana Ross, the Temptations, and Marvin Gaye.

[20]*Ibid.*, p. 15.

While the Black jazz musician has suffered rejection in many ways, the art form itself has also been rejected by many people. Blacks, with whom jazz is correctly associated, are a low-status group in the United States. Consequently, jazz has a low status and, as a result, is often rejected by American society.

It is interesting to note, however, that as rhythm and blues and rock and roll gain ascendency in terms of money and general popularity, jazz, which was becoming a lost art form in many circles, is gaining in respectability, just as the *gavotte, sarabande,* and other dance forms gained respectability. This new respectability of jazz is evidenced in many ways. More and more music educators are stressing jazz through the formation of stage bands in schools throughout the country. Many Young Audiences groups are engaging jazz ensembles to give concerts in schools, in addition to the usual classical music groups. Duke Ellington was given much-deserved honorary degrees by Washington University in St. Louis in 1965 and Columbia University in 1973. It is highly ironic that as jazz has seemed to wane in general popularity, it has gained in respectability.

The Black Musician and Symphony, Theatre, and Television Orchestras

The Black musician has been denied employment in various kinds of orchestras in this country. The symphony orchestras, both major and minor, those orchestras employed by Broadway shows in New York City, and the orchestras operated by the television networks have been reluctant to hire Black musicians.

In the last few years, however, many of the major orchestras[21] have been eager to hire at least one Black musician, perhaps to present him as an example of their "non-biased" hiring policy. Usually the practice has been to hire only one, and at the most no more than two, Black musicians at any given time. Presently, Black musicians are playing or have played with the major symphony orchestras of Denver, St. Louis, Boston, Cleveland, Philadelphia, Dallas, Baltimore, Buffalo, Kansas City, Los Angeles, and New York among others.

The overt exclusion of Blacks by Whites from these orchestras is only one facet of the problem. Indirectly, Blacks have been excluded from symphony orchestras because of the length of time needed to be trained as an orchestral instrumentalist. A classical musician must start training at an early age with an excellent teacher and a good instrument, advantages generally unavailable to Blacks for social and economic reasons.

[21]The "Major orchestra" classification was defined as of June 30, 1971, by the Major Symphony Managers' Conference as referring to those orchestras operating on annual budgets of $1,000,000 and over, and which pay their musicians on a weekly basis under a season contract. There are twenty-eight major orchestras in the U.S.

In addition, there are so few jobs available to Black musicians in the concert field that there is little incentive to study instruments like the violin, oboe, or bassoon. Many Blacks who are potentially able to play in symphony orchestras do not continue studying because they see no opportunities in this area.

When the Black child attends a symphony concert, he has few figures to emulate, since there is often no Black person on stage. Consequently, he may not be motivated to become an orchestral musician.

It is difficult for the Black musician to get the experience necessary for important jobs. A musician generally works his way up to an orchestra like the New York Philharmonic through the minor orchestras,[22] but chances for the Black musician to do this are limited. (By contrast, Black singers or solo pianists can learn the repertoire on their own, since they perform alone or with a single accompanist.)

While this situation has changed somewhat, it has changed much too slowly. The Chicago Symphony Orchestra does maintain a first-rate training orchestra that has several Blacks enrolled. In St. Louis, the Gateway Symphony Orchestra, a community orchestra under the baton of William Schatzkamer, has had Black musicians among its membership since its inception in 1963. The late Benjamin Steinberg, former conductor of the Symphony of the New World in New York, not only trained many Black musicians but placed a few of his players in orchestras such as the Syracuse, Baltimore and American Symphony Orchestras. In addition, Black musicians perform with the orchestras at Tanglewood, Massachusetts, and Interlochen, Michigan.

Black Conductors. There has been a similar lack of job opportunities for Black conductors. Until recently, the door has been completely closed to those Blacks who aspired to become conductors of concert orchestras in the United States.

Dean Dixon (1915–76) left this country in 1948 because of his inability to secure a permanent post as conductor. He had a decade of conducting experience behind him, including highly praised appearances with the NBC Symphony Orchestra and the New York Philharmonic. Opportunities were said to be opening up in America for American conductors, but they were not opening up for him. He moved to Europe and spent twenty-eight years conducting in Europe and Australia. He was conductor of the Göteborg Symphony in Sweden from 1953 to 1960 and resident

[22]The minor orchestras are divided into two categories—Metropolitan Symphony Orchestras and Urban Symphony Orchestras. The Metropolitan Orchestra classification includes those orchestras operating on annual budgets of between $100,000 and $500,000. The Urban Orchestra classification includes orchestras operating on annual budgets of between $50,000 and $100,000. These orchestras have been surveyed to determine to what extent Black musicians are employed. With about half of the orchestras responding in the survey, the rate of employment of Blacks was found to be about equal to that of the major orchestras.

Dixon: (Photo courtesy New York Public Library, Schomburg Collection of Negro Literature.)

Black conductors of concert orchestras include Dean Dixon, Isaiah Jackson, Henry Lewis, Paul Freeman, and James De Preist.

Jackson: (Photo courtesy Whitestone Photo, New York.)

Lewis: (Photo courtesy New Jersey Symphony Orchestra.)

Freeman: (Photo courtesy Detroit Symphony Orchestra.)   De Preist: (Photo courtesy ICM Artists, Ltd.)

conductor of the Hesse State Radio Orchestra in Frankfurt, West Germany, from 1961 to 1975. Dixon also conducted in Sydney, Australia, and has been invited back to the United States in recent years to make guest appearances as conductor with various major orchestras.

Everett Lee is another Black conductor who tried unsuccessfully to pursue a career in America. Lee became a successful conductor of the Norrköping Symphony in Sweden and the Symphony of the New World in New York. Another frustrated Black conductor is George Byrd. He seems resigned to continuing his musical career in Europe. He has conducted major orchestras in London, Paris, and Berlin.

Five young Black conductors have felt some of the same frustration experienced by Dixon, Lee, and Byrd. Karl Hampton Porter has been conductor of the Harlem Youth Philharmonic, an orchestra whose players range in age from eighteen to twenty-five and are mostly Black. Porter came to New York from Pittsburgh after graduating from the Carnegie Institute of Technology and the Peabody Conservatory in Baltimore. His expertise on the bassoon won him Peabody and Juilliard scholarships and has supported him comfortably despite the difficulties experienced by most Black musicians in securing employment.

Isaiah Jackson graduated *cum laude* from Harvard in 1966. He then received a Master of Arts degree from Stanford in 1967 and a Doctor of Musical Arts degree from Juilliard in 1973. While at Juilliard, Jackson conducted the pre-college orchestra and taught orchestral repertoire. In 1969, he was appointed music director of the Youth Symphony Orchestra of New York, a training orchestra that has given concerts in Carnegie Hall. During the 1970–71 concert season, Jackson served as assistant conductor of Leopold Stokowski's American Symphony Orchestra and associate conductor of the American Ballet Company, and was founder and conductor of the Juilliard String Ensemble. During the 1971–73 seasons, he served as assistant conductor of the Baltimore Symphony Orchestra. Since 1973, Isaiah Jackson has been associate conductor of the Rochester Philharmonic Orchestra, conducting eighty concerts a year. He also holds the part-time post of conductor of the University of Rochester Symphony Orchestra.

Jackson has also made a number of guest appearances as conductor. They include: Spoleto Festival (Italy), Dallas Symphony, National Symphony, Vienna Symphony, the Radio-televisione Italiana Orchestra (Rome), Los Angeles Philharmonic, New York Philharmonic, the Dance Theatre of Harlem (Covent Garden), and the Buffalo Philharmonic. In addition, Jackson has conducted several operas.

Harold Wheeler, a native of St. Louis, conducted the musical *Promises, Promises* during the first six months of its run; he was probably the first Black conductor to open a Broadway show. Having a great interest in composition, he left *Promises, Promises* to create the dance music for *Coco*, and he later orchestrated *The Wiz*. It is Wheeler's desire to continue to combine the two careers of conductor and composer or orchestrator.

Coleridge-Taylor Perkinson came out of the Manhattan School of Music with a Master's degree and became conductor of the Brooklyn Community Orchestra attached to Brooklyn College. He later served as music director of Jerome Robbins' American Theater Laboratory during the two years of its existence, did music for the Negro Ensemble Company productions beginning with *Song of the Lusitanian Bogey,* and in 1969 was conductor for the Alvin Ailey Dance Theater in its season at the Brooklyn Academy of Music.

In 1969, at the age of twenty-nine, James Frazier of Detroit became the first American and the youngest conductor ever to win the Guido Cantelli International Competition at La Scala in Milan, Italy. When the members of the orchestra voted to determine the best of the twelve competition finalists, seventy-six out of eighty-five chose him. A few days later, he and the orchestra won nine curtain calls for their performance. Frazier has conducted the Indianapolis Symphony, the Los Angeles Philharmonic, the Detroit Symphony, the Leningrad Philharmonic, and the London Philharmonic Orchestras.

While Black conductors have been given a few opportunities to conduct symphony orchestras in this country, it was not until 1968 that a Black man was given the permanent post of musical director of a professional orchestra in the United States. The man was Henry Lewis, and the orchestra was the Newark-based New Jersey Symphony Orchestra.

Born in 1932 in Los Angeles, Lewis began his rapid climb to international recognition at the age of sixteen by distinguishing himself as a double-bass player with the Los Angeles Philharmonic. When he resigned to devote his full attention to conducting, one of his first triumphs came with the same Los Angeles Philharmonic. Among his many accomplishments, he has served as Music Director of the Los Angeles Opera Company and has conducted at the Metropolitan Opera and the symphony orchestras of Detroit, Chicago, San Francisco, Boston, and in the Hollywood Bowl. In Europe, he has been heralded for performances at La Scala and with the London Symphony and Royal Philharmonic Orchestras. His Decca/London recordings include a series with his wife, soprano Marilyn Horne, and symphonic repertoire with the Royal Philharmonic Orchestra.

The Albuquerque Symphony Orchestra brought in Denis M. de Coteau as guest conductor during the 1969–70 concert season. Dr. de Coteau had received his Bachelor's and Master's degrees in Music from New York University. In 1964, he received the Doctor of Musical Arts degree in orchestral conducting from Stanford University. He has been the assistant conductor of the Brooklyn Chamber Orchestra, conductor of the San Francisco Youth Baroque Orchestra, associate conductor of the Stanford University Symphony Orchestra, conductor of the Grinnell College Orchestra, and conductor of the El Camino Youth Symphony Orchestra. He has conducted the San Mateo Community Orchestra, has served as associate conductor of the San Francisco Chamber Orchestra, and was appointed music director of both the San Francisco Ballet and Oakland Symphony Youth Orchestra. Dr. de Coteau, a well-known viola soloist, is the recipient of several honors: In addition to winning the Pierre Monteux Conducting Award and the ASCAP National Award for Adventuresome Programming, Dr. de Coteau was also named Outstanding Black American Musician in 1973.

Dr. Paul Freeman, after two years as associate conductor of the Dallas Symphony Orchestra, was elected to fill the post of conductor-in-residence with the Detroit Symphony. In 1978, Dr. Freeman became music director of the Victoria Symphony Orchestra in Canada.

Dr. Freeman, who received his Ph.D. from the Eastman School of Music in 1963, was given his first conducting position in Rochester, New York, as head of the Hillel Little Symphony. A second-prize winner of the 1967 Dimitri Mitropoulos Conducting Competition, he has had guest conducting engagements in Minneapolis, New Orleans, Baltimore, Oklahoma City, Birmingham, Chicago, San Francisco, Atlanta, and St. Louis. Dr. Freeman has begun a recording career with Serenus/Vox and Orion, and he was involved in the "Black Composer" series on Columbia Records.

James De Preist, a first-prize winner in the Mitropoulos Competition, was selected by Leonard Bernstein to be an assistant conductor of the New York Philharmonic during the 1965–66 season. In 1969, he made his European debut in Holland, which proved so successful that many guest

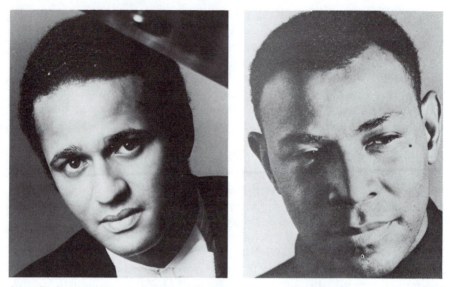

Among Black concert instrumentalists of exceptional ability are André Watts (left) and Eugene Haynes (right), pianists. (Photos courtesy Alix B. Williamson and Thea Dispeker, respectively.)

conducting engagements followed. He had a triumph with the Stockholm Philharmonic that booked him for return engagements. He then added Norway, Belgium, and Italy to his musical conquests. Mr. De Preist first conducted the National Symphony in Washington in 1970, and the following season became its associate conductor. In the fall of 1976, he was appointed music director of L'Orchestre Symphonique de Quebec. In 1980, Mr. De Preist was appointed resident conductor of the Oregon Symphony in Portland. His career has included guest conducting appearances with the Philadelphia Orchestra, New York Philharmonic, Boston Symphony, Chicago Symphony, and Cleveland Orchestra, among others. Mr. De Preist has recorded several compositions by Ravel, Debussy, Mozart, Hindemith, and Pergament with major orchestras.

Compared with the past, orchestras today appear to be eager to engage Blacks as guest conductors. Such action is long overdue, and they have a long way to go before their collective neglect of the Dixons, Lees, Byrds, and others can be forgotten. While there are at least twenty-eight major orchestras in the United States, up until now few of them have found it possible to encourage and aid in the development of Black talent through assistant or associate positions. Among those that have done so are the New York, Dallas, St. Louis, Detroit, and National orchestras. Most of the twenty-eight major orchestras have yet to take notice of Black conductors at all.

Broadway has hired at least two Black female conductors. Joyce Brown was musical director of the musical *Purlie*. Margaret Harris, a multi-talented individual, conducted the Broadway musical *Hair* and has guest-conducted with the Minnesota, St. Louis, and San Diego orchestras. In addition, she has appeared as pianist with the Los Angeles Philharmonic and is a composer as well.

The Black concert instrumentalist has not gained as much acceptance on the American concert stage as the Black singer. This may be partly because of the reason already cited—the length of time required to develop a performer of outstanding ability.

Although they are comparatively few in number, Black concert instrumentalists have demonstrated exceptional ability. Among them are André Watts, pianist; Sanford Allen and Barbara Campbell, violinists; Harold Jones, Antoinette Handy, and John Jackson, flutists; Selwart Clarke and Alfred Brown, violists; Harry M. Smyles, oboist; Kermit Moore, cellist; Joseph Wilder, trumpeter; and Richard Davis and Warren Petty, double bassists. Natalie Hinderas became the first Black pianist to appear on a major season program under the management of Columbia Artists. Two other highly gifted pianists are Armenta Adams and Eugene Haynes.

The Black musician has fared only a little better in finding employment in the theater orchestras of Broadway musicals, as an examination of the theater orchestras of Broadway musicals today indicates. From 1956 to 1958, there were twenty-six musicals presented on Broadway, employing together approximately 650 musicians. Only fourteen Blacks performed in the pit orchestras of these shows. Black musicians are usually employed when the musical has a Black theme or the star of the production is Black.[23] It would seem that "employment for the Negro musician is most often secured at the insistence of the Negro Headliner, a liberal producer, theatre owner, or pressures exerted by the Negro musician."[24]

After increased pressure from Black musicians for an increase in job opportunities with Broadway shows, more Blacks began to be used as substitute musicians. One Black musician noted, "We aren't qualified, they say, for permanent posts, but we're good enough to come through the spotlighting and pressure of being a substitute who may be unfamiliar with part of what the orchestra is playing."[25]

It must be pointed out in all fairness that it is also extremely difficult for the White musician to obtain employment in the orchestra of a Broadway musical, since whenever replacements are needed, whether permanent or temporary, the musicians of the orchestra will recommend their relatives or friends to fill the vacant position. This practice excludes all those

[23]Douglas G. Pugh, "Job Status of the Negro Professional Musician in the New York Metropolitan Area" (Urban League of Greater New York, May, 1958), p. 5 (mimeographed).
[24]*Ibid.*, p. 4.
[25]Nat Hentoff, "The Strange Case of the Missing Musicians," *The Reporter* (May 28, 1959), p. 26.

Anderson: (Photo courtesy Fisk University Library's Special Collections.)

Robeson: (Photo courtesy New York Public Library, Schomburg Collection of Negro Literature.)

Hayes: (Photo courtesy Fisk University Library's Special Collections.)

Arroyo: (Photo courtesy Thea Dispeker.)

Black singers in the European tradition include Marian Anderson, Roland Hayes, Paul Robeson, Martina Arroyo, Reri Grist, Leontyne Price, William Warfield, and Dorothy Maynor.

Grist: (Photo courtesy Columbia Artist Management.)

Warfield: (Photo courtesy Columbia Artist Management.)

Price: (Photo courtesy Fisk University Library's Special Collections.)

Maynor: (Photo courtesy New York Public Library, Schomburg Collection of Negro Literature.)

musicians who are not "insiders," and merely compounds the difficulties experienced by the Black musician.

Some Black composers have enjoyed great success on Broadway via the musical. In almost every instance, however, the Broadway show has been all-Black. Seldom has a producer seen fit to employ a Black composer to write the music for an all-White or racially mixed show. Will Vodery (1885–1951) and William Grant Still (1895–1978) were among the exceptions.

This writer made an attempt to determine the extent of employment of Black musicians by the three major television networks. NBC failed to respond. The Director of Music Operations for CBS replied, in part:

> In the area of staff employment I would estimate that over 10% of the men employed have been black with this percentage varying over the years. Combined with our free-lance employment it would be my guess that between 20%–25% of the cumulative employment is Black.
> . . . We were among the first to utilize the creative talents of such writers as Quincy Jones, Ulysses Kay, Oliver Nelson and Luther Henderson—to cite just a few.[26]

ABC responded as follows:

> . . . The American Broadcasting Company does not employ musicians. All our series are the products of individual production companies. Music and recordings utilized in our series are handled by the individual production companies.[27]

During the last decade, Blacks have been employed to a very limited extent as musical directors of continuing series. Among them are Oliver Nelson, who composed the background music for the productions "Mr. Broadway" and "The Six Million Dollar Man," and Quincy Jones, composer of the background music for "Sanford and Son" and "Roots."

The Black musician has also enjoyed some success via syndicated television series (shows produced by an independent company and then sold to individual television stations). "The Barbara McNair Show" had Coleridge-Taylor Perkinson as musical director; "The David Frost Show" employed Billy Taylor, a pianist, as musical director; and "The Allen Ludden Show" used arranger-composer H. T. Barnum in the same capacity.

Just as Black singers and actors have enjoyed increased opportunities on television in the last few years, it appears that the Black musician is also enjoying greater acceptance in this medium.

[26]Letter from Louis I. Teicher, Director of Music Operations, CBS Television Network, New York, New York, April 30, 1970.

[27]Letter from E. Y. Waite, Assistant Manager of Audience Relations, American Broadcasting Company, New York, New York, April 24, 1970.

The Black Singer in Concert and Opera

While the Black classical singer has received limited recognition in this country for several decades, it was not until 1955 that the Metropolitan Opera Company engaged a Black singer—Marian Anderson, the noted contralto. While this was not the first instance in which a Black person had performed with a major American opera company, the Black singer's acceptance in this area has been limited.

There have been many outstanding Black classical singers in the twentieth century. Among them are Ellabelle Davis, Lillian Evanti, Camilla Williams, Caterina Jarboro, Todd Duncan, Lawrence Winters, Margaret Tynes, Robert McFerrin, Roland Hayes, Paul Robeson, Grace Bumbry, Martina Arroyo, Reri Grist, Felicia Weathers, Charlotte Hollman, George Shirley, McHenry Boatwright, Abbie Mitchell, Minto Cato, Florence-Cole Talbert, André Montal, Eugene Jones, Annabelle Bernard, Kathleen Crawford, Mattiwilda Dobbs, Charles Holland, Rhea Jackson, Junette Jones, Ella Lee, Vera Little, William Ray, Gwendolyn Simms, William de Valentine, Leontyne Price, Adele Addison, Shirley Verrett, Betty Allen, William Warfield, and Dorothy Maynor.

The Black Musician and the
Musicians' Union

Former slaves who had been freed by the Emancipation Proclamation were refused admittance to labor organizations because of the color of their skin. Since these White unions refused to unionize the Blacks or support their demands for reforms, the former slaves formed an organization of their own in 1869, the National Colored Union.

This group did not concentrate only on the economic problems of Black workers but concerned itself with the political, social, and economic problems of Black people as a whole. The National Colored Union supported the Republican party, which had been largely responsible for freeing the slaves. In so doing, they relied on it completely to solve all their problems and became no more than an appendage of the party. Because this organization paid little attention to trade union problems, it did not build a strong, permanent union. Failing to meet the needs of Black workers, it faded into oblivion after a few years.

In the late 1880s and early 1890s, the American Federation of Labor was faced with the problem of what to do with Black workers in the South. Organizers and representatives continually asked their leader, Samuel Gompers, for answers to the race issue. Gompers replied that Blacks should be organized and admitted to membership in a local union, and that efforts should be made to eliminate discrimination against Blacks joining local unions. Still, he held that it would be in the best interests of the union to have Black workers organized into separate locals but attached to the same national organizations with the same rights, duties, and privileges as all other locals.

This approach was to be temporary, to be employed only when no other method could be used to bring Black workers into the Federation. For a few years, unions desiring to affiliate were required to eliminate the color clause from their constitution. In later years, however, as the A.F. of L. became openly discriminatory in its policies, separate locals came to be regarded as the preferred way of permanently organizing Black workers. Gompers now contended that the separation of Black and White workers was best for both groups and for the entire labor movement, since it afforded less chance of arousing bitterness between the two groups.

As soon as discrimination in the labor movement became the rule rather than the exception, it was inevitable that the same would develop in employment. Not only did union leaders condone the racism that most employers practiced in their hiring, but the leaders actually participated in a conspiracy to perpetuate it. As was the practice with other unions, the A.F.M. at first organized Blacks into auxiliary locals. It was not until 1940 that the twelve remaining Black auxiliaries were granted equal status with the White locals. As late as 1960, the A.F.M. probably had more segregated locals throughout the United States than any union except the Railway Clerks.

Segregated locals remained the rule until after 1945, when there arose increasing Black opposition to segregation. Some of this opposition was because of inadequate job opportunities—especially work with symphony orchestras. The greatest opposition within the A.F.M. seems to have come from a few Black leaders who opposed segregation on principle. Leadership in this cause was provided by the Los Angeles Black local whose representatives introduced a resolution at the 1957 A.F.M. convention calling for the elimination of segregated locals, claiming they violated the union's constitution due to a provision that there could be only one local in an area. Because of considerable opposition from a majority of Black delegates, who believed that the larger Black locals would lose the financial assets they had accumulated through many years of hard work, action on the resolution was postponed.

The Los Angeles Black local merged with the White local in 1953, after threatening a lawsuit. At first it was thought that the musicians would profit by this move because of increased job opportunities in the studio orchestras motion picture and recording industries, and with the Los Angeles Philharmonic. But many of the Black members of the merged locals now believe that they are worse off than before the merger. Job opportunities have not improved and the Black musicians have a smaller voice in union affairs because they are in the minority.

All remaining Black and White locals were merged in 1970, over the opposition of many Black members who had become aware of the experiences of those Blacks who had previously merged and realized that integration by itself would not solve the problems of employment for Black musicians. It is the view of the administration of many of the larger locals that it is not the responsibility of the union to secure jobs for musicians. Black musicians take an opposite view. They feel that the union should include a nondiscrimination clause in all contracts with management and modify their hands-off policy with respect to job discrimination.

The fact remains that the American Federation of Musicians has done little to help implement a fair hiring policy by employers of musicians. When it should be asserting itself in a role of leadership, it has remained silent. A change in policy is long overdue.

chapter five

American Black Composers in the European Tradition

The story of the Black composer begins considerably after the advent of the Blacks to the colonies of the New World. This delay was partly because Africans came to the New World from many different points and tribes on the West Coast of the African mainland and spoke a variety of languages. Unable to read and write and strangers in a new culture, Blacks were denied any formal education. Only when liberal-minded masters began to educate individual Blacks and free them did they have an opportunity to turn to the formal composition of music.

Beginning in the eighteenth century, the Black composer began to make his presence felt musically, not only in America but in Europe as well. Joseph Boulogne, Chevalier de Saint-Georges, whose compositions were discussed earlier, became one of France's outstanding composers of that period.

George Augustus Polgreen Bridgetower (1779–1860), a native of Poland whose father was African, became a violin virtuoso and composer and a close friend of Beethoven. Beethoven's *Kreutzer Sonata* was first dedicated to Bridgetower.

Samuel Coleridge-Taylor (1875–1912), born to an African father and English mother, produced compositions in many genres. He was widely published in his native England, and he made visits to this country, which undoubtedly inspired American Blacks to pursue careers in composition.

200

Among other non-American Black composers were Ignatius Sancho (1729–1780), who composed many works and wrote a *Theory of Music* (no longer extant); and José White (1833–?), born in Cuba, a virtuoso on the violin as well as a composer.

NEW ORLEANS COMPOSERS

In the mid-nineteenth century, many American Blacks became interested in composition. Many tried to emulate the classical style of their White contemporaries, while others were concerned with the minstrel-type songs of the American stage.

In New Orleans, many of the offspring of the union of Black women and White men were given excellent educations, which included music. While some were educated in that city, many others were sent to France for their schooling. Consequently, New Orleans boasted a large number of Black composers. Although their music was not of lasting quality, it does indicate successful attempts at emulating White composers of that period.

Basil Bares (1846–?), born in New Orleans, was a piano student of Eugène Prévost, and in 1867 he spent some time in France as a performer. Among his compositions were dance and salon pieces, the best known of which were *Les Cent Gardes, Minuit Polka de Salon,* and *Basile's Galop.*

Samuel Snaer (ca. 1834–?), active as a violinist, cellist, and pianist, was also born in New Orleans. In addition to becoming a teacher of piano and violin, Snaer also devoted considerable time to composition. His first work, *Sous Sa Fenêtre,* was published by Louis Gruenwald. Other works include *Rapelle-Toi, Le Vampire, Le Bohémien,* and *Le Chant des Canotiers.* Snaer also composed works in the popular dance forms of that period—polkas, waltzes, mazurkas, and quadrilles.

Richard Lambert (ca. 1828–?), an important conductor and teacher, was father of a highly musical family. His eldest son Lucien received his first musical instruction in New Orleans, where he became known as a pianist, teacher, and composer. He later went to Paris to continue his study. He became the chief musician of the court of Dom Pedro of Brazil before entering the piano manufacturing business in that country. Among his compositions are *La Bresiliana, L'Américaine, Paris Vienne, Le Niagara, La Juive,* and *Le Départ du Conscrit.*

Sidney Lambert, a brother of Lucien, was also a pianist and composer. He was decorated by the King of Portugal for his piano method book, and he became a musician of the court. He later went to Paris where he taught and continued to compose. *Murmures du Soir, Anna Bolean, L'Africaine,* and *Transports Joyeux* are among his compositions.

One of the most widely known Black musicians of New Orleans was Edmund Dédé (1829–1903). After receiving instruction on the violin, Dédé was sent to Mexico in 1841 to acquire a musical education. He went to

England in 1857, and then to Paris, where he entered the Conservatory and became a pupil of Halévy and Alard. His works include *Les Faux Mandarins, La Sensitive,* and *Le Palmier Overture,* all for orchestra. His last composition was an opera in four acts, *Sultan d' Ispahan.*

While New Orleans was a center of cultural activity, other cities produced their share of Black composers during the nineteenth century. Violinist Edwin Hill, the first Black man to be admitted to the Philadelphia Academy of Fine Arts (1871), composed over one hundred songs and anthems. Justin Holland (1819–86) wrote many guitar compositions, as well as two popular instruction manuals for the guitar: *Holland's Comprehensive Method for the Guitar,* published in 1874 by J. D. Peters of New York, and *Holland's Modern Method for the Guitar,* published in 1876 by Oliver Ditson of Boston. Frank Johnson (1792–1844) composed over 150 pieces, including many marches.

Other early Black composers were J. Hemmenway, who lived in Philadelphia in the 1820s; A. J. Conner of Philadelphia, who published a number of compositions between 1845 and 1850; and Thomas Green Bethune, better known as "Blind Tom," who composed approximately twenty pieces.

It is significant that Blacks were able to make these contributions to American music against heavy odds. In spite of their social environment and the role delegated to them by American society, Blacks proved capable of composing music in the European idiom as soon as they were given the opportunity.

SYNTHESIZERS OF TWO TRADITIONS

At the turn of the twentieth century, many Black composers were making a conscious effort to synthesize two musical traditions—the folk music of the Black tradition and the musical forms of the European tradition—into one music. Specifically, these composers sought to employ characteristic Black melodic idioms and dance rhythms within the context of European forms.

These composers had received excellent training at conservatories such as Oberlin in Ohio and the National Conservatory in New York, or privately with European-trained White musicians in this country and abroad. They had learned how to write music in traditional European styles, yet they seemed determined to create Black-oriented compositions.

There appear to be three major influences that caused these composers to utilize folk materials in their compositions. First, the success of the Fisk Jubilee Singers and their repertoire of spirituals caused many Blacks to take another look at these songs and to rediscover their great beauty. The pride that they began to take in this aspect of their cultural heritage had an impact on Black composers some years later.

The second major influence was the result of Antonín Dvořák's arrival in this country in 1892 to become director of the National Conservatory of Music in New York. In the *New York Herald* of May 21, 1893, an article by Dvořák appeared, "Real Value of Negro Melodies,"[1] which was to be of major significance. Stating that his interest in Black music had grown deeper during his first year in America, Dvořák now claimed that "the future music of this country must be founded upon what are called Negro Melodies." He stated further, "This must be the real foundation of any serious and original school of composition to be developed in the United States." It was his contention that "the beautiful themes" found in Black music were "products of the soil." Dvořák also believed that in order for America to "express the true sentiment of the people," the folk songs of the American people would have to be examined. He considered the folk tradition to be of the utmost importance in revealing the true identity of a nation, and he felt deeply that Black melodies could aid the composer to "get in touch with the common humanity of his country." His remarks inspired Black composers to utilize their folk materials in a manner befitting the dignity that Dvořák had bestowed on these "products of the soil."

The third major influence on the twentieth-century Black composer was the Black Renaissance, also known as the Harlem Renaissance and the New Negro movement.

After World War I, the Black populace had become disillusioned concerning their plight in the United States. Increasingly aware that the democracy for which they had fought in Europe did not exist for them in this country, they became more militant and more articulate in expressing their displeasure about social and economic conditions.

New York's Harlem became the center of Black intellectual life. Writers, poets, painters, and musicians joined ranks in protesting against social conditions. This movement was primarily a literary one, inaugurated by James Weldon Johnson with the publication of his *Fifty Years and Other Poems* in 1917. Books by other writers and poets soon followed, among them collections of poems, novels, and prose by Jean Toomer, Countee Cullen, William S. Braithwaite, Jessie Redmond Fauset, Claude McKay, Langston Hughes, Walter White, and others. National periodicals published articles about the renaissance movement by such writers as W. E. B. Du Bois, George Schuyler, E. Franklin Frazier, Benjamin Brawley, Joel A. Rogers, Arthur Schomburg, and Alain Locke. Two Black periodicals, *Crisis* and *Opportunity,* offered prizes that stimulated literary activity among young writers such as Gwendolyn Bennett, Montgomery Gregory, Eric Walrond, Georgia Douglas Johnson, Rudolph Fisher, Clarissa M. Scott, Zora Neale Hurston, Kelly Miller, and Angelina Grimke. Charles

---

[1]Antonin Dvořák, "Real Value of Negro Melodies," *New York Herald* (May 21, 1893), quoted in Merton Aborn, "The Influence on American Musical Culture of Dvořák's Sojourn in America," (unpublished Ph.D. dissertation, Indiana University), pp. 183–84.

Leaders of the Black Renaissance included James Weldon Johnson (top left), Jean Toomer (middle left), Langston Hughes (top right), Claude McKay (middle right), and Countee Cullen (bottom). (Johnson photo courtesy Fisk University Library's Special Collections; all other photos courtesy New York Public Library, Schomburg Collection of Negro Literature.)

Spurgeon Johnson made efforts to help young writers by interesting publishers in the serious development of a body of literature about Black life.

> Black musicians participated in the movement by turning to the folk music of the race as a source of materials in composition and performance. To be sure, some black composers had been drawing on such materials for a number of years—particularly those who had been associated with the musical nationalism advocated by Dvořák in 1895—but now they became more race conscious than ever. The composers used poems by black poets in their art songs; they exploited the rhythms of Negro dances and the harmonies and melodies of the blues as well as spirituals, and of the newer music called jazz in their composed concert music. Almost without exception black concert artists began to include on their programs the folk and composed music of Negroes, and some artists staged recitals consisting exclusively of Negro music.[2]

This renaissance of the arts, which began in 1917, lasted for approximately a decade and ended in 1929 with the crash of the stock market. Many of the Black literary figures were being sponsored by White patrons; when the economic depression wiped out fortunes, many of the sponsors were left without funds to support the arts. Consequently, this illustrious period in American Black history came to an abrupt end.

Each of the aforementioned factors seems to have influenced the use of Black material within European musical forms in its own way. The activities of the Fisk Jubilee Singers tended to erase the shame that the educated segment of the Black population associated with the Black spiritual and to make them proud of their musical heritage for the first time. Dvořák's efforts in championing Black music as a foundation for nationalism seemed to act as a catalyst, encouraging both Black and White composers to incorporate Black melodies and rhythms in their compositions.[3] And finally, the Black Renaissance of the 1920s served to make Blacks more race-conscious than ever, and helped sustain the Black composer's interest in the use of Black materials.[4]

[2]Eileen Southern, *The Music of Black Americans: A History* (New York: W. W. Norton and Company, 1971), p. 413.

[3]Among the White composers who utilized Black melodic and rhythmic materials in their compositions were John Alden Carpenter, George Chadwick, Aaron Copland, Eric De Lamarter, Henry F. Gilbert, Leopold Godowsky, Rubin Goldmark, Ferde Grofé, Louis T. Gruenberg, Edward Burlingame Hill, John Tasker Howard, Charles Ives, Arthur Walter Kramer, Daniel Gregory Mason, John Powell, and Leo Sowerby.

[4]The criteria used in arriving at the decision of which composers are most significant are many. Those composers who have been widely published, whose works have been recorded and programmed by symphony orchestras and concert performers, and who have received favorable reviews about their compositions have been deemed the most significant of this period. While these criteria are sociological in nature, they are in accord with the hypothesis of P. R. Farnsworth (*Musical Taste, Its Measurement and Cultural Nature*, Stanford, Cal.: Stanford University Press, 1950, p. 3) who states, ". . . musical taste is a phenomenon of the social sciences, rather than a conglomeration of chance responses or a set of absolutes. Like all other folkways, musical taste is peculiar to a group of people, a particular place, and a particular period of history. No music, then, can be inherently good or bad, for goodness is

It is always dangerous to set dates for the beginning and end of a period of musical history, for, as in the other arts, change generally takes place gradually over a number of years. The dates between which the practice of compositional synthesis by Black composers reached its zenith, however, were from around 1900 to about 1940. There is evidence of synthesis a considerable time before 1900, and there were composers long after 1940 who continued to employ Black materials in their compositions. Nevertheless, this stylistic characteristic of music by Black composers enjoyed its greatest prominence in the first forty years of the twentieth century.

Clarence Cameron White

The violinist and composer Clarence Cameron White (1880–1960) was born in Clarksville, Tennessee. After his family moved to Washington, D.C., he attended the public schools and, later, Howard University. He then studied at Oberlin Conservatory of Music (1896–1901).[5] His goal was to become a concert violinist. Upon graduation from Oberlin, White returned to Washington to teach violin at the Washington Conservatory of Music, as well as to teach in the public schools. In 1906 and from 1908–11, he studied violin with the Russian violinist Zakarevich and composition with the Black composer Samuel Coleridge-Taylor.

After three years abroad, White returned to America in 1910 and located in Boston where he divided his time between teaching in his private studio, concertizing, and composition. As his skill in composition grew, he sought to utilize the Black folk idiom in a synthesis with classical musical forms. He was especially interested in adapting this material for violin. In addition, he made arrangements of spirituals for voice. Compositions written during his stay in Boston were published by the Carl Fischer Company.

White was able to combine four careers for a number of years—administrator, teacher, composer, and, occasionally, concert violinist. From 1924–30, he was director of music at West Virginia State College.

It was during his tenure there that White's musical interest turned toward opera. In the summer of 1928, White and John F. Matheus, pro-

---

only an evaluation by a group of men trained to accept a particular set of standards." John H. Mueller (*The American Symphony Orchestra*, Bloomington, Ind.: Indiana University Press, 1951, chaps. 1 and 2) also believes that the determination of the worth of any composition is culturally derived.

[5]It is interesting to note that a number of Black musicians attended Oberlin Conservatory of Music in Ohio. Certainly, Oberlin was a first-class school during this period, but there were many other first-rate music schools throughout the country. Probably one reason was the social attitudes of the citizens in that part of the country. During slavery, that area was one of the stations along the "underground railroad"—that network dedicated to helping Blacks escape from slavery. Undoubtedly, many Blacks thought that Oberlin possessed an excellent racial climate in which to continue their studies.

Violinist-composer Clarence Cameron White.
(Photo courtesy New York Public Library,
Schomburg Collection of Negro Literature.)

fessor of Romance languages and writer of short stories and plays, visited the republic of Haiti. The purpose of the visit was to study the folklore and music indigenous to that land. As a result of the visit, Matheus wrote a two-act play, *Tambour*, using White's published score of the same name as incidental music.

In 1930 and 1931, White was awarded a Rosenwald Fellowship for creative work, and a leave of absence from his duties at West Virginia State College was secured for the purpose of foreign study while writing an opera. The opera, *Ouanga*, with a libretto by Matheus, was based on the life of Dessalines, Haitian liberator and first ruler. *Ouanga* received performances by the American Opera Society in Chicago (concert form, 1932); the Burleigh Musical Association of South Bend, Indiana (1949); the Dra-Mu, a Black opera company of Philadelphia (1950); and the National Negro Opera Company (concert version, 1956).[6]

Ouanga. The Opera *Ouanga* was written for solo voices (soprano, contralto, tenor, and bass), mixed chorus, and ballet. White makes appropriate use of native themes and dances while utilizing rhythmic patterns indigenous to the Caribbean. The orchestration is done with clarity and a great amount of variety, never seeming to overshadow the soloists or chorus.

The one characteristic that permeates this work from beginning to end is the torrid, primitive rhythms indigenous to Haiti. The rhythm accompanying the dancers as they perform the Meringue is typical.

[6]Southern, *The Music of Black Americans*, pp. 289–90.

EXAMPLE 5.1   Meringue rhythm, *Ouanga*

White also employs native instruments to add to the realism of the opera. They include voodoo drums, pebble shakers, and a steel bar which is struck.

EXAMPLE 5.2   Native instruments, *Ouanga*[7]

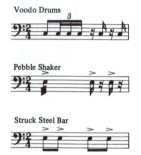

Voodo Drums

Pebble Shaker

Struck Steel Bar

For *Ouanga,* White was awarded the David Bispham medal, an honor awarded to composers of operas of outstanding merit that constitute important contributions to American opera. He continued to employ the Black idiom in his compositions throughout his career, which included serving as director of music at Hampton Institute from 1931 to 1935, and as an organizer of community music programs for the National Recreational Association from 1937 to 1941. In addition to the Rosenwald grants and the Bispham Medal, he was the recipient of several prizes and awards: the Harmon Foundation Award (1927), an honorary Doctor of Music degree from Wilberforce University (1933), and the Benjamin Award (for his *Elegy,* 1954).

While writing *Ouanga,* White studied composition and orchestration with the noted French composer, Raoul Laparra, in Paris. While studying with Laparra, White also wrote compositions for violin. His string quartet, *Prelude, Dawn, and Jubilee Hallelujah,* which is based on Black themes, was performed at the Ecole Normale de Musique by faculty members of the school. Among his other compositions are works for violin, piano, solo voice, chorus, orchestra, band, chamber ensemble, and organ. The best

[7]Sole agents, Sam Fox Publishing Company, Palm Desert, California. Used by permission.

known of his works are the *Bandana Sketches* for violin (1920), *Cabin Memories* (1921), and *From the Cotton Fields* (1921), all of which are based on Black folk songs or folklike material. His orchestral compositions include *Piece for Strings and Timpani, Kutamba Rhapsody,* and *Symphony in D Minor.* Other works are a ballet, *A Night in Sans Souci,* and the *Violin Concerto No. 2 in E minor.* Among the spirituals arranged by White are two collections: *Forty Negro Spirituals* (1927) and *Traditional Negro Spirituals* (1940), for voice and piano accompaniment. White's arrangements of spirituals for violin and piano were held in high regard in the twenties and thirties and were programmed by such noted violinists as Fritz Kreisler, Albert Spalding, and Irma Seydel.[8]

Robert Nathaniel Dett

One of the great champions of the movement to synthesize the Black and European idioms was Robert Nathaniel Dett (1882–1943). Born in Drummondsville, Ontario, Dett was the youngest of three brothers. He attended Oberlin Conservatory, graduating in 1908 with the Bachelor of Music degree in composition. In later years, he continued his musical studies at the American Conservatory of Music in Chicago, Columbia University, the University of Pennsylvania, and Harvard University.

After his graduation from Oberlin, Dett taught at Lane College in Tennessee (1908–11) and Lincoln Institute (later Lincoln University) in Missouri (1911–13). He then went to Hampton Institute, Hampton, Virginia, as director of music (1913–35). In 1920, he secured a leave of absence for one year so that he could pursue his musical studies in Boston. He studied piano under the pianist-composer, Arthur Foote, and composition at Harvard. At Harvard, Dett won the Boote prize in composition, as well as the Bowdoin prize for an essay, "The Emancipation of Negro Music."

In the summer of 1929, Dett studied in Paris under the noted teacher, Nadia Boulanger, at the American Conservatory at Fontainebleau. Returning to Hampton Institute, he molded the choir of this institution into a remarkable group with a high level of musicianship. The choir made a successful European tour in 1930, after which it toured the United States in 1931 to critical acclaim.

In 1932, Dett left college teaching to open a music studio in Rochester, New York. He did, however, resume a career in teaching on two occasions—in 1935 at Sam Houston College (then in Austin, Texas) and in 1937 at Bennett College in North Carolina.

During the years when Dett was developing fine choral groups at his various colleges, he was also involved in arranging and composing. He not only arranged many Black spirituals and folk songs for solo voice and chorus, but he also composed many original works.

[8]Southern, *The Music of Black Americans,* p. 290.

Robert Nathaniel Dett, champion of the synthesis of Black and European music. (Photo courtesy New York Public Library, Schomburg Collection of Negro Literature.)

Dett was one of the first Americans to utilize Black folk tunes for classic development. Best known among his works are five piano suites—*Magnolia* (1912), *Enchantment* (1922), *In the Bottoms* (1926), *The Cinnamon Grove* (1928), and *Tropic Winter* (1938); three motets—*Listen to the Lambs* (1914), *I'll Never Turn Back No More* (1938), and *Don't Be Weary, Traveler* (1921); two songs—*Magic Moon of Molten Gold* (1919), and *A Thousand Years Ago or More* (1919); and three choral works—*Music in the Mine* (1916), and the oratorios *The Chariot Jubilee* (commissioned by the Syracuse University Chorus, 1919), and *The Ordering of Moses*.

The Ordering of Moses.   This composition, the second of Dett's two oratorios, was written for soprano, contralto, tenor, and bass, mixed chorus, and orchestra. It is based on the spiritual *Go Down Moses*.

EXAMPLE 5.3   *Go Down Moses*

The introduction begins with a motive that permeates the entire composition. It is often used in its original form, but sometimes merely alluded to.

EXAMPLE 5.4   Opening Motive, Introduction, *The Ordering of Moses*

The motive derives from the second phrase of the chorus of *Go Down Moses*. While the rhythm is not an exact duplication, the pitches are identical.

EXAMPLE 5.5 *Go Down Moses*

Way   down   in   E - gypt's   land,—

Dett often uses the first two notes of the opening motive in diminution, then the last two notes of the motive in augmentation.

EXAMPLE 5.6 Diminution and augmentation of opening motive, *Go Down Moses*

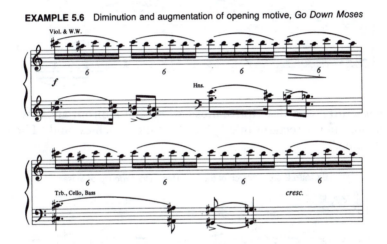

He seems to be enthralled with the interval of a fourth for he uses it throughout this composition.

EXAMPLE 5.7 Use of an interval of a fourth, *The Ordering of Moses*

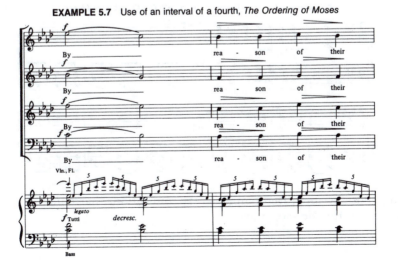

Dett has written very descriptive music where it is appropriate. It is used in this manner in the sections titled "March of the Israelites" and "The Egyptians Pursue."

EXAMPLE 5.8   "March of the Israelites," *The Ordering of Moses*

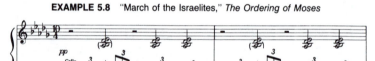

EXAMPLE 5.9   "The Egyptians Pursue," *The Ordering of Moses*

In his choral writing, Dett employs very conventional harmonies, avoiding dissonances for the most part.

EXAMPLE 5.10 Representative harmonies, *The Ordering of Moses*[9]

The Ordering of Moses was perhaps the finest result of Dett's successful synthesis of the Black and European musical traditions. It was performed at the Cincinnati Festival of 1937 and at the Worchester (Massachusetts) Festival of 1938; by the Oratorio Society in New York in 1939; and at Carnegie Hall in New York in 1941. This work was subsequently recorded by the Voice of America for distribution overseas. In 1969, Dett's oratorio was chosen for performance at the Golden Jubilee Convention of the National Association of Negro Musicians held at St. Louis, Missouri.

In addition to his original compositions, Dett published two collections of spiritual arrangements: *Religious Folksongs of the Negro* (1926) and *The Dett Collection of Negro Spirituals,* 4 volumes (1936).

Dett received many honors during his lifetime. Besides the Bowdoin and Francis Boote prizes mentioned earlier, he won the Harmon Foundation Award for composition in 1927; an honorary Master of Music degree from the Eastman School of Music in 1931; and honorary doctorates from Oberlin Conservatory and Howard University. He received the Palm and Ribbon Award from the Royal Belgium Band, by order of the Queen of Belgium. In 1938, the Columbia Broadcasting Company awarded Dett a commission to write a work for radio.[10]

Dett was also a member of several professional organizations, including the National Association of Negro Musicians. Besides being one of its founding members, he served this organization both as president and treasurer, a further indication of his dedication to both his art and his heritage.

---

[9]Copyright owner, Belwin-Mills Publishing Corporation, Rockville Center, New York. Used by permission.

[10]Southern, *The Music of Black Americans,* p. 293.

William Grant Still

William Grant Still (1895–1978), was born in Woodville, Mississippi, the only child of William Grant Still, Sr. and Carrie Lena Fambro Still. Both parents were well educated and both were musicians. The father died when the son was only three months old, after which the mother moved to Little Rock, Arkansas, where she taught in the public schools until her death in 1927.

There were three significant factors in his early life that influenced Still's musical development. His stepfather, a lover of operatic music, owned a phonograph and records, which afforded Still the opportunity to hear excellent music performed by the finest musicians.

Around 1910, at a time when brass bands were popular, Still chose to study violin rather than a wind instrument. This study provided a basis for his later knowledge and understanding of stringed instruments. (It undoubtedly reflects the cultivated tastes of his parents as well, since study of the violin by a Black boy was quite unusual.)

The third significant facet of Still's early life was the intellectual atmosphere into which he was born. This environment was as important a part of his early education as was his public-school training.

Still attended Wilberforce University in Ohio. It was during this period of his life that he became seriously interested in music. He desired to become a composer but was forbidden to do so by his mother. While in college, however, Still used every opportunity to further his training in music. He joined the university choir, played with the university's string quartet, and wrote some arrangements for the latter group. He was also a member of the university band, and it was here that he learned to play the oboe and clarinet. While yet a student, he became the bandmaster and learned to play various other instruments of the band. This experience gave him firsthand knowledge of the capabilities and qualities of various instruments and formed an invaluable part of the background needed for his future work.

William Grant Still, composer of both classical and popular music.

The first complete recital of his compositions was given at Wilber-force in 1915. The program, which consisted of songs and compositions for band, was enthusiastically received, a reception that helped Still to decide to pursue a career in music in spite of his mother's objections.

Still left Wilberforce two months before graduation because of a dis-agreement with his mother. He was now free to devote all his time to preparing for a career in music.

After spending two years as a performer and arranger for W. C. Handy's band, Still entered Oberlin Conservatory in 1917. Because he demonstrated great promise in composition, Still was granted free tuition and the opportunity to study with Dr. George W. Andrews.

After leaving Oberlin in 1920, Still continued to serve as an arranger for the firm of W. C. Handy. His next important engagement was in the orchestra of the musical show *Shuffle Along* in 1922, which enjoyed a sus-tained run in both New York and Boston. While in Boston, Still decided to study at the New England Conservatory, where he was granted a scholar-ship and received free lessons in composition from the prominent com-poser George W. Chadwick.

In 1923, he accepted the position of recording director with the Black Swan Phonograph Company of New York. While in New York, Still began to study with the French-American avant-garde composer, Edgard Varèse. His association with Varèse lasted for two years and led him into new and untried paths of musical expression.

During this period, Still was beginning to receive recognition as an arranger and orchestrator. Will Vodery, one of the first Black arranger-composers to secure a foothold in the commercial arranging field, was instrumental in creating contacts between Still and potential employers. At the same time, Still's serious compositions were being brought to the atten-tion of the public. In 1924, he composed a work for chamber orchestra and three women's voices, *The Land of Dreams*, which received its first perfor-mance in 1925 at an International Composers' Guild Concert in New York City, with Vladimir Shavitch conducting.

While studying with Varèse, Still continued to play in various musical shows. He became the conductor of the orchestra at a New York nightclub. He also accepted jobs as orchestrator for various musical shows, among them, *Vanities, Rain or Shine,* and *Running Wild,* and made special arrange-ments for Sophie Tucker, Don Voorhees, and Paul Whiteman.

Still's fame as an arranger, composer, and orchestrator had begun to spread. Because he was receiving so much work, Still no longer found it necessary to continue performing in order to make a living.

It is very rare for a musician who first wins recognition in the popu-lar-music field to gain acceptance in circles concerned with classical music. Still was able to do so, perhaps, because he never stopped composing music in the European tradition while he was arranging for radio and Broadway. Examples of the diversity of Still's works are many. In 1927, he arranged and recorded a fantasy on *St. Louis Blues*. During the same year, he composed his first ballet, *La Guiablesse,* which was later performed in both New York and Chicago. Even as early as 1924, when he was doing the orchestration for musical shows, his composition *Darker America* won a publication prize at the Eastman School of Music. In 1929–30, Still orchestrated for the Paul Whiteman orchestra's performances on the "Old Gold Radio Hour." It was during this period that his second ballet, *Sahdji* (1930) was composed. In 1930, he began to do orchestrations for the "Deep River Hour," which originated in New York. This assignment led to his becoming the first Black musician in America to conduct a White orchestra, the Deep River orchestra. He remained in this position until 1934. During this period, Still composed two symphonies—*Africa* and *Afro-American Symphony,* two works that were to become part of a trilogy with the completion of the *Symphony in G minor: Song of a New Race* (1937). He was associated with Columbia Pictures in the mid-thirties and with Warner Brothers Studios in the early forties. He also did a considerable amount of orchestration for Dmitri Tiomkin as late as 1945. In 1944, he was commissioned by the Cleveland Orchestra to write his *Poem for Orchestra;* his *Festive Overture* won the Cincinnati Orchestra Jubilee Season Prize.

During his early period, Still's compositions were constantly subjected to press criticism. His emulation of the style of Varèse appeared not to be very successful. After writing *From the Journal of a Wanderer* in 1925, he decided to abandon this style and instead to use his racial heritage as a basis for his music. *Africa, The Afro-American Symphony,* the ballet, *Sahdji,* and *From the Black Belt* all were written following this decision. His first attempt at composition in the new idiom, however, was a suite for chamber orchestra with soprano solo, *Levee Land.* The work was performed at an International Composers' Guild concert at Aeolian Hall in 1926; the conductor was Eugene Goossens and the soloist was the vaudeville star Florence Mills. In general, the work received favorable reviews.

In 1934, Still was awarded a Guggenheim Fellowship. That year is also significant in another respect. Until 1934, his compositions were predominantly orchestral works. Commencing that year, he began to write compositions for orchestra with soloist and/or chorus. *The Black Man Dances,* for piano and orchestra, was one of the first. In 1935, he wrote *Kaintuck,* for piano and orchestra. *Song of a City,* for chorus and orchestra (a version of his theme music for the New York World's Fair) followed in 1939. In 1940, he composed *And They Lynched Him on a Tree,* for contralto soloist, mixed double chorus, narrator, and orchestra.

The diversification of media that began in 1934 was accompanied by another turning point in the career of this composer. Still now decided to abandon the racial idiom that he had adopted in 1926, feeling that such an idiom should not be an end in itself, and he embarked upon a highly eclectic period. During this third period, Still utilized a variety of styles, media, and subject matter. The styles ranged from nineteenth-century romanticism to twentieth-century polytonality. His genres were expanded to include opera, chamber music, solo, and choral works. Prior to this period, the subject matter was primarily racial; subsequently, it included folk material from countries other than Africa and America, as well as abstract texts.

While Still no longer wrote compositions in a purely racial idiom, he did compose racially oriented works as late as 1957, such as *Four Indigenous Portraits* for string quartet and flute. One of the better known of his works, the opera *Troubled Island*, composed in 1941 and produced at the City Center in New York in 1949, also was based on a racial theme.

Of Still's nine operas, the libretti for seven of them are by his second wife, Verna Arvey. The libretto for his first opera, *Blue Steel,* is by Bruce Forsythe, while *Troubled Island* is based on a libretto by Langston Hughes.

Other compositions by Still include thirty works for orchestra, five of them symphonies; three for concert band; four ballets; fourteen works for piano or other solo instruments and small ensembles; and a large number of solo songs and choral works.

Afro-American Symphony.   As stated earlier, the *Afro-American Symphony* is a part of the trilogy comprising (1) *Africa,* (2) *Afro-American Symphony,* and (3) *Symphony in G Minor.* This work, which consists of four movements, was composed in 1930 and performed by the Rochester Philharmonic Orchestra in Rochester, New York in 1931 and 1932. Dr. Howard Hanson introduced it in Berlin, Stuttgart, and Leipzig in 1933.

After the symphony was composed as an abstract work, Still decided to invent a program for it, feeling that this would make it easier for audiences to understand its meaning. He prefaced each movement with an excerpt from the poems of Paul Laurence Dunbar. The first movement was titled *Longing;* the second, *Sorrow;* the third, *Humor;* and the fourth, *Aspiration.*

The poetry associated with the movements is as follows:[11]

I. Moderato assai

"All my life long twell de night has pas'
Let de wo'k come ez it will,
So dat I fin' you, my honey, at last,
Somewhaih des ovah de hill."

II. Adagio

"It's moughty tiahsome layin' 'roun'
Dis sorrer-laden earfly groun'
An' oftentimes I thinks, thinks I
An' go 'long home."

III. Animato

"An' we'll shout ouah halleluyahs,
On dat mighty reck'nin day"

[11]William Grant Still, *Afro-American Symphony* (London: Novello & Co., Ltd., 1969).

IV. Lento, con resoluzione
"Be proud, my Race, in mind and soul.
Thy name is writ on Glory's scroll
In characters of fire.
High mid the clouds of Fame's bright sky
And truth shall lift them higher."

The instrumentation includes the following:

Woodwinds: 3 flutes, 2 oboes, English horn, 3 clarinets in B-flat, bass clar-
            inet, and 2 bassoons
Brass: 4 horns in F, 3 trumpets in B-flat, 3 tenor trombones, and tuba
Percussion: timpani, vibraphone, triangle, wire brush, small cymbal, cym-
            bals, snare drum, bass drum, and celesta
Strings: violins, violas, violoncellos, contra-basses, and harp

The first movement is in A-flat major and $\frac{4}{4}$ time. The introduction
consists of a six-measure passage played by the English horn.

EXAMPLE 5.11 Introduction, *Afro-American Symphony*

The blueslike character of the introduction reflects the title of this
movement, "Longing." In measure 4, Still uses a typical blues chord to
further intensify the blueslike character. It is an ambiguous chord that may
be interpreted as a dominant chord with both a major and a minor third, or
a ninth chord with an enharmonic spelling of a raised ninth.

EXAMPLE 5.12 Blues chord, *Afro-American Symphony*

The first theme, which is also similar to the blues in character, is
introduced by a solo trumpet at measure 7, and subsequently dominates
the entire composition.

EXAMPLE 5.13 First theme, *Afro-American Symphony*

The theme is repeated except that the strings and woodwinds now play a consistent quarter-note pattern of chords containing fluctuating major and minor thirds; in effect, there also are blues chords.

The second theme is introduced by the oboe at measure 45.

EXAMPLE 5.14   Second theme, *Afro-American Symphony*

Commencing in measure 56, the second theme appears in the flutes in three-part harmony.

The development section begins at measure 68. This material, which is derived from the first theme, is announced by the strings.

EXAMPLE 5.15   Developmental material, *Afro-American Symphony*

The development section also utilizes material derived from the second motive of the first theme in measure 74.

EXAMPLE 5.16   Developmental material, *Afro-American Symphony*

The recapitulation commences in measure 104. The themes, however, reappear in reverse order to their presentation in the exposition; the second theme is followed by the first theme, both now in A-flat major.

The first theme of this movement is used in the later movements in various ways. Sometimes Still sees fit to derive a secondary theme from it, as in the introduction to the second movement and in the finale.

EXAMPLE 5.17   Introduction to second movement, *Afro-American Symphony*

At other times, the theme is simply stated in a transformed version, as is the case just before the coda in the third movement. In this instance, the first theme of this movement is restated for the final time at measure 88. Still transforms the first theme of the first movement and uses it as an accompanying figure in the trumpet.

EXAMPLE 5.18 Third movement, *Afro-American Symphony*

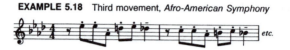

Although it is true that Still is utilizing a racial idiom in this work, none of the themes of this symphony consists of the actual quotation of genuine folk melodies, but rather are original themes written in the spirit of Black music. Some themes are reminiscent of spirituals (with banjolike accompaniment), short songs, and jazz tunes.

The first theme of the third movement is placed in the strings and accompanied by the banjo. The theme is lively, and very much in the character of a jubilant spiritual that one would hear at a camp meeting during congregational singing.

EXAMPLE 5.19 First theme, third movement, *Afro-American Symphony*[12]

There are special ways in which Still handled certain basic aspects of this composition. The dominant rhythmic motive in the *Afro-American Symphony* is the use of the tie and/or syncopation. (See Example 5.11). Another quality that characterizes Still's melodies is the importance he attaches to the interval of a third.

Still's harmonic language is traditional here except when he is interested in effecting a blues color. Chords such as that in Example 5.12 are used in a somewhat ambiguous manner, which leaves it unclear whether they are meant to be blues chords with opposing major and minor thirds, or ninth chords.

This movement follows the design of the sonata-allegro form. The first movement may be outlined as follows: (1) a short, slow introduction in the tonic key; (2) an exposition with related key schemes; (3) a development section; and (4) a recapitulation in the tonic key.

William Levi Dawson

William Levi Dawson (b. 1899), a native of Anniston, Alabama, attended Tuskegee Institute as an agricultural student. Before graduating in 1921, he had learned most of the orchestral instruments, could play piano well, and had studied music theory.

[12]Copyright owner, Novello & Co., Ltd., London, England. All examples used by permission.

William Dawson, composer of the *Negro Folk Symphony*. (Photo courtesy New York Public Library, Schomburg Collection of Negro Literature.)

His first teaching position was that of director of music at Kansas Vocational College in Topeka, Kansas, where he taught instrumental music and conducted the band. While filling this position, Dawson studied composition and orchestration at Washburn College in Topeka.

In 1922 Dawson became director of music at Lincoln High School in Kansas City, Kansas, a position he occupied for four years. His duties included supervising instrumental music in the grade schools and conducting school choirs. Dawson continued to acquire a knowledge of theory and composition by studying with Carl Busch and Regina G. Hall at the Horner Institute of Fine Arts. He graduated from this institution with honors in 1925; his *Trio in A* for violin, violoncello, and piano was performed at the graduation program.

Following his graduation, the composer went to Chicago to continue his studies in composition. Dawson won a scholarship to the American Conservatory of Music, where he studied composition with Adolph Weidig. After earning a Master of Music degree in 1927, he decided to remain in Chicago to do further study in composition with Thorvald Otterstrom and later with Felix Borowski of the Chicago Musical College faculty.

Dawson served as first trombonist in the Chicago Civic Orchestra from 1926 to 1930, under the leadership of Frederick Stock and Eric De Lamarter. In 1929 Dawson won a contest conducted by the Chicago *Daily News* for the position of bandmaster for the World's Fair, to be held in 1933. In addition, his musical activities included arranging, editing, conducting, and performing for radio broadcasts.

Dawson returned to Tuskegee in 1930, organized the music curriculum at Tuskegee Institute, and assumed the position of conductor of Tuskegee's famous choir. He served in both of these positions until his retirement in 1955. During his first and second years after his return to his alma mater, Dawson won the Rodman Wanamaker contests in music composition.

In 1932, Dawson initiated concert tours of the Institute's choir. Under his leadership, this group participated in many outstanding events: a four-week engagement at Radio City Music Hall in New York at its opening (1932–33); a concert at the White House for President Hoover (1932); performances for the birthday festivities of President Roosevelt (1933); a concert at Carnegie Hall (1933); and broadcasts over the NBC (1937–38), CBS (1940–46), and ABC (1946–51) radio networks.

The first major performance of a Dawson work occurred in 1934 when the Philadelphia Orchestra, under Leopold Stokowski, premiered his *Negro Folk Symphony* (1932), a composition based in part on themes from familiar Black spirituals.

Dawson was granted a sabbatical leave in 1952–53 to study the native music of several countries in West Africa. Upon his return from West Africa, he revised his symphony, imbuing it with rhythms strongly derived from those of African music.

After his retirement in 1955, Dawson was awarded an honorary doctorate by Tuskegee Institute. Shortly thereafter, he was sent to Spain by the Department of State for the purpose of training choral groups there.

Despite his many successes, Dawson also felt some of the frustration faced by Black and White American composers. Even though the performance of his *Negro Folk Symphony* was an artistic success, the composer sought in vain to interest American orchestras in further performances. After a number of frustrating experiences, Dawson discontinued his efforts in this direction, for his career had taken a decisive turn toward choral music. This was partly because of his decision to teach and conduct the chorus at his alma mater, a small and impecunious college without an orchestra. Consequently, after writing *Interlude* for piano and orchestra in 1943, he did not utilize this medium again.

Other orchestral compositions by Dawson include *Scherzo* (1930) and *Negro Work Song* (1940). Among his chamber works are the *Trio in A* for violin, violoncello, and piano and the *Sonata in A* for violin and piano. Choral works other than spirituals include *Hail Mary* (1946) and *Lovers Plighted.*

Negro Folk Symphony.   It had been Dawson's ambition "to write a symphony in the Negro folk idiom, based on authentic Negro folk music but in the same symphonic form used by the composers of the romantic-nationalist school."[13] His work contains rich, full orchestration. This symphony is in three movements and is programmatic, with the first and third movements in sonata form.

The instrumentation of the Negro Folk Symphony is as follows:

Woodwind: 2 flutes, piccolo, 2 oboes, English horn, E-flat clarinet, 2 clarinets in B-flat and in A, bass clarinet, 2 bassoons, and contrabassoon

Brass: 4 horns in F, 3 trumpets in B-flat and in A, 3 trombones, and tuba

Percussion: timpani, gong, chimes, African clave—*Adawura,* triangle, tenor drum, side drum, xylophone, cymbals, and bass drum

Strings: harp, violins, violas, violoncellos, and contrabasses

The first movement is titled "The Bond of Africa." It is Dawson's view that ". . . a link was taken out of a human chain when the first African was taken from the shores of his native land and sent to slavery."[14] This work opens with a motive sounded by the French horn and symbolizes the "missing link."

EXAMPLE 5.20   Motive in Introduction, *Negro Folk Symphony*

The motive appears in all three movements, sometimes fully stated, and at other times in the form of subsidiary themes or other transformations. On other occasions, the motive is only alluded to in the inner voices. This motive is very similar to the motive used by Dett in his *Ordering of Moses* oratorio (Example 5.4).

The first theme of Dawson's composition is an original melody that is written in the style of a spiritual.

EXAMPLE 5.21   First theme, first movement, *Negro Folk Symphony*

It is announced by the French horn. In contrast to the first theme, the second is based on the Black spiritual *Oh, m' littl' soul gwine-a shine.* It is introduced by the oboe.

---

[13]George Jellinek, record liner notes, *Negro Folk Symphony* (Decca Records DL 10077).
[14]*Ibid.*

EXAMPLE 5.22   Second theme, first movement, *Negro Folk Symphony*

The second theme is followed by a section that is strongly animated and is highly suggestive of rhythmic hand-clapping.

EXAMPLE 5.23   Rhythmic episode, first movement, *Negro Folk Symphony*

This rhythmic figuration appears again in the recapitulation. The two themes appear in the recapitulation in reverse order from the manner in which they were presented in the exposition.

The second movement is named "Hope in the Night." This movement opens with three strokes of the gong, symbolizing the Trinity. The English horn introduces a songlike theme against an unvarying harmonic background of pizzicato strings. This unchanging sound suggests ". . . the monotonous life of people who were held in bondage for two hundred and fifty years."[15]

EXAMPLE 5.24 First theme, second movement, *Negro Folk Symphony*

A contrasting theme is presented in the Allegretto section of the second movement by the oboes again. This theme symbolizes the play of children.

EXAMPLE 5.25 Second theme, second movement, *Negro Folk Symphony*

Each of the themes in the second movement is original with the composer.

The "missing link" motive is heard again on two different occasions in this movement, which comes to a close as it started—with three strokes of the gong.

[15]*Ibid.*

The third movement bears the title "O Le' Me Shine!" Both themes of this movement are based on the Black spirituals *O le' me shine, le' me shine, lik' a morin star,* and *Hallelujah, Lord, I been down into the sea.*

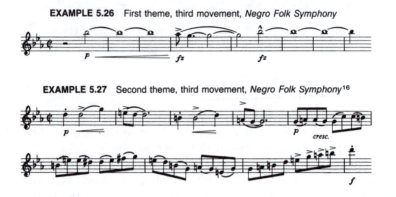

EXAMPLE 5.26   First theme, third movement, *Negro Folk Symphony*

EXAMPLE 5.27   Second theme, third movement, *Negro Folk Symphony*[16]

After the recapitulation, a coda concludes the movement as the brasses sing out with *O le' me shine lik' a morin' star.*

THE ECLECTICS

The term *eclectic* is generally applied to composers who choose from several sources and styles the materials and techniques to be used in their compositions. In contrast to the composers discussed in the previous section, who took most, though not all, of their material from the Black folk idiom, the eclectics feel free to choose whatever materials and techniques they believe suitable for the composition at hand. It may include Black material, either folk or jazz, serial or aleatory techniques, or be multifarious in nature.

The young Black composers who emerged around and after the middle of this century refused to have their compositions delimited by racial self-consciousness and felt it imperative to their freedom of expression that they draw freely upon widely divergent styles and sources in their writings.

Contemporary with the emergence of this group of composers was a high degree of race consciousness among many young Blacks of this country. These young Blacks began to define all facets of American culture in terms of "how Black it is" or "how White it is." Music was no exception. Many young Blacks have followed a hard line in espousing the view that the only true Black music is music written in forms indigenous to the race, such as blues, jazz, and gospel songs. It would appear that the majority in this group are nonmusicians.

[16]© 1931. Licensing Agent, Shawnee Press, Delaware Water Gap, Pa. All examples used by permission.

On the other hand, the eclectic composers take a completely opposite view. As an example, Olly Wilson, one of this country's promising young composers in the electronic medium, offers the definition that Black music is simply music written by Black people.

No definition of Black music will be made here other than that stated earlier—"Black music" will be used to designate that music indigenous to Blacks and that music which has been composed by Black composers.

One fact does become increasingly apparent, however: Black music appears to exist on a continuum. That music which utilizes music genres indigenous to Black culture—such as blues or soul music—sounds "very Black." Music of Black culture that is synthesized with traditional European musical forms sounds "less Black" than the former, but the "Blackness" is discernable. Finally, that music which employs twentieth-century compositional techniques, forms, and media sounds "least Black" of all. (It is interesting to note that the same difficulty arises in trying to delineate the music of *any* nationality or culture when twentieth-century compositional techniques, form, and media are utilized.)

It is primarily the Black nonmusician who has become very restrictive in defining Black music and who has labeled much of the music of the eclectics as nothing more than an attempt to imitate White music. Be that as it may, the contemporary Black composer writes music that corresponds to his artistic emotions, within a framework of harmony, counterpoint, and orchestration that provides him with the broadest range of expression.

Howard Swanson

Howard Swanson's (1907–78) devotion to the craft of composition through long and serious study culminated in his winning the coveted New York Critics' Circle Award in 1952 for his *Short Symphony* (1948). The path to this success had been long and arduous.

Swanson, born in Atlanta, began the study of piano at the age of twelve. In 1917, his family moved to Cleveland. He entered the Cleveland Institute of Music at the age of twenty, where he studied composition with Herbert Elwell. He was able to support himself while in school by working in the Cleveland post office.

Swanson completed his studies in 1937 and was awarded a Rosenwald Fellowship for further musical study in Europe with Nadia Boulanger, the renowned teacher of composition. Upon his return to the United States in 1939, Swanson obtained a job as a file clerk in the Bureau of Internal Revenue, but after three years he resigned the position to devote all of his time to composition.

Swanson first attracted attention as a composer with a bright future when one of his songs, *The Negro Speaks of Rivers* (poem by Langston Hughes), was sung by Marian Anderson in a recital in 1950. In the spring

Howard Swanson, 1952 winner of the coveted New York Critics Circle Award. (Photo courtesy New York Public Library, Schomburg Collection of Negro Literature.)

of that year, several of his songs were selected for performance at a concert of the American Composers' Festival held in New York. Then came his big breakthrough: Dimitri Mitropoluos, impressed by the quality of Swanson's music, gave the first performance of his *Short Symphony*. The coveted New York Music Critics' Circle Award followed, honoring his work as the best new orchestral work played in New York in the previous year. This was the first time that the competition had been opened to works by composers of all nationalities instead of being limited to American composers, and it was the first time the award had been won by a Black composer.

Among other honors that came to Swanson were a grant from the Academy of Arts and Letters and a Guggenheim Fellowship.

In comparison to many other composers, Swanson's list of works is small. He was a meticulous worker and often composed in an intense and expressive harmonic idiom. The *Short Symphony* is actually Swanson's second; the first one has been neither published nor performed. Other works include the *Symphony No. 3*, which was commissioned by the Symphony Orchestra of the New World and given its premiere performance in 1970; *Concerto for Orchestra* (1954); *Concerto for Piano and Orchestra* (1956); *Night Music* (1950); and *Sonata for Violoncello and Piano* (1973). Smaller works include *Music for Strings* (1952); *Sound Piece for Brass Quintet* (1952); a suite for violoncello and piano (1950); a piano sonata (1950); *Nocturne* for violin and piano (1952); *The Cuckoo,* a scherzo for piano (1949); *Fantasy Piece* for soprano saxophone and strings (1969); *Vista No. II* for string octet (1969);

and *Trio for Flute, Oboe, and Piano* (1975). He has set to music poems by Carl Sandburg—*Still Life* (1950), *The Junk Man* (1950), and *Cahoots* (1950); Vachel Lindsay—*Ghosts in Love* (1950); Langston Hughes—*The Negro Speaks of Rivers* (1942), *Joy* (1946), *Pierrot* (1946), *In Time of Silver Rain* (1947), and *Night Song* (1948); Paul Laurence Dunbar—*A Death Song* (1943); T. S. Eliot—*Four Preludes* (1947); May Swenson—*Saw A Grave Upon A Hill* (1952), *Snowdunes* (1955), *I Will Lie Down in Autumn* (1952); Robert Seymour—*Nightingales* (1952); Norman Rosten—*Songs for Patricia* (1952); and Charles E. Markham—*The Valley* (1951). A noteworthy characteristic of many of Swanson's songs is their dramatic and brooding quality.

Besides Marian Anderson, his songs have been sung by William Warfield, Kenneth Spencer, Lawrence Winters, Everett Lee Tyler, and Helen Thigpen.

Short Symphony. Swanson's best-known work is the *Short Symphony*. It is in three movements and is scored for 2 flutes, 2 oboes, 2 clarinets, 2 bassoons, 2 horns, 2 trumpets, trombone, timpani, and strings. The work is predominantly neoclassical in style.

The first movement is in sonata form but uses a little fugato as the first theme. The theme is heard first in the winds, then in the strings, and finally in the brass.

EXAMPLE 5.28 Fugato theme, *Short Symphony*

The first theme is later chromatically altered. Although this work is basically neoclassical, it contains jazzlike elements in some passages.

EXAMPLE 5.29 Jazzlike passage, first movement, *Short Symphony*

The second theme is also treated in a fugal fashion.

EXAMPLE 5.30 Second theme, first movement, *Short Symphony*

In the development section, first one theme and then the other are developed independently of each other. As the two theme groups are transposed to various keys, the themes are usually restated tonally and not in an exact replica of the original exposition.

The texture is rarely thick; when the entire orchestra is employed, which occurs on three occasions, it does not last for longer than six measures. The texture is contrapuntal and the meter remains in $\frac{4}{4}$ throughout the movement. The first movement ends as it starts, with the first theme being restated before the last chord.

The second movement is in three-part form (ABA).

EXAMPLE 5.31 Second movement (Part A of ternary form), *Short Symphony*

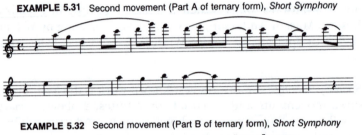

EXAMPLE 5.32 Second movement (Part B of ternary form), *Short Symphony*

This ABA form is asymmetrical in that the repeat of the A section contains only the first three measures of the six-measure A theme.

At the conclusion of this movement, the themes are restated in a kind of reverse order. The B portion of the theme is stated first, the last three measures of the A portion of the theme follow, and the first three measures of the A portion of the theme conclude the movement.

This movement begins in a major tonality and ends on a minor chord. The texture is again medium to light; in only two measures does the entire orchestra perform simultaneously.

The last movement is in rondo form. It begins with the rondo theme in the bassoons.

EXAMPLE 5.33 Rondo theme, last movement, *Short Symphony*

In the rondo form, there are three sections that correspond to the exposition, development, and recapitulation of a sonata movement, and two episodes of which the first returns in the dominant and the second is actually the development. The form is AB (dominant) AC (development) AB (tonic) A.

The theme of the B section appears in the clarinet at its first entrance and in the violas at its last.

EXAMPLE 5.34   Theme of the B section, third movement, *Short Symphony*

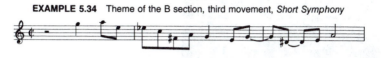

The texture is contrapuntal, and, again, the entire orchestra is seldom employed simultaneously. One meter is used throughout the movement.

Swanson employs a modern, somewhat dissonant harmonic language that utilizes major sevenths and minor seconds frequently.

EXAMPLE 5.35   Representative harmonies, first movement, *Short Symphony*[17]

Ulysses Kay

Ulysses Simpson Kay was born in Tucson, Arizona, in 1917, the son of a barber. His musical family stimulated an interest in music while Kay was still young. He is the nephew of the celebrated jazz pioneer King Oliver, who he often visited in Chicago.

He graduated from the University of Arizona in 1938 and studied at the Eastman School of Music, where he received a Master of Arts degree in composition. He studied further with Paul Hindemith at Yale and at the Berkshire Music Center.

Kay served in the U.S. Navy from 1942 to 1946. During this time, he did a considerable amount of arranging and found some time to compose.

Following the war, Kay received a Ditson Fellowship to study composition at Columbia University. He then received several other awards: a Julius Rosenwald Fellowship; a Prix de Rome for residence at the American Academy in Rome for the seasons of 1949–50 and 1951–52; a

---

[17]Copyright owner, Weintraub Music Company, New York, N.Y. All examples used by permission.

Ulysses Kay, who usually employs traditional forms in his compositions. (Photo courtesy New York Public Library, Schomburg Collection of Negro Literature.)

Fulbright scholarship to Italy for 1950–51; and grants from the American Academy of Arts and Letters and the National Institute of Arts and Letters.

Kay has been the recipient of several prizes for his compositions, including first prize from Broadcast Music, Inc., for his *Suite for Orchestra;* a Gershwin Memorial Prize for *A Short Overture;* and an American Broadcasting Company prize for *Of New Horizons.* Other honors and awards include a Guggenheim Fellowship and honorary doctorates from Lincoln University in Pennsylvania (1963), Illinois Wesleyan University (1969), Bucknell University (1966), and the University of Arizona (1969). Kay was one of four composers who visited the Soviet Union in 1958 under the terms of the United States State Department Cultural, Educational and Technical Exchange Agreement.

Many musical organizations have commissioned works by Kay, including the Stanley String Quartet of the University of Michigan, the Koussevitzky Music Foundation, the Louisville Orchestra, the *a cappella* choir of Cornell University, the New Orleans Symphony Orchestra, the Meadow Brook Music Festival of the Detroit Symphony Orchestra, and the Atlanta Symphony Orchestra. His works have been performed by the Detroit, Chicago, Rochester, Brooklyn, and Cleveland symphony orchestras, the Columbia Broadcasting Company String Orchestra, the Naples Radio Orchestra, the West Berlin Radio Symphony, and the Moscow State Radio Orchestra.

Kay has been a visiting professor at Boston University and at the University of California at Los Angeles. He has been a consultant and lecturer at such institutions as the Juilliard School of Music, Hartt College of Music, Fisk University, Millikin University, Cornell University, and others. Before accepting the position of professor of music at the Herbert Lehman College of the City University of New York in 1968, Kay worked as music consultant for Broadcast Music, Incorporated.

Kay has been a prolific composer since the performance of his first important work, the overture *Of New Horizons* (1944), by the New York Philharmonic. He has composed for a variety of solo instruments and ensembles, among them, full orchestra, string orchestra, chorus or voice and orchestra, chamber ensembles, band, opera, organ, chorus, and piano.

Among the compositions most typical of Kay's musical style are the cantata *Song of Jeremiah* (1947), the *Piano Quintet* (1949), *Three Pieces after Blake* (1952), the *Serenade for Orchestra* (1954), and the *Second String Quartet* (1956). (Two movements from the string quartet are instrumental rearrangements of *Three Pieces after Blake*.) Each of these works represents the salient characteristics of Kay's mature style.

Among Kay's more recent compositions are the *Epigrams and Hymn*, anthem for chorus and organ (1975); *Jubilee*, opera in three acts (1974–76); *Quintet Concerto* for solo brass quintet and orchestra (1974); *Southern Harmony* for orchestra (1975); *The Western Paradise* for narrator and orchestra (1976); and *Prologue and Parade* for band (1977).

Even though Kay's melodic line often contains large intervals such as major sevenths or major ninths with dissonant harmonic implications, they usually evolve or converge toward a tonal center through the use of smaller intervals. Conversely, small intervals may be used to expand the tonality from the central tonal area. Kay rarely follows the strict procedures of fugal imitation in his polyphonic writing; rather, he varies the imitation rhythmically or tonally. Through chromatic manipulation, Kay expands or contracts his harmonies. His scoring for instruments, while sparse, is nevertheless colorful. While using a medium-sized orchestra, Kay has been very successful in utilizing it to best advantage. He uses rhythm in a natural way. When an acceleration is desired, Kay adds a unit to a subdivision, progressing from two to a beat, to three or four to a beat.

Kay usually employs traditional forms in his compositions. Among them are overtures, concertos, suites, symphonies, quartets, and cantatas. His best-known works include the film score for *The Quiet One* (1948); *Brass Quartet* (1952); *Fantasy Variations* (1963); *Umbrian Scene* (1964); and *Theater Set* (1968).

Fantasy Variations.   While the form of this composition might be called theme and variations, "variations and theme" would be more appropriate. After an introduction in which a principal motive is presented, thirteen variations are derived from that motive. A theme derived in turn from the thirteen variations is presented at the conclusion.

This orchestral work utilizes a multitude of meters in the presentation of the various musical ideas. In fact, in only one variation, including the introduction and conclusion, does one meter prevail throughout the entire section.

The instrumentation includes the following:

Woodwinds: 2 flutes (flute II alternating with piccolo), 2 oboes, 2 clarinets (B-flat), and 2 bassoons
Brass: 4 horns (F), 3 trumpets (C), 3 trombones, and tuba.
Percussion: timpani, glockenspiel, vibraphone, bell, snare drum, tenor drum, bass drum, crash cymbals, suspended cymbal, small gong, tambourine, tam-tam, triangle, and wood block.
Strings: violins, violas, violoncellos, and contrabasses

Kay presents several motives in the introduction of this work. Among them are the following:

EXAMPLE 5.36 Opening horn motive, *Fantasy Variations*

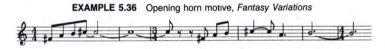

EXAMPLE 5.37 Other motives (A, B, and C), Introduction, *Fantasy Variations*

In Variation I, the thematic material is derived from the opening French-horn motive (Example 5.36). The theme is presented alternately in the oboe, flute, bassoon, and clarinet. The strings participate very little in this section. The texture is contrapuntal.

EXAMPLE 5.38 Thematic material, Variation I, *Fantasy Variations*

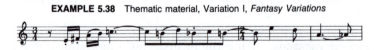

In Variation II, the thematic material is also derived from the opening motive, but this time it is presented in augmentation in the strings. The brass section plays chords as a background to the theme, giving this variation a character different from the first. The woodwinds are utilized sparingly.

Variation III employs a theme in the French horns against a triplet eighth-note figure in the woodwinds. The theme is subsequently given to the violins and violas against the same woodwind background. The texture is essentially homophonic.

The fourth variation presents the thematic material in the violins and violas. The background is agitated, consisting of triplet eighth- and sixteenth-notes, as well as quintuplet sixteenth-notes.

The fifth variation is derived from the last two measures of the C motive. (See Example 5.37.)

EXAMPLE 5.39   Theme, fifth variation, *Fantasy Variation*

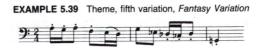

The theme is introduced in the second bassoon, cello, and double bass. The variation has a scherzolike quality.

Variation VI is derived from an inversion of the opening motive. In contrast to the previous section, this one is performed legato. The violins play a unison passage that utilizes octave leaps. The texture is quasi-contrapuntal.

In the seventh variation, the clarinet introduces the thematic material against a sustained chordal background in the strings.

The eighth variation has the trombones presenting the opening motive of the introduction in augmentation. The predominant instruments in this section are the French horns, trombones, and percussion. The texture is quite thin because the strings and woodwinds are hardly employed.

In the ninth variation, the main thematic idea is introduced in the violins against a sixteenth-note background in the violas. Later in this variation, a contrapuntal idea is introduced in the bassoons against the theme, which is now in the cellos. This is one of the few sections in which the entire orchestra is employed, though for only a few measures.

The tenth variation is marked *Largo assai,* and it is written in a homophonic style with a thick texture. The theme is presented in the strings and oboes simultaneously.

Variation XI is very agitated in character. The theme is presented in the violins, and the woodwinds provide the accompaniment. The texture is homophonic, with the woodwinds punctuating the theme with staccato announcements. Later in this variation, the strings and woodwinds are employed as contrasting groups.

For the second time in this work, Kay presents the thematic material in the trombones against a French horn background. Later, in Variation XII, the woodwinds play sustained tones while the strings utilize nervous unison figures. The theme of this variation is then played in an augmented version in the French horns and trumpets.

In the thirteenth variation, the principal thematic material is introduced in the cellos against an agitated background in the woodwinds and strings. Eighth-note triplets are used continually throughout this variation.

At the conclusion, the trumpets present the theme that has been derived from the thematic material presented in each of the foregoing variations.

EXAMPLE 5.40 Theme, *Fantasy Variations*

In a final pronouncement, the French horns end the composition as it began. It is as if the sounding of the opening motive is a reminder that all that has gone before is derived from the introductory material.

Kay utilizes vibrant harmonic progressions that are strongly supported by an imaginatively outlined bass, continually expanding or contracting his chords through the use of chromaticism.

EXAMPLE 5.41 Representative harmonies, Introduction, *Fantasy Variations*[18]

George T. Walker

George Theophilus Walker (b. 1922), composer, pianist, and music educator, was born in Washington, D.C. He attended Oberlin College and graduated from that institution in 1941. Walker received an Artist Diploma in piano and composition from the Curtis Institute of Music in 1945 after studying piano with Rudolf Serkin and composition with Rosario Scalero; a diploma in piano from the American Academy in Fountainebleau, France in 1947, after studying with Casadesus; and the Doctor of Musical Arts degree from the Eastman School of Music in 1957. Under Fulbright and John Hay Whitney Fellowships, he studied composition with Nadia Boulanger in Paris in 1957–59 and studied piano with Clifford Curzon in 1958 at Fontainebleau.

After a Town Hall debut in New York in 1945, Walker concertized extensively for several years under the management of National Concert Artists and Columbia Artists. His tours carried him to Europe (Sweden, Denmark, Holland, Germany, Italy, and France) in 1950–53 and again in 1958 and 1963. He embarked on a West Indian tour during the summer of 1956.

In between concertizing, Walker has been engaged in teaching since 1947. He did private teaching in New York and Philadelphia for three years; was pianist in residence at Dillard University in New Orleans; was coach in the opera workshop at the Eastman School of Music (1955–57); was instructor of piano at the Dalcroze School of Music, New York; taught

George T. Walker, who had his debut at Town Hall in New York in 1945.

aesthetics at the New School for Social Research, New York (1960); and taught at Smith College and the University of Colorado before taking a position at Rutgers University in 1969. In 1974, he was appointed to the faculty of the University of Delaware as Distinguished Visiting Professor. In addition, Walker has published articles in several scholarly journals.

Walker's compositions include *Address for Orchestra* (1959), which was commissioned by the Symphony of the New World and subsequently performed by the Atlanta, Baltimore, and Minneapolis orchestras; *Gloria in Memoriam* (1963), his first published work; *Perimeters* for clarinet and piano (1966), commissioned by Leroy Johnston for performance at the Juilliard School of Music; *Five Fancies* for clarinet and piano (four hands, 1974), commissioned by the David Ensemble for performance at Alice Tully Hall; *Music (Sacred and Profane)* for brass quintet (1975), commissioned by the Hans Kindler Foundation; a symphony; two string quartets; several sonatas for piano and violin, violoncello, and clarinet; a trombone concerto; and a number of piano compositions, including *Spatials* (1961), *Spektra* (1971), and *Piano Concerto* (1975). His *Psalm 81* received the Religious Arts Award in 1961, and his *Sonata for Two Pianos* won the Harvey Gaul Prize in 1963. A second piano sonata was published in 1966; a third piano sonata was commissioned by the Washington Society for the Performing Arts and Leon Bates for a performance by the latter at the Kennedy Center in 1975.

Walker is eclectic in his approach to composition, using both folk and nonfolk material. The folk material may or may not be Black in origin. His music has a contemporary sound and abounds with dissonance.

Piano Sonata No. 1.   The first movement, *Allegro energico,* is written in traditional sonata form with a clearly delineated first theme.

EXAMPLE 5.42   First theme, first movement, *Sonata No. 1*

After the exposition of the first theme, a transitional section consisting of triplets and sixteenth notes with the fourth as the predominant interval leads to the second theme. The second theme is more lyrical than the first.

EXAMPLE 5.43   Second theme, first movement, *Sonata No. 1*

After a short codetta, the development commences with material from the codetta and the transition section. The basic developmental technique is one of continuous expansion. Both themes are skillfully manipulated simultaneously, often reappearing without transformation. The development section is characterized by a strong rhythmic drive.

In the recapitulation, the thematic material is presented in the same manner as in the exposition. Except for some slight notational changes, the entire thematic material reappears, corresponding in number of measures with the exposition.

The second movement, a theme with six variations, is based on the Kentucky folksong *Oh Bury Me Beneath the Willow.* It is ten measures in length, in $\frac{6}{8}$ meter, and of uneven phrase lengths.

EXAMPLE 5.44 Theme, second movement, *Sonata No. 1*

The use of irregular units permeates all of the variations. In general, binary form prevails throughout the variations. Each of the variations is of the same length as the theme.

Variation I uses fifths and fourths in sixteenth-note patterns as the principal melodic ingredients. The second variation is strong in character and utilizes chords and the characteristic rhythmic figure (♪ ♩).

In the third variation, there is pitch repetition in octaves. This is done using sixteenth notes. This rhythmic pattern tends to act as a unifying element in the variation. The fourth variation is contrasted with the previous one by employing slower note-values, eighth and quarter notes giving it a sustained quality. The melody is carried by the inner voices.

Variation V employs several meter changes. It is scherzolike in character, and the ten measures are subdivided 4 + 6. The sixth variation utilizes a trill-like motion of sixteenth notes over which the theme is superimposed. Alternating *piano* and *forte* passages gives the variation an element of contrast.

In the final section of this movement, the theme is restated in its original simple form, altered only in the second half by octave doublings. Concluding this movement as it started, with a statement of the theme, gives the movement a kind of symmetry and balance.

The third movement, *Allegro con brio,* is a free rondo, the motive at the beginning being repeated several times throughout the movement in either hand. The most characteristic element of this motive is its rhythm.

EXAMPLE 5.45 Opening motive, third movement, *Sonata No. 1*

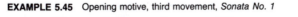

The appearance of this motive is interrupted by a series of chords in several instances.

EXAMPLE 5.46 Chord sequence, third movement, *Sonata No. 1*

The first contrasting theme is based on a folk song from Carl Sandburg's *Songbag*. The series of chords is again utilized to close this section.

EXAMPLE 5.47 First contrasting theme, third movement, *Sonata No. 1*

The next section begins with the second contrasting thematic idea in different meter.

EXAMPLE 5.48 Second contrasting theme, third movement, *Sonata No. 1*

The first contrasting theme returns for a second appearance. It also ends with a series of chord punctuations, in exactly the same sequence as before, but transposed to the dominant. The second contrasting theme also reappears in a transposed key.

The last section of the movement contains the same rhythmic motive found at the beginning. The same chord sequences are used as before to interrupt the repetition of this motive. This motivic material becomes the primary ingredient for the coda.

Walker's harmonic language throughout this composition is not very dissonant, and his textures tend to be thin and more linear than vertical in concept.

EXAMPLE 5.49 Representative harmonies, first movement, *Sonata No. 1*[19]

[19]Copyright 1972 by General Music Publishing Co., Inc. Dobbs Ferry, N.Y. Used by permission.

Julia Perry

Julia Perry (1924–79) was a native of Akron, Ohio. She was briefly a student at Akron University, but left to attend the Westminister Choir School of Princeton University through a John Knight Scholarship. Here she studied voice, piano, and composition. In 1948, Perry tied for first place in composition at the Columbus, Ohio convention of the National Association of Negro Musicians. After receiving Bachelor's and Master's degrees from the Westminster School, she was awarded a scholarship for further study in operatic conducting at Juilliard; served as coach in the opera workshop at Columbia University; did further study at the Berkshire Music Center; and studied in Europe with Luigi Dallapiccola in Florence and Nadia Boulanger in Paris. While in Europe, she organized and conducted an acclaimed series of concerts under the sponsorship of the United States Information Service.

Among her works are *Stabat Mater,* for solo voice and string orchestra (1951); *A Short Piece for Orchestra* (1952); *Pastoral,* for flute and string sextet (1959); and *Homunculus, C. F.,* for soprano and percussion (1969). Other works include *Episode,* for orchestra; *Seven Contrasts,* for baritone and chamber ensemble; *Fragments of Letters of Saint Catherine,* for solo voice, chorus, and orchestra; *Quinary Quixotic Songs,* for bass-baritone and seven instruments (1975); *Bicentennial Reflections,* for tenor, two clarinets, and percussion (1976); two operas, *The Bottle* and *The Cask of Amontillado;* several symphonies, ballet scores, and several other works for chamber ensembles and solo instruments.

Perry received a Fontainebleau Award and a Boulanger Grand Prix for her *Violin Sonata. The Cask of Amontillado* was given its first performance at Columbia University in 1954.

Julia Perry is one of the few Black women who have excelled in musical composition. Other Black women composers are Philippa Schuyler, Florence Price, Margaret Bonds, Shirley Graham, Lena McLin, Undine Moore, Mary Lou Williams, Eva Jessye, Dorothy Rudd Moore, and Betty Jackson King.

Stabat Mater.   Perry's *Stabat Mater* is composed for contralto voice and string quartet or string orchestra. It is a musical setting of the Latin poem by Jacopone da Todi (translated by the composer) and involves three characters—Jesus, Mary, and the spectator.

It is divided into ten sections. The vocal line, although dramatic and quasi-operatic in conception, is also lyrical. Chromaticism is used abundantly in the vocal line as are leaps of sevenths and ninths. Many meters are employed throughout this work.

The opening motive, which appears periodically throughout the composition, acts as a unifying element.

EXAMPLE 5.50 Principal motive, *Stabat Mater*

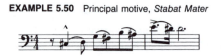

It is used, for instance, as an accompaniment for the vocal line in the first section.

The second section is sparsely orchestrated and written in a quasi-contrapuntal style.

The principal motive is used in the introduction to the third section. The texture alternates between being contrapuntal and homophonic. The fourth section features an incessant eighth-note triplet arpeggio in the second violins as an accompaniment to the vocal line. Against this figure are heard short contrapuntal passages in the cellos and double basses. The last ten measures of this section (after the termination of the vocal line) are homophonic in texture.

The most salient characteristic of section five is that the first two entries of the vocal line are answered almost note for note in the instrumental parts. Although imitative, the texture of the imitation is homophonic.

Section six employs an ostinato figure in the double basses and cellos as an accompaniment for the vocal line. There is an overlapping of the same figure in the violas and second violins.

EXAMPLE 5.51 Ostinato pattern, section six, *Stabat Mater*

In the seventh section, the principal motive is employed again as introductory material. This material is also used later in this section, which has a contrapuntal texture, as an accompaniment to the vocal line.

The eighth section is very thinly orchestrated at the beginning but increases in orchestral density and contrapuntal complexity. In the second half of this section, the composer constructs the accompanying material on a pedal point.

The half of section nine that is completely instrumental employs a whole-tone scale, which is tossed back and forth between the first violins and the cellos.

EXAMPLE 5.52   Whole-tone scale, section nine, *Stabat Mater*

After a short vocal passage, this section becomes instrumental again with most of the material derived from the principal motive. The accompaniment for the final vocal passage is homophonic in texture.

The tenth and final section has a homophonic texture. It employs continuous syncopation in the first six measures. Dynamically, this is the softest of all the sections; thus, the composition ends as it began—very quietly.

Throughout this composition, Perry employs a very dissonant harmonic language, frequently using intervals of a major seventh and ninth and minor second.

EXAMPLE 5.53   Representative harmonies, section one, *Stabat Mater*[20]

[20]*Stabat Mater* by Julia Perry. Copyright 1954 by Southern Music Publishing Co., Inc. International Copyright Secured. All Rights Reserved Including the Right of Public Performance for Profit. Used by permission.

Hale Smith

Hale Smith (b. 1925), a native of Cleveland, Ohio, attended the Cleveland Institute of Music where he studied composition with Marcel Dick. Smith received the Bachelor of Music degree in 1950 and the Master of Music degree in 1952. It was at Cleveland's celebrated Karamu Theater that he had the opportunity to write music scores for the stage productions *Yerma* and *Blood Wedding*. The Karamu Theater was also the scene, in 1955, of the first full program devoted to his compositions.

In 1958, Smith went to New York, where he took positions as music editor for E. B. Marks Music and Sam Fox Music Publishers, editor and general musical advisor for Frank Music, and consultant to the C. F. Peters Corporation. In 1968, he was appointed to the faculty of C. W. Post College of Long Island University. In 1970, Smith received an appointment as associate professor of music at the University of Connecticut at Storrs.

Smith, who gained much of his practical experience by playing in jazz groups, has managed to combine two careers—composer of concert and school music and composer and arranger of jazz. He has been active as an arranger and advisor for such jazz performers as Chico Hamilton, Oliver Nelson, Quincy Jones, Ahmad Jamal, and Eric Dolphy. Smith has received commissions from various sources: Broadcast Music, Incorporated, for *Contours for Orchestra* (1962); the Symphony of the New World, for *Music for Harp and Orchestra* (1967); Southern Illinois University at Edwardsville, for *Expansions* (for band, 1967); Robert Nagel, for *Exchanges* (for trumpet and

Hale Smith, classical composer who gained much practical experience playing with jazz groups. (Photo courtesy Charles Stewart.)

band, 1972); the Nassau County Office of Cultural Development, for *Introduction, Cadenzas and Interludes for Eight Players* (1974); Undine Moore and Altona T. Johns, for *Concert Music for Piano and Orchestra* (1972); and Tougaloo College (with the assistance of the National Endowment for the Arts), for *Comes Tomorrow* (jazz cantata, 1972).

Other works by Smith include *In Memoriam—Beryl Rubinstein*, a setting of poems by Langston Hughes and Russell Atkins for chorus and chamber orchestra (written in memory of the late director of the Cleveland Institute of Music, 1953); *Epicedial Variations* (1956); *Orchestral Set* (1962); works for band; concertos for trumpet and alto saxophone with band or orchestra; and compositions for solo voice, various solo instruments, and chamber ensembles. Smith also wrote the score for the documentary film on mental health, *Bold New Approach* (1966), and his collection of jazz piano pieces for the intermediate student, *Faces of Jazz* (1968), has been praised by educators.

Smith has been very critical of programs on which all the works performed were written by Black composers, preferring to have his works performed alongside those of White composers. It is his contention that the works of Black composers must be allowed to compete and be compared with those of composers of all cultures.

Contours.   This is a single-movement work that employs serial technique.[21] In addition to using several variants of the basic tone row, it also employs several meters.

Contours is scored for the following instruments:

Woodwinds: 2 flutes (2nd flute alternating with piccolo), 2 oboes, B-flat clarinet, bass clarinet, and 2 bassoons

Brass: 4 French horns in F, 4 trumpets in C, 2 trombones, and tuba

Percussion: cymbals, tom-tom, tenor drum, glockenspiel, snare drums, piano, and celesta

Strings: violins, violas, violoncellos, contrabasses, and harp

Smith uses the original row in the traditional retrograde, inversion, and retrograde-inversion forms, and in various transpositions.

EXAMPLE 5.54   Original row and retrograde, *Contours*

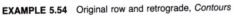

Original   Retrograde

---

[21]George Perle, in *Serial Composition and Atonality* (Berkeley: University of California Press, 1962, p. 2) offers the following postulates that govern serial music: (1) The set comprises all twelve notes of the semitonal scale arranged in a specific linear order; (2) No note appears more than once within the set; (3) The set is statable in any of its linear aspects: prime, inversion, retrograde, and retrograde-inversion; and (4) The set in each of its four transformations (that is, linear aspects) is statable upon any degree of the semitonal scale.

EXAMPLE 5.55　Inversion and retrograde inversion, *Contours*

Inversion　　　　　　　　　　　　　Retrograde-Inversion

In this composition, as in many of his others, Smith utilizes motives as his basic compositional materials. The principal motive is presented by the bass clarinet in measure five.

EXAMPLE 5.56　Principal motive, *Contours*

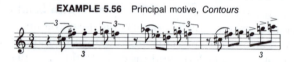

Other motives are presented in turn by the strings and by the harp and piano.

EXAMPLE 5.57　Motive (strings), *Contours*

EXAMPLE 5.58　Motive (harp and piano), *Contours*

Smith modifies the row material by often not exposing the complete row or its variants after the original exposition. He is able to construct a satisfactory, not terribly dissonant, harmonic structure utilizing the tone row.

EXAMPLE 5.59　Representative harmonies, Introduction, *Contours*[22]

Smith utilizes jazzlike rhythms in an almost subconscious way. It is his contention that this element of his musical style comes through because of his past musical experiences as a Black musician.

Smith makes versatile use of orchestral sonorities. There are raucous cries from the brass and clamorous outbursts from the percussion, in contrast to the suave sounds of the strings and woodwinds. The composition is brought to a close with a restatement of the opening motive, here given to the B-flat clarinet.

Thomas J. Anderson

Thomas Jefferson Anderson (b. 1928), born in Coatesville, Pennsylvania, had a varied background that prepared him for the career of composer. He became interested in music through his mother, an educator and musician, and was touring as a professional jazz musician by the time he was a teenager. Anderson studied at West Virginia State College and graduated in 1950; received a Master's degree in music education from Pennsylvania State University in 1951; did further work at the Cincinnati Conservatory of Music; obtained a doctorate in composition from the University of Iowa in 1958; and did postdoctoral work at the Aspen School of Music. As part of his training as a band director, Anderson learned to play most of the wind instruments, a training now evident in his excellent scoring. Anderson has studied composition with George Ceiga, T. Scott Huston, Philip Bezanson, Richard Hervig, and Darius Milhaud.

Anderson first taught at West Virginia State College. On completing his graduate study, he was appointed chairman of the music department at Langston University in Oklahoma. He accepted a professorship at Tennessee State University in Nashville in 1962. During the 1969–70 concert season, Anderson assumed the position of composer-in-residence with the Atlanta Symphony Orchestra, a position supported by a Rockefeller Foundation Grant. He also held a faculty appointment at Morehouse College in Atlanta. In 1973, Anderson was appointed chairman of the music department at Tufts University in Medford, Massachusetts.

Anderson's music is eclectic in that at times it reflects the influence of the jazz tradition, while at other times avant-grade styles are evident. He has composed works for the orchestral, chamber, piano, band, and choral media. Among his most widely performed works are the *Chamber Symphony*, commissioned by Thor Johnson and the Nashville Little Symphony (1968); *Squares,* "an essay for orchestra," commissioned by West Virginia State College for its 75th anniversary (1965); and *Personals* (1966), a secular cantata for narrator, chorus, and brass septet, commissioned by Fisk University for its 100th anniversary. Other works include *New Dances* for orchestra (1960); *Pieces* for clarinet and chamber orchestra (1962); *Five Portraitures of Two People* for piano duet (1965); *Rotations* for band (1967); *Symphony in Three Movements* (1964); *Classical Symphony* (commissioned by the Oklahoma City Junior Symphony); *Bagatelles* for harpsichord, oboe, and violin (1963); *Connections* for string quartet (1966); *Five Easy Pieces for Violin, Piano, and Jew's Harp* (1973); *Horizon '76* for soprano and orchestra (commissioned by the National Endowment for the Arts for the Bicentennial of the United States, 1975); *In Memoriam Malcolm X* for soprano and orchestra (1974); *Swing Set* for clarinet and piano (commissioned by Thomas Ayres, 1972); *Transitions: A Fantasy for Ten Instruments* (1971); and *Watermelon* for piano (1971). The Coatesville Area Senior High School commissioned *In Memoriam Zach Walker* (1969), written in memory of Zachariah Walker, who was lynched in 1911.

Among the honors received by Anderson have been MacDowell Colony Fellowships (1960–63, 1968), a Copley Foundation Award (1964), and a Fromm Foundation Award (1964).

Squares. This is a sectional work in one movement for orchestra. Each section utilizes a different meter: The first section is in $\frac{2}{4}$ meter, the second in $\frac{4}{4}$, the third in $\frac{3}{4}$, and the fourth in $\frac{6}{8}$ meter.

The instrumentation is as follows:

Woodwinds:　piccolo in C, 2 flutes, 2 oboes, 2 clarinets in B-flat, and 2 bassoons

Brass:　4 French horns in F, 3 trumpets in B-flat, 2 trombones, bass trombone, and tuba

Percussion:　timpani, snare drum, tenor drum, bass drum, cymbals, and gong

Strings:　violins, violas, violoncellos, and double basses

The material for this work is derived from the principal motive, which appears in measures three and four in the bassoons and double basses.

EXAMPLE 5.60　Principal motive, *Squares*

It is from this germ that the entire composition evolves. The motive appears again in contracted form (sixteenth-note triplets), half of it played by the bassoons and trombone, the other half by the oboes and trumpet. This motive is explored and developed throughout the first section. Usually it appears transformed, either rhythmically, tonally, or both. There is interplay between the woodwinds and strings, which toss transformations of the motive back and forth. The motive often appears disguised in sixteenth- and thirty-second notes.

Material derived from the principal motive permeates the second section as it did the first section. The motive appears in various disguises, including augmentation.

EXAMPLE 5.61 Motive in augmentation, second section, *Squares*

At other times, only the second half of the motive is employed.

In the third section, the principal motive continues to make its presence felt, but this time disguised by being fragmented among several instruments. This section is characterized by the very sparse use of instruments.

EXAMPLE 5.62 Fragmented motive, third section, *Squares*

In the fourth section, minor seconds are used in abundance. Motivic material from the first section is again utilized but is often disguised by the use of minor seconds in a vertical fashion. In addition, the motive is used in dimunition.

EXAMPLE 5.63 Principal motive in dimunition, fourth section, *Squares*

The harmonic structure of this composition is one in which linear movement takes precedence over vertical triads.

EXAMPLE 5.64 Representative harmonies, section two, *Squares*

The last five measures of this composition are the exact reverse of the first five measures, with one exception—the absence of the principal motive. The last chord is an exact replica of the first chord.

EXAMPLE 5.65   First and last chord, *Squares*[23]

Arthur Cunningham

Arthur Cunningham (b. 1928), born in Piermont, New York, began studying music at the age of six. At seven, he was writing and performing his own piano pieces, and by the age of twelve, Cunningham was writing for his own band of ten musicians. Cunningham demonstrated such a high level of musicianship that at thirteen he began the study of composition with Wallingford Riegger and theory with Sam Morgenstern at the Metropolitan Music School, which he attended from 1941 to 1945. It was here that he also studied jazz theory with Johnny Mehegan and jazz piano under Teddy Wilson. After attending summer sessions at the Juilliard School of Music, where he studied choral techniques under Peter Wilhousky, Cunningham entered Fisk University, where he studied under John W. Work III, and graduated in 1951. In 1951–52, Cunningham studied composition at Juilliard with Peter Mennin, Norman Lloyd, and Henry Brant, and choral techniques with Margaret Hillis.

The first public performance of Cunningham's works took place in 1951 on a program sponsored by the National Association of Negro Musicians. Works for solo voices and piano were presented.

Cunningham's music is as varied as his musical experiences. He has written compositions for concert performance, scores for stage works, a piano instruction book, and works for performance by children. His *Adagio*

Arthur Cunningham, whose material includes compositions for the concert idiom, scores for stage works, and works for performances by children. (Photo courtesy Elwood Emerick Management.)

for String Orchestra (1954), commissioned by the Suburban Symphony Orchestra of Rockland County, New York, was performed that year. Cunningham's first important commission, however, was *Concentrics* (1968), performed by the Symphony of the New World. Other commissions include *The Garden of Phobos* (1968), by the Rockland Community College; *Shango* (1969), commissioned by the National Theatre Company; and *Trinities* (1969, for cello and two double basses), commissioned by Arthur Davis. His other compositions include works for symphony orchestra; works for chamber orchestra and chamber ensembles; works for solo piano; and a large number of songs, both sacred and secular, for solo voice. His music for stage includes *Ostrich Feathers,* a children's rock musical (1964); *Patsy Patch and Susan's Dreams,* a musical for very young children (1963); and a one-act mini-rock opera, *His Natural Grace* (1969).

Cunningham has also written the texts for several of his works, including the libretto for a short opera, *House By the Sea* (1966). In addition, he wrote the libretto and music for the mini-rock opera, *Louey Louey* (1968).

Among his other works are the choral piece *The Garden of Phobos,* mentioned above; *Violetta,* a musical; *Engrams,* written for Natalie Hinderas' concert tour of the United States during the 1969–70 season; *Lullabye for a Jazz Baby* (1969), written for André Kostelanetz and performed throughout the South and West by the Oakland Youth Chamber Symphony Orchestra; and *Harlem Suite* (1970), composed for the 1970–71 Natalie Hinderas tour.

Lullabye for a Jazz Baby.   This is a highly sectionalized work that employs several meters. Cunningham employs conventional harmonies but in the manner they are employed in jazz; for example, he uses a great number of secondary dominants in series.

The sections of this work bear the titles "Patter of Running Feet," "Night is Falling," "Lullabye," "Serenade Lullabye," "Lullabye," "Scherzo/Blues," "Charleston," and "Lullabye."[24]

The instrumentation is as follows:

Woodwinds: 2 flutes (first flute doubles on piccolo), 2 oboes, B-flat clarinet, and bass clarinet
Brass: 2 French horns in F, 2 trumpets in B-flat, and 2 trombones
Percussion: xylophone, snare drum and bass drum
Strings: violins, violas, violoncellos, double bass, and harp

The introduction consists of a snare-drum figure that employs shifting accents, depicting the patter of running feet. This figuration is punctuated by a chord that represents a spank for the baby.

EXAMPLE 5.66 Introduction, *Lullabye for a Jazz Baby*

EXAMPLE 5.67 Lullabye, *Lullabye for a Jazz Baby*

The next new material is introduced in the section titled "Serenade." This material is then used as a background to an improvised jazz trumpet solo.

EXAMPLE 5.68 Serenade, *Lullabye for a Jazz Baby*

Following this section, the same thematic material is then played in a style reminiscent of the big-band era of the late thirties and early forties.

The next section is a paraphrase of the initial thematic material, based on the same harmonic structure. In the "Scherzo/Blues" section that follows, new thematic ideas are presented in a style completely different from the previous sections.

---

[24]These are the titles given to each section in the score. The liner notes to the album, *The Black Composer in America*, give the following titles: "Patter of Running Feet"; "Objections by the Baby"; "Spanks"; "Lullabye"; "Serenade Lullabye, Blues Scherzo/Dream/Sugar Hill Lullabye, Charleston"; and "Spanks."

EXAMPLE 5.69   Scherzo/Blues, *Lullabye for a Jazz Baby*[25]

The lullabye theme reappears in a somewhat transformed manner, to be followed by a short coda entitled "Charleston." The entire composition is based on three major thematic ideas that are presented in a manner closely related to the jazz idiom.

Frederick C. Tillis

Frederick Charles Tillis (b. 1930) was born in Galveston, Texas. After graduating from Wiley College, Tillis received his Master of Arts and Doctor of Philosophy degrees in composition from the University of Iowa. He gained considerable experience in composition and arranging as director of the 3560th Air Force Band and arranger for the Flight Training Command from 1952 to 1956. After teaching at Wiley and Grambling Colleges, he was appointed chairman of the music department at Kentucky State College at Frankfort in 1967. He subsequently joined the music faculty at the University of Massachusetts.

He has written two works under commission: *Celebration,* a concert march for band, for the centennial celebration of Morehouse College; and a work for mixed chorus, for the Kentucky State College in 1968. Tillis participated as one of the guest composers in the 1967 Symposium of Contemporary Music at Illinois Wesleyan University, where several of his chamber works were performed. He was also a part of the 1968 Festival of Contemporary Music at Spelman College, where *Design for Orchestra No. 2* was performed by the Atlanta Symphony Orchestra.

Tillis has written compositions for chamber ensembles, orchestra, band, chorus, solo voice, vocal ensembles, organ, piano, jazz bands, and the electronic medium. His works have varied widely in style, from *Three Chorale Settings for Organ* (1962) and *Passacaglia for Organ* (1962), both in Baroque style, to *Music for an Experimental Laboratory, Ensemble No. 2* (1967), in the electronic medium. Among his most performed works are *Music for Alto Flute, Violoncello and Piano* (1966); *Overture to a Dance* (1961), for band; *Halleluvah* (1966), for male glee club; and two songs, *Enogod* (1957), and *Me* (1968), for soprano and piano. Other works include *Niger Symphony* (1975); *Spiritual Cycle for Soprano and Orchestra* (1978); *Three Symphonic Spirituals* (1978); *Music for Violin, Cello and Piano* (1972); and *Pastorale for Wind Ensem-*

ble (1972). Among Tillis' electronic works are *Music for Tape Recorder No. 1*, and *Three Plus One* (1969), fo violin, guitar, clarinet, and tape.

Music for Alto Flute, Violoncello, and Piano.   In this work, Tillis utilizes the piano in a manner once considered avant-garde but now thought of in music circles as almost conventional. Tillis has given explicit directions as to how the piano should be played.

> In this composition, the pianist is to produce the sound by playing pizzicato and hammered strokes (with fingers or hand) *inside* the piano. For the most part, indeterminate pitches are used. Pitch areas are designated in the following manner as determined by the number of partitions on the sound board located inside of a grand piano:
> 1st Partition = highest section of the sound board.
> 2nd Partition = second highest section of the sound board.
> 3rd Partition = third highest section of the sound board.
> 4th Partition = lowest section of the sound board.
> Note: If the piano has five crossbars omit the highest treble partition.[26]

The piece is one movement and utilizes $\frac{4}{4}$ meter throughout, except for one measure of $\frac{3}{4}$ meter near the middle of the work. It is based on the interval of the tritone, which is used both melodically and harmonically.

EXAMPLE 5.70 Use of melodic and harmonic tritone, *Music*

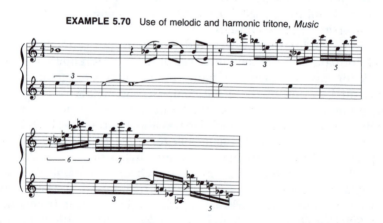

Other intervals used often are the perfect fourth and perfect fifth.

While this composition is built around a tonal center of C, the tonality does shift to the dominant before returning to C for the conclusion.

The first half of this work is performed without the piano except for a triad sounded by the suppression of the piano keys while a glissando is played in the two initial measures. Consequently, the two sections differ

---

[26]Performance notes: *Music for Alto Flute, Cello and Piano* (New York: Composers Facsimile Edition, 1968).

considerably in sound. When the piano does enter, it is played pizzicato, alternating between two indeterminate pitches played as a ground bass for sixteen measures. Once again, the composer utilizes the interval of a tritone.

EXAMPLE 5.71   Ground bass, *Music*

A cantabile theme is introduced by the alto flute against a figure in the violoncello part, which is similar to the flute theme from the beginning of the second section.

EXAMPLE 5.72   Cantabile theme (alto flute), *Music*

After the exposition of the theme in the alto flute part, the piano is used to present indeterminate pitches that help contrast the second section with the first.

EXAMPLE 5.73   Indeterminate pitches (piano), *Music*

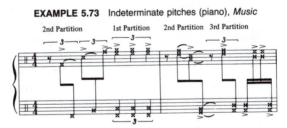

The harmony is governed by the linear movement of the voices, which proceed without regard to controlling vertical structures such as the triad. There are tonal centers that are quite apparent, however, primarily because of the reiteration of the pitch serving as the tonic (in most cases C or its dominant, G).

In the first section of this composition, the composer constantly utilizes multiples of notes in the alto flute part against notes in the violoncello part.

EXAMPLE 5.74   First section, *Music*[27]

[27]© 1968, Frederick Tillis. All Rights Reserved. All examples are used by permission.

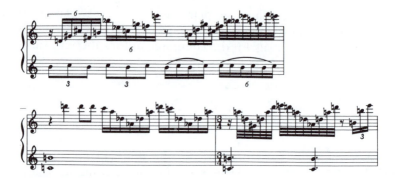

In the second section, the piano joins the ensemble, utilizing glissandi, pizzicato, and hammerlike strokes. The second melodic line in the alto flute part, however, is more legato and less chromatic, and is played in a singing style.

William S. Fischer

William S. Fischer (b. 1935) was born in Shelby, Mississippi, in the heart of the Mississippi Delta, and grew up in both Jackson, Mississippi, and New Oreleans. He began studying music at the age of seven. At the age of ten, he became interested in band instruments while living in Natchez, Mississippi, where his father was Dean of Natchez College. Three years later, Fischer began study of the alto saxophone and was soon playing in the high school band. At the age of sixteen, he was playing professionally.

William S. Fischer, who has employed electronic media with more traditional sounds. (Photo courtesy E. L. Jenkins & Co.)

Subsequently, he played in the bands of blues singers such as Muddy Waters, Joe Turner, Guitar Slim, Ivory Joe Hunter, Ray Charles, and others.

Fischer was educated at Xavier University in New Orelans and graduated with a degree in music education. He then taught high school in Virginia and Louisiana. After spending three summers at the music camp in Aspen, Colorado, Fischer entered Colorado College for further study, receiving a master's degree in composition. While at this institution, he studied with Albert Seay and Paul Doktor. Fischer did further study at the Academy of Music in Vienna and at the University of Vienna. He became composer-in-residence at Xavier University, and there he wrote various chamber and choral pieces for local performance.

Fischer's musical experiences have been varied. He has worked in the concert field as a composer and performer; played viola in the orchestras of Broadway musical comedies; and worked as a composer, arranger, and musical director with jazz groups. Among the awards he has received as a composer of concert music are commissions from the Rockefeller Foundation, a German State Grant (Deutsches Akademischer Austausdienst), and a Fulbright Fellowship. Fischer has also served as musical director at the Atlantic Record Company, on the faculty in the Theatre Arts Division of Boston University, and at the High School of Music and Art in New York City.

Fischer has composed music for many media, including orchestral, chamber, solo piano, viola, saxaphone, jazz quintet and symphony orchestra, chorus, voice, and electronic works. He also composed works in several genres, among them, ballets, operas, and musicals.

One of Fischer's most performed works is *A Quiet Movement* (1966), which was first performed on a southern tour by the Oakland Youth Chamber Orchestra in the spring of 1970. His electronic works generally call for mixtures of live and taped sound. Among them are *Batucada Fantastica* for two tapes and two percussionists (1968); *Gift of Lesbos* for violoncello, piano, and tape (1968); and *Time I* for saxophone, viola, violoncello, percussion, and tape (1966).

Fischer's opera *Jessye* was performed in Buffalo, New York, while his musical *Jack-Jack* was performed off-Broadway in New York City. Fischer has often combined two media in his compositions, as in his *Concerto Grosso for Jazz Quintet and Orchestra* (1968) and *Experience in E, for Jazz Quintet and Orchestra* (1968). In addition, he has written two string quartets, a sonata for violin and piano, and works for the solo voice. Among the latter is his *Joy of Love* (1969), based on a poem by LeRoi Jones (Imamu Amiri Baraka).

A Quiet Movement.   This composition consists of one movement and retains a single ($\frac{4}{4}$) meter throughout. Nevertheless, this work, which is closely related to the theme-and-variation form, is highly sectionalized because of the manner in which Fischer has employed families of instruments. Almost every section is dominated by one of the instrumental families.

Fischer states, "Even though this work is notated, the central idea on which it is based is to make it sound as though it is improvised and not contrived."[28] This idea comes through remarkably well throughout the composition.

Fischer employs the following instrumentation:

Woodwinds: 2 flutes, 2 oboes, 2 clarinets, bass clarinet, alto saxophone, and 2 bassoons
Brass: 4 French horns, 3 trumpets, 3 trombones, and tuba
Percussion: timpani, suspended cymbals, 4 tempered drums, and triangle
Strings: first and second violins, violas, violoncellos, double basses, and harp

After a short introduction, the principal thematic idea is introduced by the alto saxophone. The interval of a ninth, one of the salient characteristics of the principal theme, is employed as a unifying element of this work.

EXAMPLE 5.75 Principal theme, *A Quiet Movement*

After the theme has been exposed, the first section is dominated by the strings. The upper strings play a sustained background against which the lower strings (cello and double bass) play pizzicato passages.

EXAMPLE 5.76 String-dominated section, *A Quiet Movement*

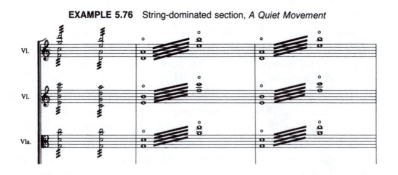

[28]William S. Fischer, telephone interview, August 3, 1971.

In the next section, Fischer uses the brass as the dominating family of instruments in the manner of *Klangfarbenmelodie*.[29] At no time do any two instruments play simultaneously, nor does any one instrument play more than one note in succession.

EXAMPLE 5.77 Brass-dominated section, *A Quiet Movement*

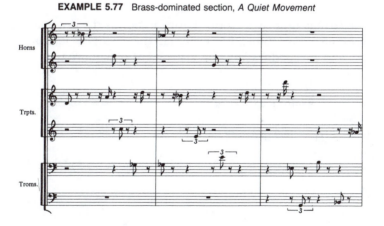

The strings return again as the most prominent instrumental group and are employed in a fashion similar to before. The upper strings continue to play sustained tones while the lower instruments use pizzicato.

The next section uses only percussion—timpani, suspended cymbal, and four tempered drums.

[29]*Klangfarbenmelodie* is a term coined by Schoenberg to indicate a succession of tone-colors related to one another in a way comparable to a relationship between the pitches of a melody.

EXAMPLE 5.78   Percussion-dominated section, *A Quiet Movement*

The strings now make a third appearance as the dominating instrumental family. This time, however, all the stringed instruments play
pizzicato, and rarely does any one instrument play more than one note in
succession.

EXAMPLE 5.79   String-dominated section, *A Quiet Movement*

The final section employs all the families of instruments, with no one group dominating.

Fischer's harmonic structure seems to be governed by linear considerations; that is, horizontal motion appears to take precedence over vertical structures. The harmony is dissonant and acrid.

EXAMPLE 5.80   Representative harmonies, *A Quiet Movement*[30]

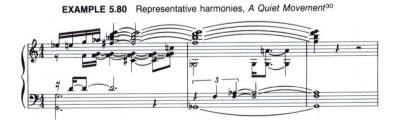

Fischer has employed a form in this composition that, in many respects, resembles variations on a theme. In a strict sense, however, he has used his principal theme as a source of inspiration and derived from it suggestions that superficially appear to have only a slight connection with it.

[30]Used with permission of the copyright owner, Bote & Bock Verlag, Berlin, Germany.

Southern has made a perceptive observation of the Black composers who reached musical maturity in the 1950s and began to make their presence felt:

> Black composers born in the 1930s were in an even better position to experiment than had been their predecessors. Almost without exception they were well trained, studying at the best musical institutions in the country, and they received help from various sources—grants from foundations; prizes won in national or international competitions; commissions from various types of organizations, particularly from symphony orchestras and college groups; fellowships and scholarships; and teaching positions that gave them time for composing.[31]

Olly Wilson

One of the outstanding composers among those who are willing to experiment with compositional techniques is Olly W. Wilson (b. 1937). Wilson's earliest attempts at composition were in the area of jazz, as an arranger and composer in high school in his native St. Louis, and later for a semiprofessional jazz quintet. After high school, he entered Washington University in St. Louis on a scholarship, where he received his first formal instruction in composition with Robert Wykes. After graduation in 1959, Wilson studied at the University of Illinois with Robert Kelley, receiving the Master of Music degree in 1960. He then attended the University of Iowa, where he studied with Philip Bezanson, and he received his doctorate in 1964.

Since his high school days, Wilson has played the double bass. He gained experience on this instrument by performing with concert ensembles in St. Louis and Cedar Rapids, Iowa.

Wilson taught at Florida A. & M. University, West Virginia University (graduate division), and Indiana University before joining the music faculty of Oberlin. In 1967, Oberlin awarded him a grant to study composition of electronically generated music at the Studio for Experimental Music of the University of Illinois. Wilson subsequently became head of the electronic laboratory at the University of California at Berkeley.

A performance of his *Sextet* (1963) by members of the Atlanta Symphony gained national publicity, and remains perhaps the most performed of all Wilson's works. Three of his works are for orchestra—*Structure for Orchestra* (1960); *Three Movements for Orchestra* (1964), his next most performed work; and *Voices* (1970), commissioned by the Boston Symphony Orchestra and the Fromm Foundation. His other works include ballets, compositions for chamber ensembles, compositions for live-tape mixtures, and works for solo voice, chorus, violin, clarinet, piano, and double bass.

[31]Southern, *The Music of Black Americans*, pp. 475–77.

Wilson has seemed to be in search of a unique sound, which might explain, in part, his interest in electronic music. He has used unusual combinations in some of his compositions, including *Wry Fragments* (1961) and *And Death Shall Have No Dominion* (1963), both for tenor and percussion ensemble, and *Chanson Innocente* (1965), for contralto and two bassoons. His *Cetus* was the winning composition at the International Electronic Music Competition held at Dartmouth College in 1968. He followed this electronic work with another, *In Memoriam—Martin Luther King, Jr.* (1969), for mixed chorus and electronic sounds.

In Memoriam—Martin Luther King, Jr.   Wilson composed this work for electronic tape and mixed chorus (SATB), which at times expands to eight parts. It is in one movement. The composition commences with electronic sounds in an unmeasured section. Using the title line from one of Martin Luther King's favorite hymns, "Free At Last," the chorus makes its entry in the bass in a continuation of the unmeasured section. As the bass voices enter, the electronic sounds die out.

With the entrance of the tenors, the composition becomes measured ($\frac{4}{4}$), with the basses and tenors subdividing into four parts.

EXAMPLE 5.81   Subdivision of male voices, *In Memoriam—Martin Luther King, Jr.*

The sopranos and altos are subdivided in a similar manner upon their entrance.

In the next unmeasured section, the electronic tape reenters against a pedal tone in the choral bass line. This time, however, the electronic sounds are definite and determinate.

EXAMPLE 5.82   Electronic sounds, *In Memoriam—Martin Luther King, Jr.*

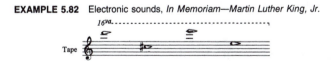

Wilson subdivides the male voices by having single pitches in both the bass and the tenor glissando to clusters that encompass all of the diatonic pitches within outer specified notes.

EXAMPLE 5.83 Subdivision of male voices, *In Memoriam—Martin Luther King, Jr.*

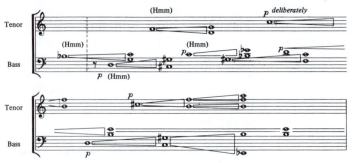

Hence, the upper basses begin on the B-flat and gradually divide while performing a glissando up or down to a cluster consisting of the notes G, A, B, and C. The lower basses begin on D and gradually sing a divided glissando up or down to the notes C-sharp, D, E, F, G, and G-sharp. Consequently, the number of parts being performed at any point varies, but by the time the full male section reaches its climactic chord (last chord in Example 5.82), each male member of an average-size choir will probably be singing a separate pitch.

Among the vocal devices in this composition is the use of whispered sounds in conjunction with a sung text.

EXAMPLE 5.84 Whispered sounds, *In Memoriam—Martin Luther King, Jr.*

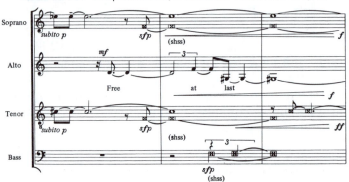

At various points, Wilson directs the chorus to turn to the left, center, and right, creating different dynamic levels and different timbres (probably depending somewhat on the hall in which it is performed). In addition, he creates a "muted choir" by instructing the performers to place their hands over their mouths while singing.

Wilson also utilizes spoken text in conjunction with sung text.

EXAMPLE 5.85 Spoken and sung text, *In Memoriam—Martin Luther King, Jr.*

The composition ends with the word "free" sung by the sopranos, in contrast to the beginning in which the basses alone sang the same word. After this final statement, the composition is brought to its conclusion by electronic sounds, just as it began.

In Memoriam—Martin Luther King, Jr. is an example of Wilson's preoccupation with novel sounds, not for their own sake but for dramatic interpretation of a deeply felt message.

EXAMPLE 5.86 Vocal texture, *In Memoriam—Martin Luther King, Jr.*[32]

John Carter

Born in St. Louis in 1937, John Carter attended the Oberlin Conservatory, where he majored in piano under Jack Radunsky. After Oberlin, while serving in the United States Army, he won two piano competitions that resulted in solo appearances with orchestras.

The principal formative influence on Carter's music has been Black folk music—spirituals, shouts and hollers, work songs, and funeral music. Carter has commented on his approach to handling this kind of material.

> My purpose in using Negro melodies is to preserve the spirit of the original, which is, after all, unique, but at the same time to bring them into the mainstream of Western music. In other words, my compositions are as distant from the conventional spiritual "arrangement" as, say, Bartók's music is from traditional Hungarian tunes.[33]

An important work by Carter is the *Requiem Seditiosam: In Memoriam, Medgar Evers,* a tribute to the murdered civil rights leader, which was first performed by the Symphony of the New World in New York's Philharmonic Hall. This work was completed with financial assistance from the American Music Center. Other works are *Kodoku,* a song cycle setting Japanese texts for voice and piano; *Cantata,* a suite that utilizes traditional Black melodies; *Epigrams,* a ballet that was choreographed by the New York City Ballet's Arthur Mitchell; *Valses Pour Les Danseurs Noir* (waltzes for Black dancers and piano); and a piano concerto. Carter's music has been performed throughout the United States and Europe by such noted singers as Leontyne Price, Martina Arroyo, Betty Allen, Adele Addison, and William Warfield. During the 1968–69 concert season, Carter served as composer-in-residence with the National Symphony Orchestra in Washington.

Cantata. This work is a five-movement suite for voice and orchestra (a version for voice and piano is also available). The five movements are titled Prelude, Rondo, Recitative, Air, and Toccata. Carter here makes use of traditional Black melodies, which are transformed considerably by the idiom of the suite.

The first movement, Prelude, has no time signature. It opens with a three-note motive that also appears at the beginning of the second movement.

EXAMPLE 5.87 Opening motive, first movement, *Cantata*

[33]Alan M. Kriegsman, "Symphony Gets Composer-in-Residence," *The Washington Post,* October 20, 1968.

EXAMPLE 5.88 Opening motive, second movement, *Cantata*

The first movement is entirely instrumental, with a contrapuntal texture.

The second movement, a rondo, is based on the spiritual *Peter Go Ring Dem Bells*.

EXAMPLE 5.89   *Peter Go Ring Dem Bells*

Pet - er   go   ring dem bells.   Pe - ter   go   ring dem bells.

Like the Prelude, the opening section of the second movement is unmetered. The melodic material of the spiritual is used as an introduction to the movement. In the next section (the A section of the rondo form), the spiritual is transformed through changes in key signature, time signature, and accompaniment texture.

The following section is instrumental and employs a meter that shifts from $\frac{6}{8}$ to $\frac{9}{8}$ and back. This is followed by a section in which the accompanying texture is homophonic, while the melodic line is again based on the spiritual, newly transformed. Since this material is very similar to the material in the opening section, it can be regarded as a return to A. The next section is also a vocal section, but it employs new material, homophonic in texture, and constitutes the C section. There is another return to the A material in the final section, again trasnformed to some degree. Thus, the form of the movement is ABACA.

The third movement is based on the spiritual *Sometimes I Feel Like a Motherless Child*, with a chordal accompaniment.

EXAMPLE 5.90   *Sometimes I Feel Like a Motherless Child*

Some-times   I   feel   like   a   moth - er - less   child.

This spiritual is stated and repeated in its entirety in its original form.

Carter uses the spiritual *Let Us Break Bread Together* as the basis for the fourth movement, Air. It is repeated in its original form, and then presented in a transformed version.

EXAMPLE 5.91   *Let Us Break Bread Together*

Let   us   break   bread   to - geth - er   on___   our   knees

The title of the last movement, Toccata, reflects the virtuosic accompaniment to the vocal line. The spiritual used as a basis for this movement, *Ride On King Jesus,* is in three-part (ABA) form.

EXAMPLE 5.92 *Ride on King Jesus*

The texture of this movement is also homophonic. The movement ends with a short instrumental section similar to the beginning of the first movement, giving the work a certain symmetry.

While his harmonic language is tonal, Carter's settings for these spirituals nevertheless contrast strongly with those of Burleigh, Dett, and White. Where the harmonic language of the older composers is romantic and traditional, Carter's is modern and dissonant.

EXAMPLE 5.93 Representative harmonies, fourth movement, *Cantata*[34]

Wendell Logan

Wendell Morris Logan (b. 1940) is a native of Thomson, Georgia. After graduating from Florida A. & M. University in 1962, he did further study at the American Conservatory of Music during the summer of 1963. Logan received a master's degree in composition from Southern Illinois University in 1964 and a doctorate from the University of Iowa in 1968. He

[34]*Cantata* by John Carter, © Copyright 1964 by Southern Music Publishing Co. Inc. All Rights Reserved Including the Right of Public Performance for Profit. All examples used by permission.

has taught at Florida A. & M. University, Ball State University, Western Illinois University, and Oberlin College.

Performances of his works include: *String Quartet,* performed at the Goucher College Summer Music Festival in 1964; *Concert Music for Orchestra,* at the Dallas Composers' Conference in 1965; *Stanzas for Three Players,* at the Center for New Music concert; *Woodwind Quintet,* at the Ball State Summer Music Festival; *Songs of Our Time,* Town Hall Concert, New York; and *Proportions for Nine Players and Conductor,* American Society of University Composers' Convention.

Songs of Our Times. This work was motivated by ". . . a concern for and reaction to current social and political conditions found in this country."[35] Logan set to music poetry by W. E. B. Du Bois, LeRoi Jones, and Gwendolyn Brooks.

From W. E. B. Du Bois, *The Riddle of the Sphinx:*[36]

And they that raised the boasters
Shall drag them down again,
Down with the theft of their thieving
And murder and mocking of men;

Down with their barter of women
And laying and lying of creeds;
Down with their cheating of childhood
And drunken orgies of war,
  down
   down
    deep down,
 Where 'neath the bloody finger-marks thy
  riven bosom quakes,
 Thicken the thunders of God's Voice and lo:
  a world awakes!

From LeRoi Jones, *The End of Man Is His Beauty:*[37]

And silence
which proves / but
a referent
to my disorder.
  Your World shakes

cities die
beneath your shape.
  The single shadow

---

[35]George Corwin, record jacket notes, *Songs of Our Time,* by Wendell Logan (Golden Crest Records, CRS 4087).

[36]Used by permission of the Ghana Universities Press, copyright owner.

[37]Copyright © 1964 by LeRoi Jones. Used by permission of the Sterling Lord Agency.

From Gwendolyn Brooks, *The Soft Man:*[38]

Disgusting, isn't it, dealing out the damns
To every comer? Hits the heart like pain.
And calling women (Marys) chicks and broads,
Men hep, and cats, or corny to the jive.
Being seen Everywhere (Keeping Alive),

Rhumboogie (and the joint is jumpin', Joe),
Brass Rail, Keyhole, De Lisa, Cabin Inn.
And all the other garbage cans.

But grin.
Because there is a clean unanxious place
To which you creep on Sundays. And you cool
In lovely sadness.
No one giggles where
You bathe your sweet vulgarity in prayer.

Logan utilizes a mixed chorus (SATB) and an instrumental ensemble consisting of flute, clarinet in B-flat, bassoon, French horn, trombone, double bass, piano, and percussion. The three percussion players perform on a variety of instruments:

Player One: bongos (2), snare drum, 2 suspended cymbals (hi-10), small tam tam, woodblocks (3), timpani, vibraphone.
Player Two: cowbells (3), wooddrums (4), brake-drums (4), maracas, triangle, glockenspiel, chimes.
Player Three: tom-toms (2), bass drum, suspended cymbals (hi-10), tam-tam, temple blocks (5), timpani, xylophone.

This composition is in three movements and utilizes several meters as well as a considerable amount of unmeasured material. The unmeasured sections are generally played as fast as possible without blurring.

EXAMPLE 5.94   Unmeasured section, first movement, *Songs of Our Time*[39]

---

[38]From *The World of Gwendolyn Brooks*, by Gwendolyn Brooks. Copyright 1945 by Gwendolyn Brooks Blakely. Reprinted by permission of Harper & Row, Publishers, Inc.

[39]All instruments are written at actual pitch and in their sounding octave.

Logan allows many of the instrumental performers a great amount of flexibility by interjecting aleatory passages for certain instruments. In his performance notes, Logan explains the degree of freedom allowed the performer.

It can be played starting at any point (left to right or vice-versa). Pattern can also be repeated several times and may be interrupted at any point. Always as fast as possible! The last note should be held for the proportionally indicated length of time.[40]

EXAMPLE 5.95 Aleatory passage, first movement, *Songs of Our Time*

[40]Wendell Logan, performance notes, *Songs of Our Time*.

Logan permits other forms of improvisation as well. Whenever material is enclosed within a square or rectangle, ". . . the performer should distribute notes and dynamics freely within the length of time suggested by the dimensions of the square or rectangle,"[41] aided by a cue from the conductor.

EXAMPLE 5.96   Improvised section (piano), first movement, *Songs of Our Time*

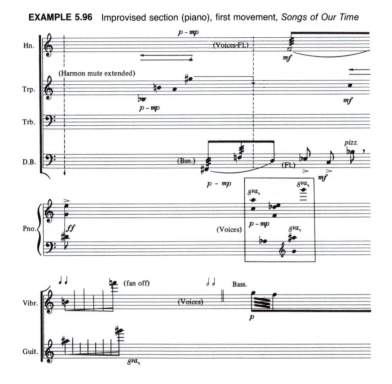

Tone clusters are employed in the piano part, requiring the performer to sound all the tones between the two indicated notes by the use of his arms or hands.

EXAMPLE 5.97   Tone cluster (piano), second movement, *Songs of Our Time*

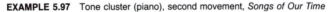

[41]*Ibid.*

Logan has utilized many vocal devices. On certain words, for example, each half of the choir sings the indicated "subsounds," in which the first or last syllable or letter of a word is enclosed in brackets and is not to be sung.

EXAMPLE 5.98 "Subsounds," first movement, *Songs of Our Time*

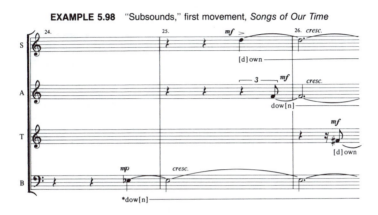

Glissandi are used effectively by Logan, their speed varying between voices.

EXAMPLE 5.99 Glissandi, first movement, *Songs of Our Time*

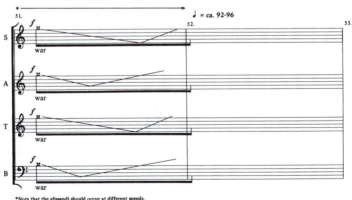

*Note that the glissandi should occur at different speeds.

Pitches sometimes depict the meaning of words, as in Example 5.99, where on the word "shakes" the voices alternate rapidly between two pitches.

EXAMPLE 5.100   Second movement, *Songs of Our Time*

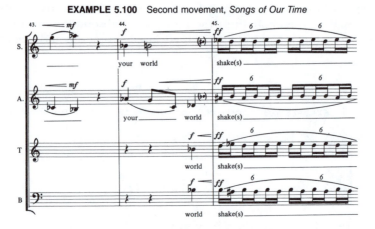

The harmonic language reflects the meaning of the texts. The harmonies are acrid and stark, and the dissonances are sometimes extreme.

EXAMPLE 5.101   Representative harmonies, first movement, *Songs of Our Times*[42]

Talib Rasul Hakim

Talib Rasul Hakim (Stephen Chambers, b. 1940) was born in Asheville, North Carolina. His formal music education includes study at the Manhattan School of Music, the New York College of Music, and the New School for Social Research, as well as private study with Robert Starer, William Sydeman, Hall Overton, David Reck, Morton Feldman, Chou Wen-Chung, Charles Whittenberg, and Ornette Coleman. His works have been performed on the "Music In Our Time" concerts held in New York at the Young Men's Hebrew Association under the direction of Max Pollikoff, as well as by college groups and some of the minor symphony orchestras.

Among Hakim's awards are the Bennington Composers' Conference Scholarships (1964–69) and ASCAP Composers' Awards (1967–69). His most widely performed compositions have been *Sound Gone* (1967) for piano; *Elements* (1967) for strings, flutes, clarinet, piano, glass and bamboo chimes; and *Sound Images* (1969) for percussion, brass, double basses, and six female voices. Other works include *Placements* (1970) for flugelhorn, French horn, trombone, tuba, two percussion, contrabass, and piano; *Uranian-Projections* (1970) for soprano, percussion, and piano; *Reflections on the 5th Ray* (1972) for narrator and chamber orchestra; *Tone-prayers* (1973) for chorus (SATB) with percussion and piano; and *Recurrences* (1974) for chamber orchestra.

Sound-Gone. In the performance of this composition, the piano is used partly in a conventional manner, but the performer must also employ a pencil, paper, fingernails, and a water glass to manipulate the strings inside the piano in various ways to produce both pitched and unpitched sounds.

This composition, while in one movement, is highly sectionalized. It begins with the use of tone clusters of determinate pitches. The piano strings are first plucked using the fingernails. A water glass is then used on the strings in such a manner as to give a glissando effect and indeterminate pitches. Sometimes the keyboard is struck with the fingers while using the water glass on the strings, producing both determinate and indeterminate pitches. At other times, the strings are plucked while partially covered by paper.

The next section utilizes traditional harmonies and a lyrical but disjunct melodic line that ranges over several octaves. In this section, an ostinato figure is employed in the bass line.

EXAMPLE 5.102 Ostinato figure, bass line, *Sound-Gone*

The third section is similar to the first in that indeterminate pitches are obtained through the manipulation of the piano strings by various extraneous objects. When determinate pitches are employed, they are generally in the context of tone clusters.

The composition ends with a chord in the upper register, while the wooden casing of the piano is struck in a rhythmic fashion with a pencil.

EXAMPLE 5.103 Conclusion, *Sound-Gone*[43]

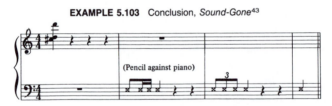

The Black composer first began to compose music in the eighteenth century. In America, his initial efforts in composition were more imitative than creative, but as his musical talent matured, he began to make his presence felt with the emergence of the twentieth century. The music indigenous to Black culture reached maturity more than a century ago. However, it took time for the Black composer to assimilate into the music of the dominant culture in this country, and, even as the assimilation process was in progress, the Black composer demonstrated a high degree of originality by synthesizing Black music materials with European forms.

At the mid-point of the twentieth century, the Black composer began using music materials not necessarily indigenous to the Black ethnic group. As has been documented, Blacks have learned their craft well. They have had to face insuperable odds in an effort to gain recognition for their outstanding contributions to American music. It appears that the recognition due them, but long overdue, is close at hand.

List of Compositions
by Composers Included
in This Study

A list of compositions by American Black composers included in this study, the medium for which they were composed, poets, publishers, dates of publication, and performances are given when this information is available.

ANDERSON, THOMAS JEFFERSON, JR., 1928–

Bagatelles for harpsichord, oboe, and violin (1963). 5 mvts.: Boea, Barcarolle, Burletta, Blues, Ballonchio. (New York: Composers Facsimile Edition, 1963). First perf.: Univ. of Oklahoma Composers' Symposium, Norman, Okla., 1963.

Beyond Silence, cantata for tenor, B-flat clarinet, trombone, viola, violoncello, and piano (1973). Text: Pauline Hanson. (New York: American Composers Alliance, 1973). First perf.: Busch-Reisinger Museum of Harvard University, 1973.

Block Songs for soprano and children's toys (chromatic pitch pipe, musical jack-in-the-box, and musical busy box), (1972). Text: Pearl Lomax. (New York: Composers Facsimile Edition, 1972).

Chamber Symphony (1968). 1 mvt. (New York: Composers Facsimile Edition, 1969). First perf.: Nashville Little Symphony, 1969.

Classical Symphony, (1961). 3 mvts. (New York: Composers Facsimile Edition, rental). Commission, Oklahoma City Junior Symphony. First perf.: Oklahoma City Junior Symphony, 1961.

Connections for string quintet (2 violins, 2 violas, violoncello), (1966). (New York: Composers Facsimile Edition, 1967). First perf.: Blair String Quartet, Nashville, 1968.

Etudes and a Fancy for wind quintet (1964). 6 mvts.: Assimilation, Compliments, Transference, Diversity, Recurrence, Fancy. (New York: Composers Facsimile Edition, 1967). First perf.: Aspen School of Music, 1964.

Five Easy Pieces For Violin, Piano, and Jews Harp (1973). (New York: American Composers Alliance, 1973). First perf.: composer's children, Winchester, Mass., 1974.

Horizon '76 for soprano and orchestra (1975). 2 mvts.: A Song (Serenades, Introductions and Overture), F Natural (Interlude, Ritornello and Fantasia). Text: Milton Kessler. Commission: National Endowment for the Arts for the Bicentennial of the United States. (New York: American Composers Alliance, 1975).

In Memorian Malcolm X for soprano and orchestra (1974). Text: Robert Hayden. (New York: American Composers Alliance, 1974). Commission: Symphony of the New World. First perf.: Lincoln Center, by the Symphony of the New World, 1974.

In Memoriam: Zach Walker for band (1968). (New York: Composers Facsimile Edition, 1968). First perf.: Coatesville High School Band, Coatesville, Pa., 1969.

Intervals for orchestra (1970–71). 7 mvts. (New York: Composers Facsimile Edition, 1972). Commission: Robert Shaw.

Introduction and Allegro for orchestra (1959). (New York: Composers Facsimile Edition, rental). First perf.: Oklahoma City Symphony Orchestra, 1959.

New Dances for orchestra (1960). 5 mvts.: Caccia (Italy), Cancan (France), Counjai (Africa), Cachucha (Spain), Country Dance (U.S.A.). (New York: Composers Facsimile Edition, 1967).

Personals, cantata for narrator, mixed chorus, and brass septet (1966). 6 parts: Once more, listening to the wind and rain; Darkness brings the jungle on our room; And now the downpour ceases; Let us dance by metal waters burned; A moment we pause to quench our thirst; Let us go back into dusk again. Text: Arna Bontemps. (New York: Composers Facsimile Edition, 1967). Commission: Fisk University, for its 100th anniversary. First perf.: Fisk University, Nashville, 1966.

Pieces for clarinet with chamber orchestra (1962). 6 movts.: Prologue, Liberaments, Dialogue, Ode, Elegy, Epilogue. (New York: Composers Facsimile Edition, 1966). First perf.: Oklahoma City Symphony Orchestra, 1962.

Portraits of Two People for piano (four hands) (1965). 5 mvts.: Canvas, Contemplation, Capriciousness, Concordance, Candor. (New York: Composers Facsimile Edition, 1967). First perf.: Nashville Unitarian Church, 1968.

Rotations for band (1967). (New York: Composers Facsimile Edition, 1968). First perf.: Tennessee State University Band, Nashville, Tenn., 1969.

Spirituals for jazz quartet, orchestra, chorus, children's choir tenor and narrator (1982). First perf.: Atlanta Symphony Orchestra, 1982.

Squares for orchestra (1965). (New York: Composers Facsimile Edition, 1966). Commission: West Virginia State College for its 75th anniversary. First perf.: Oklahoma City Symphony Orchestra, Third Annual Interamerican Festival of the Arts, Chickasha, Oklahoma, 1966.

Swing Set for clarinet and piano (1972). Commission: Thomas Ayres. First perf.: University of Iowa, Iowa City, Ia., 1973.

Symphony in Three Movements (1964). 3 movts.: Allegro, Adagio ciaconna, Vivace. (New York: Composers Facsimile Edition, 1966). First perf.: Oklahoma City

Symphony Orchestra, Festival of Twentieth-Century Music at Oklahoma City University, 1964.

This House for male chorus with 4 chromatic pitch pipes (1971). (New York: American Composers Edition, 1971). First perf.: Morehouse College Glee Club, MENC 23rd National Biennial Convention, Atlanta, Ga., 1972.

Transitions: A Fantasy for Ten Instruments for flute, B-flat clarinet, bassoon, F horn, B-flat trumpet, trombone, violin, viola, violoncello, and piano (1971). (New York: American Composers Editions, 1971). Commission: Berkshire Music Center in cooperation with the Fromm Music Foundation. First perf.: Berkshire Music Center, Lenox, Mass., 1971.

Trio Concertante, concerto for clarinet, trumpet, and trombone with band (1960). (New York: American Composers Alliance, rental). First perf.: Langston University Band, Langston, Okla., 1960.

Variations on a Theme by M. B. Tolson, cantata for soprano, alto saxophone, trumpet, trombone, piano, violin, and violoncello (1969). Text: M. B. Tolson. (New York: Composers Facsimile Edition, 1969). First perf.: Atlanta, Ga., 1970.

Vocalise for violin and harp (1980). Commission: Richard Hunt. First perf.: Webster College, St. Louis, Mo., 1980.

Watermelon for piano (1971). (New York: Composers Facsimile Edition, 1971). First perf.: Indiana University, Bloomington, 1972.

CARTER, JOHN, 1937–

Cantata for high voice with orchestra (1964). 5 movts.: Prelude, Rondo, Recitative, Air, Toccata. (New York: Southern Music Company, 1964). Also published for voice and piano by Southern.

Emblemes for violin. First perf.: Lincoln Center, New York, 1967.

Epigrams, (ballet) orchestra. Choreography by Arthur Mitchell.

Kodoku for high voice with piano. First perf.: Detroit, Mich.

Requiem seditiosam for orchestra. Alternate title: *In Memoriam Medgar Evers.* Written with grant from the American Music Center. First perf.: Symphony of the New World, New York, 1967.

Saetas Profanas for medium voice with piano. Textless. First perf.: Carnegie Hall, New York.

Valses Pour Les Danseurs Noirs for piano. Waltzes for Black Dancers.

CUNNINGHAM, ARTHUR, 1928–[1]

Adagio for oboe and strings (1954).

Amen for mixed chorus (1962).

Amen Amen for mixed chorus (1965).

Ballet for jazz quartet and string quartet (1968).

Beginner's Piano Book (1964). Twenty-eight pieces.

Concentrics for orchestra (1963).

The Cossack for mixed chorus (1964). Text: Arthur Cunningham.

---

[1]These works are available from the composer through rental: Arthur Cunningham, 4 North Pine, Nyack, New York 10960.

Dialogue for piano and chamber orchestra (1966).

Dim Du Min for English horn (oboe) and chamber orchestra (1968–69).

Eclatette for cello (1969).

Engrams for piano (1969).

Fifty Stars for women's chorus (2 parts).

Four Shadows for piano (1950).

Four Songs for soprano and piano (1967). 4 parts: Purple Grapes, Green Figs and Dewberries; Thisby Dying; I Do Wander Everywhere; Lovers and Madmen. Text: William Shakespeare (*A Midsummer Night's Dream*).

Fragment for 3 French horns, 3 trumpets, 3 trombones, 5 temple blocks, maracas, claves, tambourine, cymbal, snare, 3 timpani, bass drum (1968).

From Where I Stand for mixed chorus (1950; rewritten, 1964). Text: Arthur Cunningham.

Fruitful Trees More Fruitful Are for mixed chorus (1965). Text: George Herbert (1593).

Garden of Phobos, The for mixed chorus (1968). Text: Life sounds. From the Moons of Mars Suite.

The Gingerbread Man for men's chorus (1955; rewritten, 1964). Text: Arthur Cunningham.

Harlem Suite for piano (1970). (Bryn Mawr: Theodore Presser Company, 1973). Rewritten for SATB chorus and ballet.

He Met Her at the Dolphin for mixed chorus (1963). Text: Arthur Cunningham. (New York: Remick and Witmark).

His Natural Grace, one-act mini-rock opera (1969). Book, music and lyrics by Arthur Cunningham.

House by the Sea, one-act opera (1966).

Hymn of Our Lord at the Last Supper for mixed chorus (1962). Text: Acts of St. John.

In the Year Seventeen for mixed chorus.

Into My Heart for mixed chorus (1964). Text: A. E. Housman.

Jabberwocky for soprano and piano (1960). Text: Lewis Carroll.

The Leaden Eyed for soprano and piano (1956). Text: Vachel Lindsay.

Let the Day Begin for women's chorus (1964).

Loveliest of Trees for mixed chorus (1964). Text: A. E. Housman.

Lullabye for a Jazz Baby for orchestra (1969). Commission: André Kostelanetz.

Minakesh for violoncello and strings (1969).

Night Lights for orchestra (1955).

Octet for percussion ensemble (5 temple blocks, 4 timbales, 3 timpani, snare drum, tambourine, suspended cymbal, maracas, guiro, claves, bass drum; 1968).

Omnus for string orchestra (1968).

Organ Prelude and Hymn, Lead Us Still and Guide Us for mixed chorus and organ (1965). Text: Arthur Cunningham.

Ostrich Feathers, children's rock musical comedy (1964). Text: Arthur Cunningham.

Pale Moons Rise for mixed chorus (1955). Text: Arthur Cunningham.

Patsy Patch and Susan's Dream, musical comedy for very young children (1963). Book and lyrics by Arthur Cunningham.

Prometheus for bass and piano or orchestra (1967).

Ring Out Wild Bells for mixed chorus (1965). Text: Alfred, Lord Tennyson.

Septet for piccolo, flute, oboe, English horn, clarinet in B-flat, bass clarinet, bassoon (1968).

Serenade for violoncello and piano (1950).

Sing Children Sing for mixed chorus (1964). Text: Arthur Cunningham.

Song of Songs for soprano and piano (1951). Text: Wilfred Owen.

Sugarhill for two double basses and violoncello or solo piano (1969).

Theatre Piece for orchestra (1966).

Then the Cricket Sings for mixed chorus and soloists (1957; rewritten in 1964).

Thisby Dying for violoncello and flute (1968).

Trio for violin, viola, and violoncello (1968).

Trio for flute, viola, and bassoon (1952).

Trinities for two double basses and violoncello (1969).

Turning of the Babies in the Bed for baritone and piano (1951). Text: Paul Laurence Dunbar.

Two Haitian Play Dances for two pianos (1951).

Two Inventions for two double basses (1952).

Violetta, musical comedy (1963).

Volume of Sixty Piano Pieces for piano (1966).

The West Wind for mixed chorus (1962). Text: John Masefield.

When I Was One and Twenty for mixed chorus (1963). Text: A. E. Housman.

With Rue My Heart Is Laden for mixed chorus (1964). Text: A. E. Housman.

DAWSON, WILLIAM LEVI, 1897–

Hail Mary for mixed chorus (1946).

Interlude for piano.

Jump Back, Honey for orchestra. Wanamaker prize, 1930.

Lovers Plighted for mixed chorus.

The Mongrel Yank for mixed chorus.

Negro Folk Symphony (1931; revised in 1952). 3 movts.: The Bond of Africa; Hope in the Night; O le' Shine, Shine Like a Morning Star. (Delaware Water Gap, Pennsylvania: Shawnee Press, Inc., 1965).

A *Negro Work Song* for orchestra (1940). Commission: Columbia Broadcasting System.

Out in the Fields With God for mixed chorus and orchestra. (Chicago: Neil A. Kjos Music Co., 1957).

Scherzo for orchestra (1930). Wanamaker prize, 1930.

Sonata in A for violin and piano (1927).

Trio in A for piano, violin, violoncello (1925).

DETT, ROBERT NATHANIEL, 1882–1943

Adagio Cantabile for piano.

American Sampler for orchestra.

Arietta

As by the Streams of Babylon for chorus.

Ascapetso for piano.

Ave Maria for chorus.

Beyond the Dream for piano.

Bible Vignettes for piano.

Cave of the Winds for piano. 2 movts.: March, Two-step. (Niagra Falls, New York: S. C. Fragard, 1902).

Chariot Jubilee, oratorio (1921).

Cinnamon Grove Suite for piano (1927).

City of God for mixed chorus with piano. Text: Samuel Johnson. (New York: J. Fischer & Brothers).

Dance of Desire for piano.

Enchantment Suite for piano (1922).

Follow Me for voice and piano. (Cincinnati: J. Church, 1919).

Gently Lord, O Gently Lead Us for chorus.

Go On, Mule for voice and piano.

Hampton! My Home by the Sea for mixed chorus. Text: Robert Nathaniel Dett. (Hampton, Virginia: 1914, in *The Southern Workman*).

The Hard-Won Miles for voice and piano.

Hew Down the Tree for chorus.

I'm A-Going to See My Friends Again for voice and piano.

In the Bottoms Suite for piano (1913). 5 mvts.: Prelude, Night; His Song; Honey; Barcarolle; Juba Dance. (Chicago: Summy, 1913).

Iorana for voice and piano.

The Lamb for women's chorus.

Magic Moon of Molten Gold for voice and piano.

Magnolia Suite for piano (1911). 5 movts.: Magnolias; The Deserted Cabin; My Lady Love; Mammy; The Place Where the Rainbow Ends. (Chicago: Summy, 1912).

March Negre

Music in the Mine for chorus.

My Day for voice and piano.

Now Rest Beneath the Night Shadows for chorus.

The Ordering of Moses, oratorio (1937). Text: Robert Nathaniel Dett, after folklore and the Bible. (New York: J. Fischer & Brothers, 1937). First perf.: Cincinnati Festival, 1937.

Parade of the Years for orchestra. Text: Edward Hungerford. Incidental music.

Ramah for violin.

A Song for orchestra.

Symphony, E Minor.

Tropic Winter Suite for piano (1938). 7 movts.: The Daybreak Charioteer; A Bayou Garden; Pompons and Fans; Legend of the Stoll; To a Closed Casement; Noon Siesta; Parade of the Jasmine Banners. (Chicago: Summy, 1938).

The Voice of the Sea for voice and piano.

Were Thou the Moon? for voice and piano.

Zion Hallelujah for voice and piano.

FISCHER, WILLIAM, 1935–

Away for mixed chorus (1962). Text: Robert Frost.

Batucada Fantastica for percussion and electronic sound (1962).

Concerto Grosso for jazz ensemble with orchestra (1968).

Concerto Grosso for jazz ensemble with orchestra (1969). First perf.: Austin Symphony "Pops" Concert, Austin, Texas, 1969.

Elected Silence, Sing to Me for mixed voices (1954). Text: Gerard Manley Hopkins.

Elegy for clarinet with piano (1954).

Experience in E for jazz ensemble with orchestra (1968).

Gift of Lesbos for violoncello with piano and electronic sounds (1968).

Introduction and Song for orchestra (1959).

Jack-Jack, opera (1968). Text: Megan Terry. First perf.: New York (1970).

Jesse, opera (1966). Text: William S. Fischer.

Joy of Love for women's chorus with piano (1969). Text: LeRoi Jones.

Lake of the Ozarks for piano (1955).

Movement for '65 for flute with harp (1965).

Music for Baritone Voice and Piano (1963). Text: Bible.

Music for Flute and Harp (1964).

Music for Soprano Voice and Piano (1963). Text: Anonymous.

Partials for saxophone (1966).

Piece for viola with piano (1955).

Predilections for viola music (1963).

Psalm 23 for mixed chorus with brasses (1962). Text: Bible.

Quartet No. 1 for string quartet (1954).

Quartet No. 2 for string quartet (1962).

A Quiet Movement for orchestra (1966). (Berlin: Bote & Bock, 1966).

Short Piece for violin with harpsichord (1962).

Simon Wilde for mixed media. Text: Megan Terry.

Sonata for violin and piano (1962). First perf.: Xavier University, New Orleans, La.

Statement for speaking chorus with orchestra (1964).

Suite for Three for piano, flute, and violin. First perf.: Xavier University, New Orleans.

Time I for electronic sounds, percussion, saxophone, viola, and violoncello.

Time II for electronic sounds, percussion, saxophone, viola, violoncello (1967).

Triology for women's chorus with orchestra (1964). Text: e. e. cummings. First perf.: Xavier University, New Orleans, 1965.

Trio for piano, clarinet, kettle drums, violin (1962).

Variations for orchestra (1961).

Variations No. 2 for orchestra (1964).

What Do They Mean To Us for mixed chorus (1963). Text: Arthur Rimbaud.

HAKIM, TALIB RASUL
(CHAMBERS, STEPHEN), 1940–

Contours for oboe, bassoon, horn, trumpet, violoncello, and contrabass (1966). First perf.: Town Hall, as part of Max Pollikoff's "Music in Our Time" series, 1967.

Currents for string quartet (1967).

Duo for flute and clarinet (1963). (New York: Galaxy Music, 1965). First perf.: Bennington Composers Conference, Bennington, Vermont, 1964.

Elements for flute/alto flute, clarinet/bass clarinet, violin/viola, violoncello, piano, and glass and bamboo wind and hand chimes (1967). First perf.: On "Inside Bedford-Stuyvesant," WNEW-TV, New York City, 1969.

Encounter for flute, oboe, clarinet, bassoon, horn, trumpet, and trombone (1965).

Four for clarinet, trumpet, trombone, and piano (1965). First perf.: New Music Ensemble of the University of North Carolina, 1968.

Inner-Sections for flute, clarinet, trombone, piano, and percussion (1967).

Moments for E-flat saxophone, bassoon, and horn (1966).

Music for Nine Players and Soprano Voice (1977). First perf.: 1977.

Mutations for bass clarinet, horn, trumpet, viola, and violoncello (1964).

Ode to Silence for soprano and piano (1964). Text: Talib Rasul Hakim.

On Being Still on the 8th for alto flute, French horn, bass clarinet, bassoon, violoncello, double bass, percussion, and piano (1978).

Peace-Mobile for woodwind quintet (1964).

A Piano Piece for piano (1965).

Placements for five percussion instruments and piano (1970). (Berlin: Bote & Bock [New York: Associated Music], 1975).

Portraits for alto flute, bass clarinet, 3 percussion instruments, and piano (1965).

Psalm of Akhnaton for mezzo-soprano, flute, and piano (1978). First perf.: Morgan State University, Baltimore, Md., 1978.

Quote-Unquote for bass-baritone, oboe, trumpet, and 2 percussion instruments (1967). Text: Talib Rasul Hakim.

Reflections on the 5th Ray for narrator and chamber orchestra (1972). Text: Theresa Schoenacher. Commission: Brooklyn Chamber Orchestra, 1972.

Roots and Other Things for flute/alto flute, oboe/English horn clarinet/bass clarinet, trumpet, French horn, trombone, viola, violoncello, and contrabass (1967). First perf.: Society of Black Composers, Boston, Mass.

Set-Three for soprano, violoncello, and piano (1970). Text: Talib Rasul Hakim. First perf.: Summer Convocation on the Arts, Saratoga Springs, New York, 1970.

Shapes for chamber orchestra (1965). First perf.: Oakland Youth Chamber Orchestra, 1970.

Six Players and a Voice for soprano, clarinet, trumpet, violoncello, 2 percussion instruments, and piano (1964). Text: Talib Rasul Hakim. First perf.: YMHA/YWHA, as part of Max Pollikoff's "Music in Our Time" series, 1969.

Sketchy Blue-Bop for concert jazz band (1973). Commission: University of Wisconsin (River Falls). First Perf.: University of Wisconsin, River Falls, Wis.

Song-Short for soprano, alto flute, English horn, bass clarinet, French horn, and trombone (1967). Text: Talib Rasul Hakim.

Sound-Gone for piano (1967). First perf.: Temple University, 1970.

Sound-Images for 2 trumpets, 2 flugelhorns, 4 French horns, 3 trombones, tuba, 3 percussion instruments, strings, and female chorus (1969). Text: Talib Rasul Hakim. First perf.: Society of Black Composers, New York City, 1969.

Three Play Short Five for bass clarinet, percussion, and contrabass (1965). First perf.: Max Pollikoff's "Music in Our Time" series, 1965.

Timelessness for flugelhorn, French horn, trombone, tuba, percussion, contrabass, and piano (1970).

Titles for flute, oboe, clarinet, and bassoon (1965).

Tone-Poem for soprano, percussion, contrabass, and piano (1969). Text: Langston Hughes. First perf.: Bowdoin College, 1969.

Tone-Prayers for mixed chorus with percussion and piano (1973). Text: Talib Rasul Hakim. Commission: University of Wisconsin (River Falls). First perf.: University of Wisconsin, River Falls, Wis., 1973.

Uranian-Projections for soprano, percussion, piano (1970). Text: Talib Rasul Hakim.

Visions of Ishwara for orchestra (1970). First perf.: Symphony of the New World, New York City, 1971.

KAY, ULYSSES S., 1917–

Admiral Byrd for orchestra (1960). Score for the episode "Admiral Byrd" from the CBS television series *The Twentieth Century.*

Ancient Saga for piano and string orchestra (1947). (New York: American Composers Alliance).

As Joseph Was A-Walking for mixed chorus (1943). (New York: American Composers Alliance).

Aulos for solo flute, 2 horns, string orchestra, and percussion (1967). Commission: John Solum. First perf.: Indiana University Chamber Orchestra, Bloomington, 1967.

Ballet "Danse Calinda", ballet (1941). After a story by Ridgeley Torrence.

The Birds for chorus and piano (1966). 5 songs. Commission: Burton A. Cleaves, for the Simmons College Glee Club. Text: P. J. Bailey, J. Hogg, W. Cowper, Alfred, Lord Tennyson, S. C. Taylor. First perf.: Simmons College Glee Club, Boston, Mass., 1967. (New York: Duchess Music/MCA, 1969.)

Bleeker Street Suite (piano sketch) for elementary orchestra with recorders (1968). 4 movts.: Entrata; Lullaby; Novelettes; Ostinato.

The Boor, opera in one act (1955). (New York: Associated Publishers, Inc.). After the play by Anton Chekhov; libretto by the composer.

Brass Quartet for two trumpets and two trombones (1950). (New York: Peer International Corporation).

Brief Elegy for oboe and string orchestra (1946). (New York: American Composers Alliance).

The Capitoline Venus, opera in one act (1969). Libretto: Judith Dvořák, after Mark Twain. Commission: Quincy Society of Fine Arts. First perf.: Krannert Center for the Performing Arts, University of Illinois; University of Illinois Opera Group, Champaign-Urbana, Ill.

Choral Triptch for mixed chorus and string orchestra (1962). 3 songs: *Give Ear to My Words; How Long Wilt Thou Forget Me, O Lord?; Alleluia.* Text: Biblical. Commission: Daniel Pinkham, under a Ford Foundation Grant. First perf.: Museum of Modern Art, New York City. (New York: Associated Music, 1967).

Christmas Carol for women's chorus (3 parts, 1943). (New York: Peer International Corporation.

Come Away, Come Away Death for men's chorus (3 parts, 1944). (New York: Peer International Corporation).

Concerto for Orchestra (1948). (New York: American Composers Alliance).

Concert Sketches for band (1965). 6 parts: Prologue; Parade; Promenade; Carnival; Holiday; Epilogue. Written for the Oswald Band Composition Award competition sponsored by the American Bandmasters' Association.

Dedication for mixed chorus (1946). (New York: American Composers Alliance).

Duo for Flute and Oboe (1943). (New York: American Composers Alliance).

Emily Dickinson Set for women's chorus and piano (1964). Text: Emily Dickinson. Commission: Burton A. Cleaves. (New York: Duchess Music [Leeds Masterwork Choral Series], 1965). 3 songs: Elysium Is as Far; Indian Summer; Ample Make This Bed. First perf.: Simmons College Glee Club, Boston, Mass.

The Epicure for mixed chorus and piano (1959). Text: Abraham Cowley. (New York: Duchess Music/MCA).

Epigrams and Hymn for mixed chorus and organ (1975). Text: John Greenleaf Whittier, the Reverend John Murray, and Samuel Longfellow. Commission: Princeton Theological Seminary, Bryn Mawr Presbyterian Church, and the Brick Presbyterian Church, for the Bicentennial. First perf.: Brick Presbyterian Church Choir.

Evocation for concert band (1944).

Essay on Death (1964). Television film about John J. Kennedy for WNET, New York City.

F. D. R.: From Third Term to Pearl Harbor for orchestra (1958). For the episode "F.D.R.: From Third Term to Pearl Harbor" from the CBS television series *The Twentieth Century.*

Facets for piano and woodwind quintet (1971). Commission: Eastman School of Music, for its 50th anniversary. First perf.: Eastman School of Music by the faculty ensemble Musica Nova.

The Fall of China for orchestra (1959). For the episode "The Fall of China" from the CBS television series *The Twentieth Century.*

Fantasy Variations for orchestra (1963). Commission: Portland (Maine) Symphony. (New York: Duchess Music Corporation, 1966). First perf.: Portland Symphony, 1963.

First Nocturne for piano (1973). Commission: Mrs. Eric Stein. First perf.: James Dick, 1973.

Five Mosaics for chamber orchestra (1940).

Five Portraits for violin and piano (1972). Commission: McKim Fund of the Library of Congress. First perf.: Library of Congress.

Flowers in the Valley for mixed chorus unaccompanied (1961). (New York: C. F. Peters under the sponsorship of Sigma Alpha Iota in the American Music Awards series, 1962). First perf.: Illinois Wesleyan University Choir, Bloomington.

Flute Quintet for flute and string quartet (1943). (New York: American Composers Alliance, 1943).

Forever Free for band; alternate title: *A Lincoln Chronicle* (1962). 3 movts.: Prelude; Toccata; Proclamation. (New York: Associated Music, 1975). First perf.: Lincoln Memorial, by the U.S. Marine Band.

Four Hymn-Anthems for mixed chorus and organ (1965). Text: *God, the Lord* (text by John Keble paraphrased from the Psalms of David); *Lo, the Earth* (text by Longfellow); *Love Divine* (text by Charles Wesley); *O Come Emmanuel* (Veni, Veni Emmanuel). (New York: Duchess Music/MCA, 1965; each published separately).

Four Inventions for piano (1946). (New York: Duchess Music/MCA, 1964). First perf.: Town Hall, 1947.

Four Silhouettes for concert band (1972). (New York: Duchess Music/MCA, 1973). First perf.: Lehman College Band, New York City.

Fugitive Songs for medium voice and piano (1950). 8 songs: *That Day You Came* (text by Lizette Reese); *When the Wind Is Low* (text by Cale Young Rice); *Even Song* (text by Ridgely Torrence); *The Fugitives* (text by Florence Wilkerson); *The Mystic* (text by Wittner Bynner); *Sentence* (text by Wittner Bynner); *When I Am Dead* (text by Elsa Barker). First perf.: Town Hall, New York City, 1958.

Going Home (1962). Commission: Peter Hollander. United Nations Film Department production.

Grace to You, and Peace for mixed chorus and organ (1955). (New York: H. W. Gray, 1957). Text: Biblical text adapted by Theodore Melnechuk. First perf.: Bethlehem, Pennsylvania, at the festival service for the 100th anniversary of the Moravian Church. Moravian Anthem Contest award, 1956.

Guitarra for guitar (1973). 3 movts.: Prelude; Arioso; Finale. Commission: Wilbur P. Cotton.

Harlem Children's Suite for elementary orchestra (1973). 3 movts.: Prelude; Aria; Finale. Commission: Harlem School of the Arts.

Heralds for brass octet (4 trumpets, 4 trombones) (1968). First perf.: International Music Congress, New York City, 1968.

Heralds II for three trumpets (1974). Alternate title: *Fanfare for Three Trumpets*. First perf.: Brooklyn College Brass Ensemble, 1974.

How Stands the Glass Around? for mixed chorus unaccompanied (1954). (New York: Associated Music, 1956). Text: James Wolfe. Commission: Randolph Singers.

Hymn-Anthem on the Tune "Hanover" for mixed chorus and organ or piano (1959). (New York: C. F. Peters, 1960). Text: Sir Robert Grant.

Inscriptions from Whitman for mixed chorus and orchestra (1963). 2 movts. Text: Walt Whitman. Commission: Tercentenary Commission of the State of New Jersey and the New Jersey Symphony, for the New Jersey Tercentenary. First perf.: Women's Chorus of Douglass College, the New Jersey Oratorio Society Male Chorus of Atlantic City, and the New Jersey Symphony Orchestra, 1964.

Jubilee, opera in three acts (1974–76). Libretto: Donald Door based on the novel by Margaret Walker. Commission: Opera South. First perf.: Opera South, Jackson, Mississippi, 1976.

The Juggler of Our Lady, opera in one act (1956). Libretto: Alexander King. First perf.: Xavier University, New Orleans, La., 1962.

The Land for orchestra (1962). Score for an NBC news documentary featuring Chet Huntley.

A Lincoln Letter for mixed chorus and bass soloist (1953). Text: attributed to Abraham Lincoln. First perf.: College Choir of Lincoln College, Lincoln, Illinois.

The Lion, the Griffin, and the Kangaroo for orchestra (1951). Commission: Peter Hollander. Filmscore, Hollander-Tait Productions, Inc.

Markings for orchestra (1966). Commission: Meadow Brook Festival, Oakland University (Rochester, Minnesota). First perf.: Meadow Brook Festival, Oakland University, by the Detroit Symphony, 1966. Written in memory of Dag Hammarskjöld and dedicated to Oliver Daniel.

A New Song for mixed chorus unaccompanied (1955). Texts: Biblical. 3 songs: *Sing Unto the Lord; Like As A Father; O Praise the Lord.* (New York: C. F. Peters, 1961;

published separately). Commission: Illinois Wesleyan University College Choir, Bloomington. First perf.: Illinois Wesleyan University Annual Symposium on Contemporary American Music, by the Illinois Wesleyan Collegiate Choir, 1956.

New York, City of Magic for orchestra (1958). Commission: WNET (New York City). For film, produced by WNET, first showing at the Museum of Modern Art, 1961.

Nosotros for orchestra (1962). Commission: Peter Hollander. United Nations Film Department production.

Of New Horizons for orchestra (1944). (New York: C. F. Peters, 1961, parts on rental). Commission: Thor Johnson. First perf.: New York Philharmonic Symphony Orchestra, New York City. American Broadcasting Company Award, 1946.

Once There Was A Man for narrator, mixed chorus, and orchestra (1969). Text: Randal Caudill. Commission: Worchester (Mass.) Music Festival. First perf.: Detroit Symphony, Detroit, Mich., 1969.

Organ Suite No. 1 (1958). 3 movts. Commission: Marilyn Mason. First perf.: St. Paul's Chapel, New York City.

Parables for mixed chorus and chamber orchestra (1970). 2 songs: *The Old Armchair; The Hell-Bound Train.* Texts: Anonymous. Commission: American Choral Directors Association. First perf.: First Annual Convention of the American Choral Directors Association, by the Kansas State University Concert Chorale, and the Kansas State University Chamber Orchestra, Kansas City, Mo., 1971. (New York: Duchess Music/MCA, 1970, parts on rental).

Partita in A for violin and piano (1950). 4 movts.: Prelude; Burlesca; Interlude; Echo. First perf.: American Academy in Rome, 1952.

Phoebus, Arise for soprano, bass, mixed chorus and orchestra (1959). 7 parts: *Prelude* (text by the composer); *No!* (text by Thomas Hood); *Tears, Flow No More* (text by Lord Herbert of Cherbury); *Phoebus, Arise* (text by William Drummond); *The Epicure* (text by Abraham Cowley); *Epilogue* (text by the composer). Commission: International Music Council of New York City. First perf.: Town Hall by the Interracial Fellowship Chorus and Orchestra, 1959.

Pieta for English horn and string orchestra (1950). First perf.: Town Hall as part of the 19th Annual Festival of American Music.

Piano Quintet for piano and string quartet (1949). (New York: American Composers Alliance).

Piano Sonata (1940). (New York: American Composers Alliance). First prize, Phi Mu Alpha Competition, 1940.

Pentagraph for women's chorus and piano (1972). 5 movts.

Portrait Suite for orchestra (1948). 5 movts.: Prologue; Asymmetric; Reclining Figure; Blossoming; Epilogue. First perf.: Erie Philharmonic, Erie, Pa., 1964. Award for best composition by a native Arizonian, 1948.

Prelude for solo flute (1943; revised in 1974) (New York: Pembroke/Carl Fischer, 1976).

Presidential Suite for orchestra (1965). Commission: Greater Boston Youth Symphony. First perf.: Greater Boston Youth Symphony, Boston's Symphony Hall, 1965.

Prologue and Parade for concert band (1977). (New York: Carl Fischer, Inc., 1978).

The Quiet One Suite for orchestra (1948). Alternate title: *Suite from the Quiet One.* 4 movts.: Joys and Fears; Street Wanderings; Interlude; Crisis. First perf.: New York Little Symphony, 1948.

Quintet Concerto for brass quintet (2 trumpets, horn, and 2 trombones; alternate part for tuba is available) and orchestra. 3 movts. Commission: Juilliard School of Music. First perf.: Juilliard School of Music, 1974.

Reverie and Rondo for orchestra (1964). Alternate title: *Two Pieces for Orchestra*. First perf.: Flint Symphony Orchestra, Flint, Mich., 1968.

The Rope for solo dancer and piano (1946). Commission: Eleanore Goff; revised for piano and string orchestra as *Ancient Saga*. First perf.: New York City, 1947.

Scherzi Musicali for chamber orchestra (1968). Commission: Chamber Music Society of Detroit for its 25th anniversay. First perf.: Princeton Chamber Orchestra and the Interlochen Arts Woodwind Quintet, Detroit, Mich., 1969.

Serenade for Orchestra (1954). (New York: Associated Music, 1955). Commission: Louisville Philharmonic Society. First perf.: Louisville Orchestra, 1954.

The Shape of Things for orchestra (1960). Score for the NBC news program "World Wide 60."

A Short Overture for orchestra (1946). (New York: Duchess Music/MCA, 1973, parts on rental). First perf.: New York City Symphony, 1947. Third Annual George Gershwin Memorial Contest Winner, 1947.

Short Suite for concert band (1950). 5 movts.: Fanfare; March; Interlude; Lyric; Finale. (New York: Associated Music, 1957). First perf.: Baylor University Golden Wave Band, Baylor University, 1951.

Sinfonia in E for orchestra (1950). (New York: Pembroke/Carl Fischer). First perf.: Eastman-Rochester Symphony Orchestra, 1951.

Six Dances for string orchestra (1954). Alternate Title: *American Dances*. 6 parts: Schottische; Waltz; Round Dance; Polka; Promenade; Galop. (New York: Duchess Music [Leeds Contemporary Classics for Strings series] 1965). First perf.: CBS radio "String Serenade."

Solemn Prelude for concert band (1949). (New York: American Composers Alliance). Commission: Baylor University Band. First perf.: Baylor University Golden Wave Band, Baylor University, 1950.

Sonatina for Violin and Piano (1942). (New York: American Composers Alliance).

Song of Ahab, cantata for baritone voice and ten instruments (1950). Commission: Quincy Fine Arts Society, Quincy, Ill.

Song of Jeremiah for baritone, mixed chorus, and orchestra (1945). Text: Biblical. First perf.: Fisk University Choir, Nashville, Tenn., 1954.

Southern Harmony for orchestra (1975). (New York: Pembroke/Carl Fischer, 1976). Commission: Southeastern Regional Metropolitan Orchestra Managers Association. First perf.: North Carolina Symphony Orchestra, 1976. Based on themes and motives from William Walker's "The Southern Harmony" of 1835. 4 mvts.: Prelude: Land of Beginnings; Fifes and Drums; Variants; Elysium.

Stephen Crane Set for mixed chorus and instrumental ensemble (flute, oboe, English horn, clarinet, bass clarinet, bassoon, 2 horns, 2 trumpets, tenor trombone, bass trombone, and percussion; 1967). 4 parts: Black Ryders; Mystic Shadow; A Spirit; War Is Kind. Text: Stephen Crane. Commission: Chicago Musical College of Roosevelt University, in honor of its 100th anniversary. First perf.: Chicago Musical College, 1968.

String Quartet No. 1 (1949). (New York: American Composers Alliance).

String Quartet No. 2 (1956). 4 movts. First perf.: University of Illinois (Champaign-Urbana) by the Walden String Quartet.

String Quartet No. 3 (1961) Commission: University of Michigan. First perf.: Stanley Quartet, 1962.

Submarine! for orchestra (1959). Score for the episode "Submarine!" from the CBS television series *The Twentieth Century.*

Suite for Brass Choir for 4 trumpets, 4 horns, 3 trombones, tuba (1943). (New York: American Composers Alliance).

Suite for Flute and Oboe (1943). (New York: Duchess Music/MCA, 1964). 4 movts.: Prelude; Air; Minuet; Gigue. First perf.: Composer's Forum concert, New York City, 1947.

Suite for Orchestra (1945). 4 movts.: Fanfare; Three-four; Scherzo; Olden Tune: Finale. (New York: Associated Music, 1948). First perf.: Town Hall, by the American Youth Orchestra, New York City, 1950.

Suite for Strings for string orchestra (1947). 4 movts. First perf.: Baltimore Chamber Orchestra, Baltimore, 1949.

Suite in B for oboe and piano (1943). 3 movts.: Prelude; Recitative and Air; Dance. First perf.: American Academy in Rome, 1949.

Symphony (1967). 4 movts. Commission: Illinois Sesquicentennial Commission. First perf.: Chicago Symphony Orchestra, Chicago, 1968.

Tears, Flow No More for women's chorus and piano (1959). (New York: Duchess Music/MCA). Text: Lord Herbert of Cherbury. Arrangement of "Tears, Flow No More" from *Phoebus, Arise.*

Ten Short Essays for piano (1957). Alternate title: *Ten Pieces for Children.* 10 pieces: So Gay; Tender Thought; Sprite's Dance; Little Tune; Old Lament; Make Believe; Two Voices; Playing, Playing; Slumber Song; March Song. (New York: Duchess Music/MCA, 1965).

Theater Set for orchestra (1968). 3 movts.: Overture; Ballad-Chase Music; Finale. (New York: Duchess Music/MCA, 1971). Commission: Junior League of Atlanta for Robert Shaw and the Atlanta Symphony Orchestra. First perf.: Atlanta Symphony Orchestra, Atlanta, 1968.

A Thing of Beauty for orchestra (1966). Commission: Fisk University. A Trafco production film.

Three Fanfares for Four Trumpets (1942). (New York: Duchess Music/Leeds Music, 1964). First perf.: Composer's Forum concert, 1947.

The Three Musketeers (television score) for orchestra (1960). Commission: David Susskind. A Talent Associates, Ltd. production.

Three Pieces After Blake for high voice and orchestra (1952). 3 pieces: *To the Evening Star; Mad Song; Contemplation.* Text: William Blake. First perf.: 1955.

To Light That Shines for chorus and organ (1962). Text: Samuel Johnson. Commission: New York Society for Ethical Culture. First perf.: New York City, 1962.

Trigon for wind orchestra (1961). 3 movts.: Prelude; Canticle; Toccata. Commission: American Wind Symphony. First perf.: American Wind Symphony, Pittsburgh, Pa., 1961.

Triple Set for male chorus unaccompanied (1971). Three parts: *Ode: To the Cuckoo* (text by Michael Bruce); *Had I a Heart* (text by R. B. Sheridan); *A Toast* (text by R. B. Sheridan). (New York: Belwin Mills, 1972).

Triptych on Texts of Blake for high voice, violin, violoncello, and piano (1962). Reduction by the composer of *Three Pieces After Blake: To the Evening Star; Mad Song; Contemplation.* Commission: Kermit Moore. First perf.: Winston-Salem Teachers College, by the Clarmoor Quartet, Winston-Salem, North Carolina, 1963.

Triumvirate for male chorus unaccompanied (1953). 3 parts: *Music* (text by Ralph Waldo Emerson); *Children's Hour* (text by Henry Wadsworth Longfellow); *Night*

March (text by Herman Melville). (New York: Peer/Southern Music, 1954). Commission: Leonard dePaur for the dePaur Infantry Chorus. First perf.: The dePaur Infantry Chorus, Hunter College, New York City, 1954.

Two Dunbar Lyrics for mixed chorus unaccompanied (1965). (New York: Duchess Music/MCA [Masterwork Choral Series], 1966). Text: Paul Laurence Dunbar. Commission: 75th anniversary of West Virginia State College. First perf.: West Virginia State College, 1965.

Two Meditations for organ (1950). (New York: H. W. Gray [Contemporary Organ series, #27], 1951). First perf.: Fisk University, 1952.

Two Short Pieces for piano (4 hands; 1957). (New York: Franco Columbo).

Two Songs for Children for voice and piano (1966). (New York: Published separately: *Where the Boats Go;* published by Canyon Press [Juilliard Project Collection], 1970; *The Little Elf-Man;* published by Duchess Music). 2 songs: *Where the Boats Go* (text by Robert Louis Stevenson); *The Little Elf-Man* (text by John Kendrick Bangs). Commission: Juilliard School of Music, for the Juilliard Repertory Project.

Umbrian Scene for orchestra (1963). (New York: Duchess Music/MCA, 1965). Commission: Edward B. Benjamin. First perf.: New Orleans Philharmonic, 1964.

Visions for piano (1974). New York: *The Black Perspective in Music,* 3 (May, 1975).

The Western Paradise for narrator and orchestra (1976). 5 movts. Commission: National Symphony, for the Bicentennial. First perf.: National Symphony, Washington, D.C., 1976.

What's In A Name? for mixed chorus unaccompanied (1954). Text: Helen F. More. First perf.: Randolph Singers, 1955. Originally part of a work entitled *Two Madrigals.*

A Wreath for Waits for unaccompanied mixed chorus (1954). 3 parts: *Noel; Lully Lullay; Welcome Yule.* Text: Anonymous. Commission: Cornell University A Cappella Chorus. First perf.: Ann Arbor, Michigan, 1954.

LOGAN, WENDELL, 1940–

Beats for Duke, Cannon and Oliver for percussion and tape.

Blues for Mr. Charley for jazz ensemble (tenor saxophone, double bass, piano, 2 percussionists) and soprano.

Brass Quintet.

Concert Music for Orchestra.

Duo Exchanges for clarinet and percussion (1979). First perf.: University of Redlands.

Evocation for harmonica and magnetic tape.

For Cannon for jazz band.

From Hell to Breakfast for jazz group, dancers, singers, tape, and lights.

Hughes Set for men's choir (1979). Text: Langston Hughes. First perf.: Morehouse College Glee Club, Cleveland, Ohio, 1979.

Ice and Fire for baritone, soprano, and piano.

Malcolm, Malcolm for mixed chorus with electronic tape (1979). First perf.: Shaw High School Choir, Cleveland, Ohio, 1979.

Music for Brass.

Five Pieces for Piano (1978). First perf.: Oberlin Conservatory, 1978.

Polyphony I for Orchestra.

Praise Ye the Lord for women's chorus and timpani.

Proportions for Nine Players and Conductor.

Sketch I for jazz band.

Songs of Our Time for chorus and chamber orchestra (1969).

Stanzas for Three Players.

String Quartet.

Suite for Brass.

Textures for piano.

To Mingus for vibraphone and any improvising instrument (1979). First perf.: Oberlin Conservatory of Music, 1979.

Variations on a Motive by John Coltrane for jazz ensemble.

What Time Is It? for voice and piano.

Woodwind Quintet.

PERRY, JULIA 1924–79

Bicentennial Reflections for tenor, 2 clarinets, and percussion (1976).

The Bottle, opera.

The Cask of Amontillado, opera (1954). Produced at Columbia University, 1954.

Children's Symphony for orchestra (1978).

Episode for orchestra.

Fragments of Letters of Saint Catherine for solo voice, chorus, and orchestra.

Homunculus, C. F. for soprano and percussionists (1969).

How Beautiful the Feet for voice and piano (1954). Text: Isaiah 52:7.

Our Thanks To Thee for mixed chorus and alto soloist (1951). (New York: Galaxy, 1951).

Pastoral for flute and strings (1959).

Quinary Quixotic Songs for bass-baritone and 7 instruments (1975).

Seven Contrasts for baritone and chamber ensemble.

A Short Piece for orchestra.

Simple Symphony for strings, 3 clarinets, 3 trumpets, and percussion (1973).

Song of Our Saviour for mixed chorus (1953).

Stabat Mater for contralto and string quartet or string orchestra (1951). (New York: Southern Music Publishing Co., 1954). Text: Jacopone da Todi (translated by Perry).

Ye Who Seek the Truth for mixed chorus and tenor. Text: Julia Perry.

SMITH, HALE, 1925–

Anticipations, Introspections, and Reflections for piano (1971). First perf.: International Piano Festival, University of Maryland and New York City, 1971.

Beyond the Rim of Day for high voice and piano (1950). (New York: E. B. Marks, 1970). Text: Langston Hughes. 3 songs: *March Moon; Troubled Woman; To a Little Lover-Lass, Dead.* First perf.: Karamu Theater, Cleveland, Ohio, 1955.

Blood Wedding, chamber opera (1953). Commission: Karamu Theater, Cleveland, Ohio. First perf.: Karamu Theater. Play by Garcia Lorca (main characters are non-singing parts).

Bold New Approach for orchestra (1966). Music for a documentary film on mental health; Irving Jacoby, producer.

By Yearning and By Beautiful for string orchestra (1961). First perf.: Richmond Symphony Orchestra, 1972. Suggested by Russell Atkins's poem "By Yearning and By Beautiful."

Comes Tomorrow, jazz cantata for mixed chorus, soloists (soprano, contralto, tenor, and bass-baritone), and jazz ensemble (1972; revised in 1976). Text: Hale Smith. 4 movts.: *Exhortation; How Lucky I Am; Every Day Is A New Day; What Good Is a World?* (New York: E. B. Marks, 1976). Commission: Tougaloo College (Tougaloo, Mississippi), Tougaloo College Concert Choir, the Jackson College instrumental ensemble, 1972.

Concert Music for Piano and Orchestra (1972). Commission: Undine Moore and Altona T. Johns. First perf.: Richmond Symphony Orchestra, 1972.

Contours for orchestra (1962). (New York: C. F. Peters, 1962). Commission: Broadcast Music, Inc., in celebration of its 20th anniversary. First perf.: Louisville Symphony Orchestra, 1962.

Duo for Violin and Piano (1953). 3 movts. (New York: C. F. Peters, rental). First perf.: Karamu Theater, Cleveland, Ohio, 1955.

Epicedial Variations for violin and piano (1956). (New York: E. B. Marks, rental). First perf.: Cleveland, Ohio.

Evocation for piano (1965). (New York: C. F. Peters, 1966; International Library of Piano Music). First perf.: Cleveland, Ohio.

Exchanges for trumpet and band (1972). Commission: Robert Nagel. First perf.: Lehigh University Band, Bethlehem, Pa. (New York: E. B. Marks, rental).

Expansions for band (1967). (New York: E. B. Marks, 1967). Commission: Symphonic Band of Southern Illinois University at Edwardsville, 1967. First perf.: Symphonic Band of Southern Illinois University at Edwardsville, 1967.

Faces of Jazz for piano (1968). 12 parts: My Scarf Is Yellow; The Broken Saxophone (for Eric [Dolphy]); Pooty's Blues; Day's End (for Eric [Dolphy]); Off-Beat Shorty; Blooz (for Ahmad Jamal); Following (for John Lewis); Scrambled Eggs and Ernie (for Ernie Wilkins); That's Mike; An Asphodel for Marcel; Goin' in A Hurry (for Ahmad Jamal); Come to My Party (for William Randall). (New York: E. B. Marks, 1968).

For One Called Billy for piano (1975). (New York: E. B. Marks, 1975), *The Black Perspective in Music,* 3 (May, 1975).

I'm Coming Hime for mixed chorus with optional piano and/or rhythm section (1974). (New York: E. B. Marks, 1974). Text: Hale Smith.

In Memoriam Beryl Rubinstein for mixed chorus and chamber orchestra or piano (1953; orchestrated 1958). 3 movts.: *Moderato* (text is a vocalise); *Poeme D'Automne* (text by Langston Hughes); *Elegy* (text by Russell Atkins). (New York: Highgate Press [Galaxy Music], 1959, as part of the Cleveland Composers Guild Publication Series).

Introduction, Cadenzas, and Interludes for Eight Players for flute/alto flute, oboe, clarinet, harp, piano, violin, viola, and violoncello (1974). (New York: E. B. Marks, 1976). Commission: Nassau County Office of Cultural Development. First perf.: Sea Cliff Chamber Players, 1974.

Lysistrata (incidental music for Aristophanes' *Lysistrata;* 1952). Commission: Karamu Theatre, Cleveland, Ohio. First perf.: Karamu Theatre, 1952.

Music for Harp and Orchestra (1967). (New York: E. B. Marks, rental). Commission: Symphony of the New World. First perf.: Carnegie Hall, by Symphony of the New World, New York City.

Nuances of Hale Smith for small orchestra (1967–68). 7 short pieces. (New York: Sam Fox Music Publishers). Commission: Sam Fox Music Publishers. Television and radio background music.

Orchestra Set for orchestra (1952). 4 pieces. (New York: C. F. Peters, rental). First perf.: Symphony of the New World, 1974. This work was part of the composer's Master's thesis.

Ritual and Incantations for orchestra (1974). (New York: C. F. Peters, rental). Commission: Thorne Music Fund. First perf.: Houston Symphony Orchestra, 1974.

Somersault for concert band (1964). (New York: Frank Music, 1964). Commission: Frank Music Corp., as part of their *Adventures in Form* series. First perf.: Midwest Band Clinic, Chicago, 1964.

Sonata for violoncello and piano (1955). 3 movts. Commission: Kermit Moore. First perf.: (Europe) by Kermit Moore; (America) Donnell Auditorium, New York City.

Take a Chance for concert band (1964). (New York: Frank Music, 1965). Commission: Frank Music Corp., as part of their *Adventures in Form* series. An aleatoric episode for band.

Three Brevities for solo flute (1960). First perf.: Circa 1961, Cleveland, Ohio. Originally written for Eric Dolphy and Jerome Richardson.

Trinal Dance for concert band (1968). (New York: Duchess Music/MCA, 1968). Commission: Lewis Roth.

Two Kids for unaccompanied mixed chorus (1950). (New York: E. B. Marks, 1973). Text: Nicholas Guillén (translated by Langston Hughes and Ben Frederic Carruthers from "Cuba Libre").

Two Love Songs of John Donne for soprano, string quartet, and woodwind quintet (1958). 2 songs: *Confined Love, The Computation.* (New York: E. B. Marks, rental). Text: John Donne. First perf.: Donnell Library Composer's Forum, New York City, 1958.

The Valley Wind for medium voice and piano (1955). 4 songs: *The Valley Wind* (text by Lu Yün, translated by Arthur Waley); *When Daisies Pied* (text by Shakespeare); *Envoy in Autumn* (text by Tu Fu, translated by Powys Mathers); *Velvet Shoes* (text by Elinor Wylie). First perf.: Karamu Theatre, Cleveland, Ohio. *Envoy in Autumn* and *Velvet Shoes* were part of the composer's Master's thesis.

Variations for Six Players for woodwind quintet and piano (1975). (New York: E. B. Marks, 1976). Commission: William Scribner. First perf.: Bronx, New York, 1975.

Yerma, incidental music for Garcia Lorca's play *Yerma.* (1951). Commission: Karamu Theatre, Cleveland, Ohio. First perf.: Karamu Theatre, 1951.

STILL, WILLIAM GRANT, 1895–1978

Afro-American Symphony (1931). (Glen Rock, New Jersey: J. Fischer).

All That I Am, for voice and piano (1955).

The American Scene for orchestra (1959).

And They Lynched Him to a Tree for chorus (1940). (Glen Rock, New Jersey: J. Fischer).

Archaic Ritual for orchestra (1946).

Aria for accordion (1960). (New York: Sam Fox).

Bayou Home for voice and piano (1948). (New York: Robbins Music Corporation).

A Bayou Legend, opera in 3 acts (1940).

Bells for orchestra (1940). (New York: Leeds Corporation).

Breadth of a Rose for voice and piano (1940). (New York: G. Schirmer, Inc.).

Caribbean Melodies for voice and piano (1947). (Bryn Mawr, Pennsylvania: Oliver Ditson Co.).

Carry Him Along for chorus (1947). (Bryn Mawr, Pennsylvania: Oliver Ditson Co.).

Danzas de Panama for orchestra or string quartet (1950). (New York: Southern Music Co.).

Darker America for orchestra (1928). (New York: Carl Fischer).

Deserted Plantation for piano (1936). (New York: Robbins Music Corporation).

Dismal Swamp for orchestra (1937). (New York: American Music Center).

Elegy for organ (1963). (Los Angeles: *The Los Angeles Organist*).

Fanfare for the 99th Fighter Squadron for orchestra (1942).

Festive Overture for orchestra (1949). (Glen Rock, New Jersey: J. Fischer).

Fifth Symphony (1954).

Five Animal Sketches for piano. (Morristown, New Jersey: Silver Burdett Co.).

Folk Suite No. 1 for string quartet, flute, and piano (1952).

Folk Suite No. 2 for flute, clarinet, violoncello, and harp (1953).

Folk Suite No. 3 for flute, oboe, bassoon, and piano (1954).

From A Lost Continent for chorus (1945).

From the Black Belt for orchestra (1946). (Glen Rock, New Jersey: C. Fischer).

From the Delta for band (1950). (New York: Leeds Corporation).

Grief for voice and piano (1955). (Bryn Mawr, Pennsylvania: Oliver Ditson Co.).

Here's One for chorus or voice and piano (1950). (Bryn Mawr, Pennsylvania: John Church Co.).

Highway Number One, opera in one act (1963).

Incantation and Dance for oboe and piano (1945). (New York: Carl Fischer, Inc.).

Kaintuck for orchestra (1935).

La Guiablesse (ballet) for orchestra (1953). (New York: Carl Fischer, Inc.).

Lament for voice and piano. (Morristown, New Jersey: Silver Burdett Co).

Lenox Avenue (ballet) for orchestra (1938). (Glen Rock, New Jersey: J. Fischer and Bro.).

Little Red Schoolhouse for orchestra (1935).

Little Song for orchestra (1945).

Marionette (U.S.A.) for piano (1940). (New York: Leeds Corporation).

Minatures for oboe, bassoon, and piano (1960).

Miss Sally's Party (ballet) for orchestra (1946).

Mississippi for voice and piano (1948).

Mota, opera in 3 acts (1951).

Old California for orchestra or band (1945). (New York: Carl Fischer, Inc.).

Out of the Silence for orchestra (1946). (Glen Rock, New Jersey: J. Fischer & Bro.). Orchestrated version of *Seven Traceries*.

Pages from Negro History for orchestra (1953). (New York: Carl Fischer, Inc.). 3 parts: Africa; Slavery; Emancipation.

The Pillar, opera in 3 acts (1956).

Plainchant for America for voice and piano (1941). (Glen Rock, New Jersey: J. Fischer & Bro.).

Poem for Orchestra (1955). (New York: Leeds Corporation).

A Psalm for the Living for chorus (1961).

Quit Dat Fool'nish for piano (1936). (Glen Rock, New Jersey: J. Fischer & Bro.).

Reverie for organ (1961). (Los Angeles: *The Los Angeles Organist*).

Rhapsody for soprano and orchestra (1950).

Rising Tide for chorus (1938). (Glen Rock, New Jersey: J. Fischer & Bro.).

Romance for saxophone and piano (1958).

Sahdji (ballet) for orchestra (1931). (Rochester, New York: Eastman School of Music).

Serenade for orchestra (1957).

Seven Traceries for piano (1940). (Glen Rock, New Jersey: J. Fischer & Bro.).

Song for the Lonely for voice and piano (1950).

Songs of Separation for voice and piano (1952) (New York: Leeds Corporation).

A Southern Interlude, opera in 2 acts (1950).

Symphony in G Minor (1937). (Glen Rock, New Jersey: J. Fischer & Bro.).

Symphony No. 4 (1951).

Those Who Wait for voice and piano (1951).

To You, America for orchestra (1951). (New York: Southern Music Co.).

Troubled Island, opera in 3 acts (1949).

Two Choral Episodes (1949). (Glen Rock, New Jersey: J. Fischer & Bro.).

Up There for voice and piano. (Morristown, New Jersey: Silver Burdett Co.).

Victory Tide for orchestra or band (1943). (Glen Rock, New Jersey: J. Fischer & Bro.).

Vignettes for oboe, bassoon, and piano (1960).

The Voice of the Lord for voice and piano (1946). (New York: Witmark).

The Wailing Woman for voice and piano (1941).

Winter's Approach for voice and piano (1940). (New York: G. Schirmer, Inc.).

Wood Notes for orchestra (1954). (New York: Southern Music Co.).

SWANSON, HOWARD, 1907–1978

Cahoots for voice and piano (1950). (New York: Weintraub Music, 1951). Text: Carl Sandburg.

Cello Suite for violoncello and piano (1951). (New York: Weintraub Music Company).

Concerto for Orchestra (circa 1957). 3 movts. (New York: Weintraub Music, 1970). Commission: Louisville Symphony Orchestra. First perf.: Louisville Symphony Orchestra, 1957.

The Cuckoo for piano (1948). (New York: Leeds Music, 1949).

A Death Song for voice and piano (1943). (New York: Weintraub Music, 1951).

Fantasy Piece for Soprano Saxophone and Strings (1969). (New York: Weintraub Music, rental). Commission: Thorne Music Fund.

First Symphony.

Four Preludes for voice and piano (1947). (New York: Weintraub Music, 1952). Text: T. S. Eliot. 4 songs.

Ghosts in Love for voice and piano (1950). (New York: Weintraub Music, 1950). Text: Vachel Lindsay.

I Will Lie Down in Autumn for voice and piano. (New York: Weintraub Music, 1952). Text: May Swenson.

In Time of Silver Rain for voice and piano (1947). (New York: Weintraub Music Company, 1950). Text: Langston Hughes.

Joy for voice and piano (1946). (New York: Weintraub Music Company, 1950). Text: Langston Hughes.

The Junk Man for voice and piano (1950). (New York: Weintraub Music Company, 1950). Text: Carl Sandburg.

Music for Strings for string orchestra (1952). (New York: Weintraub Music Company, rental). First perf.: The Little Orchestra Society, Town Hall.

The Negro Speaks of Rivers for voice and piano (1942). (New York: Weintraub Music Company, 1950). Text: Langston Hughes.

Night Song for voice and piano (1948). (New York: Weintraub Music Company, 1950).

Night Music for chamber orchestra (flute, oboe, clarinet, bassoon, horn, and strings; 1950). (New York: Weintraub Music Company, rental). First perf.: Locust Valley Music Festival, 1950.

Nightingales for unaccompanied male chorus (1952). (New York: Weintraub Music Company, 1952). Text: Robert Seymour Bridges. Commission: Leonard dePaur.

Nocturne for violin and piano (1948). (New York: Weintraub Music Company, 1951).

Piano Sonata (1950). (New York: Weintraub Music Company, 1951).

Pierrot for voice and piano (1946). (New York: Weintraub Music Company, 1950). Text: Langston Hughes.

Saw A Grave Upon A Hill for voice and piano (1952). (New York: Weintraub Music, 1952). Text: May Swenson.

Short Symphony (1948). 3 movts. (New York: Weintraub Music Company, rental). First perf.: Carnegie Hall, by the New York Philharmonic, 1950. New York Critics' Circle Award for best orchestral work of the 1950–51 season, 1951.

Snowdunes for voice and piano. (New York: Weintraub Music Company, 1955). Text: May Swenson.

Sonata for Violoncello and Piano (1973). 3 movts. First perf.: Alice Tully Hall, New York City, 1973.

Sonata No. 1 for piano (1948). 3 movts. (New York: Weintraub Music Company, 1950).

Sonata No. 2 for piano (1976). 3 movts.

Sonata No. 3 for piano (1976). 3 movts.

Songs for Patricia for voice and string orchestra or piano (1952). Four songs: *Darling, Those Are Birds; No Leaf May Fall; One Day; Goodnight.* (New York: Weintraub Music Company, 1952). Text: Norman Rosten.

Soundpiece for Brass Quintet (1952). (New York: Weintraub Music Company, 1953).

Still Life for voice and piano (1950). (New York: Weintraub Music Company, 1950). Text: Carl Sandburg.

Suite for Violoncello and Piano (1949). 4 movts.: Prelude; Pantomine; Dirge; Recessional. (New York: Weintraub Music Company, 1951). Commission: Bernard Greenhouse.

Symphony No. 1 (1945). 4 movts. (New York: Weintraub Music Company, 1951). First perf.: Symphony of the New World, Lincoln Center, New York City, 1951.

Symphony No. 3 (1970). 3 movts. Commission: Symphony of the New World. First Perf.: Symphony of the New World, 1970.

To Be Or Not To Be for voice and piano (1951). (New York: Weintraub Music Company, 1951). Text: Anonymous.

Trio for Flute, Oboe, and Piano (1975). 3 movts. (New York: Weintraub Music Company, rental). Commission: New World Trio.

Two Nocturnes for piano (1967). (New York: Weintraub Music Company, rental).

The Valley for voice and piano (1952). (New York: Weintraub Music Company, 1951). Text: Charles Edwin Markham.

Vista No. II for string octet (1969). (New York: Weintraub Music Company, rental).

TILLIS, FREDERICK C., 1930–

Alleluia for mixed chorus (1969).

The Blue Express for jazz ensemble (1973). First perf.: University of Massachusetts Jazz Workshop, 1973.

Blue Stone Differencia for jazz ensemble (1972).

Brass Quintet (1962).

Capriccio for Viola and Piano (1960).

Celebration for concert band (1966).

Concert Piece for Clarinet and Piano (1955; revised in 1960).

The Cotton Curtain for student orchestra (1966).

Designs for Orchestra (1963). 2 movts.

The End of All Flesh for baritone voice and piano (1960).

Five Spirituals for Chorus and Brass Choir (1976). Text: Gwendolyn Brooks. First perf.: University of Massachusetts Chorale and Brass Choir, European tour, 1976.

Freedom for mixed chorus (1968). Memorial to Dr. Martin Luther King, Jr.

Gloria, Music for an Experimental Laboratory, Ensemble No. 2, electronic (1967).

Hallelujah for male glee club (1966).

Metamorphosis on a Scheme of J. S. Bach for jazz ensemble (1972).

Militant Mood for brass sextet (1961). Alternate title: *In a Spirited Mood.* (Joshua Corporation, 1978).

Motions for trombone and piano (1964).

Music for Alto Flute, Cello and Piano (1966). (New York: American Composers Alliance).

Music for an Experimental Laboratory, Ensemble No. 1, electronic (1967).

Music for an Experimental Laboratory, Ensemble No. 3, electronic (1970).

Music for Recorders (1972). 2 pieces.

Music for Tape Recorder, No. 1, magnetic tape (1968).

Music for Violin, Cello and Piano (1972). (Joshua Corporation, 1978).

Navarac for jazz ensemble (1974).

Niger Symphony (1975). (Joshua Corporation).

One Dozen Books, Inc. for jazz ensemble (1971).

Overture to a Dance for band (1961). (New York: American Composers Alliance).

Passacaglia for Brass Quintet (1950). (Joshua Corporation, 1978).

Passacaglia for Organ (1962).

Phantasy for Viola and Piano (1962).

A Prayer in Faith, Psalms for baritone voice and piano (1960).

Pastorale for wind ensemble (1974). (Joshua Corporation, 1978).

Poems for Piano (1970).

Quartet for Flute, Clarinet, Bassoon and Cello (1952).

Quintet for Four Woodwinds and Percussion (1962).

Reflections for medium voice and piano (1973).

Ring Shout Concerto for Percussionist and Orchestra (1973–74). First perf.: University of Massachusetts Symphony, 1973.

Saturn for jazz ensemble (1978).

Seasons for women's chorus (1972–73). Commission: Regis College Glee Club with support from the Massachusetts Council on the Arts and Humanities.

Secrets of the African Baobob for jazz ensemble (1976). First perf.: University of Massachusetts, 1976.

Sequences and Burlesque for student string orchestra (1966).

Seton Concerto for Trumpet for trumpet and jazz ensemble (1973).

String Trio for violin, viola, and violoncello (1961).

Three Chorale Settings for Organ (1962).

Three Movements for Piano (1964).

Three Plus One for violin, guitar, clarinet, and tape recorder (1969).

Three Showpieces for viola (1966).

Three Songs from Shadows and Distance Nowhere for voice and piano (1971). (Joshua Corporation, 1978). Text: Langston Hughes.

Two Songs for Soprano and Piano (1967–68). 2 songs: *Enogod; Me.*

WALKER, GEORGE, 1922–

Address for Orchestra (1959). 3 movts. Commission: Symphony of the New World. First perf.: Mons Festival (Mons, Belgium), 1971. The Symphony of the New World performed movements I and III at Lincoln Center in 1968. The Belgian performance was the first performance of the work in its entirety.

Antiphonies for Chamber Orchestra for flute, oboe, B-flat clarinet, bassoon, horn, C trumpet, trombone, percussion, and strings (1968). First perf.: Bennington College Chamber Orchestra.

The Bereaved Maid for medium voice and piano (1953). (New York: General Music, 1971; distributed by Frank Music). Text: Anonymous. First perf.: Paris, 1958.

Concerto for Trombone and Orchestra (1957). 3 movts. (New York: General Music, agent). First perf.: Rochester Philharmonic, 1957.

Dialogues for Cello and Orchestra (1976). Commission: Cleveland Orchestra. First perf.: Cleveland Orchestra.

Five Fancys for Clarinet and Piano (four hands; 1974). (New York: General Music, agent). Commission: David Ensemble. First perf.: Alice Tully Hall, New York City, by the David Ensemble.

Gloria In Memoriam for women's chorus with organ (1963). (New Valley Music Press, 1963). First perf.: Smith College Choir, 1964.

I Went To Heaven for medium voice and piano (1953). (New York: General Music, 1971; distributed by Frank Music). Text: Emily Dickinson. First perf.: Paris, 1958.

Lament for medium voice and piano (1971). (New York: General Music, 1975). Text: Countee Cullen.

Lyric for Strings for string orchestra (1946). First perf.: American Foundation Orchestra, Paris, 1958. An arrangement of the slow movement of *String Quartet No. 1.* Work has undergone several title changes; previous titles include *Lament for Orchestra, Lyric for M. K.,* and *Lyric for String Orchestra.*

Mass for soloist, chorus, and orchestra (1977–78).

Music for Brass—Sacred and Profane (1975). 4 movts.: Invocation; Dance; Chorale; Dance. Commission: Hans Kindler Foundation. First perf.: American Brass Quintet, Washington, D.C., 1976.

Music for Three for violin, violoncello, and piano (1970). (New York: General Music, 1972). First perf.: National Gallery of Art, by the University of Maryland Trio, 1970.

Parameters for Clarinet and Piano (1966). 3 movts. (New York: General Music, 1972). Commission: Leroy Johnston. First perf.: Juilliard School of Music.

Piano Concerto (1975). 3 movts. (New York: General Music, 1976; piano score only). Commission: National Endowment for the Arts and the Atlanta Symphony Orchestra. First perf.: Minneapolis Symphony Orchestra.

Prelude and Caprice for piano (1941, 1945). 2 movts.: Prelude; Caprice. (New York: General Music, 1974).

Psalm 83 for chorus. Religious Arts Festival Award, Rochester, New York.

Psalm 84 for mixed chorus with organ (1960). (New York: General Music, 1975). Text: Biblical.

Psalm 96 for unaccompanied mixed chorus (1963). (New York: General Music, 1975). First perf.: Morgan State College Choir, 1976.

Psalm 105 for women's chorus with organ (1963). (New York: General Music, 1975). First perf.: Morgan State College Choir, 1975.

Psalm 117 for mixed chorus with organ (1953). (New York: General Music, 1975). Text: Biblical. First perf.: Riverside Church, New York City, 1971.

Psalm 148 for mixed chorus with organ (1963). (New York: General Music, 1975). Text: Biblical. First perf.: Montclair State College Choir, 1971.

A Red, Red Rose for medium voice and piano (1971). (New York: General Music, 1975). Text: Robert Burns.

Response for medium voice and piano (1953). (New York: General Music, 1971; distributed by Frank Music). Text: Paul Laurence Dunbar. First perf.: Bennington College.

So We'll Go No More A-Roving for medium voice and piano (1953). (New York: General Music, 1971; distributed by Frank Music). Text: Lord Bryon. First perf.: Bennington College, 1968.

Sonata for Cello and Piano (1957), 3 movts. (New York: General Music, 1972). First perf.: American Cello Society series (Kosciusko Foundation), 1965.

Sonata For Two Pianos (1963). Harvey Gaul Prize, 1963.

Sonata for Violin and Piano (1958). 1 movt. (New York: Associated Music, 1970). First perf.: Hartt College of Music.

Sonata No. 1 for piano (1953). 3 movts. (New York: General Music, 1972). First perf.: National Gallery of Art, 1960.

Sonata No. 2, for piano (1957). 4 movts. (New York: Galaxy, 1966). First perf.: Eastman School of Music, 1958.

Sonata No. 3 for piano (1975). 3 movts. (New York: General Music, 1975). Commission: Washington Society for the Performing Arts and Leon Bates. First perf.: Kennedy Center, 1976.

Spatials for piano (1961). Theme and six variations. (New York: General Music, 1972). First perf.: Brandeis University, 1965.

Spektra for piano (1971). (New York: 1972).

Spirituals for Orchestra (1974). Introduction and 4 sections. (New York: General Music, agent). First perf.: Houston Symphony Orchestra, 1974.

Stars for mixed chorus unaccompanied (1953). (New York: Associated Music, 1968). Text: Susan D. Keeney. First perf.: University of Colorado Chamber Singers, University of Colorado, 1969.

String Quartet No. 1 (1946). 3 movts. First perf.: Juilliard School of Music, 1946.

String Quartet No. 2 (1967; revised in 1968). 4 movts. (New York: General Music, agent). First perf.: Library Museum of Lincoln Center, 1967. Rhea Soslund Chamber Music Competition Award, 1967.

Sweet, Let Me Go for medium voice and piano (1954). (New York: General Music, 1971). Text: Anonymous.

Symphony for Orchestra (1961). 4 movts. (New York: General Music, agent). First perf.: University of Colorado Symphony, University of Colorado.

Three Lyrics for Chorus for mixed chorus with piano (1958). 3 songs: *The Bereaved Maid* (anonymous text); *Take, O Take Those Lips Away* (text by Shakespeare); *O Western Wind* (anonymous text). (New York: General Music, 1971 (published separately). First perf.: University of Colorado Chamber Singers, 1969.

Three Spirituals for Voice and Piano (1975). Arrangements of 3 spirituals: *Ev'ry Time I Feel de Spirit; I Got a Letter from Jesus; Mary Wore Three Links of Chain.* (New York: General Music, 1975).

Variations for Orchestra (1971). Introduction and eight variations. (New York: General Music, 1972). First perf.: Baltimore Symphony Orchestra, 1974.

With Rue My Heart Is Laden for medium voice and piano (1953). (New York: General Music, 1972; distributed by Frank Music).

With This Small Key for unaccompanied mixed chorus (1971). (New York: General Music, 1975). Text: Sister M. Therese.

WHITE, CLARENCE CAMERON, 1880–1960

Allegretto Elegiaco for violin and piano.

American Negro Folk Songs (1928).

Bend Down Beloved for violin and piano.

Cabin Memories for violin and piano. 4 spirituals: *Nobody Knows the Trouble I've Seen; I'm Goin' Home; Bear de Burden; Down By de Ribber Side.*

Camp Songs for violin and piano.

Capriccio for violin and piano.

Caprice for violin and piano.

Characteristic Dances for violin and piano.

Concerto, E Minor for violin and orchestra.

Concerto, G Minor for violin and orchestra.

Dance Caprice for piano.

Deliverance for violin and piano.

Divertimento for orchestra.

Elegy for orchestra (1954). (New York: Sam Fox Music Co.).

Fantasie on Folk Tunes for violoncello and piano.

Great Day.

Honey Chile for violin and piano. (Philadelphia: Theo. Presser Co.).

Improvisation for piano. (Boston: Boston Music Co.).

Jubilee Song for violin and piano.

Katamba for orchestra.

Lonesome Road for men's voices. (New York: Sam Fox Music Co.).

March Triumphal for band. (Philadelphia: Theo. Presser Co.).

Mary, Do Not Weep for violin and piano.

Negro Rhapsody for orchestra.

Night at Sans Souci, ballet. Text: Arthur H. Ryder.

Ouanga, opera. (New York: Sam Fox, 1955). Libretto: Arthur H. Ryder.

Overtones for violin and piano. (New York: Sam Fox Music Co.).

Pantomine for orchestra.

Patter Without Chatter for piano. (Philadelphia: Theo. Presser Co.).

Piece, for Strings and Tympani. (New York: Sam Fox Music Co.).

Pilgrim Song for violin and piano. (New York: Carl Fischer).

Plantation Song for violin and piano. (New York: Carl Fischer).

Quartet, C Minor for string quartet. Based on Negro themes.

Reflects for piano. (Philadelphia: Theo. Presser Co.).

Remembrance for violin and piano. (New York: Sam Fox Music Co.).

Rhapsody for violin and piano.

Scotch Idyl for violin and piano. (New York: Carl Fischer).

Serenade for orchestra. (New York: Carl Fischer).

Songs for orchestra. (New York: Sam Fox Music Co.).

Suite on Negro Themes for orchestra. (New York: Sam Fox Music Co.).

Symphony, D Minor.

System of Scale Studies, for violin (method). (New York: Gamble-Hinged Music Co.).

Twilight for violin and piano.

Valse Coquette for piano.

Violinists' Daily Dozen for violin (method). New York: Gamble-Hinged Music Co.).

Worship for violin and piano.

WILSON, OLLY, 1937–

Akwan for piano/electronic piano and orchestra (1972). Commission: Richard Bunger, with a grant from the Martha Baird Rockefeller Foundation. First perf.: University of California Orchestra, Berkeley, 1973.

And Death Shall Have No Dominion for tenor and percussion (1963). Text: Dylan Thomas. First perf.: University of Iowa Percussion Ensemble, Iowa City, 1963.

Biography for soprano, flute, harp, and percussion (1966). Text: LeRoi Jones. The New Music Circle, University of Missouri, St. Louis, 1967.

Black Martyrs, electronic sound (1972). Commission: Pitzer College, Claremont, Calif. First perf.: Pitzer College, 1973. Designed especially for the Salathe Tower and the Pitzer College Quadrangle.

Black Mass, electronic music (incidental music for the LeRoi Jones play Black Mass). First perf.: University of California, Berkeley, 1971.

Cetus, electronic sound (1967). First perf.: Symposium for Contemporary Music, Illinois Wesleyan University, Bloomington, Ill., 1968. 1968 Dartmouth Arts Council Prize, awarded in the First International Competition for Electronic Compositions.

Chanson Innocente for contralto and two bassoons (1965). Text: e. e. cummings. Commission: Stephen Bassoon. First perf.: Wisconsin College Conservatory, Milwaukee, 1966.

Dance Music I for wind ensemble (1963). 3 movts. First perf.: University of Iowa Wind Ensemble, Iowa City, 1963.

Dance Music II for wind ensemble (1965). First perf.: Florida A. & M. University Wind Ensemble; danced by the university Dance Ensemble, 1965.

Dance Suite for wind ensemble (1962). First perf.: Florida A. & M. University Wind Ensemble, 1962.

Echoes for clarinet and electronic sound (1974–75). First perf.: University of Redlands (Calif.)., 1975.

The Eighteen Hands of Jerome Harris, electronic (ballet) (1971).

Gloria for mixed chorus unaccompanied (1961).

In Memoriam, Martin Luther King Jr. for mixed chorus and electronic sound (1969). Text: Olly Wilson, after Martin Luther King, Jr. First perf.: Oberlin College Choir, Oberlin, Ohio

Piano Piece for piano and electronic sound (1969). First perf.: Oberlin College.

Piece for Four for flute, trumpet, contrabass, and piano (1966). 3 movts. First perf.: Contemporary Music Festival, Oberlin, Ohio.

Prelude and Line Study for flute, clarinet, bass clarinet, and bassoon (1959). 2 movts. First perf.: Washington University Woodwind Quartet, University of Iowa, Iowa City, 1959.

Sextet for flute, clarinet, bassoon, horn, trumpet, and trombone (1963). 5 movts. First perf.: University of Iowa Sextet, Iowa City.

Soliloquy for contrabass (1962). First perf.: Florida A. & M., 1962.

Sometimes for tenor and electronic sound (1976). Work for electronic tape and tenor voice based on the spiritual *Sometimes I Feel Like a Motherless Child.* First perf.: Berkeley Contemporary Chamber Players Concert, 1976.

Spirit Song for soprano, double chorus, and orchestra (1973). Text: Adapted from traditional spirituals. 2 movts. Commission: Oakland Symphony Orchestra. First perf.: Oakland Symphony Orchestra, the Castlemont High School Choir, and the women's voices of the Oakland Symphony Chorus, 1974.

String Quartet (1960). 3 movts. First perf.: Graduate String Quartet of the University of Illinois, 1960.

Structure for Orchestra (1960). 1 movt.

Three Movements for Orchestra (1964). First perf.: University of Iowa Orchestra, Iowa City, 1964.

Trio for Flute, Cello, and Piano (1959). First perf.: Washington University Trio, at University of Iowa, Iowa City, 1959.

Two Dutch Poems for contralto and piano (1960). 2 songs: *Intervention* (text by Roland Hoist); *Marc Greets Things in the Morning* (text by Paul Van Ostaiijen). First perf.: University of Illinois, 1960.

Violin Sonata (1961). 1 movt. First perf.: Contemporary Music Festival, Central State University, Wilberforce, Ohio, 1961.

Voices for orchestra (1970). Commission: Boston Symphony Orchestra and the Fromm Foundation. First perf.: Tanglewood Festival Orchestra, 1970.

Wry Fragments for tenor and percussion (1961). 4 movts. Text: James Cunningham. First perf.: Florida A. & M. University Percussion Ensemble, 1961.

List of Recordings
of Compositions
By Composers Included
in This Study

ANDERSON, THOMAS JEFFERSON, 1928–

Chamber Symphony. Composers Recording, Inc., CRI SD-258 (Royal Philharmonic Orchestra, James Dixon, conductor).

Squares: An Essay for Orchestra. Columbia M-33434: Vol. 8, *Black Composers Series* (Baltimore Symphony Orchestra, Paul Freeman, conductor).

Variations on a Theme by M. B. Tolson. Nonesuch 71303 (Jan DeGaetani, mezzo-soprano, and the Contemporary Chamber Ensemble, Arthur Weisberg, conductor).

CUNNINGHAM, ARTHUR, 1928–

Engrams. Desto Records, DC 7102-3, *Natalie Hinderas Plays Music by Black Composers.*

Lullabye for a Jazz Baby. Desto Records, DC-7107, *The Black Composer in America* (Oakland Youth Orchestra, Robert Hughes, conductor).

Thisby. Eastern Records ERS-513, *Contemporary Black Images in Music for the Flute* (Antoinette Handy, flute).

DAWSON, WILLIAM LEVI, 1899–

Negro Folk Symphony. Decca Records DL-710077 (American Symphony Orchestra, Leopold Stokowski, conductor).

Out in the Fields. Desto Records DC-7107, *The Black Composer in America* (Cynthia Bedford, mezzo-soprano; Oakland Youth Orchestra, Robert Hughes, conductor).

DETT, ROBERT NATHANIEL, 1882–1943

In the Bottoms. Desto Records DC-7102/3, *Natalie Hinderas Plays Music by Black Composers.*

The Ordering of Moses. Silver Crest Records, TAL-42868S (Jeanette Walters, soprano; Carol Brice, contralto; John Miles, tenor; John Work, baritone; Mobile Symphony Orchestra, Talladega College Choir, William L. Dawson, conductor).

FISCHER, WILLIAM S., 1935–

A Quiet Movement. Desto Records, DC-7107, *The Black Composer in America* (Oakland Youth Orchestra, Robert Hughes, conductor).

HAKIM, TALIB RASUN, 1940–

Placements. Folkways Records, FTS-33903 (Joe Chambers, Omar Clay, Warren Smith, Barbara Burton, Wilson Moorman, percussion; Stanley Cowell, piano; Talib Hakim, conductor).

Shapes. Desto Records, DC-7107, *The Black Composer in America* (Oakland Youth Orchestra, Robert Hughes, conductor).

Sound-Gone. Desto Records, DC-7102/7103, *Natalie Hinderas Plays Music by Black Composers.*

Visions of Ishwara. Columbia Records, M-33434, *Black Composers Series, Vol. 8* (Baltimore Symphony Orchestra, Paul Freeman, conductor).

KAY, ULYSSES SIMPSON, 1917–

Brass Quartet. Folkways Records, FM-3651, *Music for Brass Quintet* (American Brass Quintet).

Choral Triptych. Cambridge Records, CRS-1416, *Four Contemporary Choral Works* (King's Chapel Choir of Boston and the Cambridge Festival Strings, Daniel Pinkham, conductor).

Dances for String Orchestra. Turnabout Records, TVS-34546 (Westphalian Symphony, Paul Freeman, conductor).

Fantasy Variations. Composers Recordings, Inc., CRI SD-209 (Oslo Philharmonic Orchestra, Arthur Bennett Lipkin, conductor).

How Stands the Glass Around? Composers Recordings, Inc., CRI-102, *Lament for April 15 and Other Modern Madrigals* (Randolph Singers, David Randolph, conductor.

Markings. Columbia Records, M-32783, *Black Composers Series, Vol. 3* (London Symphony Orchestra, Paul Freeman, conductor).

Prelude for Flute. Eastern Records, ERS-513, *Contemporary Black Images in Music for the Flute* (Antoinette Handy, flute).

Serenade for Orchestra. First Edition Records, LOU 545-8 (Louisville Orchestra, Robert Whitney, conductor).

A Short Overture. Desto Records, DC-7107, *The Black Composer in America* (Oakland Youth Orhcestra, Robert Hughes, conductor).

Sinfonia in E. Composers Recordings, Inc., CRI-139 (Oslo Philharmonic Orchestra, George Barati, conductor).

Suite for Orchestra. First Edition Records, LOU 548-9 (Louisville Orchestra, Robert Whitney, conductor).

Umbrian Scene. First Edition Records, LOU 651 (Louisville Orchestra, Robert Whitney, conductor).

What's in a Name? Composers Recordings, Inc., CRI 102, *Lament for April 15 and Other Modern Madrigals* (Randolph Singers, David Randolph, conductor).

LOGAN, WENDELL, 1940–

Songs of Our Times. Golden Crest Records, S-4087 (Ball State Chorus & Instrumental Ensemble; Corwin, conductor).

PERRY, JULIA, 1924–79

Homunculus C. F. Composers Recording, Inc., CRI SD-252 (Manhattan Percussion Ensemble, Paul Price, conductor).

Short Piece. Composers Recording, Inc., CRI 145 (Imperial Philharmonic of Tokyo, William Strickland, conductor).

Stabat Mater. Composers Recording, Inc., CRI 133 (Nokiko Asakura, soprano; Japan Philharmonic Orchestra, William Strickland, conductor).

SMITH, HALE, 1925–

Brevities. Eastern Records, ERS-513, *Contemporary Black Images in Music for the Flute* (Antoinette Handy, flute).

Contours. First Edition Records, LOU 632 (Louisville Orchestra, Robert Whitney, conductor).

Evocation. Desto Records, DC-7102/3, *Natalie Hinderas Plays Music by Black Composers.*

Expansions. New World Records, NW 211, *Winds of Change* (Southern Illinois University [Edwardsville] Band, C. Dale Fjerstad, conductor).

In Memoriam Beryl Rubinstein. Composers Recordings, Inc., CRI 182 SD, *The Cleveland Composers Guild, Vol. I* (Kulas Choir and Chamber Orchestra, Robert Shaw, conductor).

Somersault. Educational Reference Library Band Program, Vol. 2 BP-102 (Baldwin-Wallace Symphonic Band, Kenneth Snapp, conductor).

STILL, WILLIAM GRANT,
1895–1978

Afro-American Symphony. Columbia Records, M-32782, *Black Composers Series, Vol. 2* (London Symphony Orchestra, Paul Freeman, conductor).

Festival Overture. Composers Recordings, Inc., CRI SD-259 (Royal Philharmonic, Arthur Bennett Lipkin, conductor).

From the Black Belt; Darker America. Turnabout Records, TVS-34546, (Westchester Symphony Orchestra, Siegfried Landon, conductor).

Highway 1, U.S.A.: Selections ("What Does He Know of Dreams"; "You're Wonderful Mary"). Columbia Records, M-32782, *The Black Composers Series, Vol. 2* (William Brown, tenor; London Symphony Orchestra, Paul Freeman, conductor).

Sahdji. Columbia Records, M-33433, *Black Composers Series, Vol. 7*, (Morgan State University Choir; London Symphony Orchestra, Paul Freeman, conductor).

Sahdji Selections. Audio House Records, AHR 30F75 (Morgan State College Choir, Nathan Carter, conductor).

Songs of Separation. Desto Records, DC-7107, *he Black Composer in America* (Cynthia Bedford, soprano; Oakland Youth Orchestra, Robert Hughes, conductor).

Visions. Desto Records, DC-7102/3, *Natalie Hinderas Plays Music by Black Composers.*

We Sang Our Songs. Nonesuch Records, NR 2597 (Fisk Jubilee Singers, Matthew Kennedy, conductor).

SWANSON, HOWARD,
1907–1978

Concerto for Orchestra. Silhouettes in Courage, SIL-K5001/2, *The Long Quest* (Budapest Philharmonic Orchestra, Benjamin Steinberg, conductor).

Seven Songs ("Ghosts in Love"; "Joy"; "The Junk Man"; "The Negro Speaks of Rivers"; "Night Song"; "Still Life"; "The Valley"; Desto Records, DST 6422 (Helen Thigpin, soprano, and David Allen, piano).

Short Symphony. Composers Recording, Inc., CRI SD-254 (Vienna State Opera Orchestra, Franz Litschauer, conductor); and American Recording Society, ARS-116 (American Recording Society Orchestra, Dean Dixon, conductor).

Trio for Flute, Oboe, and Piano. Folkways Records, FTS-33903 (New World Trio).

TILLIS, FREDERICK CHARLES,
1930–

Music for Piano, Alto Flute and Violoncello. Eastern Records ERS-513, *Contemporary Black Images in Music for the Flute* (Trio Pro Viva).

WALKER, GEORGE THEOPHILUS,
1922–

Address for Orchestra: Passacaglia. Desto Records, DC-7107, *The Black Composer in America* (Oakland Youth Orchestra, Robert Hughes, conductor).

Concerto for Trombone. Columbia Records, M-32783, *The Black Composers Series, Vol. 3* (Denis Wick, trombone; London Symphony Orchestra, Paul Freeman, conductor).

Lyric for Strings. Columbia Records, M-33433, *The Black Composers Series, Vol. 7* (London Symphony Orchestra, Paul Freeman, conductor).

Sonata for Piano, No. 1. Desto Records, DC-7102/3, *Natalie Hinderas Plays Music by Black Composers.*

Sonata for Piano, No. 2. Composers Recordings, Inc., CRI S-270, (George Walker, piano).

Spatials. Composers Recordings, Inc., CRI S-270 (George Walker, piano).

Spektra. Composers Recordings, Inc., CRI SD-270 (George Walker, piano).

WILSON, OLLY, 1937–

Akwan. Columbia Records, M-33434. *Black Composers Series, Vol. 8* (Richard Bunger, pianist; Baltimore Symphony Orchestra, Paul Freeman, conductor.

Cetus. Turnabout Records, TV-34301, *Electronic Music, Vol. 4.*

Echoes. Composers Recordings, Inc., CRI SD-367.

In Memoriam, Martin Luther King, Jr. Oberlin College Recordings, Series 1, Vol. 19 (Oberlin College Choir, Robert Fountain, conductor).

Piano Piece with Electronic Sounds. Desto Records, DC-7102/3, *Natalie Hinderas Plays Music by Black Composers.*

Piece for Four. Composers Recordings, Inc., CRI SD-264 (Robert Willoughby, flute; Gene Young, trumpet; Joseph Schwarts, piano; Bertram Turetzky, double bass).

Sometimes. Composers Recordings, Inc., CRI SD-370.

Bibliography

BOOKS

ALLEN, FRANCIS, CHARLES PICARD, AND LUCY MCKIM. *Slave Songs of the United States*. New York: Oak Publications, 1965.

APTHEKER, HERBERT. *A Documentary History of the Negro People in the United States*. New York: Citadel, 1951.

―――. *The Negro in the Civil War*. New York: International Publishers, 1938.

―――. *The Negro People in the United States*. Vol. I, New York: Citadel, 1951.

ASHE, THOMAS. *Travels in America, performed in 1806, for the purpose of exploring the rivers Alleghany, Monogahela, Ohio and Mississippi, and ascertaining the produce and condition of their banks and vicinity*. Newburyport, Mass.: E. Sayer and Co., 1808.

AVERY, VERNA. *Studies of Contemporary American Composers*. New York: J. Fischer, 1939.

BAKER, DAVID, LIDA M. BELT, AND HERMAN C. HUDSON. *The Black Composer Speaks*. Metuchen, N. J.: Scarecrow, 1977.

BALLIETT, WHITNEY. *Dinosaurs in the Morning*. New York: Lippincott, 1962.

―――. *The Sound of Surprise*. New York: Dutton, 1959.

BARNHART, CLARENCE L., ED. *The World Book Encyclopedia Dictionary*. Garden City, N. Y.: Doubleday, 1964.

BELZ, CARL. *The Story of Rock*. New York: Oxford, 1969.

BENNETT, LERONE, JR. *Before the Mayflower: A History of the Negro in America*. Chicago: Johnson, 1966.

BERENDT, JOACHIM ERNST.   *The Jazz Book*. Trans. by Dan Morganstern and Helmut and Barbara Bredigkeit. New York: L. Hill, 1975.

BRAWLEY, BENJAMIN.   *A Social History of the American Negro*. New York: Macmillan, 1921.

BUCKINGHAM, JAMES SILK.   *The Slave States of America*. Vol. II. London: Fisher, Son, and Co., 1842.

BUTCHER, MARGARET JUST.   *The Negro in American Culture*. New York: Knopf, 1956.

CHARTERS, ANN.   *Nobody: The Story of Bert Williams*. New York: Macmillan, 1970.

CHARTERS, SAMUEL.   *The Bluesmen*. New York: Oak Publications, 1967.

———.   *Jazz: New Oreleans, 1885–1963*. New York: Oak Publications, 1958.

CHARTERS, SAMUEL AND LEONARD KUNSTADT.   *Jazz, a History of the New York Scene*. Garden City, N. Y.: Doubleday, 1962.

CHASE, GILBERT.   *America's Music*. New York: McGraw-Hill, 1955.

CHERNOFF, JOHN MILLER.   *African Rhythm and African Sensibilities: Aesthetics and Social Action in African Musical Idioms*. Chicago: University of Chicago, 1979.

CORNISH, DUDLEY TAYLOR.   *The Sable Arm: Negro Troops in the Union Army, 1861–1865*. New York: Longmans, Green, 1956.

COURLANDER, HAROLD.   *Negro Folk Music, U.S.A.* New York: Columbia University, 1963.

CRESSWELL, NICHOLAS.   *The Journal of Nicholas Cresswell, 1775–1777*. New York: Lincoln MacDeagh, Dial Press, 1924.

CRUM, MASON.   *Gullah: Negro Life in the Carolina Sea Islands*. Durham: Duke University, 1940.

CUBAN, LARRY, ED.   *The Negro in America*. Glenview, Illinois: Scott, Foresman, 1964.

CUNEY-HARE, MAUD.   *Negro Musicians and Their Music*. Washington, D.C.: Associated Publishers, 1936.

DANCE, STANLEY.   *The World of Count Basie*. New York: Scribner's, 1980.

———.   *The World of Earl Hines*. New York: Scribner's, 1977.

———.   *The World of Swing*. New York: Scribner's, 1974.

DANKWORTH, AVRIL.   *Jazz: An Introduction to Its Musical Basis*. London: Oxford, 1968.

DAVIE, MAURICE R.   *Negroes in American Society*. New York: McGraw-Hill, 1949.

DELAFOSSE, MAURICE.   *The Negroes of Africa—History and Culture*. Port Washington, N. Y.: Kennikat, 1931.

DELERMA, DOMINIQUE-RENÉ.   *Black Music in Our Culture*. Kent, Ohio: Kent State University, 1970.

DEXTER, DAVE.   *The Jazz Story*. Englewood Cliffs, N. J.: Prentice-Hall, 1964.

DICKENS, CHARLES.   *American Notes for General Circulation*. Paris: Baudry's European Library, 1842.

DIETZ, BETTY WARNER AND MICHAEL BABATUNDE OLATUNJI.   *Musical Instruments of Africa*. New York: John Day, 1965.

DONALD, HENDERSON H.   *The Negro Freedman*. New York: Henry Schuman, 1952.

DOYLE, BERTRAM WILBUR.   *The Etiquette of Race Relations in the South*. Chicago; University of Chicago, 1937.

DRIMMER, MELVIN, ED.   *Black History: A Reappraisal*. Garden City, N. Y.: Doubleday, 1968.

DU BOIS, W. E. BURGHARDT.   *The Negro*. New York: Holt, Rinehart and Winston, 1915.

———.   *The Souls of Black Folk*. Chicago: A. C. McClurg, 1903.

EISEN, JONATHAN. *The Age of Rock*. New York: Random House, 1969.

ELLINGTON, EDWARD K. *Music Is My Mistress.* Garden City, N. Y.: Doubleday, 1973.

ELLINGTON, MERCER. *Duke Ellington in Person.* Boston: Houghton Mifflin, 1978.

ELLINGTON, MERCER AND STANLEY DANCE. *Duke Ellington—An Intimate Memoir.* Boston: Houghton Mifflin, 1978.

EMERY, LYNNE FAULEY. *Black Dance in the United States from 1619 to 1970.* Palo Alto, Calif.: National Press, 1972.

EPSTEIN, DENA. *Sinful Tunes and Spirituals: Black Folk Music to the Civil War.* Urbana, Ill.: University of Illinois, 1977.

FARNSWORTH, PAUL RANDOLPH. *Musical Taste, Its Measurement and Cultural Nature.* Stanford: Stanford University, 1950.

FEATHER, LEONARD. *The Encyclopedia of Jazz in the Sixties.* New York: Russell and Russell, 1968.

———. *The Pleasures of Jazz.* New York: Horizon, 1976.

FERGUSON, BLANCHE E. *Countee Cullen and the Negro Renaissance.* New York: Dodd, Mead, 1966.

FISHER, MILES MARK. *Negro Slave Songs in the United States.* New York: Russell and Russell, 1968.

FONER, PHILIPS. *History of the Labor Movement in the United States.* Vol. II. New York: International Publishers, 1947.

FOX, CHARLES. *Jazz in Perspective.* London: British Broadcasting Corporation, 1969.

FRANKLIN, JOHN HOPE. *From Slavery to Freedom.* New York: Knopf, 1956.

FRANKLIN, JOHN HOPE, AND ISIDORE STARR. *The Negro in Twentieth Century America.* New York: Random House, 1967.

FRAZIER, E. FRANKLIN. *The Negro Family in the United States.* Chicago: University of Chicago, 1966.

———. *The Negro in the United States.* New York: Macmillan, 1957.

GALPIN, FRANCIS W. *European Musical Instruments.* New York: Dutton, 1937.

GARLAND, PHYL. *The Sound of Soul.* Chicago: Henry Regnery, 1969.

GILMAN, CAROLINE. *Recollections of a Southern Matron.* New York: Harper and Brothers, 1837.

GITLER, IRA. *Jazz Masters of the Forties.* New York: Macmillan, 1966.

GLEASON, RALPH J. *Celebrating the Duke.* Boston: Little, Brown, 1975.

GOFFIN, ROBERT. *Jazz from the Congo to the Metropolitan.* New York: Doubleday, 1944.

GOLDBERG, ISAAC. *Tin Pan Alley.* New York: Ungar, 1961.

GOLDBERG, JOE. *Jazz Masters of the Fifties.* New York: Macmillan, 1965.

HADLOCK, RICHARD. *Jazz Masters of the Twenties.* New York: Macmillan, 1965.

HANDY, W. C. *Father of the Blues.* New York: Macmillan, 1947.

HARRIS, REX. *The Story of Jazz.* New York: Grosset and Dunlap, 1955.

HARRISON, MAX. *Charlie Parker.* New York: A. S. Barnes, 1961.

HASKINS, JAMES. *The Creoles of Color of New Oreleans.* New York: Harper and Row, 1975.

HERSKOVITS, MELVILLE J. *The Myth of the Negro Past.* New York: Harper and Brothers, 1941.

HITCHCOCK, H. WILEY. *Music in the United States: A Historical Introduction.* Englewood Cliffs, N. J.: Prentice-Hall, 1969.

HODEIR, ANDRE. *Jazz: Its Evolution and Essence.* Trans. David Noakes. New York: Grove Press, 1956.

HORRICKS, RAYMOND. *Count Basie and His Orchestra.* Westport, Conn.: Negro Universities Press, 1971.

HUGHES, LANGSTON. *The First Book of Jazz.* New York: Franklin Watts, 1955.

IRWIN, GRAHAM W. *Africans Abroad: A Documentary History of the Black Diaspora in Asia, Latin America, and the Caribbean During the Age of Slavery.* New York: Columbia University, 1977.

JACKSON, CLYDE OWEN. *The Songs of Our Years.* New York: Exposition, 1968.

JACKSON, GEORGE PULLEN. *White and Negro Spirituals.* New York: J. J. Augustin, 1943.

JAMES, MICHAEL. *Dizzy Gillespie.* New York: A. S. Barnes, 1961.

––––––. Miles Davis. New York: A. S. Barnes, 1961.

JEWELL, DEREK. *Duke: A Portrait of Duke Ellington.* New York: W. W. Norton and Co., 1977.

JOHNSON, CHARLES S. *Shadow of the Plantation.* Chicago: University of Chicago, 1934.

JOHNSON, JAMES WELDON. *Black Manhattan.* New York: Knopf, 1930.

JONES, A. M. *Studies in African Music.* Vols. I and II. London: Oxford, 1959.

JONES, LeROI. *Black Music.* New York: Morrow, 1967.

––––––. *Blues People.* New York: Morrow, 1963.

JONES, MAX AND JOHN CHILTON. *The Louis Armstrong Story, 1900–1971.* Boston: Little, Brown, 1971.

JOST, EKKARD. *Free Jazz.* New York: Universal Edition, A. G. Wein, 1975.

KATZ, BERNARD, ED. *The Social Implications of Early Negro Music in the United States.* New York: Arno, 1969.

KATZ, WILLIAM LOREN. *Eyewitness: The Negro in American History.* New York: Pittman, 1967.

KEEPNEWS, ORRIN AND BILL GRAVER, JR., COMPS. *A Pictorial History of Jazz.* New York: Crown, 1966.

KEIL, CHARLES. *Urban Blues.* Chicago: University of Chicago, 1966.

KOFSKY, FRANK. *Black Nationalism and the Revolution in Music.* New York: Pathfinder, 1970.

KREHBIEL, HENRY EDWARD. *Afro-American Folksongs.* New York: Ungar, 1962.

KYAGAMBIDDWA, JOSEPH. *African Music from the Source of the Nile.* New York: Holt, Rinehart and Winston, 1955.

LANDECK, BEATRICE. *Echoes of Africa.* New York: David McKay, 1961.

LEONARD, NEIL. *Jazz and the White Americans.* Chicago: University of Chicago, 1970.

LEVINE, LAWRENCE W. *Black Culture and Black Consciousness: Afro-American Folk Thought From Slavery to Freedom.* New York: Oxford, 1977.

LOCKE, ALAIN. *The Negro and His Music.* Port Washington, New York: Kennikat, 1968.

––––––, ed. *The New Negro.* New York: Boni, 1925.

LOMAX, ALAN. *Mister Jelly Roll.* New York: Duell, Sloan and Pearce, 1950.

LOMAX, JOHN AND ALAN LOMAX. *Negro Folksongs.* New York: Macmillan, 1936.

LONGSTREET, AUGUSTUS. *Georgia Scenes, Characters, Incidents, etc. in the First Half Century of the Republic.* New York: Harper and Brothers, 1840.

LOVELL, JOHN. *Black Song: The Forge and the Flame.* New York: Macmillan, 1972.

MacDONALD, ROBERT T., JOHN R. KEMP, AND EDWARD F. HAAS. *Louisiana's Black Heritage.* New Orleans: Louisiana State Museum, 1979.

MANDELBAUM, DAVID G. *Soldier Groups and Negro Soldiers.* Berkeley and Los Angeles: University of California, 1952.

MARCUS, GREIL, ED. *Rock and Roll Will Stand.* Boston: Beacon, 1969.

MARCUSE, SIBYL. *Musical Instruments.* Garden City, N. Y.: Doubleday, 1964.

MARSHALL, RAY. *The Negro and Organized Labor.* New York: John Wiley, 1965.

MARTI, SAMUEL. *Instrumentos musicales predortesianos.* (2d ed. Mexico: Instituto Nacional de Antropologia e Historia, 1968.

MARTIN, PHYLLIS M. AND PATRICK O'MEARA., EDS. *Africa.* Bloomington: Indiana University, 1977.

MCCARTHY, ALBERT. *Big Band Jazz.* New York: Putnam's, 1974.

_____. *Louis Armstrong.* New York: A. S. Barnes, 1961.

MCNAMARA, DANIEL, ED. *The ASCAP Biographical Dictionary.* New York: Harper and Row, 1952.

MEIER, AUGUST, ED. *The Making of Black America.* New York: Atheneum, 1969.

_____. *Negro Thought in America, 1800–1915.* Ann Arbor: University of Michigan, 1963.

MEIER, AUGUST, AND ELLIOTT RUDWICK. *From Plantation to Ghetto.* New York: Hill and Wang, 1966.

MERRIAM, ALAN, P. *The Anthropology of Music.* Evanston: Northwestern University, 1964.

MEYER, LEONARD B. *Emotion and Meaning in Music.* Chicago: University of Chicago, 1956.

MILLER, WILLIAM R. *The World of Pop Music and Jazz.* St. Louis: Concordia, 1965.

MORGAN, ALUM AND RAYMOND HORRICKS. *Modern Jazz.* London: Victor Gollanca, 1964.

MUELLER, JOHN H. *The American Symphony Orchestra.* Bloomington: Indiana University, 1951.

MYRDAL, GUNNAR. *An American Dilemma.* 9th ed. New York: Harper and Row, 1944.

NEWTON, FRANCIS. *The Jazz Scene.* New York: Monthly Review, 1960.

NKETIA, J. H. KWABENA. *African Music in Ghana.* Evanston: Northwestern University, 1963.

_____. *The Music of Africa.* New York: W. W. Norton and Co., 1974.

ODUM, HOWARD W. AND GUY B. JOHNSON. *The Negro and His Songs.* Hatboro, Pennsylvania: Folklore Associates, 1964.

OAKLEY, GILES. *The Devil's Music: A History of the Blues.* New York: Harcourt Brace Jovanovich, Inc., 1976.

OLIVER, PAUL. *The Meaning of the Blues.* New York: Macmillan, 1969.

_____. *Savannah Syncopators: African Retentions in the Blues.* New York: Stein & Day, 1971.

_____. *Screening the Blues.* London: Cassell, 1968.

_____. *The Story of the Blues.* Philadelphia: Chilton, 1969.

OSTRANSKY, LEROY. *The Anatomy of Jazz.* Seattle: University of Washington, 1960.

_____. *Understanding Jazz.* Englewood Cliffs, N. J.: Prentice-Hall, 1977.

PANASSIÉ, HUGUES. *Louis Armstrong.* New York: Scribner's, 1971.

_____. *The Real Jazz.* Trans. Anne Sorelle Williams. Adapted for American publication by Charles Edward Smith. New York: Smith and Durrell, 1942.

PARRISH, LYDIA. *Slave Songs of the Georgia Sea Islands.* Hatboro, Pennsylvania: Folklore Associates, 1942.

PATTERSON, LINDSAY, ED. *International Library of Negro Life and History.* New York: Publishers Co., 1969.

PHILLIPS, ULRICH BONNELL. *American Negro Slavery.* New York: Peter Smith, 1952.

RABOTEAU, ALBERT J. *Slave Religion: The 'Invisible Institution' in the Antebellum South.* New York: Oxford, 1978.

RAY, BENJAMIN. *African Religions: Symbol, Ritual and Community.* Englewood Cliffs, N. J.: Prentice-Hall, 1976.

REDDING, SAUNDERS.   *The Negro*. Washington, D.C.: Potomac, 1967.

———.   *To Make a Poet Black*. Chapel Hill: University of North Carolina, 1939.

REUTER, EDWARD BYRON.   *The American Race Problem*. New York: Harper and Row, 1938.

RIEDEL, JOHANNES.   *Soul Music, Black and White*. Minneapolis: Augsburg, 1975.

ROBERTS, JOHN S.   *Black Music of Two Worlds*. New York: Holt, Rinehart and Winston, 1972.

———.   *The Latin Tinge: The Impact of Latin American Music on the United States*. New York: Oxford, 1979.

ROSE, AL AND EDMOND SONCHON.   *New Oreleans Jazz*. Baton Rouge: Louisiana State University, 1967.

ROSE, ARNOLD.   *The Negro in America*. New York: Harper and Brothers, 1948.

RUBLOWSKY, JOHN.   *Black Music in America*. New York: Basic Books, 1971.

RUDWICK, ELLIOTT M.   *Race Riot at East St. Louis, July 2, 1917*. Carbondale: Southern Illinois University, 1964.

RUSSELL, ROSS.   *Jazz Styles in Kansas City and the Southwest*. Berkeley: University of California, 1971.

SALK, EDWIN A.   *A Layman's Guide to Negro History*. New York: McGraw-Hill, 1966.

SARGEANT, WINTHROP.   *Jazz: Hot and Hybrid*. New York: Dutton, 1946.

SCARBOROUGH, DOROTHY.   *On the Trail of Negro Folk-Songs*. Hatboro, Pennsylvania: Folklore Associates, 1963.

SCHULLER, GUNTHER.   *Early Jazz: Its Roots and Musical Development*. New York: Oxford, 1968.

SCHWARTZ, H. G.   *The Story of Musical Instruments*. Elkhart, Indiana: Conn Band Instrument Division, 1938.

SCOTT, ALLEN.   *Jazz Educated Man*. Washington, D.C.: American International, 1973.

SHAFER, WILLIAM AND JOHANNES RIEDEL.   *The Art of Ragtime*. Baton Rouge: Louisiana State University, 1973.

SHAW, ARNOLD.   *The Rock Revolution*. London: Crowell-Collier, 1969.

———.   *The Street That Never Slept*. New York: Coward, McCann and Geoghegan, 1971.

———.   *The World of Soul*. New York: Cowles, 1970.

SIDRAN, BEN.   *Black Talk*. New York: Holt, Rinehart and Winston, 1971.

SIMPSON, GEORGE E.   *Black Religions in the New World*. New York: Columbia University, 1973.

SOUTHERN, EILEEN.   *The Music of Black Americans: A History*. New York: W. W. Norton and Co., 1971.

SPAETH, SIGMUND.   *A History of Popular Music*. New York: Random House, 1948.

SPELLMAN, A. B.   *Four Lives in the Bebop Business*. New York: Pantheon, 1966.

STAMPP, KENNETH M.   *The Peculiar Institution*. New York: Knopf, 1956.

STEARNS, MARSHALL.   *The Story of Jazz*. New York: Oxford, 1956.

STEARNS, MARSHALL AND JEAN STEARNS.   *Jazz Dance*. New York: Macmillan, 1968.

STODDARD, HOPE.   *From These Came Music*. New York: Harper and Row, 1952.

TAFT, PHILIP.   *Organized Labor in American History*. New York: Harper and Row, 1964.

TAYLOR, BILLY.   *Jazz Piano*. Dubuque, Iowa: Wm. C Brown, 1982.

TERRY, WALDO.   *This is Ragtime*. New York: Hawthorne, 1971.

THIEME, DARIUS L.   *African Music—Annotated Bibliography*. Washington, D.C.: Library of Congress, 1964.

THOMPSON, OSCAR, ED.   *The International Cyclopedia of Music and Musicians*. New York: Dodd, Mead, 1964.

THURMAN, HOWARD.   *Deep River*. Port Washington, N.Y.: Kennikat, 1969.

TILTON, JEFF TODD. *Early Downhome Blues*. Urbana: University of Illinois, 1977.
TRAIL, SINCLAIR, ED. *Concerning Jazz*. London: Faber Popular Books, 1957.
TYER, GUS. *The Labor Revolution*. New York: Viking, 1966.
ULANOV, BARRY. *A Handbook of Jazz*. New York: Viking, 1960.
_____. *A History of Jazz in America*. New York: Viking, 1952.
VIRGINIA WRITERS' PROJECT. *The Negro in Virginia*. New York: Hastings House, 1940.
WHITE, EVELYN D., COMP. *Selected Bibliography of Published Choral Music by Black Composers*. Washington, D.C.: Howard University, 1975.
WHITE, NEWMAN I. *American Negro Folk-Songs*. Hatboro, Pennsylvania: Folklore Associates, 1965.
WILEY, BELL IRVIN. *Southern Negroes, 1861–1865*. New Haven: Yale University, 1938.
WILLIAMS, ERIC. *The Negro in the Caribbean*. Washington, D.C.: Associates in Negro Folk Education, 1942.
WILLIAMS, MARTIN T., ED. *The Art of Jazz*. New York: Oxford, 1959.
_____. *Jazz Masters in Transition, 1957–1969*. New York: Macmillan, 1970.
_____. *Jazz Masters of New Orleans*. New York: Macmillan, 1967.
_____. *Jazz Panorama*. New York: Crowell-Collier, 1962.
_____. *The Jazz Tradition*. New York: Oxford, 1970.
_____. *Where's the Melody?* New York: Pantheon, 1969.
WILSON, JOHN S. *Jazz: The Transition Years, 1940–1960*. New York: Appleton-Century-Crofts, 1966.
WOODMAN, HAROLD D., COMP. AND ED. *Slavery and the Southern Economy*. New York: Harcourt, Brace and World, 1966.
WOODSON, CARTER G. *Free Negro Heads of Families in the United States in 1830*. Washington, D.C.: Association for the Study of Negro Life and History, 1925.
WOODWARD, C. VANN. *The Strange Case of Jim Crow*. New York: Oxford, 1966.
WORK, JOHN WESLEY. *Folk Songs of the American Negro*. New York: Negro Universities Press, 1969.

MUSIC SCORES

ANDERSON, THOMAS J. *In Memoriam: Zach Walker*. New York: Composers Facsimile Edition, 1968.
_____. *Squares*. New York: Composers Facsimile Edition, 1966.
CARTER, JOHN. *Cantata*. New York: Southern Music, 1964.
CUNNINGHAM, ARTHUR. *Lullabye for a Jazz Baby*. New York: Available from the composer, 1969.
DAWSON, WILLIAM LEVI. *Negro Folk Symphony*. Delaware Water Gap, Penn.: Shawnee, 1965.
DETT, R. NATHANIEL, ED. *Negro Spirituals*. London: Blandford Press, 1959.
_____. *The Ordering of Moses*. Glen Rock, N.J.: J. Fischer, 1939.
FISCHER, WILLIAM ARMS, ED. *Seventy Negro Spirituals*. Boston: Oliver Ditson, 1926.
FISCHER, WILLIAM S. *A Quiet Movement*. Berlin: Bote & Bock, 1966.
HANDY, WILLIAM C., ED. *Blues, An Anthology*. New York: Boni, 1926.
JOHNSON, HALL. *The Green Pastures Spirituals*. New York: Farrar and Rinehart, 1930.
JOHNSON, JAMES WELDON, ED. *The Book of American Negro Spirituals*. New York: Viking, 1925.
_____, ed. *The Second Book of Negro Spirituals*. New York: Viking, 1926.
KAY, ULYSSES S. *Fantasy Variations*. New York: Duchess Music, 1966.

LOGAN, WENDELL. *Songs of Our Time*. Oberlin, Ohio: Available from the composer, 1969.

NICKERSON, CAMILE L. *Five Creole Songs*. Boston: Boston Music Co., 1952.

———. *Gue-Gue Solingaie*. New York: Leeds Music, 1934.

PERRY, JULIA. *Stabat Mater*. New York: Southern Music, 1954.

SMITH, HALE. *Contours*. New York: C. F. Peters, 1962.

STILL, WILLIAM GRANT. *Afro-American Symphony*. Glen Rock, N.J.: J. Fischer, 1935.

SWANSON, HOWARD. *Short Symphony*. New York: Weintraub Music, 1951.

TILLIS, FREDERICK C. *Music*. New York: American Composers Alliance, 1968.

WALKER, GEORGE. *Sonata No. 1*. New York: General Music, 1971.

WHITE, CLARENCE CAMERON. *Ouanga*. New York: Sam Fox, 1955.

WILSON, OLLY. *In Memoriam—Martin Luther King, Jr*. Los Angeles: Available from the composer, 1968.

PERIODICALS

BERGER, MONROE. "Jazz Resistance to the Diffusion of a Culture-Pattern," *Journal of Negro History*, XXXII, 4 (October 1947), pp. 461–94.

BONTEMPS, ARNA. "Rock, Church, Rock," *Common Ground*, III, 1 (Autumn 1942), pp. 75–80.

BRIGHT, KENNETH AND INEZ CAVANAUGH. "That Harmful Little Armful," *The Crisis*, 54, 4 (April 1944), pp. 109–10.

BRUCE, JOHN E. "A History of Negro Musicians," *The Southern Workman*, XLV, 10 (October 1916), pp. 569–73.

"CONCERT MUSIC," *BMI: The Many Worlds of Music* (February 1970), pp. 4–5.

"CONDUCTORS," *Time* (December 31, 1965), p. 49.

COOK, MERCER. "Will Marion Cook: He Helped Them All," *The Crisis*, 51, 14 (October 1944), pp. 322, 328.

DUNCAN, JOHN. "Art Music by Negro Composers on Record," *Negro History Bulletin*, 31, 4 (April 1968), pp. 6–9.

———. "Negro Composers of Opera," *Negro History Bulletin*, XXIX, 4, pp. 79–80, 93.

———. "Negro Spirituals—Once More," *Negro History Bulletin* (January 1947), pp. 80–81, 95.

"EIGHTEENTH CENTURY SLAVE ADVERTISEMENTS," *Journal of Negro History*, 1 (April 1916), pp. 163–216.

EUBA, AKIN. "Nigerian Music: An Appreciation," *Negro History Bulletin*, XXIV, 6 (March 1961), pp. 130–33.

GARRETT, ROMEO B. "African Survivals in American Culture," *Journal of Negro History*, LI, 4 (October 1966), pp. 243–44.

GOLDMAN, ALBERT. "It's Hard to Fake the True Blues," *Life*, 67, 1 (July 4, 1969), p. 8.

HECKMAN, DON. "Five Decades of Rhythm and Blues," *BMI: The Many Worlds of Music* (Summer), pp. 4–31.

———. "From Steppenwolf to Booker T. to Air Force," *The New York Times*, June 14, 1970, p. 29.

HENTOFF, NAT. "John Lewis," *Broadcast Music Brochure*, 1960.

———. "The Strange Case of the Missing Musicians," *The Reporter*, 20, 11 (May 28, 1959), pp. 25–27.

HERSKOVITS, MELVILLE J. "African Gods and Catholic Saints in New World Negro Belief," *American Anthropologits*, 38 (1937), pp. 635–43.

_____. "Drums and Drummers in Afro-Brazilian Cult Life," *Music Quarterly*, XXX (1944).

"THE INTEGRITY OF GOSPEL," *BMI: The Many Worlds of Music* (February 1970), pp. 13–14.

JEZER, MARTIN. "Ornette Coleman on the Frontiers of Jazz," *Music Journal* (March 1963), pp. 77–79.

"THE JOHNSON FAMILY," *Negro History Bulletin* (November 1948), pp. 27–28.

JOHNSON, GUY B. "The Negro Spiritual: A Problem in Anthropology," *American Anthropologist*, XXXIII, 2 (April-June 1931), pp. 157–71.

KIRBY, PERCIVAL ROBSON. "A Study of Negro Harmony," *Musical Quarterly*, XVI, 3 (July 1930), pp. 404–14.

KRAJEWSKI, FRAN. "The Ellington Legend," *Music Journal*, XXVIII, 5 (May 1970), pp. 32, 63–64.

KRIEGSMAN, ALAN M. "Symphony Gets Composer-in-Residence," *The Washington Post*, October 20, 1968.

LAUBENSTEIN, PAUL FRITZ. "Race Values in Aframerican Music," *Musical Quarterly*, XVI, 3 (July 1930), pp. 378–403.

LAURENCIE, LIONEL DE LA. "The Chevalier de Saint-Georges," trans. Frederick H. Martens, *Musical Quarterly*, V, 1 (January 1919), pp. 74–85.

"LITTLE RICHARD," *BMI: The Many Worlds of Music* (March 1969), pp. 19–20.

McGREGOR, CRAIG. "So in the End the Beatles Have Proved False Prophets," *The New York Times*, June 14, 1970.

MERRIAM, ALAN P. "Music in American Culture," *American Anthropologist*, 57 (1955), pp. 1172–81.

MOLLESON, JOHN. "The Negro in Music," *Musical Anthropologist*, 57 (1955), pp. 1172–81.

MOLLESON, JOHN. "The Negro in Music," *Musical America*, LXXXIII, 12 (December 1963), pp. 24–25.

"NEW JAZZ," *BMI: The Many Worlds of Music* (March 1967), p. 23.

PAGE, EARL DAVID. "The Race Record," *Music Journal* (March 1963), pp. 44, 88.

"PHILIPPA SCHUYLER," *Opportunity: Journal of Negro Life*, XIV, 9 (September 1936), p. 262.

"THE RETURN OF THE NATIVE," *American Musical Digest*, I, 1 (October 1969), pp. 31–32.

RUSSCOL, HERBERT. "Can the Negro Overcome the Classical Music Establishment," *High Fidelity Magazine*, 18 (August 1968), pp. 42–46.

RUSSELL, JOHN D. "Colored Freemen as Slave Owners," *Journal of Negro History*, 1, 3 (July 1916), pp. 233–42.

SCHUYLER, GEORGE S. "America Caught Up With Him," *The Crisis*, 49, 6 (June 1942), pp. 3–4, 195.

SHEEN, MICKEY. "Jazz—Creative American Music," *Music Journal*, XXVIII, 5 (May 1970), p. 31.

SHERRER, CHARLES W. "Jazz in Kansas City," *Music Journal*, XXVIII, 5 (May 1970), pp. 28–29, 60–61, 64–65.

STEVENSON, ROBERT. "Afro-American Musical Legacy to 1800," *The Musical Quarterly*, 54 (October 1968), pp. 475–502.

STILL, WILLIAM GRANT. "The Men Behind American Music," *The Crisis*, 51, 1 (January 1944), pp. 12–15, 29.

VAN VETCHEN, CARL. "The J. W. Johnson Collection at Yale," *The Crisis*, 49, 7 (July 1942), pp. 222–23, 226.

VON HORNBOSTEL, E. M. "African Negro Music," *Journal of the International Institute of African Languages and Culture* (January 1928), pp. 30–62.

WATERMAN, RICHARD A.   "'Hot' Rhythm in Negro Music," *Journal of the American Musicological Society*, I, 1 (Spring 1948), pp. 24–38.

WEINSTEIN, ROBERT V.   "Black 'n Blues," *Negro History Bulletin*, 32, 5 (May 1969), pp. 13–15.

YANCY, HENRIETTA MILLER.   "The Contributions of the American Negro to the Music Culture of the Country," Part 1, *The School Musician Director and Teacher* (January 1970), pp. 55–57.

————.   "The Contributions of the American Negro to the Music Culture of the Country," Part 2, *The School Musician Director and Teacher* (February 1970), pp. 60–62.

————.   "The Contributions of the American Negro to the Music Culture of the Country," Part 3, *The School Musician Director and Teacher* (March 1970), pp. 60–61, 73.

————.   "The Contributions of the American Negro to the Music Culture of the Country," Part 4, *The School Musician Director and Teacher* (April 1970), pp. 62–63.

RECORDS

BERRY, CHARLES.   *Chuck Berry's Golden Decade, 1955–1965*. Chess Records, LPS-1514D.

BOTKIN, B. A., ED.   *Negro Religious Songs and Services*. Library of Congress, AAFS-L10.

————, ed.   *Negro Worksongs and Calls*. Library of Congress, AAFS-L8.

BOULTON, LAURA C.   *African Music*. Folkways Records, FW 8852.

COLEMAN, ORNETTE.   *Free Jazz*. Atlantic Records, 1367.

————.   *The Shape of Jazz to Come*. Atlantic Records, 1317.

COLTRANE, JOHN.   *Ascension*. Impulse Records, A-95.

————.   *Chasin' the Trane*. Impulse Records, A-10.

————.   *Giant Steps*. Atlantic Records, 1311.

————.   *Impressions*. Impulse Records, A-42.

————.   *My Favorite Things*. Atlantic Records, 1361.

COURLANDER, HAROLD, ED.   *Negro Folk Music of Albama*, Vol. I. Ethnic Folkways Library, FE 4417.

DAVIS, MILES.   *Birth of the Cool*. Capitol Records, TT 1974.

DAVIS, MILES.   *Kind of Blue*. Columbia Records, 1355.

HERSKOVITS, MELVILLE AND FRANCES S. HERSKOVITX, ED.   *Afro-Bahian Religious Songs from Brazil*. Library of Congress, AAFS-61-65.

The History of Rhythm and Blues, 1947–60.   Atlantic Records, SD 8161/4.

The History of Rhythm and Blues, 1961–67.   Atlantic Records, SD 8193/4; SD 8208/9. 8208/9.

LOMAX, ALAN, ED.   *Afro-American Spirituals, Worksongs and Ballads*. Library of Congress, AAFS-L3.

————, ed.   *Sea Island Folk Festival*. Folkways Records, FS 3841.

MERRIAM, ALAN P.   *Africa South of the Sahara*. Folkways Records, FE 4503.

PENNIMAN, RICHARD.   *Little Richard's Greatest Hits*. Okeh Records, 14121.

————.   *Here's Little Richard*. Specialty Records, 2100.

REDDING, OTIS.   *The Dock of the Bay*. Volts Records, S-419.

ROLLINS, SONNY.   *Saxophone Colossus*. Prestige Records, 7326.

————.   *Way Out West*. Contemporary Records, 3530.

Salve Regina: Choral Music of the Spanish New World, 1550–1750.   Angel Records, S 36008.

SILVER, HORACE. *Blowin' the Blues Away.* Blue Note Records, 4017.
STEARNS, MARSHALL, ED. *Negro Blues and Hollers.* Library of Congress, AFS-L59.
TAYLOR, CECIL. *The World of Cecil Taylor.* Candid Records, 8006.
TERRY, SONNY. *Sonny Terry's Washboard Band.* Folkways Records, Fa 2006.

UNPUBLISHED WORKS

ABORN, MERTON. "The Influence on American Musical Culture of Dvořák's Sojourn in America." Unpublished doctoral dissertation, Indiana University, 1965.
ALLISON, ROLAND LEWIS. "Classification of the Vocal Works of Harry T. Burleigh (1866–1949) and Some Suggestions for Their Use in Teaching Diction in Singing." Unpublished doctoral dissertation, Indiana University, 1966.
APPLEBY, DAVID PERCY. "A Study of Selected Compositions by Contemporary Brazilian Composers." Unpublished doctoral dissertation, University of Indiana, 1956.
BRAITHWAITE, COLERIDGE ALEXANDER. "A Survey of the Lives and Creative Activities of Some Negro Composers." Unpublished doctoral dissertation, Columbia University, 1952.
CARTER, ALBERT E. "The Louisiana Negro and His Music." Unpublished Master's thesis, Northwestern University, 1947.
CRAWFORD, LUCILLE H. "The Musical Activities of James Weldon Johnson." Unpublished Master's thesis, Fisk University, 1940.
DAVIDSON, FRANK. "The Rise, Development, Decline and Influence of the American Minstrel Show." Unpublished doctoral dissertation, New York University, 1952.
FAHEY, JOHN ALOYSIUS. "A Textual and Musicological Analysis of the Repertoire of Charley Patton." Unpublished Master's thesis, University of California, 1966.
GEORGE, ZELMA WATSON. "A Guide to Negro Music: An Annotated Bibliography of Negro Folk Music and Art Music by Negro Composers or Based on Negro Thematic Material." Unpublished doctoral dissertation, New York University, 1953.
GILLUM, RUTH HELEN. "The Negro Folk-Song and Its Influence in American Music." Unpublished Master's thesis, University of Kansas, 1940.
HAMMOND, STELLA LOU. "Contribution of the American Indian and Negro to the Folk-Music of America." Unpublished Master's thesis, Wayne University, 1936.
HANSEN, CHADICK C. "The Ages of Jazz: A Study of Jazz in its Cultural Context." Unpublished doctoral dissertation, University of Minnesota, 1959.
JACKSON, EILEEN STANZA. "The Use of Negro Folksong in Symphonic Forms." Unpublished Master's thesis, University of Chicago, 1941.
NICKERSON, CAMILE L. "Africo-Creole Music in Louisiana." Unpublished Master's thesis, Oberlin College, 1932.
PUGH, DOUGLAS G. "Job Status of the Negro Professional Musician in the New York Metropolitan Area." New York: Urban League of Greater New York, 1958. (Mimeographed.)
PYKE, LANCELOT ALLEN, II. "Jazz, 1920 to 1927: An Analytical Study, Vols. I and II." Unpublished doctoral dissertation, University of Iowa, 1962.
RICKS, GEORGE. "Some Aspects of the Religious Music of the United States Negro: An Ethnomusicological Study with Special Emphasis on the Gospel

Tradition." Unpublished doctoral dissertation, Northwestern University, 1960.

SHOCKETT, BERNARD IRWIN.   "A Stylistic Study of the Blues, 1917–1931, as Practiced by Jazz Instrumentalist." Unpublished doctoral dissertation, New York University, 1969.

SIMPSON, RALPH RICARDO.   "William Grant Still—The Man and His Music." Unpublished doctoral dissertation, Michigan State University, 1964.

THOMPSON, LEON EVERETT. "A Historical and Stylistic Analysis of the Music of William Grant Still and a Thematic Catalog of His Works." Unpublished doctoral dissertation, University of Southern California, 1966.

VATTEL, ELBERT DANIEL. "Ritual in Chicago's South Side Churches for Negroes." Unpublished doctoral dissertation, University of Chicago, 1940.

WATERMAN, RICHARD ALAN. "African Patterns in Trinidad Negro Music." Unpublished doctoral dissertation, Northwestern University, 1943.

Index